T0355372

Indentured Students

Indentured Students

How Government-Guaranteed Loans
Left Generations Drowning in College Debt

Elizabeth Tandy Shermer

The Belknap Press of Harvard University Press

CAMBRIDGE, MASSACHUSETTS   LONDON, ENGLAND   2021

LIBRARY OF CONGRESS CATALOGING-IN-PUBLICATION DATA

Names: Shermer, Elizabeth Tandy, author.
Title: Indentured students : how government-guaranteed loans left generations drowning in college debt / Elizabeth Tandy Shermer.
Description: Cambridge, Massachusetts : The Belknap Press of Harvard University Press, 2021. | Includes bibliographical references and index.
Identifiers: LCCN 2021001564 | ISBN 9780674251489 (cloth)
Subjects: LCSH: Federal aid to higher education—United States—History. | Student loans—United States—History. | College costs—United States—History. | Debt—United States—History. | Educational equalization—United States—History.
Classification: LCC LB2342.4.U6 S54 2021 | DDC 379.1/2140973—dc23
LC record available at https://lccn.loc.gov/2021001564

For the forty-five million of us, and counting,
who together owe more than $1.7 trillion

Contents

Introduction: Drowning in Debt 1

1 Honorably Financing College 15

2 Will Work for School 33

3 A Bill of Rights for Only Some GIs 76

4 The Fizzled Response to Sputnik 117

5 Federally Guaranteed Students 163

6 Reauthorizing the Loan Industry 202

7 Bankers Lose Their Sweetheart Deal 242

Epilogue: A Brave New World of Indentured Students 288

APPENDIX 1
Revenue Sources for Higher Education Institutions
by Academic Year, 1909–1910 to 1989–1990 303

APPENDIX 2
Median Household Income by Race and
Hispanic Origin, 1967 to 2018 304

APPENDIX 3
Consumer Debt since 1945   305

NOTES   307

ACKNOWLEDGMENTS   367

INDEX   371

Indentured Students

Introduction

Drowning in Debt

"My loans are a black cloud hanging over me," twenty-eight-year-old Jessie Suren admitted to reporters in June 2016. The Pennsylvania native knew she was just one of many feeling the pressure of outstanding student debt. One of the jobs she worked to pay off her $76,000 balance, making $12 an hour, was dialing delinquent borrowers. The jobless, broke, and even terminally ill debtors she called had taken out loans for themselves or family members to fund all sorts of degrees and majors from for-profit institutions, public universities, and private colleges. Suren's job put her in touch with just a tiny fraction of the forty-two million Americans who then owed roughly $1.3 trillion.[1]

That debt grew to $1.6 trillion by 2020, collectively owed by forty-five million borrowers ever more eager to rail against the highly profitable student loan industry some consider a "carefully constructed trap." College debt has made marriage, homeownership, parenthood, retirement, and even gainful employment seem like a pipe dream to many alumni, including cancer survivor Hillary Finne. She graduated from Loyola University Chicago Law School but the Illinois Board of Admissions to the Bar considered her spotty repayment record reason enough to refuse her application. That decision ended her dream of being an attorney and the likelihood she would ever be able to pay back her student loans. North Carolina State graduate Ashley Dale also felt hoodwinked. A financial aid officer had estimated that a federal loan of $16,400 should translate to payments of just $100 a month. But after earning his master's degree in graphic design and deferring payments for some years, Dale got his first bill for $340. "My rent at the time was $275," he recalled, "and my car payment was like $109, so it was quite a shock." Bouts of unemployment and underemployment forced more deferrals and eventually default, and penalties and interest added to the burden. Twenty-two years later, at age fifty-one, Dale faced a debt of $78,000, and learned he could clear it by making monthly payments of $535 for another thirty years—a further outflow of nearly $200,000 that was very unlikely to happen.[2]

Many of the indebted regret not having had the fine print explained to them. "I didn't understand how much money a loan could accrue," nursing school graduate Jackie Krowen admitted. "You just clicked some buttons on the computer and you had a huge check." Some had no idea that family members might also find themselves in debt. When a prolonged illness forced Vanessa McClurg to drop out of college, she took a job paying just $9 an hour in a Utah auto repair shop and soon fell behind on payments. Aggressive collectors warned her they "would immediately go after the federal benefits of the co-signor," her retired father. "My 84-year-old grandfather gave me every dime he had in his savings," she said, "so I could become current on my loans."[3]

Even for those paying on time, heavy debt takes its toll. University of New Orleans alum Danielle Aluotto said, "I feel the weight of my student loans every day." Many are depressed and anxious, including Alex, a thirty-one-year-old Iowan, who lamented that "you will forever be a slave to something you signed your life away to when you were a stupid 17- or 18-year-old." Others resent how debt limits their choices. According to Kate, age twenty-five, "I see a lot of jobs that I would love but I know I would not be able to afford everything with my loans." Even a high-profile politician can be, as US House Representative Ilhan Omar says she is, "shackled with the burdens of student debt."[4]

Comparisons to slavery, convict labor, and indenture became easy to find by the millennium's turn; such analogies pepper news stories and research papers with titles like "Slavery by Debt," "Student Debt Peonage," "Forever in Your Debt," "The Price of Opportunity," and "Is Going to College a Choice?" Some economists, reporters, and politicians dismissed those metaphors. But educational loans struck many borrowers and some experts as similar to other arrangements used across the centuries to compel young men and women, particularly those of color, to work without hope of ever escaping their debts.[5]

Such shackles should be consigned to the distant past. Yet most young people and their families do not consider skipping postsecondary schooling to be a real option. A college degree had become a prerequisite for a career even before headlines started predicting that automation and artificial intelligence would leave many less-educated workers permanently unemployed. Amid such warnings college expenses continued to skyrocket, and the number of families able to pay out of pocket declined. By 2019, more than 70 percent of students borrowed some amount to stay enrolled, and the typical student graduated owing more than $37,000. Student debt has become one of the largest categories of American consumer debt, second only to home mortgages, in the new millennium.[6]

Unequal chances of achieving the increasingly elusive American Dream have defined the twenty-first-century contours of this student debt tragedy. Americans of all ages, races, and family incomes now borrow to advance their education. Research reveals, however, that only elite schools with massive endowments tend to offer low-income and working-class applicants financial aid packages and services generous enough to keep them on track—and even in these schools, such students comprise a small part of the student body. Prestigious institutions have long competed for exceptional students, however wealthy, by offering merit scholarships. Low-income, minority, immigrant, and female applicants are less likely to apply to those institutions. They overwhelmingly turn to less well-known, but still costly, universities, community colleges, and for-profit institutions, which do not have the same tuition assistance resources. For some families, the annual bill for tuition, fees, and room and board at a four-year college can exceed that year's household income. Many parents borrow to pay fees for children who still need to devote so many hours to working part-time that they struggle to finish their degrees. Students of color, particularly women, are most likely to find themselves taking out more loans, struggling to repay them, and defaulting. African American and Latinx families generally lack the inherited family wealth that makes paying out of pocket for college possible. They spend more money over time to earn the same degrees as their wealthier peers, which only widens the racial wealth gap—a relatively new phrase that speaks to systemic inequalities far beyond the simple differences in pay that persist even among

Ivy League white and minority alumni. Gender-based salary differences have also left women owing disproportionately more. It is well known that, in recent years, women have made up the majority of American college students and often outperform their male peers. Yet, regardless of race, female students remain less likely to receive the scholarships that would reduce the cost of postsecondary education. Plus, they are still paid less for the same work as their male counterparts both during their school years and after, and are more likely to step away from paid work to care for children or elderly relatives. With interest charges racking up relentlessly, women thus take longer on average and spend more to pay off their debts.[7]

Many borrowers, regardless of age or background, do not understand the implications of what they are signing or, like Jackie Krowen, clicking through online. These complex financial products often leave students and parents making questionable choices about how much to borrow and from whom. The fact that they formally consent to the terms, however, makes it hard to police abuses even where their true understanding is dubious—as seen in some infamous schemes by certain for-profit schools. These proprietary institutions are far more eager than nonprofit colleges to accept students with less than sterling academic records—and while such students have even more reason to fear going deep into debt, they and their parents still reportedly expect college to be a good investment. After all, teachers, guidance counselors, financial aid officers, bankers, and politicians have spent decades assuring Americans, like Jessie Suren, that borrowing for a BA will lead to more opportunities and decades of higher earnings to make up for a temporary state of indebtedness.[8]

That assurance is nonsensical in an era when Americans seeking basic undergraduate degrees take on levels of debt that, in the past, only doctors, lawyers, and MBAs incurred to fund their educations. Before the Great Recession, those professionals tended to stay on top of their payments and see handsome returns on their investments. Recovery from that global economic crisis has not helped borrowers for BAs or for more advanced degrees. Even highly skilled alumni are saddled with debts that might take a lifetime to repay. It hardly helps that student debt cannot be discharged in bankruptcy proceedings. Tens of thousands of elderly Americans are also paying off student loans taken out for themselves or family members. Some have even had their social security checks garnished for defaulting. A 2019 study of borrowers who graduated in 2014 showed that a third of them had made no progress yet on repaying what they owed. Those bills often influenced the directions of lives, and the pursuit of dreams, like the homeownership and parenthood that Hillary Finne gave up on.[9]

Newspapers may publish sensational stories about universities' fancy gyms, waterparks, and luxury dorms, but the reality is that few people now mired in debt lived high on the hog while in school. In one recent survey of American students, over a third said they experienced food and housing insecurity. Millions of undergraduates, too, have jobs that give them little time to study. Dropouts, like Vanessa McClurg, are most likely to default. But researchers fear that alumni current on their loans, like Danielle Aluotto, might very well start failing to pay. By 2017, state school graduates had an 11 percent default rate, just a few points less than for-profits' percentage. Those numbers reflected that sheepskins no longer guaranteed entry into a shrinking American middle class, as Jessie Suren discovered. Graduating still improved a low-income person's economic odds and remained a strong predictor of upward mobility. Borrowing for education increases the likelihood that a student will graduate. Still, these financial obligations are putting a growing number of borrowers, and especially the women of color among them, on a path to perpetual poverty.[10]

Many have bemoaned this student debt catastrophe as the shocking coda to American higher education's storied twentieth-century expansion. The country had but 1.1 million college students in 1931; sixty years later, 14 million were enrolled. By 2015, 59 percent of the adult population had some postsecondary schooling and a third held at least a bachelor's degree. Those numbers really began to increase after Congress passed the 1944 GI Bill, with its stipends to cover tuition for World War II veterans. Next, the oft-repeated story goes, a Cold War fear of falling behind in science and engineering compelled federal lawmakers to directly fund higher education institutions. The imperative to fight a War on Poverty and build a Great Society in the 1960s inspired liberals to pass the 1965 Higher Education Act. That legislation finally devoted the money necessary to increase the seats available to aspiring undergraduates, who (thanks to the 1964 Civil Rights Act) could no longer be denied entry based on their race, religion, or sex. Expanded access fueled the academy's rapid growth and helped millions enter the middle class. Upward mobility was good for a country whose economic fortunes depended on a well-educated workforce during and after the mid-century heyday of American manufacturing. It was only at the millennium's turn, many experts believe, that partisan politics, spending cuts, spiraling costs, unscrupulous lenders, and predatory for-profits turned American higher education into the kind of curse that could reduce (not assure) aspiring undergraduates' chances of living the American Dream.[11]

Many academics and journalists want to blame the student debt crisis on digital diploma mills, which played a recent, important part in worsening a much older financial mess. The fights over segregation, religious freedom, taxing, and spending that have long divided Americans also thwarted efforts to provide the kind of robust federal aid that would have made higher education affordable. The fact is that students and parents have struggled to pay for college since the early days of the republic. College administrators and faculty have traditionally resisted some forms of substantial, direct government funding that could reduce the costs passed along to students. But most state and federal officials never considered using taxpayers' money to generously underwrite colleges and universities rather than leave them to depend on student fees and philanthropy. Since the 1930s, lawmakers have instead preferred tuition assistance programs, which provide stipends to individual students but do not fundamentally change the fee structure presented to a steadily growing number of college applicants. Government funding pitched at the individual level also did little to influence schools to open their doors to Jews, Catholics, immigrants, and citizens of color, especially if they were women. After World War II, congressional efforts to fund higher education beyond the GI Bill were derailed by interests in maintaining segregation and academic freedom, and resisting expansions of federal authority, taxation, and spending. By the late 1950s, making loans more accessible to students seemed a cheap, politically palatable way to provide equal educational opportunities. College administrators and education experts took care to craft a program of offering government-guaranteed loans that relied on the campus admissions officers who interacted with promising students to determine their borrowing needs. The program's architects designed it to jumpstart a student loan industry in the private sector, rather than have the government issue loans directly. The program guaranteed first and foremost that banks would be repaid even if borrowers defaulted, but nevertheless the financiers had to be coaxed into participating. In a good example of the political truism that "operations is policy," presidential appointees and their staffs hammered out many details in the administration of this complicated, creative financing solution that had not been formally legislated. Unfortunately, as one of the architects would lament in the mid-1970s, what began as "little more than a salamander" of a government-guaranteed loan industry turned into a "fund-eating dragon." This was true well before reporters and lawmakers uncovered rampant fraud and corruption in the early 1990s—and although those revelations included abuses by proprietary trade schools, the warning signs did not stop Democrats and Republicans from making for-profits fully eligible for federal student aid programs. In 2008, with debts and defaults escalating, laws were changed to force states, lenders, and campuses to turn over much more data about tuition charges, borrowing levels, and bankruptcy rates. There is now much greater transparency into a loan industry that has, in the view of some, enslaved or indentured borrowers for years.[12]

The intertwined histories of student debt and tuition assistance offer insights into the trajectory and fate of the entire American democratic experiment. By the end of the twentieth century, US citizens had extraordinary legal protections for equal opportunity, yet faced levels of wealth and income inequality not seen since the Gilded Age of the late nineteenth century. Americans, particularly women and citizens of color, still struggled to pay for college, as well as for housing, health care, retirement, and other basic needs that many western democracies have treated as human rights. Historians have shown how partisanship, faith in free enterprise, American federalism, misogyny, and white supremacy limited the New Deal's impact even decades before conservatives began to dismantle banking, housing, pension, and other social welfare provisions. Bitter compromises and uneven efforts to enforce the law disproportionately helped white, male, industrial workers and worsened long-standing racial and gender inequalities. Providing blue-collar workers with white-collar living standards also benefited financial services companies, which profited enormously from selling the mortgages, insurance policies, and other financial products. They were critical private partners to a public welfare system designed to bolster manufacturing workers—and by extension their families, as their aging parents and young children no longer had to work. The many Americans and immigrants denied those basic financial supports demanded equality for decades. By the year 2000, many more had access to various celebrated programs. But unemployment protections, mortgages, student loans, and other social welfare guarantees seemed woefully inadequate and even pernicious instead of being the genuine support that liberals had promised.

Some academics describe the financialization of the US economy as a shift that began after the 1970s. Yet finance has been a vital part of American life since colonial times. Financial products like insurance buoyed the Gilded Age and Progressive Era's growing middle and professional classes, who largely came from white, Protestant stock. Access to those private, employer-offered, or state-run credit arrangements, financial products, and insurance policies was later expanded by New Deal reforms. Many Depression-era experiments mitigated the risk of extending credit to blue-collar workers by making the national government the payer of last resort in public-private financial arrangements that required employees and employers to fund pension, unemployment, savings, and mortgage programs. Such creative financing inspired new financial products after World War II, by which point 1930s regulations had made banking safer. Private-sector options slowly supplemented and sometimes took the place of public pensions, federally guaranteed home loans, and unemployment or disability compensation policies during and after the stagnant 1970s. With a wave of deregulation and austerity policies, precarity steadily supplanted the postwar prosperity that only some Americans had enjoyed.

By now, all citizens have become accustomed to receiving help through tax deductions. Such breaks, however, shrink the revenues available for the kind of targeted spending that might actually reduce racial, gender, and class inequities—by addressing systemic problems that lawmakers have assumed government-guaranteed financial products would vanquish. Many studies have shown that in the aftermath of supposedly universal government programs, like student loans, inequality has instead worsened.[13]

The story of the American financial sector and the federal loan guarantees designed to nurture it stretches back decades before bankers embraced lending to undergraduates in the mid-1970s and for-profit schools gained more access to federal tuition assistance programs in the 1990s. It is a long, tragic tale featuring fears of federal expansion, complicated public-private social welfare programs, lawmakers eager to offer Americans government-guaranteed financial products, and incendiary power struggles. As Congress fought the executive branch and both major political parties underwent fraught, bitter, twentieth-century realignments, citizens struggling to pay for housing, health, education, and other basic needs bore the real costs of Capitol Hill showdowns and shutdowns that rarely ended with agreements to attack the inequality built into American life.

More than a century ago, working-class and middle-class Americans (particularly women, immigrants, minorities, Jews, and Catholics) began demanding access to the country's colleges and universities. The academy had long been a bastion of white, Protestant men who could marshal the resources to devote time to studies. Schools had always accommodated some talented but poor undergraduates by finding ways for them to cover their fees and living expenses, often by working or committing to pay after they had graduated. Even in the speculative 1920s, only wealthy colleges and a few philanthropists offered upfront loans, which epitomized risk. Collecting payments from either graduates or dropouts could be challenging, and their degrees and credits could not be repossessed.

Nonpayment just added to the many financial challenges that campuses faced during the Great Depression. Many postsecondary schools teetered on the brink of bankruptcy but the Roosevelt administration never considered offering the academy a New Deal. Such a bailout would have been unimaginable. Many Southern Democrats feared federal assistance would require campuses to desegregate, which would undermine Jim Crow. But Catholic school administrators pressured lawmakers to make their institutions also eligible for government support—an arrangement some viewed as at odds with the US Constitution's separation of church and state. Many presidents of elite colleges and universities, including Harvard's James Conant, nonetheless recoiled at some liberals' eagerness for mass higher education. Academics across the country feared that accepting government money would give politicians power over them, which would threaten their academic freedom and their institutions' autonomy.

New Dealers subsequently focused on the needs of students through a "work-study" program, not a lending scheme. The National Youth Administration used government funds to pay them for campus-managed projects and tasks so they could continue their studies. This support intentionally kept young men and women in school and out of competition with adults for scarce jobs. Federal officials never attempted to force colleges to enroll more impoverished students, let alone ones who were female, African American,

Jewish, or Catholic. The nonprofit public and private postsecondary schools that participated in the program may have agreed with the New Dealers' hope that part-time work would go to the neediest students. But, with strict limits on the percentage of enrollees that could be supported in this way, the jobs doled out by campus staff generally went to white men. In all, the program distributed $93 million to help more than 600,000 students afford tuition, living expenses, and books, enabling many campuses to remain open during the Depression.

Much beloved by its beneficiaries, the work-study program dramatically ended in 1943, a casualty of ongoing fights over segregation, academic freedom, taxing, spending, and federal power. The 1930s experiment nevertheless set an important, uniquely American precedent that would shape federal higher education policy and campus financing for decades. Both Republicans and Democrats had proven themselves willing, albeit in many cases begrudgingly, to give federal tuition assistance to aspiring students, not to the universities that admitted them.

Lawmakers used that approach to create another option for the millions of soldiers returning to a job market that many feared would be flooded. They could pursue an education. Many Americans wanted to see veterans taken care of, but the American Legion and the White House really fought for them to have a chance to go to college. Moderate and right-wing senators and representatives agreed to include the education entitlement in the Servicemen's Readjustment Act of 1944 only because surveys suggested that fewer than a million returnees would take advantage of it. Administrators at some elite schools still shuddered at the thought of admitting what they presumed would be a large number of incapable students tempted by the generous stipend to apply. Cash-strapped colleges and universities would clearly be incentivized to admit and keep them on campus, turning once-respected institutions, as University of Chicago president Robert Hutchins warned, "into educational hobo jungles."[14]

Indeed, the new law handsomely rewarded postsecondary institutions for participating and accepting large numbers of GIs by setting the reimbursement rate for tuition at a much higher rate than even Harvard charged. Because many campuses immediately hiked their fees, it represented an indirect infusion of cash to pay for the campus expansions needed to welcome a tidal wave of veterans, and later to educate larger generations of Americans.

The GI Bill is now storied, but this federal financial assistance to expand educational opportunities had some dire, unintended consequences. In fact, its long-term effects epitomize the danger that a supposedly universal program can serve to perpetuate an inequality that lawmakers expect it to reduce. More than two million veterans enrolled, defying most lawmakers' and academics' low expectations. But as campuses were inundated with this mostly white male population, women students tended to be crowded out. Many Jewish, Catholic, and white ethnic veterans struggled to find campuses that would admit them. Even fewer options existed for African American service personnel, who also found themselves largely shut out of the GI Bill's guaranteed home loan benefits. The clearly unequal outcomes of a supposedly color-blind law only increased the racial wealth gap, leaving African American families relatively less able to afford college in subsequent decades. Meanwhile, civilian students and their families bore the brunt of the tuition hikes the GI Bill encouraged—which ultimately contributed to falling enrollments and declining tuition revenues in the GI Bill's final years. Frightened college staffs across the country recognized that fee increases had placed higher learning out of reach for more of America's high school graduates in the postwar years—even as it became obvious that future generations would have less chance of entering or staying in the middle class without a degree.

The GI Bill, both in its successes and its shortcomings, inspired Americans to demand more federal aid to those seeking higher education after that legislation expired in the 1950s. But despite today's nostalgic accounts of a Cold War education boom, many efforts to expand access to postsecondary schooling were stymied by political fights over desegregation, the separation between church and state, and the growth of federal power. Those fights almost derailed the passage in 1958 of the National Defense Education Act. The Soviets' launch of Sputnik in the fall of 1957 had a galvanizing effect, but federal aid to campuses and students did not follow immediately. Disagreements between and within the Democratic and Republican parties caused negotiations to drag on for almost a year, and yielded a final bill that was hardly generous. The intentionally temporary legislation focused on cultivating strengths in specific areas—education, science, math, engineering, and modern foreign languages—and did nothing to force or encourage desegregation of colleges facing an increasing number of court challenges and protests. The law's greatest legacy was its hastily arranged compromise to support undergraduates not with "free ride" scholarships but with loans, a form of student assistance that had not been seriously considered in the 1930s and 1940s.

That provision opened a Pandora's Box. Students and parents unexpectedly embraced a limited, temporary program that had an unexpectedly long life. That widespread enthusiasm also encouraged Democrats and Republicans to embrace lending as a much cheaper way than grants to encourage and expand access to higher education. They proceeded to extend and expand the National Defense Education Act's lending provisions and experiment with additional student loan programs at the state level—and subsequently made lending to students a key component of the 1965 Higher Education Act.

Textbooks usually describe the 1965 legislation as a historic breakthrough that guaranteed federal funding for postsecondary schools, not students. In reality, lawmakers devoted the most money to the new Guaranteed Student Loan Program, later renamed the Federal Family Education Loan Program. Aides to President Lyndon Johnson modeled it on earlier state experiments with student lending and on the New Deal's still wildly popular mortgage assistance program. Johnson particularly liked government-guaranteed loans, which he and many other liberals hoped would spawn a new private industry focused on student lending. Again, enabling more Americans to take on debt to cover college fees seemed a relatively inexpensive way of expanding access to higher education. Cost was important in a moment when Johnson was also promising to wage a War on Poverty and to build a Great Society while still funding a costly military campaign in Vietnam. But liberals did not sell student lending as a low-cost social policy or way to tinker with the labor market. Democrats from northern and western states, as well as moderate Republicans, instead saw it as a way to guarantee equal opportunities to all Americans, because many quietly assumed it would lift many minorities, particularly African Americans, into the middle class. The law's supposedly color-blind features never fooled southern Democrats and conservative Republicans. But the loan program's fiercest critics were the bankers, who lobbied hard against, what they considered, an unnecessary government intervention in the private sector.

Financiers embraced guaranteed lending only after 1972, when Congress reauthorized the Higher Education Act of 1965. In terms of milestones in American higher education, 1972 is usually recalled for Title IX, which made it illegal to deny opportunities to students on the basis of sex, and Pell grants, which were designed as subsidies to poor students and expected by lawmakers to go mainly to African Americans. Alongside these celebrated provisions, the 1972 amendments made it easier for more for-profit schools to qualify as institutions that students could use federal tuition assistance options to attend, and created a new, quasi-governmental agency, the Student Loan Marketing Association (SLMA or, as it is usually called, Sallie Mae). That government-sponsored enterprise was designed to operate the business of issuing and servicing the government's loans to students, but also to make a market for student debt that private-sector bankers would find more attractive to participate in. Essentially Sallie Mae made the program's promised return on bankers' investment irresistible in the stagnant 1970s economy. This new secondary market encouraged banks to experiment with other student aid financial products, since the lack of profit risk on the federal loans could offset the substantial risks of private student lending. The effect was to greatly expand the student loan portfolios of many financial services firms.

The student loan industry grew exponentially after Sallie Mae's 1972 creation. Even as increasing numbers of borrowers defaulted on their loans, lawmakers did not rein in that expansion but instead encouraged it through the 1970s and 1980s. Congress considered policing it only after a major lender collapsed in 1990. Subsequent investigations uncovered abuse, corruption, and profiteering that ran throughout the entire sector but were particularly egregious among the small number of for-profit schools eligible for federal student assistance programs.

Continued fights over equality, taxing, spending, regulation, and federal power prevented genuine reform for decades. Most lawmakers balked at better regulating the already powerful student loan industry even after a 1992 change to federal budget reporting revealed that the guaranteed-loan program cost the government far more than it would to directly lend money to students and parents. The parties' realignment made lending money directly to undergraduates a partisan issue even though it would save taxpayers, campuses, and students a lot of money. Student loan industry lobbyists almost stopped the creation of a small direct-loan pilot program in 1992 and used their sizeable power to thwart efforts to expand direct lending in the 1990s and 2000s. Lawmakers helped by easing restrictions on for-profit schools' eligibility for federal tuition assistance programs. Those schools' alumni were already disproportionately likely to default. But Democrats and Republicans could agree to give them access to this indirect aid because these institutions still disproportionately served the immigrants, citizens of color, women, and nontraditional students who struggled to find a place in the country's community colleges, state schools, and private universities. Policing for-profits and safeguarding direct lending seemed unlikely to many during the early months of the Great Recession when borrowers finally started to publicly admit they were drowning in student debt. This growing outcry helped a slim Democratic majority permanently replace the guaranteed-loan program with direct lending during the tense 2010 budget reconciliation process that more famously enacted Obamacare.

President Barack Obama certainly celebrated ending guaranteed lending, which he labeled a "sweetheart deal in federal law that essentially gave billions of dollars to banks." He and others quickly learned the limits of that legislative jujitsu. The 2010 reconciliation process did not resolve the political fights that had robbed colleges of direct funding that would end their historic reliance on fees. By 2017, most states expected their public colleges and universities to be funded primarily by revenue from students. Most Americans wanting postsecondary degrees continue to have little choice but to borrow sums that will take years to pay back. That budget legislation also did not tackle the inequities that leave women, citizens of color, and immigrants paying more for degrees no longer guaranteeing well-paying jobs. Student debt and unequal pay have instead continued to ensure the persistence of the historic wealth gap between men and women, as well as between white households and families of color. The legislation did nothing to forgive the student debts Americans have struggled to repay since colleges first started offering them two hundred years ago.[15]

1

Honorably Financing College

"I was one of the lucky ones," President Lyndon Baines Johnson noted when he signed the 1965 Higher Education Act at his alma mater in San Marcos, Texas. He had enrolled at Southwest Texas State Teachers College in the mid-1920s because it was cheap and close to his family's home. Like a lot of ambitious young Americans, the Texan had still taken on debt for the studies that were his pathway out of poverty. "I lived in a tiny room above [college president] Dr. Evans' garage," he recalled, for "three years before the business manager knew I occupied those quarters and submitted me a bill." He sometimes "wondered what the next day would bring that could exceed the hardship of the day before." Even though Johnson shaved and showered in a gymnasium down the road and "worked at a dozen different jobs, from sweeping the floors to selling real silk socks," he graduated with a student loan debt of $220 in 1930 (equivalent to over $3,400 today). He took pride in signing this legislation on the campus where "the seeds were planted," he told the crowd, for "my firm conviction that, for the individual, education is the path to achievement and fulfillment; for the Nation, it is a path to a society that is not only free but civilized; and for the world, it is the path to peace."[1]

That road was hardly straightforward in the early twentieth century, when hundreds of thousands of Americans wanted more schooling to escape factory work or the family farm. Tuition may have been cheap by twenty-first-century standards, but those seemingly low rates obscure how unaffordable higher education has been since the nation's founding, when, generally, only the country's white, male gentry enrolled in colleges and universities perpetually teetering on the brink of bankruptcy. Fees and donors provided far more revenue than government support throughout the nineteenth century. History and geography subsequently limited opportunities for the growing number of ambitious men and women applying in the early twentieth century, when better-paying white-collar jobs required at least some college coursework. Opportunities were especially limited for laborers, immigrants, Catholics, Jews, and African Americans seeking credentials or college degrees. Most American institutions of higher learning remained rarified, remote, private colleges heavily dependent on donations and fees. Even the urban public universities willing to admit those outside the Protestant elite needed strivers, like Johnson, to scrape together money for tuition, books, and basic necessities. Only the wealthy could really afford the expense and time college required. Needy undergraduates had to hope for the growing number of scholarship, work, and loan programs that philanthropies, state governments, and universities offered before the stock market's 1929 crash upended the academy's already precarious financing.

A Land of Few Opportunities

Even before the Great Depression, few Americans could easily pay for higher learning. Vermont's Justin Morrill, a House Republican and staunch abolitionist, had reshaped higher education in America to provide more access with his celebrated 1862 Land-Grant College Act. Designed "to establish at least one college in every State upon a sure and perpetual foundation, accessible to all, but especially the sons of toil," it donated the proceeds from federally owned lands for schools to be built or expanded that focused on agricultural sciences and other practical pursuits rather than the classics. The Morrill Act represents the first federal aid to higher education, but did not concern itself with controlling the expense of attending a land-grant institution. Only in the first half of the twentieth century did a few states (most notably California) provide enough taxpayer support to allow public institutions to not charge tuition.[2]

No one at the time called that "financial aid." Before World War II, this phrase described direct funding from government or donors to underwrite the costs of running a campus. It evolved to include "student aid" during the Cold War. Only toward the end of the twentieth century did financial aid come to mean, at least colloquially, support for individual students. A century before that linguistic shift, the real financial sacrifice for enrollees and their families had been time, not money. Hours devoted to school came at the expense of those used to increase household income, especially in decades when factory and field work was so much easier to find than white-collar or professional jobs.[3]

Fees barely kept land-grant schools, small liberal arts colleges, or even Ivy League universities solvent. Most postsecondary institutions did not charge the full cost of instruction. Campus histories, as one scholar puts it, "almost always contain the story of anxiety-producing periods when the end seemed near." Many institutions were forced into temporary closures. Fires were a constant source of crisis; by 1890, sixty-two postsecondary schools in America had lost a main building (in many cases, their only building) to flames, and some never recovered from such disasters. The Civil War also caused many colleges in the South to suspend classes, after which a number failed to reopen. Colleges and universities have used a variety of means to survive such threats to their bottom lines. They sought donations, sold buildings, and spent endowment funds to cover debts and pay for daily operations. Some switched religious commitments or peddled subscriptions which were essentially prepayments for later studies. Campus heads held expenses down by having instructors and students attend to day-to-day maintenance and operations, or, in some cases, by relying on slave labor. They developed creative ways of competing for applicants able to pay—or, especially at new schools, attracted students by not initially charging tuition or extending financial help generously, to build the alumni base required for healthy donations in the future. They accepted applicants whose religion did not match the school's affiliation, who were unprepared for advanced study, or who were older (or sometimes younger) than the norm. Many of those tactics were restorative in the short term and some were transformative in the long term, but they did not make colleges and universities, public or private, immune to economic downturns, wars, pandemics, population changes, and environmental disasters.[4]

Tuition revenue did much to supplement meager state allocations and private donations. Most postsecondary institutions have relied on a mix of philanthropy, state funds, and student fees to stay open; the support of government officials and private benefactors for higher education has generally been inconsistent and insufficient on its own. That mix continued even as Americans increasingly made distinctions between public and private campuses after the Civil War. Colonial governments and early state legislatures created but did not generously fund colleges modeled on medieval universities like Oxford, Cambridge, and Heidelberg. In 1790, President George Washington urged Congress to start a new college in the nation's capital to provide the civic education required for a democratic republic to succeed, but the idea was rebuffed. Some thirty years later, New Hampshire's legislature decided that Dartmouth College should become a public institution with governor-appointed trustees, but Dartmouth faculty revolted. The case went to the US Supreme Court, whose 1819 ruling sided with the professors—a win for the educators' prized institutional autonomy but one that did nothing to encourage government support. Even when state schools were founded in Maryland, North Carolina, and other states to meet growing demand for professional education in the antebellum years, they were unevenly supported. As the number of postsecondary schools in the United States grew to 250 in those decades, only the University of Virginia and University of South Carolina received regular appropriations from their state governments. Most institutions were stand-alone denominational colleges established along the moving frontier (including a handful founded by wealthy patrons and educators for the instruction of women or African Americans).[5]

Midwesterners especially stood out in those pre–Civil War years for creating the prototypes of the modern American university. New states sold enough government land before the Civil War to create twenty public schools. Michiganders notably embraced the German research model to transform the University of Michigan between 1853 and 1863. In 1855, the state's legislators also created America's first school devoted to the agricultural sciences, the Agricultural College of the State of Michigan. That college, lawmakers later decided, would reap the benefits of the 1862 Morrill Act, which enabled states to use the revenues from the sale of federal lands to establish new or fund already existing colleges dedicated to agricultural, military science, and engineering (then called the mechanical arts).[6]

While historians of Michigan State University tend to celebrate that institution's claim to be the first of the land-grant universities, the land-grant legislation's legacy is far more complicated. Historian Robert Lee and journalist Tristan Ahtone, for example, have decried this federal investment in education as a "massive wealth transfer masquerading as a donation" because the "Morrill Act worked by turning land expropriated from tribal nationals into seed money for higher education." Much of the eleven million acres of western land the government distributed as eighty thousand parcels had been purchased by it, for less than $400,000, but more than a quarter of those parcels had been "confiscated through outright seizure or by treaties that were never ratified by the federal government." Justin Morrill did not mention these land grabs when he dedicated his legislation to "the sons of toil" whom he considered in need of more education. Sale proceeds did not offer young people tuition assistance but instead directly supported schools. Some of the beneficiaries, like New York's Cornell University, were not institutions Americans would now consider public schools. Bay State legislators also used this legislation to help the founders of the Massachusetts Institute of Technology open that now expensive, prestigious private school in 1865. It had first been discussed in the 1840s but was not chartered until 1861.[7]

The land-grant legislation offered a blood-soaked foundation for many campuses, but not robust, continuous financial aid. Congressional delegation size determined how many acres a state received. By selling this land, states gained money that could only be used to endow public colleges and universities. Only five southern assemblies split their endowments between white and Black institutions. As states proceeded to sell the land, most got far less per square foot than they had hoped. (The average across the country was $1.65 an acre.) Land sales also took time; the University of California regents, for example, still held unsold parcels in 1900. The principal had to be conserved and invested to sustain land-grant campuses but lawmakers could transfer endowments to other schools. (Both Brown's and Yale's grants were reassigned to state institutions in the 1890s.) Interest income was used to establish new colleges, reopen shuttered ones (like the preparatory school that became the University of Minnesota), and keep struggling institutions afloat—including the Michigan Agricultural College (later to be named Michigan State University). Nothing in the law forced state legislators to provide additional, ongoing funding to sustain institutions established with land-grant proceeds.[8]

Neither did Congress provide much additional help to campuses. The 1887 Hatch Act injected new funds into land-grant schools, but only to support agricultural experiment stations and other programs focused on farming and manufacturing. In 1890, the Second Morrill Act (as it came to be known) provided for annual appropriations to states to support land-grant colleges, while also stipulating that no state receiving such funds could exclude African American students—a rule that caused states unwilling to end segregation to create the separate institutions, some of which endure today as historically Black colleges. By 1910, funds tied to those laws accounted for more than a third of the income of most land-grant colleges, in part because state legislatures spent so little on their schools.[9]

Only a handful of legislatures had managed to create outstanding public universities before World War I. Illinois, Wisconsin, Michigan, and California lawmakers all passed permanent property taxes to fund their state schools. Wisconsinites especially stood out for their ambitious experiment in making the university of use to the public.[10]

Some politicians doubted their state universities' value. For example, Ben Tillman, the Democrat who won the 1890 South Carolina gubernatorial election, stripped funds from the University of South Carolina, seeing it as too elitist. (His opponent was an alumnus.) Even in Wisconsin, where expert faculty members were consulted for advice on governance issues, lawmakers were suspicious about how Madison campus staff spent their time and state resources, and launched investigations throughout the 1890s and 1900s. At the University of California, administrators found it easier to gain support of donors as they sought to rapidly expand the Berkeley campus at the turn of the century.[11]

Major philanthropists did a lot to overhaul American postsecondary schooling in the decades before World War I. Private institutions still dominated the Northeast, but vied with state schools in the South and Midwest, and were hard to find out West. That scholastic mix hardly met the needs of a nation that had emerged as a leading manufacturing power during the Gilded Age. Industrialists since the early nineteenth century had been eager to underwrite the science and engineering instruction that would improve their operations. College administrators, particularly in the Ivy League, had been reluctant to accept gifts underwriting courses outside the classical or religious curricula their schools offered. They became far more amenable in the late nineteenth century. By then, tycoons were offering to bankroll programs of study that interested them, to build new schools (as Andrew Carnegie, Johns Hopkins, and Leland Stanford did, as well as John D. Rockefeller and Marshall Field with the University of Chicago), and to transform existing ones (as tobacco magnate James B. Duke did to a small college in North Carolina). Their charitable foundations also provided much-needed aid to schools willing to improve their finances, standardize their course offerings, offer degrees in subjects of practical value, and generally operate in a more professional, businesslike manner.[12]

Even these powerful men and their philanthropies could not immediately transform the American academy. Overall, they spent far more in the Northeast than other areas of the country and lavishing money on the elite campuses where their peers and children studied rather than donating in ways that might improve the overall quality of American higher education. Most college and university faculty members had not earned a PhD and even fewer conducted anything approximating original research.[13]

More students started to demand access to these schools during their overhauls in the Gilded Age and Progressive Era. Few had been eager to enroll before those pivotal decades. The generally remote land-grant universities did not see the flood of applicants Morrill had anticipated. Many aspiring undergraduates, including some who enrolled, had little interest in the practical scientific training the senator thought more Americans needed. The country's twenty oldest colleges increased admissions by only 3.5 percent in the 1870s, while the overall population surged by 23 percent. The student population continued to grow with the addition of new colleges and universities, but the total number of undergraduates remained unimpressive. Even with a 60 percent increase in matriculation, in the first decade of the twentieth century the portion of the entire population enrolled moved only from 4.01 to 4.48 percent. In 1910, there were about a thousand postsecondary schools in the country, but only a handful could accommodate more than two thousand undergraduates and graduates, and the total number of students was just 300,000.[14]

Proprietary schools were responsible for much of the growth in the early twentieth century. These for-profit, degree-granting institutions first emerged in the Gilded Age and thrived through the Progressive Era and Roaring Twenties. Popular demand for more schooling drove their growth in cities across the country. Relatively inexpensive to attend, these schools initially offered commercial training to white middle-class Americans who did not have the social connections to matriculate in well-established colleges. Jews, Catholics, immigrants, African Americans, and other minorities soon flocked to evening classes teaching the kind of skills needed for better-paying, more-respectable, white-collar jobs. Women especially gravitated to institutions that could prepare them for jobs teaching, typing, bookkeeping, and taking shorthand. Though some enrollees complained about the expense and the quality of the instruction, many alumni offered glowing praise for alma maters that helped move them from the factory floor to the front office.[15]

The success of these schools and their alumni irked educators at the helm of the country's most prestigious public and private institutions. For example, Harvard University president Charles Eliot, having read a study of New York's fast-growing assortment of business colleges, took to the pages of the *Boston Herald* to damn them as "sham institutions" run by a "multitude of humbugs" who "outrageously abused the name 'college' to which none of them had any right." Certainly, there were "money-making rackets" in this era, yet Eliot's and other elites' denunciation of these schools also seemed disdainful of the men and women these institutions saw fit to train. Perhaps it was prejudice and fear of competition that spurred Eliot and other Ivy League administrators to push for a change in the public school system instead, whereby young people could gain business training through an expanded set of high schools. Meanwhile, established universities started new schools of education, law, and business on their own campuses, offering students interested in those practical fields more illustrious degrees. These premier academic credentials would, of course, be unavailable to most Americans, leaving the majority of students to enroll in proprietary programs. The exclusivity of Harvard's and other elite institutions' offerings, in which students could not simply choose to enroll if they had the money to pay, kept the academy overwhelmingly white and male, and also made it very likely that anyone reaching the top tiers of the country's business and politics would be so, as well.[16]

As established colleges waged their war on what can now be seen as the precursors to today's for-profit schools, enrollments soared. Matriculation doubled in the 1920s, when more Americans could afford to send their children to college. Young people, like the youthful Lyndon Johnson, increasingly saw that investing the time and money to earn a degree paid off in the chance to enter the growing ranks of professionals and managers.[17]

Aspiring undergraduates had more options but certainly not enough. Reporters often celebrated the 1920s as an era when self-made men and women were paying their way through college. The majority of enrollees in nonprofit institutions remained white men from the middle and upper classes. At state schools the children of urban professionals greatly outnumbered farmers' kids. Elite private universities were even more restrictive. They needed tuition revenue but refused to substantially increase admission rates to meet demand. Administrators instead limited enrollments, often on the basis of race, religion, and ethnicity. Quotas on the number of Jews and Catholics as well as the general exclusion of African Americans cultivated a rarified atmosphere, which reflected how college remained a privilege even as applications and enrollments exploded at other types of institutions.[18]

As blue-collar strivers flocked to junior colleges, teachers colleges, urban universities, and proprietary schools after World War I, those institutions grew in size and number. Applicants clamored for the full- and part-time programs in engineering, home economics, and business that they considered useful. By 1930, municipal schools had eclipsed the public and private research universities in size. The College of the City of New York, for example, had irregular enrollments but nevertheless grew to 24,000 students in the 1920s. Those numbers transformed the American student population, which still included the children of wealthy industrialists and professionals but also now featured a growing number of working-class Jewish, Catholic, and African American men and women. Widespread eagerness for more education often surprised educational leaders and policymakers. For example, Wisconsin legislators had included postsecondary education benefits in a bonus bill for WWI soldiers but failed to predict how popular those perks would be. Veterans crowded into college classrooms, particularly for courses in what they considered practical fields.[19]

All schools, not just the for-profits, desperately needed these students. Many public and private universities expanded facilities in the 1920s when donations increased, business and federal funding for scientific research grew, and the number of applications soared. States did increase their support for public universities. Michigan legislators raised university appropriations by 50 percent in 1921, the same year legislators earmarked $5.1 million for capital improvements to the Ann Arbor campus. Tuition revenue still remained vital, however. State schools in the Roaring Twenties still relied on student fees for 22.5 percent of revenue, whereas private institutions used tuition to cover 54.2 percent of expenses. Even though seventeen out of thirty-one public universities reported waiving tuition for residents, most (unlike the University of California and University of Wisconsin) levied other fees. Most campuses still charged less than administrators spent educating students. A surge in state support ensured that fees only had to cover roughly half the University of Michigan's payroll. But tuition revenue paid for 63 percent of Columbia's operating expenses and almost 90 percent of those costs at the University of Pennsylvania and the Massachusetts Institute of Technology.[20]

Student Self-Help

Enrollees still needed help affording college. The country hardly had a robust tradition of student aid, which increased but never kept pace with enrollment. American campuses imported a tradition from Europe of offering scholarships, discounts, jobs, and loans to the talented poor, particularly if they promised to dedicate themselves to something virtuous after graduation. Thomas Jefferson, for example, insisted that the University of Virginia (founded in 1819) provide grants for gifted but destitute residents. Some nineteenth-century colleges charged no tuition in their early years but levied fees as they began to attract wealthier applicants and needed to pay for expansions. Stanford, for example, was tuition-free for more than thirty years. Staff billed students $60 for non-academic services as early as 1919 but only started charging tuition in 1920, when the university had established itself enough to easily compete with nearby Berkeley for applicants.[21]

While donors often find it most appealing to fund new buildings or academic programs rather than contribute to attracting or supporting students, there have always been some benefactors happy to establish scholarships. These grants were awarded to students first identified for their talent and then found to be financially needy. Harvard recorded such a gift in 1643. "Charity funds" became commonplace in the early 1800s, including at private New England institutions like Williams College. Wealthy Americans increasingly endowed such funds after the Civil War, when the country's industrialization provided both the money for such gifts and the need for a more educated workforce. The Gilded Age's philanthropists spent even more money on students. The Peabody Education Fund, for example, distributed $580,660 in scholarships in the last decade of the nineteenth century, most of them to help promising students in the South become capable schoolteachers. Those charities donated even more after World War I, when industrialists created more than ten foundations prioritizing student aid. As such, the private money available for undergraduate and graduate scholarships rapidly grew from an estimated $105,351 in 1921 to almost $1.5 million in 1930.[22]

Students received far less state help. The federal government did not provide direct assistance until after World War I, and even then designated it only for disabled veterans. Massachusetts and Maryland had started state aid programs after the Revolution. In the nineteenth century, legislatures usually tied such support to specific institutions. For example, New York officials offered to help some enrollees in Cornell's state programs and departments. Other legislatures joined donors and alumni in starting scholarship pools for public universities and land-grant colleges. Still, even during the 1927–1928 academic year, only 402 schools offered a total of 34,013 scholarships.[23]

Undergraduates have historically had an easier time finding jobs. Colonial colleges employed enrollees for a variety of tasks, including bell-ringing. By the end of the nineteenth century, staff commonly helped students find work on or near campus. Some universities even created offices dedicated to finding a form of aid described as "self-help" by the early twentieth century. This uniquely American phrase quickly became as ubiquitous as "working one's way through college," which better described the students who squeezed in evening classes at for-profits after factory shifts. At nonprofit institutions, in contrast, enrollees held a range of jobs. University of Chicago students at the turn of the century, for example, spent their time clerking, lighting street lamps, minding children, reading to the elderly, working in railroad stations, staffing newspaper offices, and even collecting debts.[24]

Undergraduates did not really begin borrowing for their educations until the speculative Roaring Twenties. Elite schools had been the first to lend. After all, these rarified institutions had the funds to do so. But they had a long tradition of rarely extending credit. Dartmouth, for example, stood out in 1806 for graduating thirty-three students (out of a class of thirty-nine) who together owed their alma mater $1,222.18. A century later, most Association of American Universities members loaned money to just 1 percent of their student bodies. Yet campus loan officers tended to be generous. They often only charged interest after graduation, putting the revenue toward guaranteeing future resources for the next cohort of needy applicants.[25]

Administrators became more interested in lending programs in the 1920s. Stanford trustee Herbert Hoover, for example, suggested borrowing to quell student protests over charging and then quickly raising tuition. He considered many undergraduates' flashy cars proof that most could easily afford the $225 required to enroll, which was on the high end of what other private institutions charged at the time. Everyone else, he suggested, should be offered a loan, not a scholarship, because he had wanted but was unable to borrow from Stanford as a student.[26]

Hoover was hardly alone in considering credit more dignified than charity in the 1920s. As lenders offered consumers more credit and experimented with installment plans, college administrators across the country toyed with charging students the full cost of instruction and letting them pay over time. Lending seemed an easy, reliable way to ensure the enrollment and revenue needed to pay for campus expansions and improvements that neither states nor donors reliably covered. These advances epitomized this infamously speculative era. Admission alone was a student's collateral. Neither degrees nor college credits could be repossessed. Plus, loan officers did not necessarily have systems in place to collect payment. Some only asked that undergraduates repay them when and if they could. Twenty-five percent of debts made under such agreements proved uncollectable. Women alumni tended to be better about paying off liens, at least until marriage. If they left the workforce, contract terms sometimes made it unclear whether or not their husbands were responsible for their educational debts. Schools with stricter agreements also struggled to recoup funds. Staff had to dun 15 percent of borrowers, turning 1 percent of delinquencies over to lawyers.[27]

Those difficulties did not stop clubs, business associations, churches, individuals, and philanthropies from lending. Foundations gave a sizeable amount. Money often went directly to elite schools, which ensured tuition assistance largely went to the white men who made up the vast majority of top institutions' student bodies. Donors did not place onerous rules on campus loan funds. The Cambridge Foundation, for example, did not demand that Harvard charge specific interest rates, impose uniform repayment rules, or set standards to assess the likelihood of repayment in 1916, when the du Pont Fund also declined to set similar restrictions on grants to the University of Virginia for student aid. Even the American Banking Association's Foundation for Education only suggested guidelines, since, as a representative admitted, "even with the best of judgment it has not always been possible to estimate correctly either the desire or the ability of the student to repay his obligation."[28]

Only a few of the roughly seventy-five philanthropies imposed stringent rules on the money they lent directly to students in the 1920s. Whitney Benefits staff extended the foundation's income to students but never charged interest. The Feild Cooperative Loan Fund, in contrast, required borrowers to take out life insurance policies to guarantee repayment. The harshest was perhaps New York realtor William Harmon's eponymous foundation. He considered scholarships morally bankrupt. His staff intended credit from the Division of Student Loans to ensure that both students and colleges would be able to support themselves through a revolving loan fund that charged 6 percent interest. These financial products guaranteed that schools "running at a deficit" could "balance their budgets by charging" the full cost of instruction, which would also teach students about "business obligations" far better than the "semi-charitable" grants upon which too many depended. Harmon considered that strategy successful. The poorest students did a better job repaying their obligations to his foundation because their "earning power" had been so "enhanced as a result of their education."[29]

The Harmon Foundation contributed but a portion of the roughly eight to ten million dollars in credit available to students in 1930. Campuses provided a lot. The University of Chicago's fund, for example, was almost nonexistent in 1920 but grew steadily from $5,498 in 1921 to $111,365 in 1932. By then, half the American student body financed their studies by working part-time and taking out loans, usually ranging somewhere between $25 and $200. Lending had become so commonplace that *New York Times* reporter Dorothy Woolf celebrated the "changed attitude of borrowers and lenders. No longer can the loan be considered an act of charity," she enthused. "Today it is held an honorable and praiseworthy means of financing higher education."[30]

Collegiate Crash

Loan funds could hardly save the many campuses facing bankruptcy during the Great Depression. Enrollments had almost doubled in the 1920s but, in the 1930s, a record number of Americans were out of work and could not afford tuition. College loan officers, private lenders, and philanthropic organizations were deluged by inquiries in 1930, as students after the stock market crash found themselves without funds or many options for part-time work. The country's student population shrank dramatically after 1932, when budgets set earlier had expired. Because schools' endowments, private donations, and state allocations had shrunk, most raised tuition rates to try to make up for the shortfall. Between 1930 and 1936, for the nation as a whole, the share of state school budgets contributed by legislatures dropped from 22.3 percent to 14.4 percent. Between 1932 and 1934, national enrollment fell 8 percent, but total tuition revenue plummeted by 61 percent. Numbers declined far more in professional programs, teachers' colleges, and urban schools. New York University, for example, lost ten thousand of its almost thirteen thousand students between 1929 and 1934. Two years later, thirty-one schools had closed, while twenty-two others had merged. Most of the shuttered colleges were private; only two were four-year institutions. For-profits struggled as much as the remaining 1,700 nonprofit public and private institutions. Some proprietary schools vigorously advertised for students, others tried to become degree-granting nonprofits, and more than a few simply closed. Elite private institutions fared the best in these years when they feverishly competed for the country's wealthiest children, including applicants whom Wesleyan's president labeled "white dullards."[31]

Desperation led less prestigious campuses to try anything to stay open. More than 10 percent of private colleges and universities accepted IOUs. Some administrators bartered for admission. Illinois's Carthage College accepted coal, and the University of North Dakota allowed students to cover fees with produce. Some college officials continued to promise that students could split their time between working and studying. The number of part-time matriculates increased overall in the 1930s but many students complained that college officials reneged on promises of decent hours and pay. Reports surfaced of malnourishment, homelessness, and depression among students, including a Kansas University undergraduate who lived off one quart of milk and a sweet roll each day. Some state schools provided housing at extremely low cost or charged ten or twelve cents for dinners, but even that was too expensive for many students. Investigators found an undergraduate budgeting just fifty cents for food and another sleeping in an abandoned car. They grimly concluded that many undergraduates "would have been no better off anywhere else. At the colleges they could suffer undernourishment in attractive surroundings; and in the classrooms and college libraries they could at least find warmth."[32]

A few could also receive grants and loans. The amount and availability of money was still small (just a 38 to 44 percent increase between the 1928–1929 and the 1936–1937 academic years). Administrators desperately fundraised in order to increase aid but the amounts were not nearly enough to stop students from dropping out. After all, the high levels of unemployment, particularly for youth, hardly seemed to make enrollment worth the expense. DePauw University student reporters even suggested the school hand out hot dogs instead of degrees since hungry, unemployed alumni could not eat their sheepskins.[33]

Neither students nor campuses received much assistance in the early years of the Depression. President Hoover certainly made overtures. He assembled an advisory group dominated by professional educators but also marbled with public officials, corporate executives, and civic leaders to make recommendations just before the stock market crashed in 1929. Two years later, this National Advisory Committee on Education submitted a report calling for federal assistance without any significant oversight. They wanted government "cooperation," in line with Hoover's preferred governing style and the hands-off tradition that the Supreme Court had upheld in 1819 and the first Morrill Act had continued. Committee members emphasized that the country's industrialization had left local and state governments unable to adequately educate citizens who needed schooling now more than ever. As such, educators needed a continuous flow of unrestricted funds and a new Department of Education, whose head would be a part of the president's cabinet. That appointee would not oversee faculty and staff but safeguard educators' autonomy while giving them much-needed leverage in Washington.[34]

The committee's proposals kept with past political precedent. The executive branch's Department of the Interior already included a small Office of Education, whose staff generally compiled statistics and generated reports.

The Advisory Committee certainly wanted a bureaucracy with more gravitas to reflect how important they considered schooling but members hardly wanted a Department of Education to have much power over them. Neither did Office of Education appointees. In the 1920s, staff tended to come from the ranks of leading educational organizations, like the National Education Association (NEA).[35]

NEA members included primary, secondary, and postsecondary teachers as well as education experts. They generally shared a reverence for keeping schooling the provenance of local and state governments and jealously guarded their autonomy and academic freedom. Scientists and engineers also had more faith in manufacturers, who, before World War II, had done more to support them than the federal government. These research scientists also tended to view liberal policymakers' growing embrace of the social sciences with suspicion. Such misgivings also reflected the conservative Republican bent of many college administrators, who advocated minimal state interference. Their ranks included the heads of land-grants and private institutions, such as Kenyon College president Gordon Chalmers, Columbia president Nicholas Murray Butler, and Harvard president James Conant.[36]

Conant, a celebrated chemist, was a dominant figure in American higher education during the Depression, World War II, and early Cold War. He personified the contradictions that epitomized the academy's fraught relationship with the federal government. He has long been lauded for his work on the Manhattan Project, influence over the National Science Foundation's creation, and role in making Harvard and the rest of American higher education more meritocratic. He spent World War I helping the Bureau of Chemistry develop poison gases but resisted the lure of lucrative industrial work. As he explained to his fiancée in the early 1920s, he first wished to become a leading organic chemist, then president of Harvard, and "after that, a Cabinet member, perhaps Secretary of the Interior." Those ambitions seemed fitting for a determined Yankee raised in Boston's immigrant suburbs, almost denied admission to Roxbury Latin, and dedicated to making a place for himself in the Harvard student body's rigid social hierarchy. He managed to best the Boston Brahmins vying to run Harvard in 1933 when trustees, he later remembered, assumed "you couldn't raise money for anything." The newly inaugurated Conant immediately roiled the school and its Ivy League competitors by establishing a generous scholarship program to ensure that talented, needy students could enroll. Conant never forced Harvard to practice the need-blind, full-aid, standardized-testing meritocracy he routinely preached. He rejected the "Jacksonian" view that "affirmed all men were born equal, envied intellectual pre-eminence, and preached the doctrine of equal educational privilege for all." He instead envisioned admissions officers cultivating a "natural aristocracy of talent and virtue," whose members came from all segments of society, including the poor. He frequently referred to Jefferson's vision for the University of Virginia, but nevertheless insisted that private colleges were duty-bound to find, train, and fully fund the talented young people who performed well on tests but could not afford fees.[37]

Conant exemplified why much of the academy, including those on its seemingly progressive edges, did not celebrate Franklin Delano Roosevelt's triumph over Hoover in 1932. They certainly wanted to be, as the NEA's James Rule put it, "within the beneficent sphere of the New Deal," but many professors and administrators bitterly opposed the federal interventions to relieve and reconstruct the nation. NEA staffers convened emergency committees and urged lobbyists to keep teachers, the public, and Congress abreast of any threats to American education. Faculty and administrators openly aired their frustrations throughout Roosevelt's first term. Nicholas Murray Butler admitted in 1935 that FDR did "a great service when he took selfish, organized big business off our necks," but Columbia's president still denounced policies that seemed poised to let "selfish organized big labor . . . take its place." Others upbraided the administration for violating the sacrosanct checks and balances that were supposed to be performed by other branches of government, as well as the traditional powers of state and local authorities, voluntary organizations, and private citizens. Conant spoke publicly against executive branch intrusions, particularly in institutions of higher learning. "Nowhere is liberty and freedom more prized and more essential than in an academic community," he warned in 1934. "To coerce it is to enslave it."[38]

Some professors and students nevertheless begged the president to aid the academy. A University of Oklahoma zoology professor urged Roosevelt to denounce spending cuts during his fireside chats. A University of South Carolina faculty member asked him "in the name of downtrodden and oppressed teachers" to do "something for us, the forgotten men and women of America." Chicago junior college students wanted the president to use his influence to stop their campus from closing in July 1933. A father asked Roosevelt to personally donate money to his daughter's struggling Christian college in Massachusetts. A young Floridian suggested federal relief funds could "send college boys back to school" in order to take "youths out of the contest for jobs needed by married men and giving youths . . . an education so they will be fitted properly for jobs when the times comes." He received a boilerplate reply, which epitomized New Dealers' initial disinterest in aiding the academy.[39]

Higher education never topped the Roosevelt administration's agenda. FDR and his aides did want to offer a New Deal for youth but never considered the kind of radical, top-down postsecondary overhaul leading academics dreaded. Both political traditions and geographic realities made such a bailout unimaginable to New Dealers facing fierce opposition to their many initiatives to relieve the citizenry and reconstruct the nation. Only a few top appointees quietly worked to open the door to the male-dominated Ivory Tower. They had help from young upstarts like future president LBJ, who had struggled to pay for college in the 1920s, when blue-collar, immigrant, Jewish, Catholic, African American, and female applicants had found themselves largely shut out of elite schools waging war on the for-profits willing to offer the credentials they needed to compete for well-paying work.

2

Will Work for School

South Carolina housewife Mrs. C. L. Melton desperately wanted to send her son to college in the fall of 1933. But after her husband's salary as a state detective was reduced, his wages barely covered the family's everyday expenses in the little town of Cheraw. Her "greatest ambition" remained "to educate my only child." So she wrote to the new president, Franklin Delano Roosevelt, for help. The White House replied with brochures and pamphlets for scholarships available through the many private and religious organizations that had ratcheted up student aid after World War I. She wrote back not to the staffer who mailed these but to "His Excellency," pointedly informing FDR that she had sent inquiries to such organizations but had been told by all that there were "no funds available." She had already considered giving up her "very attractive little rented brick house" to cover college costs because she could not "afford to let my son meet the problems of life unprepared, as I have done in being uneducated." How, she asked, "can we hope to raise serviceable Americans without educations?" Melton wished this administration "would provide some plan by which worthy boys and girls would borrow money from our government for an education."[1]

Her request for a federal student loan is one of few in the official files.[2] Her letters arrived shortly after the president's now-famous first hundred days, when lawmakers passed an extraordinary amount of legislation. Several years of state budget cuts, declining enrollments, and reports of starving students had not placed the academy on packed White House and congressional agendas. The country seemed to have far more pressing needs. Top New Dealers also doubted that pursuing higher education was a priority need or desire of the majority of Americans. The eagerness of ordinary citizens like Melton, however, helped push the Roosevelt administration to start weaving postsecondary schooling into the expansive New Deal to relieve and reconstruct the nation.

The White House never pursued a real academic overhaul. Experiments instead kept within the general spirit of the New Deal, which delicately expanded federal power, relied on the private sector to help carry out a lot of public reforms, and prioritized keeping Americans off unemployment rolls. The disastrous labor market, not the academy's poor financial health, inspired New Dealers to fashion a new work-study arrangement—a program that would thrill young people but annoy some higher education leaders and the conservative lawmakers who opposed the Roosevelt administration well into World War II. It was not that they hated the creative financing involved, which would become the hallmark of federal higher education aid. The problem was the encroachment of federal power into a realm traditionally left to states, churches, and private organizations, and for some, the threat that expanded access to education posed to white supremacy.

Jobs, Not Schools

A program like work-study was unimaginable in the early days of the Roosevelt administration. FDR had grown up a world away from the working-class and immigrant strivers increasingly eager to enroll in the country's relatively few colleges, universities, and proprietary schools. He had been tutored at home before his parents sent him to Groton, matriculated at Harvard, and went on to pursue his law degree at Columbia.[3]

FDR nevertheless prized pragmatic training. As an undergraduate, he had embraced Harvard's social scene and his role as editor of the *Crimson*, but later he felt he might have benefited from courses on the "practical idea of workings of a political system—of the machinery of primary, caucus, election, and legislature." He dismissed government courses focused on theory as "like an electric lamp that hasn't any wire." Real-world concerns mattered most to him as a politician. For example, in a speech at Oglethorpe University, he made a case for more central planning of the economy by pointing to "the vocation of higher education itself," where the market laws of supply and demand did not seem to be working. "You and I know," the presidential candidate insisted, "that the number of trained teachers needed in the nation is a relatively stable figure." Campuses across the country were nevertheless turning out "annually far more trained teachers than the schools could possibly use or absorb." As governor of New York, he had seen seven thousand qualified teachers "out of work, unable to earn a livelihood in their chosen profession because nobody had the wit or the fore-thought to tell them in their younger days that the profession of teaching was gravely oversupplied." That frustration helped explain his enthusiasm for the University of Wisconsin's mission to be of service to the state and its people. The conviction on that campus that social "science must aid in the making and administration of law," was also the spirit of his New Deal planning. Such sentiments did not endear him to "the school crowd"—the label that FDR and his aides privately applied to those running the nation's older, more traditional schools.[4]

Many top New Dealers shared the president's sentiments. The Roosevelt administration has long been remembered for welcoming academics into an executive branch tackling the country's many pressing problems. They staffed bureaucracies and ran relief programs but also provided the president with advice. This new generation of government bureaucrats seemed starkly different than their predecessors from the country's elite business circles. But many of the academics in the storied Brain Trust had graduated from or even taught in top institutions. Their politics certainly made them outsiders among the largely Protestant academic elite. Yet this cohort, whether from the nation's white middle- and upper-classes or from striving white-ethnic or minority working-class communities, only really knew northeastern or midwestern collegiate customs. Many, including Iowan Harry Hopkins, were thus ill-informed or even unaware of the academy's broader contours as well as the social, economic, and political conditions in the rest of the country.[5]

After Roosevelt entrusted Hopkins to oversee the nation's relief programs, the Grinnell College alum in turn asked famed journalist Lorena Hickok to traverse the country in 1933 and report back. Two years of letters provided a searing portrait of a country in crisis. Her brief mentions of far-flung colleges and universities in some ways confirmed what New Dealers presumed about the academy. One University of North Carolina sociologist—a Civil

Works Administration (CWA) appointee, no less—dismissed Hickok's concern that a Raleigh interracial commission was unrepresentative of the state's population. He assured her that its two-to-one ratio of whites to African Americans captured the town's dynamics even though the audience she saw there had triple the number of African Americans. The head of Clemson's agriculture department and the president of Furman College told Hickok that the CWA could pull out of South Carolina by May 1934. Hickok had more faith in a University of South Carolina sociologist, then on leave to administer such help, who warned that residents would need federal assistance for the foreseeable future. But Hickok admitted doubts about the young people graduating from these institutions. She relayed the concerns of a well-regarded social worker who regretted hiring recent University of Nevada alumni. Hickok, too, considered them unready. "I seriously question the wisdom," she wrote, "of turning these youngsters, no matter how excellent their technical training, loose on these people." She insisted that "maturity, the judgment that comes with maturity, cannot be acquired in any classroom."[6]

But Hickok applauded the work done by agricultural extension faculty. They were the only ones willing to make the treacherous day-long trip to reach remote communities in Knox County, where she encountered an old Kentuckian "half dead from pellagra." After speaking briefly, Hickok turned to leave and the woman "reached out and laid her hand on my arm and said in a voice that was hardly more than a whisper: 'Don't forget me, honey! Don't forget me.'" Hickok noted that University of West Virginia agricultural experts remembered the many families on relief. The school's subsistence garden program had "organized the people into self-governing garden clubs, and it has done marvels for their morale." One such club had taken its cooperation further than growing food. Working together, these out-of-work miners had "fixed their cabins all up, had cleared land and made a park and a baseball diamond, and were planning to make a swimming pool and build a tennis court for themselves."[7]

Hickok's early letters arrived when New Dealers had more urgent concerns than near-bankrupt schools and destitute students. The administration did create an Emergency Education Program for unemployed illiterates, which eventually included vocational training. But the president also suggested slashing federal funding to land-grants, a proposed 1933 cut that farm and state school lobbyists fought hard to restore. The White House pushed harder for a lot of emergency legislation in those early months but let bills to create a Department of Education and spend $75 million on scientific research languish in Congress, even though a third of the money was to be spent in research universities, like Wisconsin Madison.[8]

Those choices reflected the administration's priorities as well as White House insiders' assumption that the poverty stricken did not need or want more education. That sense shaped the evolution of the Civilian Conservation Corps (CCC). It initially offered out-of-work young men food, work, and fresh air. Higher-ups had expected recruits to learn by doing in camps dedicated to conservation work but soon discovered that many enlistees required basic literacy courses. Pressure and encouragement led many to sign up for courses, which were an immediate success. Congress set aside money for each camp to have a school in 1937. Just two years later, 90 percent of CCC volunteers had enrolled. The agency ended up employing 1,500 teachers, who taught more than 300,000 eager young men. A third of them chose academic, not vocational, subjects, including literature, history, and the fine arts.[9]

CCC recruits' needs and demands helped transform New Dealers' thinking about the usefulness of universities. Aides began to realize that schooling was not a waste of money but a tool to help with the larger effort to reconstruct the nation. Higher learning soon became part of other iconic New Deal initiatives, including the Tennessee Valley Authority. TVA head David Lilienthal unabashedly celebrated the agricultural extension classes offered to impoverished southerners desperate for water and electricity. Knowledge, he maintained, was the best way to empower citizens to use this massive infrastructure project to put "Democracy . . . on the March."[10]

Other Roosevelt insiders considered continuing education classes in the fine arts, humanities, and social sciences essential. More schooling opportunities would offer relief to the country's eighty thousand unemployed teachers, who could educate other Americans in the same broad range of subjects increasingly available to eager CCC recruits. Secretary of the Interior Harold Ickes considered such experiments necessary for students and teachers. "Whenever men and women who are on relief have the opportunity to teach others or to prepare themselves better for jobs and for better living," he observed, "they will preserve their self respect and make more profitable use of their times." He even suggested that Hopkins tap the services of University of Akron president George Zook, Roosevelt's appointee to head the Office of Education.[11]

Hopkins had no interest in advice from someone who had come from the established teaching circles that openly criticized the administration. He instead wanted to work with Hilda Smith, who ran Bryn Mawr's Summer School for Women Workers. That program was an integral part of the 1920s labor education movement dedicated to offering the working class much more than vocational training or the sort of classical education at elite institutions loath to admit blue-collar applicants. Hopkins liked Smith's July 1933 one-page proposal for a broad adult education program. Soon the Workers Education Project was launched (later to be renamed the Workers Service Program) and found Americans eager to both learn and teach. It received applications for adult education courses from unions, voluntary groups, settlement houses, and Boards of Education, whose members worked with the program to develop specific plans for their areas. Many Americans also applied to teach, but Smith did not fill her ranks with local, professional teachers. She and her staff openly rejected the Ivy League's rigid pedagogy. Her instructors would "sit around a table . . . as one of the group" as opposed to "a class in formal rows with the teacher obviously in authority" over a broad range of courses including current events, history, public speaking, English, journalism, drama, music, and science. Both teachers and students contributed to this ten-year program's success and popularity. "A group of miners in Iowa is being taught English by the daughter of an Italian miner," Smith celebrated, while "farmers in Wisconsin and Minnesota are studying cooperative marketing and the problems of consumers" and urban "textile workers, taxicab drivers, shop girls, and ditch diggers are discussing problems of trade-unionism and questions raised by current State and Federal legislation."[12]

The Workers Education Project and other schooling experiments also began to lessen the antagonism and mistrust between the Roosevelt administration and at least some wings of the academy. The top-down interference that so many academics feared never materialized. For example, federal officials and philanthropies together compensated the forty-five campuses that agreed to host the program's summer training centers. New Dealers also used academics' research to craft policies and programs dedicated to improving the country's economic health and the citizenry's welfare. New Dealers implicitly recognized their work's importance when they championed the 1935

Bankhead-Jones Act, which greatly increased federal support for land-grants in order to bolster research, teaching, and extension work, which, as Hickok had noted, helped impoverished local communities. The country's almost six hundred public teachers' colleges, land-grants, and universities also benefited from the money that New Dealers were increasingly willing to match for construction, repair, and even expansion. Hopkins's Works Progress Administration generally supplied workers for projects, leaving schools to cover material expenses. But the Public Works Administration fronted half the costs for public colleges and universities able to cover the rest, partnerships that funded $200 million worth of dorms, classrooms, labs, and libraries.[13]

Will Work for School

Directly bailing out the country's far-flung, patchwork quilt of public and private postsecondary schools nevertheless remained unimaginable throughout the 1930s. FDR, despite what his critics feared then and Americans have generally assumed since, remained in favor of keeping citizens off the dole, making work a condition of relief, balancing the budget, preserving federalism, and taming capitalism in order to save it. The president, of course, gave his appointees tremendous leeway to experiment, but many New Dealers, Hilda Smith included, drew inspiration from earlier private and state efforts to stabilize the economy and improve social welfare. Overhauling postsecondary schooling would have required an uncharacteristic, fundamental rethinking of the federal government's relationship to the academy, particularly the for-profit, religious, and private nonprofit schools ineligible for public-works projects. Ruling those institutions out deepened the distinction between them and state institutions, even though all nonprofits still relied on a mix of student fees, state appropriations, and donations. The country's roughly 600 state institutions understandably remained a low priority even as New Dealers became increasingly interested in what more learning could do for the country. Normal schools, teachers' colleges, and research universities educated less than half the country's 1.12 million undergraduate and graduate students.[14]

There were many more unemployed Americans than college students. Record-breaking unemployment subsequently put the labor market at the top of the White House's agenda. In the Roosevelt administration's early years, New Dealers made work a condition of relief even though many economists doubted there would be enough jobs for every American then or in the future. A range of initiatives endeavored to reduce the number of citizens competing for jobs and depending on government support, which even Roosevelt insiders maligned as being on the dole. Historians have noted the distinctly public-private character of these iconic experiments. Workers and employers, for example, paid taxes to support the 1935 Social Security Act's many pathbreaking programs, including the public pension system for the elderly as well as a welfare program for single mothers. That legislation complemented the 1935 Wagner Act, which guaranteed the rights of employees not toiling in homes, fields, or government offices. This landmark labor legislation, in effect, enabled private-sector workers to form and join government-certified unions to bargain collectively for higher wages and other benefits. Families could trust banks with their savings by 1936 because a series of banking acts offered deposit insurance and regulated the financial market that had proved so risky in the 1920s. White, working-class men could still get lines of credit, which were much more restrictive than the student loans that had become more common in that speculative era.[15]

Experts have only recently noticed how much of the New Deal's celebrated social welfare guarantees actually relied on creative financing. Government-guaranteed financial products gave working Americans access to the safeguards that white middle- and upper-classes had been buying since the Gilded Age to protect their livelihoods and fortunes. The Federal Deposit Insurance Corporation, for example, protected at least some of the savings blue-collar men needed to buy a home through the 1934 National Housing Act's well-regulated mortgage program. Federal guidelines assured bankers that the low-interest, fixed-rate, long-term loans would be repaid. That legislation also ensured that the mortgage industry would be profitable for financiers who could buy and sell debt through the Federal National Mortgage Association, a privately owned, federally chartered financial institution that became known as FNMA or Fannie Mae. New Dealers patterned this and other government-sponsored enterprises after the Federal Farm Credit Banks established in 1916 to generate much-needed loans for farmers. But homeowners got more than the mortgages that would become the template for federal student loans thirty years later. Mortgage holders could take advantage of a decades-old deduction for interest paid, the kind of write-off Democrats and Republicans later favored to make higher education more affordable and student debt manageable. There would be many more Americans eligible for college when Congress permitted those deductions in the 1990s because the 1938 Fair Labor Standards Act included a prohibition outlawing child labor, among the many other sections devoted to improving life on the job.[16]

But New Dealers had many reasons for offering young people more immediate assistance, which the Roosevelt administration's public-private, creatively financed zeitgeist shaped. Reports of radical fascist and communist youth movements roiling European politics terrified Edward Filene and Charles Taussig. The Great Depression had shaken many Americans' faith in reform, democracy, and capitalism. These businessmen considered the country's youth to be especially vulnerable to homegrown socialists, communists, fascists, and demagogues, including the tyrannical Louisiana governor Huey Long and the charismatic radio priest Father Coughlin. Young people's discontent concerned many New Dealers. Hickok's final report to Hopkins warned that while "only among the young is there evidence of revolt" but that "these young people are growing restive. Out of some 15 weekly reports from industrial centers all over the country, hardly one omitted a paragraph pointing out that these young people may not tolerate much longer a condition that prevents them from starting normal, active, self-respecting lives, that will not let them marry and raise families, that condemns them to idleness and want." Hickok emphasized in January 1935 that federal investigators feared that "our present day crop will constitute a lost generation, sold out by a depression they didn't make." Hilda Smith shared such concerns and particularly worried that disaffected young people might turn to crime. She subsequently shared Hopkins's desire for programs that would give young people the opportunity to both envision and shape their futures.[17]

There were many ideas that New Dealers could have experimented with to help young people. The Wisconsin legislature created a loan program in 1933 to help students who were eager to enroll in colleges that sorely needed revenues. Long, in contrast, pledged to educate every white young man in Louisiana. Taussig instead suggested courses in political theory, parades to celebrate the New Deal, and finding more ways to involve citizens in the democratic process before they turned twenty-one and gained the right to vote. Some leading academics hoped for scholarship and job programs, whereas University of Chicago president Robert Hutchins demanded a national borrowing scheme. When college heads met with the president in August 1933, they pressed for minimal federal oversight of the $30 million to fund such assistance.[18]

That fruitless summit occurred after FDR had largely accepted a job plan for students that Hopkins had recently brought him. A Columbia sociology professor had proposed to the Federal Emergency Relief Association that undergraduates earn roughly $7 a week for twenty hours of work. That quid pro quo epitomized the spirit of the New Deal's efforts to emphasize relief, work, and solid financing over scholarships, loans, and directly funding campuses. Hopkins and FERA staff never intended this experiment to save colleges or educate more Americans. The assistance was, as one aide explained, an effective way to "take thousands of young people out of the ranks of job seekers" while keeping them off the dole. Hopkins even suggested limiting the program to just 100,000 of the nation's brightest young people, who would have to take a test to prove their merit. FDR hated the idea of an exam, which seemed an affront to growing public support and demand for some kind of undergraduate aid program open to anyone. But he liked the idea of the federal government sending checks to students, not universities. Undergraduates would have to use the money to pay for living expenses, books, and the fees upon which colleges depended. Recipients would also be providing universities with labor, much needed by campuses generally short of funds to pay for basic upkeep.[19]

New Dealers quickly commenced planning. FDR presented Hopkins's memo to the National Recovery Council just one day after he met with academics asking for far more than the administration ever considered offering. Hopkins entrusted Emergency Education Program director Lewis Alderman and his assistant Cyril Klinefelter to design a plan that would primarily help undergraduates but also indirectly bolster college finances. This approach seemed a clever way to avoid charges of un-American federal interference in higher education, particularly its private realm. Such circuitous aid also enabled New Dealers to implicitly reward schools willing to admit striving impoverished men and women, whom elite institutions had been loath to admit even before the stock market crashed.[20]

Alderman and Klinefelter never considered lending to students. Federal officials knew that undergraduates had been borrowing to finance their studies, and that educational associations found the loans had "proved good financial risks." But a lending program seemed likely to exclude far too many young people who had neither the academic records nor the credit histories for lenders to assess if they genuinely needed loans, could excel academically, and would pay back their debts. That same worry about exclusion made scholarships unimaginable to the planners. They believed both approaches had "restricted college opportunities to a small and select segment of American youth," like those admitted to James Conant's theoretically meritocratic Harvard. Work-study, by contrast, seemed "a broader and more democratic" form of financial assistance.[21]

Work-study also avoided the control academics feared. Nonprofit institutions were never forced to participate in or provide tuition assistance to the Jews, Catholics, immigrants, and citizens of color who had little choice but to enroll in proprietary schools before the Depression. Federal money and matching state grants paid student workers, who were selected, assigned work, and overseen on the job by school staff. The Roosevelt administration still expected college personnel to lower fees for recipients, but staff could not give any awardee a free ride. Alderman and Klinefelter also specified that applicants' eligibility could have nothing to do with their academic potential. Undergraduate and graduate students only qualified for support if they could not afford to enroll without financial assistance. Schools also could not assign them jobs that might go to a full-time adult employee.[22]

Those rules hardly hampered the wildly successful December 1933 trial run at the University of Minnesota. College presidents begged for a meeting with FDR in order to convince him to expand the program. Hopkins quickly allocated more than $5 million to help 100,000 students at any nonprofit, tax-exempt, accredited school. The earmarks opened up the program to all public and private postsecondary institutions, as long as they were not the for-profits elite academics had been disparaging for decades. FERA personnel initially promised to help 10 percent of a university's student body in early 1934. Eligibility rules also cunningly worked around fears of federal control and restrictions on public money. Dollars went directly to students, not the public and private colleges charging them tuition or employing them. Like the Federal Deposit Insurance Corporation that did not force banks to participate, no institution *had* to offer this tuition assistance. Only the previous academic year's full-time enrollment numbers determined how much an individual campus's staff received.[23]

This experiment expanded when demands for a New Deal for every young person increased from both within and outside Roosevelt's inner circle. East Coast journalists, politicians, and social reformers became especially vocal about a federal hand-up in 1934, seeing that youth, particularly women and citizens of color, continued to have a much higher unemployment rate. The many Americans demanding FDR do something did not just demand help paying for college. *New York Times* editors drew attention to the "millions . . . on the verge of manhood and womanhood" who "see no gainful job immediately ahead." State officials, reporters, philanthropists, and charity heads all presumed young people "want to work," as Massachusetts Child Council appointees argued. Yet they could no longer "Go West," New York relief administrator Homer Burt reminded listeners in a forum on the "youth problem." The frontier, after all, had vanished.[24]

Americans inside and outside Washington could hardly agree on concrete solutions to the youth crisis. For example, by October 1934, Hopkins wanted state relief workers to oversee work, recreation, and schooling opportunities for Americans between the ages of sixteen and twenty-five but without any additional federal outlays. The National Student Federation's John Lang proposed a much more ambitious Federal Youth Service in 1934. That North Carolinian had no interest in putting the new agency under the Office of Education's purview, leaving oversight instead to schools and surrounding communities. The federal government would only provide information and coordinate efforts, not run the actual apprenticeships and courses on democratic values. Education Office staffers had no interest in this plan, which had won over faculty and staff from New York University, Carleton College, University of North Carolina, and even the National Education Association (NEA). FERA officials too paid little attention to Lang's suggestion but instead fought bitterly over the so-called Michigan Plan, which offered public-service apprenticeships to high school graduates desirous of more education. Abandoned CCC camps would also house a work-relief initiative for those uninterested in more schooling. Labor Secretary Frances Perkins only entered the fray after senators began investigating what the government might do for Americans under thirty. Her Children's Bureau personnel did the research for her $96 million proposal for referral services, apprenticeships, experimental camps, CCC courses, and work-study eligibility increases.[25]

That idea enraged the Office of Education's new head, whose hostility reflected the continued antagonism between New Dealers and the highbrow school crowd they despised. FDR had appointed John Studebaker after Zook had resigned, even though both had come out of rarified education circles. Like Conant, Studebaker desperately wanted to keep the federal government out of the nation's classrooms. The former Iowa teacher feared schools had not given children adequate civic lessons, and he felt the country needed a "people's university," modeled off land-grant extension services, so students could discuss American values. His celebrated Des Moines Forum received support from the Carnegie Foundation and gave him entree into the school crowd. Studebaker did little to ingratiate himself with top New Dealers when he took to the airwaves to counter Perkins's proposal. He wanted $288 million for a Community Youth Program that, he promised, would help at least two million young Americans (almost twice the number Perkins offered to assist but at almost triple the cost). They would not receive direct federal aid or a job but instead gain advice, recreation, and tuition assistance from government funding handed out by local and state education boards working in cooperation with community councils, not federal appointees. Studebaker's proposal, his first real opportunity to offer policymaking suggestions, frustrated Roosevelt, who told Hopkins it was far too costly.[26]

Roosevelt instead looked to his unofficial advisory committee on unemployed youth, an ad hoc group epitomizing the New Deal's public-private character. It included First Lady Eleanor Roosevelt, lawyer Adolf Berle, and leading manufacturers, including RCA and General Electric executives, as well as Taussig. The president of the American Molasses Company seemed an unlikely person to advise the president on this subject, especially as the wealthy businessman had never gone to college. Some recoiled at his expensive ideas for aiding young people. Reacting to one of them, an administration staffer wrote to FDR's personal secretary Louis Howe that "the press would heap so much ridicule on the Administration" that he personally "wouldn't touch it with a ten-foot pole." Taussig also had far more concerns about youth radicalism than FDR's Brain Trust did, or the CEOs offering suggestions to the president. The latter were far more interested to see young people receive apprenticeships, tuition benefits, and even jobs. But Taussig had the president's ear because he had spoken openly about young people's struggles, including on the radio. He also had a good relationship with a leading academic, Charles Judd, president of the American Psychological Association and dean of the School of Education at the University of Chicago. Taussig's exchanges with Judd had convinced him that the academy was not a monolithic, retrograde school crowd that assumed all federal aid was a form of government control.[27]

"Something Hard to Do"

Taussig also got along well with the president, his wife, and other leading officials, who shared a tremendous faith in Aubrey Williams. Hopkins tasked this young New Dealer with turning competing ideas for helping youth into one ambitious experiment. Williams had a broad vision of what the federal government could and must do for the citizenry in general and young people in particular. The Alabama native had actually voted for a socialist, Norman Thomas, in 1932 and generally remained to the left of most leading New Dealers, who rarely shared his disdain for corporations and monopolies or his desire for the government to do far more to ensure equal opportunities for all.[28]

Those convictions reflected his remarkable path from a Birmingham slum to 1930s Washington. Williams first went to work at the age of seven, after only one year of school, not yet able to read or write. A pastor's wife offered to teach him after he finished work in the evenings. The church gave him strong religious convictions but Williams also learned about the evils of Jim Crow at home and on the job. An African American woman sometimes helped his mother and never shied from telling him about the discrimination she and others faced. She taught me, Williams later recounted, "to look upon Negroes as persons," a sentiment few white southerners shared at the turn of the century. Williams prayed for "something hard to do" to fix these evils but ultimately found his calling outside organized religion. He assiduously saved to enroll in Maryville College, where he finished the high school coursework required to enroll in its undergraduate ministry program. He worked part-time to afford the Tennessee school and enlisted as a soldier during World War I in the hope he would earn enough to finish his studies.

Taken to France by the war, he restarted school at the University of Bordeaux and even finished a *diplôme d'études supérieur* despite struggling with French. He returned to Cincinnati to finish his ministerial studies only to find the University of Cincinnati's courses on urban issues more interesting, and part-time work at a recreational center more rewarding. After he graduated, Williams took a job with the Wisconsin Conference of Social Work, which he later characterized as a "watchdog" since it sought to improve public agencies that made social policy. With the University of Wisconsin's Extension Division unofficially supporting it, the group had, by the early 1920s, more than 1,200 people (most of them wealthy, white, and female) affiliated with it in one way or another. Williams found himself moving in the nation's philanthropic circles. Although he soon tired of courting donors, he learned eagerly from the academics he encountered— including the esteemed labor economist John Commons, who had a very different vision of the services that universities might provide to citizens and civil servants. Eventually, Williams became convinced that government bureaucracies could do much more than voluntary groups, and moved on from Madison.[29]

Yet the Depression did not initially inspire Williams to offer the destitute more education. He feared unemployment, hated the dole, and never deviated from the basic principle that "relief shall be in the form of wages for work done." He carried that conviction into his service with the Hoover administration, which hired him in 1931 to convince southern and western governors to accept aid. On the road, Williams promoted a program of decentralized work-relief that did not go through private charities, which contradicted the president's initial faith in having the federal government coordinate private aid. Williams could, nevertheless, largely do what he pleased far from Washington. He set up a structure for a federal relief effort in Mississippi that had nothing to do with the Red Cross. Since the Depression disproportionately hurt African Americans, he made sure to hire a substantial number of African American caseworkers to manage the aid their communities desperately needed.[30]

Williams subsequently struck Hopkins as the kind of person he needed among the thousands of young professionals who flocked to Washington for the chance to experiment under the New Deal's auspices. Williams and his wife, Anita, made friends with many of these young idealistic newcomers, especially those on the left, including Clifford and Virginia Durr, Beardsley Ruml, and Elizabeth Wickenden. But, unlike many southern white liberals, Williams never hid his politics or disgust for racism. He openly praised striking cotton workers, causing at least one Arkansas politician to complain to an intrigued FDR. The president invited Williams to a White House dinner for FERA officials and asked him to stay after to discuss his views on the agency. Williams moved quickly up the ranks of that rapidly expanding bureaucracy. The first college student program came under his purview, and he already knew it was not enough before Hopkins saddled him with the monumental task of fashioning a new executive bureaucracy just for the country's youth.[31]

FDR expected a lot but offered very few stipulations. He wanted a decentralized effort that efficiently acted on priorities signaled by policymakers in the agency's DC offices. Roosevelt also insisted on an executive committee that included staffers from every agency involved in the relief offered. That decision in some ways placated the escalating turf war between educators, career civil servants, and newly arrived New Dealers, like Williams, who also mistrusted the school crowd that included Education Office head Studebaker. FDR also wanted appointees to consult with outsiders, like those who informally counseled him on what youth needed.[32]

When Taussig and the first lady first met with Williams in May 1935, they discovered that the southern radical and the molasses CEO had similar ideas. Neither, for example, had any interest in involving the Office of Education. The proposal Williams submitted to the president on June 5 wanted all youth programs, except for the CCC, to be moved under the newly created Works Progress Administration (WPA), which Hopkins headed, stripping Studebaker of any authority over initiatives to help young people. Williams justified the proposal on the grounds that the new agency was intended primarily to offer relief, not education, even though it included the original work-study initiative that blended both. This plan also reflected his desire to coordinate efforts with other New Deal agencies, not the long-standing bureaucracies (like Studebaker's Office of Education) hostile to New Deal experiments. Studebaker made his complaints in a letter addressed to Hopkins but also sent to FDR, neither of whom shared his doubts about "the wisdom of announcing . . . a National Youth Program and setting up a new administration to operate it." Even Interior Secretary Ickes, who oversaw the Office of Education, did not want to give Studebaker any authority over the program.[33]

Taussig and Williams also wanted Roosevelt to use an executive order to create the National Youth Administration. Both feared that the president would be asking Congress to undertake too much in one calendar year. By June 1935, lawmakers had already secured passage of bills in the House or Senate (in some cases both) for some of the New Deal's major legislative achievements, including the 1935 National Labor Relations, Social Security, and Banking Acts. Those laws, and many others already passed, had required lawmakers to accept a substantial increase in the executive branch's size and authority. No one could be sure Congress would approve more, especially something involving postsecondary schooling. A few senators and representatives had indicated support for improving colleges and aiding young people but an outspoken contingent also fought the president's reform agenda, a growing coalition that included Republicans and Democrats from across the country.[34]

Even if Congress created an agency to help young people, Roosevelt appointees could hardly expect it to go unchallenged by the president's many critics. University presidents, like Harvard's James Conant and Columbia's Nicholas Butler, were just one contingent of the administration's many outspoken skeptics, fierce opponents, and aggressive challengers who bedeviled FDR's reform agenda even during the supposed high-water marks of his presidency in the mid-1930s and war years. Many of them considered even FDR's moderation too far to the left and continually made him out to be a would-be dictator poised to upend democracy, federalism, and capitalism. Such charges made the very creation of an agency for youth risky, especially since European dictators relied on the kinds of classes, parades, and civic celebrations Taussig had suggested and Roosevelt, Hopkins, and Williams never even entertained, even though all feared fascism's and communism's spread.[35]

New Dealers also had no guarantee that they would be able to ensure all young people, including women and minorities, could benefit from a congressionally created agency. Southern and rural western Democrats were a powerful contingent in the growing coalition pushing back against the New Deal. Their many seats on Capitol Hill had already forced liberals to compromise their reform agenda by excluding from New Deal legislation Americans working in domestic, agricultural, and public sectors. Such seemingly color-blind rules effectively prevented many women and people of color from receiving a New Deal, which only compounded inequality over time. The decentralized nature of many experimental agencies hardly helped federal officials carry out costly compromises. DC-based staff struggled to ensure that local appointees followed the letter of the law. At the same time, powerful business organizations, notably the American Liberty League, continually funded court challenges to New Deal initiatives, many of which the Supreme Court ruled unconstitutional well into FDR's second term.[36]

Executive Order 7086 subsequently strove to shield the administration from criticism while endeavoring to meet growing demands that New Dealers do something for young people. FDR cited the 1935 Emergency Relief Appropriation Act to allocate $50 million for a new WPA agency, the National Youth Administration (NYA). "The yield on this investment," FDR assured reporters, "should be high." The June 26, 1935, directive placed Williams in charge of NYA projects for unemployed Americans between the ages of sixteen and twenty-five who were no longer in school. He was expected to work with state and local officials and answer to Hopkins, WPA's head. An executive committee of six representatives from other federal agencies and a president-appointed National Advisory Committee (NAC) would also oversee Williams's efforts.[37]

The range of responses to the executive order highlighted how much New Deal programs divided a country Hickok famously considered just one-third a nation. *Washington Post* reporter Hannah Fried celebrated that, finally, "a voiceless section of the Nation's unemployed received their due from the New Deal." She had tremendous faith in Williams, "a brown, bespectacled Scot" whose "life of work and hardship . . . fits him well to understand the problems of youth." *Collier's* George Creel likewise deemed "the lean, bronzed Appalachian" to be "the most efficient and the most popular" of "the mad mob summoned to Washington by the New Deal." The editor of *Parents* magazine even predicted the agency would ensure there "shall be no 'lost generation' floundering hopelessly in the clutch of depression." Several student organizations, including the National Student Federation of America and the National Student League, also embraced this relief.[38]

But the plan bothered some undergraduates. The leaders of the radical American Youth Congress, which had more than eight hundred affiliated groups and more than one million members, immediately objected: their organization would prefer to be a part of an "adequate program, democratically controlled." The group did not mince words in an open letter to Williams: "The N.Y.A. is more interested in using [its funding] to entrench itself than to help the unemployed youth for which it was appropriated. . . . The entire program lowers the existing wage-scale and is no more than a paltry sop handed to the youth of the land as a gesture to build the popularity of the Washington administration." The Socialist Party–affiliated Student League for Industrial Democracy issued a similar statement disdaining the "attempt on the eve of a presidential election to make us feel that we have a stake in the Roosevelt administration, not by a bold and generous program of relief, but by a shuffling of administrative agencies." While the effect would be a "slight increase in the total number of youth beneficiaries," members still insisted, the program remained "totally inadequate in the light of the 3,000,000 unemployed young people."[39]

Academics denounced the program for far different reasons. A reporter covering the NEA and American Library Association's annual conventions warned aides days before FDR issued the executive order that leaders were "outraged that the President . . . count[ed] Studebaker out. . . . Everybody out here was asking him when he is going to resign." Educators also publicly shared their fears of federal control. The president of Columbia University's Teachers College warned teachers and school administrators that the decree was "setting the groundwork for a Fascist pattern of education in America."[40]

NAC did not offer much help navigating this political minefield. Taussig headed a motley crew that included flying ace Amelia Earhart, American Federation of Labor president William Green, Congress of Industrial Organizations leader Sidney Hillman, and Olympic runner Glenn Cunningham. FDR had appointed some, like publisher Bernarr Macfadden, to repay political debts but members were generally well-regarded private citizens who expressed concern about young people. Their ranks included educators like University of Kansas chancellor E. H. Lindley, executives such as General Electric's Owen Young, and civic leaders including the Jewish Welfare Board's David de Sola Pool. Taussig also reached out to African Americans presiding over historically Black colleges and universities (later nicknamed HBCUs), including Mary McLeod Bethune and Mordecai Johnson.[41]

When Williams and Hopkins met with NAC on August 15, the director immediately sensed the advisers were good at public relations but not policymaking. Delegates agreed only that African Americans should fully participate in the agency's offerings, that communities should cover some of the costs for campus improvement projects, that programs should guard against the spread of fascism among young people, that work had to be required for relief, and that youth needed to be kept out of the labor market for as long as possible. Hillman particularly stressed that "we must find a way not to have the youth competing with the grownups and we must not exploit the youth." Thereafter, the group met infrequently, membership changed, and even Taussig only received the occasional letter from FDR or ten-minute update. That modus operandi bothered some appointees, one of whom complained the NAC "should not be merely a 'front.'"[42]

Even if the advisory board had been more substantive, Williams lacked the time and money to implement many suggestions. The executive order had given him $10 million less than he thought necessary to offer young people something more than relief. He remarked to one group that, given the disappointments the youth of America had already suffered through the Depression, he would be lucky to have "his shirt" much less his "character" still intact when his stint at the NYA ended. Hopkins, whose health was declining, had tasked him with winding up FERA's operations, moving its initiatives over to WPA, and serving as WPA deputy administrator. "You can keep the N.Y.A.," Williams recalled Hopkins saying, "but get an assistant to handle the details."[43]

Williams, despite New Dealers' complaints and historians' later assessments, achieved a lot in a remarkably short period of time. NYA's basic structure had taken shape by mid-August, less than two months after FDR's executive order. Williams had help from WPA employees collecting statistics, making rules and safety regulations, handling accident and composition claims, and managing payrolls. But the director still had to set up the national office, appoint state directors, and establish communications with local and state organizations, which were supposed to be involved in the advisory committees operating at district, county, and community levels.[44]

Williams wanted to hire men and women involved in relief or education, which made finding staff open to schooling initiatives difficult. For example, NYA deputy director Richard Brown had once been a University of Denver sociology professor, making Williams's right-hand man knowledgeable about social welfare but also skeptical that the agency could do much for postsecondary education. Selecting state directors proved even trickier. Williams had to clear all the nominees with leading Democrats in each state. The chosen men and women tended to have some college experience, such as Arkansas director J. W. Hull (head of the Arkansas Polytechnic Institute), Kansas director Anne Laughlin (an Illinois University professor), and Oklahoma director Houston Wright (that state's superintendent of high schools). But some of them, including Williams's close friend Lyndon Baines Johnson, had spent very little time in higher education. The young Texan had only taught for a few years before getting into politics, after which he joined Congressman Richard Kleberg's staff and began to earn the respect of New Dealers.[45]

State directors found themselves more frustrated with than inspired by Williams during NYA's early months. When he first met with them on August 20, 1935, they received pep talks from Hopkins and Eleanor Roosevelt, but Williams offered no specifics about wage rates and job opportunities. He could confidently assert that NYA would not be akin to European youth leagues since it was "not designed to be or to become a youth movement in any sense of the word." He also reminded appointees, "We have our back to the wall here . . . fighting for this group of people."[46]

The meeting left state directors completely unprepared for a flood of applications for a work program existing only on paper. By October, Ohio director Burns Weston openly complained, "We are still without any definite word as to the scope of N.Y.A. projects and the procedure in regard to them," which threatened "the tremendous support in local communities of N.Y.A." His counterparts across the country considered Williams unreachable. Pennsylvania's director even begged Taussig to intervene. Yet neither NAC's chairman nor the First Lady could convince FDR to broach the subject with Williams. When the exasperated New York director, Fairfield Osborne, Jr., decided to quit, he boldly released his resignation letter to the press. "I have been terribly hurt to have as many as fifty or sixty young people in here every day looking for what they expect and they get nothing," he wrote. "I don't think you have had the time to give to the Youth Act . . . it has been humanely impossible with your other duties." In turn, Williams responded publicly to Osborne's insinuation. "I don't know anything he wanted to do that he wasn't able to do," he said, adding that "the whole country knows that it takes time to get a program like this organized."[47]

Still, the public rebuke helped turn NYA into the kind of far-reaching agency Roosevelt and his inner circle had vaguely envisioned. "I have given at least a quarter of an hour to it for the last month," Williams admitted. He blamed delays on other New Dealers, including those who had not quickly authorized expenditures. His deputy also frustrated him. Brown had been unable to immediately move to Washington and only arrived just as Eleanor Roosevelt had managed to pressure Williams to spend more time on NYA. Even though Williams only managed to use $35.5 million of the $50 million allotted by the end of the first year, NYA staff finally had wage scales, work project guidelines, community contribution plans, vocational guidance services, and job placement procedures. Work-study had even been expanded to include high school students as well as graduate students over the age of twenty-five. By September 1936, DC staff had even released an exhaustive list of appropriate jobs to participating campuses, which had been asking for clarification since the agency's infancy.[48]

Williams also spent those months trying to ensure that NYA offered youth equal opportunities. The agency had always, unlike the CCC, been open to women but regulations specifically stipulated recipients had to be citizens, who could not be discriminated against based on race, religion, or country of origin. Williams took those rules seriously. He quickly met with a group of African American leaders to discuss what NYA could do for minority youth. He also explained to state directors that African Americans had not been "getting a fair deal on government projects." He pushed appointees to be inclusive in staffing offices and distributing aid. Many complied but few did so willingly. Government pamphlets nevertheless emphasized the agency's commitment to promoting the welfare of African American youth through "full integration and participation of young Negro people," then 10 percent of those between the ages of sixteen and twenty-five. By October 1936, African Americans served on project units across the country, on twenty-two State Advisory Committees, and in seventeen state offices. Five thousand African American students had also received student aid.[49]

That progress did not satisfy Williams. Federal reports in 1936 indicated that African American youth suffered far more than their white counterparts. The southern radical had no interest in a color-blind attack on systemic inequality. He instead created a special fund that provided additional help for needy African American undergraduate and graduate students in the

1936–1937 academic year. Any participating school was expected to include a "fair allocation" of minority enrollees in its work-study quota. Only then could eligible students apply to a college or university for this special assistance. Staff could then use those requests to ask state NYA offices for more money. Federal officials scrutinized petitions that ended up providing almost $610,000 to more than four thousand pupils. Most of that money went to HBCUs in southern states, where Jim Crow segregation left African Americans with few postsecondary options.[50]

Overall assessments of NYA remained mixed. The president of the National Student Federation of America reported at an April 1936 NAC meeting that young people, and not just those in youth organizations, "constantly reiterated . . . that the National Youth Administration is not adequate, that there are no representatives of youth on Councils, and that there are certain discriminations in awarding the workships and scholarships." WPA higher-ups, including Williams, still considered "student aid . . . perhaps the most favorably received aspect of the N.Y.A." Hopkins, however, deemed the entire agency "one of the most popular things that the Government is doing. It almost rivals the C.C.C. and I should like to see anybody ever stop the C.C.C." By May 1936, the five-month-old work program had helped 210,000 young people. NAC members subsequently called for Williams to expand offerings that same month, when state directors also wanted more freedom and funding to experiment. Taussig pushed FDR to allocate more, warning him against "a false sense of security." The businessman had "been in close contact" with "intelligent, well organized and active" young Communists but he still feared that "the philosophy of Fascism" would attract "the millions of unorganized youth." He made his position clear: "Education without jobs will only make the problem more acute."[51]

Williams still considered the additional $21 million the president included in NYA's one-year extension inadequate for anything more than expanding services. The director used the money to give the central office more oversight, adopt stricter project approval rules, allocate more money for programs that taught skills, and drop restrictions on out-of-school projects in order to give young people different types of jobs and experiences. The number of students aided also increased by more than fifteen thousand between the 1936–1937 and 1937–1938 academic years, when the number of participating schools rose from 1,594 to 1,669.[52]

The Roosevelt administration's preference for public-private, decentralized experiments that respected American federalism gave colleges enormous discretion over work-study. Any nonprofit, tax-exempt postsecondary school could receive enough money to pay a small monthly salary to a sliver of enrolled undergraduate and graduate students. The wage rate and number of recipients fluctuated with the amount allocated yearly in Washington, which never altered educators' considerable authority over work-study. Campus personnel assigned jobs, decided hours, set wages, and oversaw student workers. They also decided whether one person or a committee determined who qualified for help even though NYA staff created the application form colleges had to use. Awardees were supposed to be young people studying more than part time and unable to stay in school without the opportunity to work. Paperwork subsequently included educational and financial records (including past, present, and potential earnings). Candidates also had to explain family size and need. They often had to find reputable witnesses who could vouch for their inability to afford fees, books, and basic living expenses.[53]

NYA officials, like many New Dealers, struggled to make sure campuses followed federal guidelines. They admitted their ranks were too small to develop clear work standards and ensure compliance in the agency's early years, when officials feared the program might be used to cheaply replace college staff or assign useless tasks critics could label "leaf raking." State directors eventually started reviewing schools' work-study plans but, even then, federal officials could really only guarantee that no student earned more than the rules allowed since the government sent recipients their paychecks. But NYA personnel never protested if campuses failed to use all allocated funds, limited hours to help more pupils, or offered work-study awardees additional assistance through any campus scholarship, loan, and tuition-reduction programs that had survived the stock market crash.[54]

That complicated process did not stop students from applying for work-study. Pursuing an advanced degree remained unaffordable even though fees, like rates in the Roaring Twenties, would seem cheap just a few decades later. Most schools received double, sometimes triple, the number of applicants permitted by their quotas. One urban university had 1,160 candidates for just 161 slots. For the 1936–1937 school year, the number of undergraduate applications was almost double the roughly 119,000 opportunities available nationwide. The 5,726 graduate-student quota also fell far short of demand.[55]

Work-study still helped a lot of impoverished students enroll and stay in school. The vast majority had parents, like the Meltons, who could hardly help with expenses. During the 1939–1940 academic year, almost 25 percent of recipients came from families making less than $700 a year (roughly two-thirds had annual incomes of less than $1,500). African American work-studiers were the most impoverished; 82 percent of their families made less than $700 annually. That money did not go very far since most of those households included at least five people, two or three of whom were school age. Most families had only one employed member but, in roughly a fifth of families, everyone was unemployed. Just 8 percent of students had deceased, retired, or disabled parents.[56]

Paychecks, averaging $6 to $10, subsequently meant a lot to the many students facing extraordinary hardships. Only a few awardees, generally those who lived at home or studied in rural areas, made enough to pay all their fees and expenses. At the University of Idaho, two hundred students managed to live entirely off their $18-a-month work-study paycheck. But most recipients only earned 10 to 50 percent of what they needed. Money went furthest at public institutions, especially those that followed the University of Iowa's lead in setting up cooperative housing. Three hundred Hawkeyes paid just $15 a month for room and board.[57]

Many recipients subsequently had to scrounge and work in order to study. Goucher College, for example, admitted two sisters whose minister father had lost his savings. Scholarships, loans, summer babysitting jobs, and work-study positions kept them enrolled and active in their Baltimore church. One of their classmates performed secretarial work for a faculty member, which added to the stenography skills NAC investigators predicted would make her "self-supporting when she graduates." They had just as much hope for a University of Kentucky law student, one of eight children in a destitute family. An MIT student from a Midwestern family of eight surviving on just $1,620 a year used NYA money to make up the difference between the loans and scholarships the school provided. Ten dollars a month also helped an East Coast boy earn a "straight A" record and degree at the Montana School of Mines, far from Princeton, where his brother depended on the little money his parents could spare from their $2,000 annual income. An African American railroad laborer making just $90 a month managed to give $6 to his son at the University of Illinois, which provided a small scholarship and work in a laboratory to this "brilliant" undergraduate who would have dropped out without work-study, even though he also had another job that gave him meals.[58]

That work-studier's success was typical. Reports indicated that seemingly paltry sums helped turn many mediocre students into exceptional pupils with excellent job prospects. A twenty-three-year-old orphan had started school alternatively living in a park and a University of Illinois building. He almost dropped out before staff gave him a work-study job and found him a room. He ended up finishing the term with top marks. Student aid was also a lifeline for Oklahoma Agricultural and Mechanical College students, including the president of the state's chapter of the Future Farmers of America. He had abandoned his studies after the Depression destroyed his family's finances. Only work-study enabled him to re-enroll. NYA also enabled a Mississippian to matriculate at Decatur's East Central Junior College. She quickly proved herself, according to reports, "the best student of music ever to attend," and a four-year state school recognized her talent with a sizeable scholarship. A Rutgers student who had only joined his father in America in 1929 also excelled. He cobbled together money through work-study and odd jobs. Staff labeled him "truly a man of rare promise" because he completed his degree in just three years and intended to pursue graduate study in Romance languages. Professors also considered a Polish-American Minnesotan "astonishing." He had shown mathematical talent in high school but his father, who earned $80 a month, could not afford to send him to college. Work-study helped this young man attend the University of Minnesota, where "on his own initiative" he mastered mathematics "far beyond the level of the ordinary" major. NYA paid him to assist a math professor with research, intriguing Princeton, which awarded him a fellowship to pay for graduate school. A University of North Dakota undergraduate won a Rhodes Scholarship after work-study met some of his expenses, which his widowed mother could not cover while trying to support her two younger children. NYA assistance also allowed a Vanderbilt undergraduate with nine brothers and sisters to give up his partial football scholarship. Investigators celebrated that he could finally focus on courses that "more nearly suited his ideas for the future." After graduation, he immediately found work in a bank in a large southern city. The federal program also enabled a young woman to hone teaching skills at Butler University that she used to good effect back in her hometown Indianapolis schools. Staff were sure she "would never have had her worth brought to light had it not been for NYA."[59]

Recipients considered the work that NYA paid them for to be as worthwhile as studying. NAC analysts noted that many of the early jobs "undoubtedly were routine in character or were frivolous 'boondoggling' or were hardly more than camouflage." Yet 90 percent of students in an Ohio State University survey considered the tasks they did educationally valuable. Roughly 60 percent considered their jobs as beneficial as their courses, reflecting the connection they saw between their classes and work-study assignments. Indeed, more than 20 percent of all awardees helped with research, including compiling statistics and making surveys. Recipients really kept campuses running in an era of extremely tight budgets. On-campus maintenance and community service in public libraries and government agencies rounded out the top three job categories. Many students subsequently found themselves working in academic departments, libraries, and laboratories, where they served as clerics, construction workers, janitors, printers, photographers, graders, and tutors.[60]

Such mundane labels belied how useful those assignments actually were. Students helped test new ceramic glazes, mount art exhibits, build machine tools, repair library books, remodel buildings, repair windows, transcribe legal debates, edit manuscripts, prepare atlases, improve teaching materials, and reshape agricultural practices. Young University of Wisconsin medical students performed vital cancer research, Ohio State undergraduates studied streams to help with government efforts to manage flooding, and Howard University sociology majors compiled data on African American communities in Washington, DC. NAC factfinders especially crowed that a University of Minnesota NYA fish scale study "will lead to radical changes in the methods of fish-feeding and stocking." Cornhuskers were not going to be outdone; twelve University of Nebraska work-studiers built an observatory with a revolving base. Undergraduates often took pride in both the monumental and the seemingly mundane. Almost 90 percent of Ohio State University's work-study beneficiaries considered their duties worth the money the government spent on them.[61]

Staff often celebrated how well awardees performed on the job and in classrooms. "Outside employers," Ohio State higher-ups reported, "are not interested in the student's personal development." They lamented that most un-

FIG 2.1 University of Illinois students surveying the Urbana-Champaign campus around 1938. Though few work-study recipients earned enough to cover all their expenses, many considered the tasks useful and the paychecks critical. Image 0004438.tif, Student Surveying (1), ca. 1938, Carlysle Pemberton Jr., Photographs, Record Series 26/30/7, Box 1, University of Illinois Archives.

dergraduates toiled as "dish washers, furnace tenders, rakers of leaves, and general handymen." Hundreds of NYA students, however, learned skills "educationally and vocationally of considerable significance." Work-study also caused many faculty and staff to change their minds about who could and should be educated. *Fortune* reporters had presumed in 1936 that "security is the *summum bonum* for the present college generation" but recipients immediately proved themselves intellectually curious. Many came from poor rural communities and the striving immigrant, Jewish, Catholic, and African American working classes who had little choice but to enroll in proprietary schools before work-study incentivized nonprofit institutions to accept them. Eighty percent of participating institutions reported that work-studiers generally outperformed their peers. Only 12 percent of college seniors received the aid in 1938 but awardees made up more than half of the Miami University Ohio graduates inducted into Phi Beta Kappa and almost a third of those receiving Commencement Day honors at Indiana State Teachers College. "A year ago I thought the sooner NYA was abandoned the better," an Iowa State official admitted in 1937, but "since studying this matter of aid to needy students for the whole country, I am convinced . . . we must have as much federal assistance as possible." The University of Colorado president admitted in 1937 that "there has never been a time in my experience when students have been so eager, so earnest, and so hard-working." A Temple University administrator even ventured that "government aid had a tendency to strengthen rather than weaken the moral fibre" of students, who could study and work "knowing they have an assured monthly income." By 1937, he said staff were more inclined to "believe that an intelligent society, through the N.Y.A. or some other form of aid, should provide its best minds with an education," especially since many promising youth were "often not . . . from the homes of the well-to-do."[62]

Some faculty and staff, particularly at elite schools, remained hostile. More than 230 eligible institutions refused to participate in the program in 1935. Hamilton College trustees, according to the school's paper, decided they could manage without the indirect aid. Hamilton's president, like many other disinterested administrators, cited concern about spending but also "the close control of education by the government." But many Ivy League institutions eventually signed on. Bryn Mawr, Vassar, Princeton Seminary, and Yale did not agree to use work-study until well into the fall 1935 semester, and past that point what Hopkins termed "snobbery" kept still other elite institutions from using this aid. Yale officials balked at "certain restrictions and technicalities" in what New Dealers first offered to colleges, which "made it appear impracticable for Yale." Only "the apparent value of such aid to . . . students," they insisted, "governed" in the end "the university's attitude regarding the use of Federal funds."[63]

NYA's director hardly courted such disdainful academics. At a 1936 meeting of Chicagoland professors, Williams accused trustees and school boards of aiding and abetting "the further enslavement of the masses," who needed the chance to learn. He also attacked administrators who accepted work-study but "are turning the money over to the wrong sort of persons for handling" or putting recipients "into jobs that should belong to regular employees."[64]

Those frustrations did not dampen Roosevelt insiders' enthusiasm for work-study or growing appreciation for what higher education could do for the country. The White House even convened a 1938 educational commission the chairman deemed "a committee of laymen." Representatives from the labor movement, federal government, farming sector, and business community dominated the group, whose studies outlined legal precedents for federal involvement in all levels of schooling. One report on existing collegiate opportunities proclaimed that higher education could "equalize the condition of men" but cautioned that government inaction could make postsecondary schooling "a force to create class, race, and sectional distinctions," whose "effect on American culture and representative political institutions may be appalling." That assessment complemented another confidential report that recommended extending eligibility for work-study to age thirty, to help "a substantial number of students capable of rendering significant social and intellectual contributions." The group's final report advised that NYA had "uncovered a reservoir of competent youth desirous of continued education for whom almost no provision has been made in the past."[65]

This committee had, in effect, discovered what many had overlooked when the number of college applications had exponentially increased after World War I. Mass higher education was clearly possible, desirable, and beneficial. That assumption undergirded the commission's proposal to extend work-study until 1945, when a decision could be made on making it as permanent as Social Security, FDIC, and the mortgage program.[66]

Work for Study and Defense

Sweeping reports, impressive statistics, and public communications still could not shield Williams, the NYA, or the New Deal from political conflicts brewing at home and abroad. But the director also contributed to the turmoil that imperiled work-study. He had long been known for unapologetically left-wing convictions and a "shoot-from-the-hip" style the press habitually highlighted. Williams made headlines when he declared, just after being appointed NYA's head, that African Americans were the "worst victim of the Depression" and needed to be protected from "some conscious and some unconscious discriminatory practices in the administration of relief." He promised at a November 1935 gathering of twenty-three African American organizations that government officials would be investigating charges of discrimination in public programs and reserving NYA grants for minority applicants. He also did not shy from telling members of the United Parents' Association in 1937 that educators must "teach their pupils the facts behind distribution of wealth" because the wealthy "block every measure that would equalize opportunity."[67]

Offhand remarks eventually cost him dearly. Williams intimated at a June 1938 Workers Alliance for America gathering that the president was involving himself in the upcoming midterm elections, which New Dealers hoped might purge Congress of the southern and western Democrats frustrating the administration's reform agendas. Journalists reported what Williams said, which only heightened interest in the investigations of campaign spending. Reporters mocked the young New Dealer as a left-wing sympathizer, a vote buyer, or just a fool. Williams never could edit himself. Weeks later, he made headlines again for unscripted statements that seemed to urge class warfare. Hopkins would not accept his offer to resign, but FDR could not appoint Williams to head the WPA when Hopkins became the new commerce secretary in December. That decision devastated Williams, who confided to his father-in-law, "I have lost the power I formerly had to help a lot of destitute, struggling men, women, and children." Williams regretted that, as he put it to a friend, "I didn't handle this thing so that I wasn't unhorsed."[68]

The decision was as controversial as NYA's director. *Time* magazine seemed to delight in the Roosevelt insider's political downfall. "He shut himself away from the press," it noted, after FDR chose "first-rate politician" and West Point graduate Francis Harrington. The latter knew "how to coddle Congressmen," it noted, and that was a talent that "single-minded Aubrey Williams" seemed to lack, given "his public talk about class war and the political privileges of Reliefers." But others, particularly the college staff and WPA officials who worked closely with Williams, regretted the president's choice. Ernest Lindley defended Williams's "few indiscreet remarks" in the *Washington Post*. The director's honesty had just made him "unpopular with too many favor-seeking politicians." Such outspokenness didn't bother Workers Alliance president David Lasser, who feared that Harrington represented "the Army type of mind which does not, in our opinion, embody the qualifications necessary to administer a civilian undertaking involving so many social and labor relations." North Dakota WPA staffers also promised Williams that he would be missed. The head of North Carolina College for Negroes was also disappointed. "Your name is of importance in many homes," he reminded

Williams, since "color and creed mean nothing to you." But Cornell's president was among those excited that Williams would fully devote his time to the NYA, which had already achieved "highly significant results."[69]

The director had no choice but to become the agency's full-time policymaker, champion, and defender after the 1938 midterms decimated New Dealers' power in Congress. Historians have long blamed the political setback on FDR, who focused his energies on balancing the budget just as the nation started to recover. That push had even included a cut to the work-study program, which college officials across the country had begged FDR to avoid for the sake of the fifty thousand students who would be left without support. But the president also wanted Congress to allow him to name many more judges to the Supreme Court. The infamous court-packing plan reeked of the kind of undemocratic executive overreach that critics labeled proof of FDR's dictatorial tendencies. Liberal Democrats subsequently lost a number of congressional seats, which turned the once fledgling coalition of anti–New Deal Republicans and Democrats into a force to be reckoned with once lawmakers reconvened in early 1939.[70]

Turmoil overseas helped social welfare experiments continue after the president declared that Doctor New Deal would step aside for Doctor Win-the-War. Even before the midterm elections, Roosevelt insiders fully expected that the country would soon be embroiled in another world war. Officials eventually used this national emergency as an opportunity to offer new employment rights and union guarantees to war production workers, many of whom were men and women of color. Turning the country into an arsenal of democracy also required vastly improving the country's productive capacity, basic infrastructure, and workforce. The latter was particularly important to military leaders and Roosevelt aides, who had learned, after years of trading relief for work, that the citizenry was unprepared to both fight with and arm the nation's allies.[71]

Foreign wars subsequently helped New Dealers protect controversial but vital agencies like NYA. It had the attention of military advisers by August 1938, when Assistant Secretary of War Louis Johnson informed FDR that "studies . . . and recent conversations with manufacturers" indicated a serious "shortage of skilled workmen." It was clear to him: "Private industry cannot afford to train beyond its immediate needs." FDR immediately asked Hopkins to set up a meeting that already presumed NYA's involvement in much-needed vocational training. Loftier goals to aid, educate, and integrate young people into civil society were quickly set aside in the interest of readying the country for war. Williams met with state directors in November to warn that "there will be needed a large number of young people as operatives and others in this whole undertaking." He assured them that "we are not going to turn the Youth Administration over to the Army" but suggested, "we have an opportunity here to participate in a program affecting national defense in a manner that should be acceptable to us." Participation was not optional since "we are at the point where the test of whether a democratic form of government can function effectively is being historically applied."[72]

Work-study's fate was subsequently unclear. NYA staff turned much of their attention toward vocational education. They scoured junkyards, army surplus stores, and factories for the machinery needed for such training before Roosevelt officials reorganized the government in 1939. They placed NYA under the Federal Security Administration (FSA), a name that implied the sprawling bureaucracy served the country's long-term economic health at home, not defense from foreign powers. Faculty across the country subsequently feared a drop in the enrollments upon which they still depended. A number of students considered dropping out in order to enlist or take war production jobs. Many college heads were accordingly relieved when federal officials in summer 1940 implored young people to finish their degrees. Even after the government lowered the draft age to 18 in 1942, White House press releases continued to emphasize that the country needed young people to study in order to become the doctors, engineers, and other skilled workers needed to win the war and then safeguard peace.[73]

But rehousing NYA endangered that agency, its popular work-study program, and its director. Senators and representatives now had the power to set NYA's budget, and they gleefully cut spending for the 1939 fiscal year. But Lyndon Johnson, just recently reelected to the House, helped ensure $100 million for NYA. "Among those who have habitually looked at Mr. Williams from time to time and figured Beelzebub must be back from vacation," the congressman noted from the floor, "I suppose it is because at last the National Youth Administration has touched some heart and life close to theirs and, touching it, has touched them." Lawmakers deemed NYA a defense agency that received appropriations in the name of the war effort in both September 1940 and March 1941. That money helped Williams start a youth work defense program, which offered 180,000 young men and women three months of training in facilities that approximated conditions in war production plants during the 1941–1942 fiscal year. Those well-trained recruits, defense contractors continually reported, proved invaluable in arming the Allies.[74]

Such success hardly pleased those in the school crowd, especially Studebaker. The Education Office's director had never stopped demanding authority over schooling initiatives. Weeks after FDR ordered NYA created, Studebaker begged the president for more money and authority for his bureau, whose small staff was "discouraged and embarrassed." Williams continually scoffed at requests from a man "at least partially responsible for the attacks being made on the Administration." He sounded a note of frustration: "I don't think anything is finally going to satisfy him short of having administrative control of all educational activities," so that "he can thwart and defeat the whole program." Studebaker in fact found himself relegated to collecting data. He barely had enough funding to fulfill his desire of turning the Des Moines Forum into a genuinely nationwide program for teaching civics to citizens. He unsurprisingly wanted control of all wartime vocational education programs, much to the outrage of Williams and other NYA higher-ups.[75]

But Williams compromised to save both the agency and his political career in August 1940. He gave the "school people," whom he still privately detested, purview over all "off-the-job" training for NYA enrollees. The official agreement only allowed state offices of education to determine if "it is not feasible to furnish such instruction." Only then would NYA oversee such schooling opportunities. The decision enraged staff, one of whom even quit. The olive branch scarcely pleased Taussig or the First Lady, who told Williams she was "a little disturbed." The director still hoped congressional approval of this arrangement would protect NYA, since "in the long run we have a greater category for usefulness in what we can work out for young people in our end of it." His staff, after all, maintained control of on-the-job training, which he considered most important. He also hoped the agreement might stop the "trend among educators to close in on us and attempt to restrict us at every possible point."[76]

By then, academics' opinions of NYA, federal aid, and the Roosevelt administration varied wildly. Many historians have credited the New Deal's haphazard, evolving higher education policies with tilting the Ivory Tower's politics from right to center or even all the way to the left. The three university presidents on NAC had actually convinced Taussig that New Dealers had won over the entire academy. Many campuses cooperated with the workers' education program, applied for campus improvement projects, and participated in work-study, which many administrators considered essential for their institutions' survival. The president of North Central College even said the indirect aid was as innocuous as the government exempting the Illinois school from taxes. But other college personnel remained convinced that work-study threatened academic freedom. For example, the head of Dickinson College claimed that "the possibility of control is present." But Ivy League administrators, philanthropists, and Office of Education appointees especially hated being relegated to the policymaking sidelines and openly recoiled at the 1938 education commission's expansive plans. Some, including Princeton's president and trustees, still considered work-study a necessary evil. A Harvard official even urged his colleagues to "conserve independent financial strength, even at the expense of material sacrifices." He, like other hostile educators, considered indirect aid a Faustian bargain that, a Dartmouth professor claimed, made poor students see colleges "as an easy mark." He blamed "the general Rooseveltian philosophy that the world owes an individual something even though the particular individual does not make any effort himself to contribute his share."[77]

FDR suspected that academics remained hostile to his administration. "Do a little investigating," the president instructed Williams, "and let me know who, in what we call 'the school crowd', is behind this opposition." Williams found only a small number of educators actively campaigning against NYA. Unfortunately, those opponents had enormous influence. Studebaker had managed to "appoint them to all key committees" where "these people have been able to prevent what could have been a nation-wide integration in the whole field of education of the facts, the measures, the results of your administration."[78]

Williams warned FDR when college administrators had already begun covertly orchestrating a public assault. The scandal started when the president of Harding College, George Benson, asked the state's student-work coordinator to remove twenty students from work-study at his small, private Arkansas college. "We have plenty of work about the college," Benson explained in his January 1942 letter, "we could replace every N.Y.A. job without the loss of a single student." Benson received the standard reply explaining that support would be "reallocated to other institutions which will use them to employ students who otherwise will be compelled to drop out of school because of lack of funds." NYA's Arkansas office then heard from Harding students, who begged that the money "not go to some other college where the students could likely find employment." They also sent their "spontaneous" request and "contribution to the defense of our nation" to the president and Treasury secretary. Benson wrote to Arkansas NYA officials in support of undergraduates "demonstrating the old American spirit," and wanted assurance that they would not discover "this money being used by students in some other community where they too could probably get along without it." Harding's president never received a response and happily went to the press. A *Chicago Tribune* editorial praised him and the students for wanting "to save a few dollars for the federal government." Williams, the editor surmised, was "one of those advanced social thinkers who don't like to see self-reliance in the people."[79]

Williams subsequently spent several months going back and forth with Harding students, as well as reporters, senators, and outraged Americans. Typical was the packet he sent to Wisconsin Republican senator Robert La-Follette, Jr. It contained material showing Benson's hostility to the NYA, Arkansas college officials' insistence that the press had the story wrong, and research evidence suggesting that ending work-study would force some sixteen thousand young people, including 179 Arkansans, to drop out. Williams and the entire NYA continued to be attacked, including by Virginia senator Harry Byrd. That retrograde southern Democrat placed the undergraduates' letter into the Congressional Record and quoted the transcript of a conversation with the *Washington Daily News* in which Williams denounced Benson as a "ringleader in the so-called economy drive." The director had actually asserted that "Benson admits this action was a part of a so-called economy drive of which he is the ringleader." The Capitol Hill thrashing angered some college officials, who appreciated Williams's determination to "stand by your guns" during "either a publicity stunt or the work of an economic royalist." But the sparring concerned some citizens who asked for an explanation. One wondered why the director had reportedly disapproved of students' choice to opt out of work-study, an allegation Williams had already proven false. But the director, true to his shoot-from-the-hip style, could not help but add that Benson was notoriously hostile to the NYA, despite his request to participate in work-study.[80]

The college president's scheme somewhat backfired. No one had reason to suspect the undergraduates had not written Roosevelt. At this time, the student body, especially at rarified institutions, had the reputation of being critical of the New Deal, despite radical contingents at a handful of campuses like the City College of New York. For example, Harvard faculty estimated that 90 percent of the School of Business Administration's students voted for Herbert Hoover in 1932. Only ongoing national attention encouraged journalists to dig deeper into the Harding College scandal. They discovered that Benson and a businessman on the Board of Trustees had pressured the undergraduates to be involved in a larger organized campaign to slash government spending. Coverage nevertheless emphasized that the White House seemed uninterested in cost-cutting. Publishers also ran editorials and letters to the editor attacking Williams, the NYA, and the Roosevelt administration, not Benson and the businessmen trustees who orchestrated the scheme.[81]

The slanderous campaign coincided with serious politically driven congressional inquiries. Like so many of the wartime attacks on the New Deal, Byrd started his Joint Committee on the Reduction of Non-essential Federal Expenditures in 1941 to examine specific programs and policies in order to assail the entire administration. Committee members overwhelmingly came from the southern wing of the conservative coalition that had solidified after the 1938 midterms. Lawmakers scrutinized NYA in 1941 for any proof of past extravagances to justify cutting current projects that did not aid in the war effort. They demanded NYA stop anything unrelated to defense, which Williams had already done. Lawmakers still slashed his appropriations, leaving NYA able to aid only half as many college students in the first months of the 1941–1942 fiscal year, when twenty thousand had to drop out.[82]

The Roosevelt administration could do little to shield either the NYA or Williams from political persecution. The entire executive branch had to fight both a war abroad and one at home. Erstwhile New Dealers did not just face a hostile Congress but a press corps that had never been all that favorable to the president and had certainly ceased being so by the early 1940s. Williams's politics had made him and his agency particularly vulnerable, especially by

1942, when Senator Kenneth McKellar called for investigations into the threats New Deal projects had posed to southern race relations. Having first targeted TVA and CCC, the Tennessee Democrat next went after NYA, even though he had supported robustly funding it in June 1941. McKellar quickly concurred with the Byrd committee assessment: NYA seemed to be a wasteful, redundant agency headed by someone who clearly had communist sympathies and was too eager to provide additional relief to African Americans. On the Senate floor, McKellar charged that the government was "making mollycoddles out of our people." He reported that a student had asked him to save work-study so he could "keep out of the Army." That sensational accusation hardly reflected what was happening on campuses across the country. College higher-ups and Roosevelt officials found themselves struggling to convince undergraduates to finish their educations during World War II.[83]

The press still picked up on a charge that fed their hostility toward Williams, NYA, and the Roosevelt administration. *Minneapolis Times-Tribune* editors said the war was being used as "an excuse" to save a "Depression-born" agency that had "outlived its usefulness" now that there was no need to "keep youth off the labor market." A *Wall Street Journal* editorial claimed NYA "never justified its existence, much less its continuance." The *Chicago Tribune* observed that dismantling the agency would finally put an end to Williams's "vote buying." More than that, it would eliminate "one of the principal havens for those who are pledged to the destruction of our government from within."[84]

Fighting did not cease after the administration placed NYA under the War Manpower Commission in 1942, which failed to hide the bureau or its director from public scrutiny in the winter and spring of 1943. The White House received letters and telegrams urging the survival of work-study, but well-publicized congressional investigations continued. Some academics rushed to defend the agency. In the *School Review*, Maurice Hartung scoffed at his peers' insistence that NYA was a waste; the shortage of skilled workers and doctors made work-study indispensable to the war effort. Yet business groups, particularly local Chambers of Commerce, declared NYA unnecessary, which shocked Williams. He knew that war contractors regarded it as priceless. Some hostile newspapers also urged Congress to defund NYA. The

Chicago Tribune, for example, disparaged the agency as something that "was started to buy the 'youth vote' for the New Deal" whose well-paid bureaucrats were now threatened by "the end of its existing boondoggling projects" and scrambling to restyle it as "an 'essential' war agency." Editors intimated that vastly scaled-back NYA payroll was, in fact, bloated with "economic lame ducks" who had never had such a cushy job in their lives and were "not going to let go of it, war or no war, as long as congress is foolish enough to provide funds for them."[85]

The polarizing agency did not survive the congressional budget battles in summer 1943. "I am literally sweating blood over this thing," Williams confided to one of the state directors whom he ended up having to let go to stave off criticism that NYA was redundant, expensive, and top-heavy. Williams had reason to be fearful. Roosevelt's cabinet could not agree if NYA warranted saving. Williams begged liberal Democrats in Congress, including LBJ, for help. They could do little once leading educators publicly called for "an immediate campaign to put pressure upon Congress to abolish the National Youth Administration." That May 1943 appeal resulted in thousands of telegrams being sent to senators and representatives. One congressman reported receiving over 8,000, mostly from educators who feared NYA might, as the school crowd had continually warned, set up a "federally controlled and federally operated system of schools." Williams still fought to convince the subcommittees overseeing budget negotiations to protect NYA, one of the many New Deal experiments then under the guillotine. NYA's funding was struck and put back in and reconsidered again during full committee votes, floor debates, and conference committee meetings. Congress ended up laying waste to many New Deal agencies in those tense July 1943 negotiations. The casualties included NYA and CCC, which Hopkins had once called unstoppable. Hostile media particularly celebrated the demise of NYA, which the *Los Angeles Times* summed up as "an expensive nuisance" run by that "pinko, Aubrey Williams."[86]

Schools and students suffered after Congress stopped funding NYA. There were far fewer defense jobs in 1944 and certainly by 1945. Even though unemployment fell in the early 1940s, many Americans feared its return. The war effort had already started to wind down in 1943, when federal officials started canceling orders with military contractors. The executives quickly started decreasing production and staff in the more remote factories that had employed the men and women who had not gone overseas to serve or stayed in school to study.[87]

War production workers received no help from a small federal student loan program started in 1942. This aid finally involved the Office of Education in federal tuition assistance, which mixed the features of the work-study program and the risky financial products increasingly offered to undergraduates in the Roaring Twenties. That assistance helped students two years away from completing degree programs considered important to the war effort. Applicants had to be enrolled but colleges and universities, unlike work-study, did not decide who received aid. Students applied directly to the federal government, which, at most, lent $500 directly to a needy pupil. The loans had a 2.5 percent annual interest rate but the government did not require anything up front or during enrollment. Three million dollars in credit helped roughly eleven thousand recipients pay fees at just 287 schools. Awardees only had to promise to join the war effort in some capacity after graduation. Repayment started a year after finishing unless a borrower was actively serving in the military or pursuing another degree under the GI Bill. Deferments did not stop interest from accruing, so obligations would not be paid off for more than a decade. Federal officials considered this short-lived loan program crucial for a war effort that still needed thousands of engineers, scientists, doctors, dentists, and pharmacists to creatively finance their training after work-study's sudden demise.[88]

NYA had dwarfed that two-year program's size and scope. Despite a slow start and fierce opposition, young people in the out-of-school work program laid fifteen hundred miles of road, added fifty-seven thousand acres of community park land, planted 12.5 million trees, built six thousand community buildings, and repaired eighteen thousand public hospitals, schools, and libraries. Youth also produced five thousand tons of food, 6.5 million articles of clothing, and millions of medical bandages. Their work was pivotal in turning the United States into the much-celebrated arsenal of democracy. In 1941 alone, the Army made use of thirty-five thousand hand tools, ninety-six thousand machine parts, and thirteen thousand gun components manufactured in NYA facilities.[89]

The small checks that work-study students received also made a huge difference. NYA paid $89,014,982 for undergraduate and $4,263,294 for graduate student salaries. Roosevelt and Congress never allocated enough to help everyone in need but, at its height, work-study supported one of every eight college students. In the end, more than two million young people received aid to stay in school, 620,000 of them college students. It mattered who was in charge of the details. Income eligibility rules helped crack open the academy's door for impoverished Americans, who had proven, as NYA staff had constantly intoned, that the "financial need of students had little bearing on their intelligence or ability." That point was underscored in the agency's final report, along with the assessment that "the return on the Government investment was high." That money had helped both students and postsecondary schools teetering on the brink of bankruptcy in the early 1930s. Academics had become at least somewhat more amenable to—some even hopeful for—the federal aid that a growing number of government officials deemed important for reasons other than quelling youth radicalism. National Resources Planning Board experts in fact suggested the president and Congress consider offering educational grants to promising young people because "our economy must provide work for all who are able and willing to work." That argument was consistent with NYA staffers' view that "An adequate youth program is a special responsibility . . . which should be an integral part of any government undertaking to establish [economic] security." Charles Taussig's March 1942 NAC report likewise emphasized that it would "be the height of folly to scrap an entity that will most certainly be needed" to help with demobilization. The businessman stressed the need for young GIs and civilians to have "equal educational opportunity" to gain the skills needed by "peace-time industry," and argued the agency could ensure that.[90]

But NYA, like so many New Deal experiments, never lived up to promises to help everyone, and likely even exacerbated long-standing inequities. Researchers have argued that most awardees would have likely tried to enroll in college, following in the footsteps of LBJ and the record number of college hopefuls applying in the 1920s. One analysis suggests that NYA unintentionally drove much of the 60 percent hike in state school tuition rates that occurred between 1932 and 1940. Schools could charge more as portions of the student body earned additional money to afford fees, books, and living expenses. Higher costs made degrees even more unaffordable for those long excluded from the academy and less likely to receive the work-study aid New Dealers had allowed college staff to assign. Women, for example, were only roughly 40 percent of undergraduate work-studiers until formal US entry into WWII, when their numbers rose from 48 percent of the student body in the 1941–1942 academic year to 58 percent in the next. Men still accounted for 75 percent of graduate student awardees throughout the program. Despite Williams's efforts, whites also benefited far more from work-study. He openly admitted to Mary McLeod Bethune months before NYA's demise "that Negro youth have not had equitable participation." He regretted that many of his appointees had let staff in state NYA offices spend "all available money for projects for white youth." He had let them blame "'local conditions' and community attitudes" even though rules had stipulated everyone be treated equally. Even after he had set up work-study funds for which only young African Americans would be eligible, the director had known more needed to be done. But his staff had only looked at racial disparities in the 1939–1940 and 1942–1943 academic years, when "other-than-white youth," most of whom were African American, were but 6.3 percent or 7.9 percent of collegiate work-studiers despite being 10 percent of young people.[91]

Williams understood, better than any of his contemporaries, the long-term consequences of NYA, its limitations, and its demise. He publicly called the agency's abrupt termination a "very unfortunate happening." But he privately blamed the "small coterie" who "have from the N.Y.A.'s inception done everything . . . to hamper, malign, and destroy it." They had "committed a dastardly and enduring crime against the present and future promises of American life." "We were caught empty-handed as we faced several million young people," Williams remembered in his official final report. "The schools had no answer to their plight." But "we fought and you fought and thousands of others fought," he confided to an NAC member, "with everything we had." "We shall keep fighting," the disgraced New Dealer continued, "but we should not be fooled into believing that the other side will not keep fighting too."[92]

The political war at home in fact continued as the Allies steadily prevailed abroad. The end of the 1943 budget battles did not stop politicians, policymakers, and private citizens from fighting over how the country would demobilize and how conversion to a peacetime economy would unfold. Concerns about the labor market and unemployment dominated discussions. Federal control, economic inequality, and segregation subsequently remained incendiary topics in broad discussions of what citizens could expect from their government and to what veterans had a right. Despite work-study students' stellar grades and outstanding achievements, Roosevelt's aides, lawmakers, veterans, and academics still debated whether or not more Americans could or should continue their studies in the months after NYA's defunding. That unresolved question came up repeatedly in the contentious hearings over the 1944 GI Bill of Rights. Its celebrated educational guarantees offered limited, direct tuition assistance so that eligible veterans would stay out of the labor market and still be able to afford the fees upon which most colleges and universities depended.

3

A Bill of Rights for Only Some GIs

"The conditions under which GI Joe is forced to acquire his education parallels that of the concentration camp," Thomas Wicks fumed in a 1946 telegram to President Harry Truman. The newspaper editor demanded that something be done so that veterans could receive the aid intended to help them stay in colleges, like the University of Missouri campus near Wicks. "Why must [veterans] live in mud," he wondered, or "in a room with three other men that was built for two, living in unhealthful conditions, trying to study in a poorly illuminated room." He was not the only one concerned about "the future leaders of America being treated on par with dogs." The White House received reports from all over the country that former enlistees had not received the educational benefits guaranteed to them under the 1944 Servicemen's Readjustment Act. Some complained that they or their spouses had been taking classes for months under the so-called GI Bill of Rights without seeing the stipends promised to support them and their families. College remained prohibitively expensive for many. An Oklahoman wrote that 20 percent of the veterans at a nearby agricultural college had been barely surviving while they waited months for government checks. Such widespread delays forced former service personnel to dip into their savings, ask parents for help, cash in war bonds, take part-time jobs, procure loans, or just drop out.[1]

When Americans reminisce about the famed GI Bill, few bring up overcrowded classrooms, shoddy dorms, and late payments. They also rarely mention that GIs almost did not get their Bill of Rights. The larger war over government spending, federal authority, and economic security had not ended when Congress abruptly defunded New Deal agencies, including the National Youth Administration (NYA) and Civilian Conservation Corps (CCC). Many in Washington already feared what would come with the pending demobilization of eleven million service personnel amidst a haphazard, uneven transition to a peacetime economy. They could not agree on who should be helped or how. Many doubted that a large number of returnees would want or need additional education, but recognized that offering schooling opportunities would at least take some pressure off a situation where too many job-seekers came back to not enough jobs. Some lawmakers worried that higher education stipends would create incentives to be idle rather than productive. Veterans groups, conservative reporters, and right-wing congressmen managed to set aside their differences to thwart the Roosevelt administration's plan to use what remained of the New Deal's bureaucratic apparatus to oversee a set of benefits, which liberals quietly hoped would eventually be made available to all civilians. Skillful congressional maneuvering instead put the small Veterans Administration in charge of that help, which included a number of government-guaranteed financial products. The VA was ill-equipped to oversee many of the initiatives, including a tuition assistance program that shared many characteristics with work-study but was even more convoluted.[2]

Only GIs stopped that college aid from becoming a total boondoggle. More than two million veterans flocked to cramped classrooms where, like work-studiers, they excelled despite low expectations, meager stipends, and deplorable living conditions. But the well-known success stories do not include the 80 percent of veterans who did not take advantage of a short-lived program that, like many Roosevelt-era experiments, promised equal opportunities upfront but actually exacerbated long-standing inequities over time.

The War Over Peace

Many doubted during the war that there would be prosperity in the future. A 1945 *Fortune* poll found that most citizens expected another depression within a decade. In another survey, 70 percent anticipated not doing as well economically after the war. An even higher percentage predicted fewer employment opportunities. GIs also doubted there would be enough work for them when they returned home. An Army Information and Education Division survey found that 50 percent of soldiers considered "the problem of earning a living" their greatest challenge once the war ended. Widespread memories of lost jobs and impoverished WWI veterans fueled fears of returning to "ditch digging and bread lines." Another GI even predicted "11 million apple salesmen." The country's educational elite shared their concerns. Harvard's James Conant openly feared that rapid demobilizing "could well sow the seeds of a civil war within a decade" if "accidents of geography and birth" seemed to decide veterans' fates.[3]

The challenges of the GIs' return, the labor market, and the economy also drove ongoing executive branch efforts to plan for peace. Roosevelt ordered the seven-year-old National Resources Planning Board (NRPB) to begin strategizing in November 1940. By 1942, staff had crafted ambitious plans for postwar demobilization and long-term economic growth for specific regions and the entire nation. Suggestions for southern and western states emphasized a need for more investment, vocational training, higher education, progressive taxation, public transportation, and social services. NRPB higher-ups also hoped for full employment, which 1930s labor laws and social welfare programs had tried to narrow to men between the ages of twenty-five and sixty-five. Planners nevertheless prioritized equal access, for every American, to health, housing, and education, which erstwhile New Dealers now deemed vital to economic security and social democracy. Those suggestions complemented ideas for postwar retraining and employment coming out of critical parts of the Federal Security Administration (FSA), which included the NYA, CCC, Office of Education, and Social Security Administration. Public opinion shaped staff's speedy efforts to plan for peace. Surveys indicated that 86 percent of voters (regardless of their party affiliation) supported providing more schooling for soldiers. As such, White House insiders pushed for a retraining bill that friendly Democrats could introduce to cajole Congress into providing the kind of aid soldiers would need and citizens seemed to want.[4]

That and other White House proposals operated on the principle that, as historian Keith Olson surmised, "the economy and not the veteran needed adjusting." Roosevelt and his aides had no interest in just giving soldiers a reward for services rendered. Fears of another Bonus March made that idea unpalatable but mustering-out pay also went against the very spirit of the 1930s experimentation that had continued during WWII. White House insiders wanted improved, sustained, permanent economic security for everyone, not just special classes of citizens, like veterans.[5]

That desire underlay the earliest public promises made to GIs. For example, the 1940 Selective Service Act lowered the draft age to eighteen and included provisions to help veterans find jobs. FDR emphasized the need to ensure that anyone forced to drop out must be given the chance "to resume their schooling." The government, the president added, must ensure "equal opportunity for the training and education of other young men of ability after their service in the armed forces has come to an end."[6]

Roosevelt and his aides wanted to provide ample help to soldiers and civilians but struggled to agree on what was to be done and how, particularly in regard to education. As with the 1930s discussions of creating a youth agency, FDR sought advice and policy proposals from several committees, which included NRPB staffers, business executives, social scientists, and military officers. This disparate crew's wide-ranging ideas showed how much remained unresolved after work-study's abrupt end. Advisers could only really agree that schooling provisions must take into consideration the country's manpower needs. Some considered it sufficient that veterans be mustered out slowly so civil society could more easily absorb them. Others recommended a federal unemployment compensation system to supplement state offerings for every American (not just veterans) and a short paid furlough before the military officially discharged a combatant. That proposal included at least a year's worth of education or training, which could be extended to four through a competitive examination process. Still others supported a federal provision for only one year of education because they "did not believe that all the load of education should be taken off the States." One plan wanted to expand the limits on eligible degree programs beyond those that explicitly trained GIs for occupations that clearly needed more skilled workers. That plan seemed too generous to those who believed "the primary objective . . . is to do what is necessary to overcome the educational shortages created by the war." This faction wanted to limit schooling benefits even more, so that only GIs who had served at least six months could receive a year of education or training support, and only "exceptionally able ex-service personnel" with demonstrated "unusual promise and ability"—of which they estimated there might be roughly a hundred thousand—would qualify for additional grants, and maybe even loans.[7]

White House personnel also disagreed over who should be in charge of administering these benefits. Some, including Bureau of the Budget staffers, presumed the VA would oversee services, particularly for education. An increasingly contrarian Congress seemed unlikely to allow any civilian executive branch bureaucracy to handle such an expansive initiative, even recommending that the president let lawmakers hash out the details. Other insiders presumed that Congress could not be trusted to pass FDR's reported vision for a veterans bill to serve as an "entering wedge" that might someday open the door to an even more expansive social safety net for every American.[8]

Erstwhile New Dealers understood that oversight was a critical matter. All these experiments' fates, as in the case of work-study, hinged on which agency housed them and who awarded benefits. By 1942, top advisers had already been discussing how to convince a majority of lawmakers not to give the VA control of returnees' benefits. Entrusting that department with new entitlements would have continued the long-standing American tradition of treating service personnel as a special class of citizens. There would be no hope of someday turning those temporary rewards for soldiers into permanent entitlements for civilians. The VA also seemed ill-equipped for this undertaking. Its small staff had little experience administering the kind of services and government-guaranteed financial products that the Roosevelt administration's alphabet-soup agencies had become increasingly adept at running, particularly help for the unemployed. FSA, which had briefly housed NYA, seemed a much more appropriate choice. Advisers even hoped entrusting FSA with overseeing veterans' entitlements might protect this fledgling bureaucracy in an era when the entire social welfare apparatus liberals had constructed seemed vulnerable to congressional conservatives eager to dismantle what remained of the New Deal.[9]

Congress gutted a lot of the bureaucratic framework in July 1943. The CCC, NYA, and NRPB did not survive tense budget negotiations. NLRB's untimely demise symbolized how, despite popular memory and academic assumptions, the transition to a peacetime economy was hardly smooth and coordinated. Demobilization was instead a piecemeal, haphazard, and politically fraught undertaking involving local and state governments, voluntary organizations, business groups, trade unions, and farming associations as well as the federal officials and Washington lawmakers still at war with each other.[10]

FDR gave no hint of such acrimony in a fireside chat just weeks after Congress unceremoniously defunded chunks of his administration. His update included the first public proposals for aiding veterans. The president explained that "the returning soldier and sailor and marine are a part of the problem of demobilizing the rest of the millions of Americans who have been (working and) living in a war economy since 1941." He subsequently promised legislative proposals tackling "food, manpower, and other domestic problems" plaguing all Americans because GIs must "not be demobilized into an environment of inflation and unemployment." Veterans should instead return to an expansive list of services, which would include (at the very least) mustering-out pay, job placement help, unemployment insurance, and an opportunity to study. Disabled service personnel, the president emphasized, also needed better pensions and medical services. "Congress will help," FDR hoped, "for obviously the Executive Branch of the Government cannot do it alone." Renowned radio broadcaster Raymond Gram Swing also urged lawmakers to act decisively. The presidential laundry list must not become "a partisan measure," he declared. "A program like this is something a democratic nation owes not only to its youth but to itself."[11]

Battling Over Rights

The president's olive branch seemed only to provoke journalists and congressional leaders long disdainful of the administration's social welfare experiments. Although *Newsweek* described FDR's "shrewd maneuver" of slipping these proposals into a fireside chat as a "coup that caught the President's political foes flat-footed," his Capitol Hill enemies were, in fact, quick to attack the recommendations that FDR did not actually specify and send over until months later. New Hampshire Senator Styles Bridges still chastised FDR for daring to "dangle before the eyes of soldiers the gift of their own tax money." GOP national chairman Harrison Spangler admonished "the Commander-in-Chief [for] stooping to this type of politics" when Roosevelt should be "thinking only of winning the war."[12]

Yet many lawmakers eagerly made proposals for peace after the president shared his administration's general plans. They, too, wanted to prevent the kind of political unrest and economic downturn that had followed World War I. Maury Maverick, a famously liberal former representative from Texas, argued that allowing widespread unemployment, particularly for service personnel, would put the nation on a path to "dictatorship." Conservative Republican Hamilton Fish, representing New York's Hudson Valley, shared that fear. If GIs "come home and sell apples as they did after the last war," he warned, "we would have chaotic and revolutionary conditions." The almost thirty bills introduced included a simple plan for six months of pay after discharge, a public works program for former GIs, lending for farms, education, and debt repayment, as well as Utah Democratic Senator Elbert Thomas's generous college benefit bill. The University of Utah political scientist had a record of supporting opportunities to help young people, like the 1933 Emergency Conservation Work legislation that had created the CCC. Yet he did not propose to underwrite schools to provide more seats for veterans but instead wanted, like White House liberals, to provide them with tuition assistance. But this devout Mormon had the power to shepherd his veterans education bill into law. S180 entrusted the Office of Education to oversee the program, which ensured debate would be before the Senate Education and Labor Committee he chaired.[13]

The American Legion embraced crucial aspects of Thomas's bill but recoiled at letting his committee hold hearings. Scholars have disagreed over how much credit the American Legion deserved for the GI Bill's success, but Legionnaires labored mightily to make the public and Congress prioritize veterans' care. The million-strong American Legion stood at the forefront of veterans groups, which also included the much smaller Veterans of Foreign Wars and Disabled American Veterans. All these organizations included plenty of WWI doughboys, now in middle age, who remained indignant about how little help they had received after the war, during the postwar recession, and in the years after the 1929 stock market crash. But Legionnaires' politics had made them infamous. Army officers had started the nationwide organization to "carry into the new life that effective teamwork and mutual support . . . so thoroughly learned in the army." Postwar labor unrest concerned the Legion's middle-class members far more. Its leaders denounced strikers in various settings. For example, when Boston police officers, forbidden to form a union, walked off the job in September 1919, the Massachusetts branch of the Legion issued a prompt resolution condemning any sympathetic strikes, seeing any such action "under the circumstances as a radical injury to and the abrogation of civil rights and liberty." That pledge inspired thousands more veterans to join the group. Their reputation for vigilantism, opposition to the New Deal, and red-baiting frightened many in the 1930s, when radical journalist Upton Sinclair joined others in labeling the Legion part of the worrisome spread of fascism in America.[14]

Such political sensibilities shaped the Legion's demands for WWII veterans. Top Legionnaires opposed anything resembling Depression-Era experimentation and feared the kind of entry wedge for which some Roosevelt insiders hoped. Legionnaires wanted no one else but soldiers to receive substantial help for a limited amount of time. As such, leaders publicly committed the organization to drawing up an expansive plan for the reintegration of all soldiers back into civil society. They considered such a program "a sound investment," but not for the nation's well-being, as Roosevelt's advisers imagined. Legionnaires instead wanted to single out soldiers as a special class of deserving citizens, the kind of designation White House insiders opposed. The Legion's national commander, Warren Atherton, reasoned that "If we can spend hundreds of billions to wage war, we should be able to spend a few billions to make that war worth winning for those who win it." The Legion's DC offices spent ten months cataloging the many bills introduced in Congress to ensure that every soldier get, as one Legionnaire put it, "a decent break, a chance to stand on their feet and be master of their own fate." They feared delay or derailment because plans would be heard before different committees. So Legionnaires, along with the other veterans groups, pressured Congress to adopt a parliamentary proposal that designated only two committees (one each in the House and the Senate) to debate all bills for veterans (including Thomas's education proposal).[15]

Legionnaires also crafted a single comprehensive bill laying out everything introduced in Congress. Its leaders entrusted that formidable task to men who shared the organization's political sensibilities, including former Illinois governor John Stelle. This Democrat had connections to the Roosevelt administration but his workgroup included Arkansas US Attorney Sam Rorex, Detroit banker W. B. Waldrip, Californian R. W. McCurdy (vice chairman of the Legion's National Rehabilitation Committee), and Kansan Harry

Colmery, who Stelle said "jelled all our ideas into words." The task suited Colmery, a University of Pittsburgh Law School alumnus who specialized in contracts, insurance, and business law. A former WWI Army Air Service instructor and pilot, he had become a successful lawyer and staunch Republican, even chairing the Wendell Willkie War Veterans National Committee during the 1940 presidential election. Colmery and other members of the so-called Stelle Committee also reached out to a known opponent of the administration's labor policies to carefully craft their proposal. Stanley Rector suggested onerous rules, including a five-year eligibility cap. He went so far as to recommend the Legion's bill "be labeled plainly for what it is," which was "a temporary program of definite duration to meet the special problems of a special group."[16]

The Stelle Committee suggested calling the final bill "the Servicemen's Readjustment Act" or "the Omnibus Veterans' Relief Bill," which hinted at how it was both expansive and limited. Even though Colmery and the Legion deeply opposed the New Deal, their proposals offered much more than many liberals wanted to give veterans and more than they had been able to secure for the citizenry during the 1930s and early 1940s. Colmery constantly worried about being too generous. On the drafts he even penciled in "is this too liberal?" next to postsecondary provisions that seemed unnecessary, burdensome to colleges, easy to abuse—"which may be disadvantaging"—and having the potential to "authorize a vast scheme of education without source / relation to the ability of the veteran." The final proposal nevertheless ended up providing vocational training and college support that borrowed heavily from Thomas's bill. Only honorably discharged veterans, who had served at least nine months and had their studies disrupted, would qualify for a year's worth of support. The government would provide only $300 for fees and a monthly subsistence allowance of $50 ($75 for married GIs). Only the VA could decide if GIs with "exceptional ability or skill" could have an additional three years of support. But nowhere did Legionnaires offer help for campuses expected to enroll GIs. The group's wish list instead included a lot more provisions for soldiers, including generous mustering-out pay, a weekly $35 unemployment stipend, and lending for homes as well as small businesses and farms. Those benefits reflected how controversial 1930s social welfare experiments remained, including government-guaranteed financial products. Legionnaires argued the offers must expire, never to become as permanent as the New Deal's mortgage, pension, and unemployment insurance programs then seemed. Colmery also wanted the VA to oversee everything so liberals could not extend any of these services to civilians, including the war production workers crucial to transforming the country into an arsenal of democracy.[17]

Legionnaires found an invaluable ally in securing passage and thwarting the White House's agenda before they finished crafting their proposal. William Randolph Hearst had been a muckraker and two-term congressman, famous for progressive trustbusting. By the early 1940s, this septuagenarian had built a media empire through the ruthlessness captured in the 1941 film *Citizen Kane*. The newsman's power had grown as his politics had taken a sharp turn to the right. Like the Legionnaires, Hearst detested Roosevelt, opposed the New Deal, and feared the spread of Communism—and he made his many newspapers toe that line. He "set the topics, dictated the tone, and edited all the editorials in his papers," his biographer David Nasaw writes, and "he proudly proclaimed that while other newspapers merely reported the news, his newspapers 'made' it." The chief's stable of right-wing journalists also did a lot to shape public opinion about liberal policies and programs, much to the delight of those continuing to fight them both inside and outside Washington.[18]

The "Hearstlings," as Legionnaires liked to call his reporters, made good on the chief's reported assurances that he would back the Legion "with all we've got." Editors of *Chicago American*, *Boston American*, and *New York Journal American* assigned correspondents and commissioned cartoonists to ensure the public knew about the "Shame of a Nation." Daily coverage urged readers to demand their congressional representatives do something to help the country's troops. Editorials became more incendiary after Congress failed to act quickly. "There is nothing to DEBATE about, nothing to BARGAIN about, nothing to justify a further WASTE OF TIME," a typical *Journal American* editorial pronounced.[19]

Widespread coverage and catchy branding kept the public interested after the Legion released its draft bill on January 8, 1944. Historians have disagreed over who came up with the name "GI Bill of Rights," but all agree it was far catchier than the Stelle Committee's pedestrian suggestions. Those, as the Legion's acting publicity director reportedly warned, had "all the political sex of a castrated mule." (Some have credited the quip instead to one of three journalists Hearst had sent to Washington to help the Legion promote the complicated legislation.) It is also uncontested that whoever thought up the much snappier label for the Servicemen's Readjustment Act made a major contribution to shaping the mythology and reverence that still surround the law.[20]

The Legion spared no expense lobbying Congress. "We didn't organize the American Legion to be a savings bank for a last man's club," Commander Atherton reasoned, "The best way to use every dime in our treasury is in the assistance to the veterans coming out of this war." Funds helped more than twenty thousand Legion posts and auxiliary units flood congressional mailboxes with written demands to pass the Legion's omnibus legislation. The national office also sent advice on how to promote the bill in print or through petition drives. Veteran voices for the so-called "Magna Carta" also peppered four hundred ads played on the radio and shown before movies. Hearst's media empire did not charge anything for stories that stressed how much soldiers had sacrificed, issued dire warnings against inaction, and castigated lawmakers for dithering. His journalists did far more than keep the public apprised of the Legionnaires' efforts; they played an instrumental part in what some considered at the time to be "the most powerful lobby that has ever been organized." Hearst entrusted the *Chicago American*'s Roy Topper to handle promotion and ordered *Boston American* reporter Frank Riley to keep track of congressional support. Riley did so not in Massachusetts but in the Legion's DC offices, where one room had a wall covered from floor to ceiling with a chart tallying lawmakers' support.[21]

Passage was hardly guaranteed. FDR had little interest in endorsing the Legion's legislation. He still met with leaders but hoped staunch liberals, like Thomas, would be able to secure enough votes for an entering wedge of benefits. The president could not put Thomas, Texas representative Sam Rayburn, Massachusetts representative John McCormack, or Kentucky senator Alben Barkley in charge of this undertaking. The ongoing war consumed FDR's attention, especially as his health began its serious decline. His influence over legislation also remained controversial. The president could not get too directly involved in congressional fights, much less intervene after the House Rules Committee sent the Legion's bill onto the specially designated veterans legislation committees.[22]

Some of Roosevelt's staunchest southern critics chaired those panels. Mississippi Democrat John Rankin, for example, was known as "a little man with bushy hair and a Hallelujah voice" that added a special lilt to his open disdain for Jews, Communists, immigrants, and trade unionists. He had served in the House since 1921 and had already spent more than a decade at the helm of its veterans committee. He had hated the New Deal long before he led the effort to override FDR's veto of 1935 legislation giving former dough-boys US savings bonds instead of bonuses. Rankin had insisted that his House Committee on World War Legislation conduct all hearings on any legislation related to veterans, including the parliamentary proposal the American Legion and other veterans groups had pressured Congress to adopt. Legionnaires could trust the committee's top Republican, Edith Nourse Rogers. Dubbed "the Angel of Walter Reed," she had proved herself a staunch advocate for military hospitals after joining Congress in 1925, when the GOP had urged her to run for the Massachusetts seat left open by the death of her husband, Legionnaire John Rogers.[23]

Rankin's counterpart chairing the Senate Finance Committee's World War Veterans Legislation subcommittee shared Rogers's and Rankin's convictions. Senator J. Bennett "Champ" Clark, a founder of the Legion, warned his colleagues that he had never seen veterans groups "so much wrought up, as unanimous, and as bitter, about any proposition, as they are about the proposal to take a simple matter of veterans' rehabilitation and pitchfork it into a general scheme of social rehabilitation affecting all of the people of the United States." His father had been Speaker of the House when Clark, who had opposed US entry into the Great War, enlisted. The retired colonel practiced law before Missourians elected him to the Senate in 1932 and was a Democrat who never rubber-stamped any administration proposals. For example, even though he agreed that the United States should enter the war after the attack on Pearl Harbor, Clark wanted military spending limited and the president's power curbed. Those opinions undermined his clout and authority in Congress even before FDR picked Missouri's other senator, Legionnaire Harry S Truman, to be his 1944 running mate.[24]

Bennett could still count on support from the growing anti-Roosevelt co-alition that had felled the NRPB, CCC, and NYA and heralded the two major parties' steady postwar realignment. Like the Roosevelt administration and much of the public, this cohort of Republican and Democratic congressmen feared massive unemployment and political instability, the ingredients for another calamitous depression. Yet, unlike liberals in Congress and the executive branch, these conservatives insisted that more social welfare provisions, public services, and earmarked funds were a recipe for political and economic disaster, not keys to preventing catastrophe and safeguarding democracy. They feared exactly the kind of opening wedge some in the White House wanted. Wisconsin Republican Senator Alexander Wiley shared the concern of his constituents that the "Federal Government was liable to use this as an opportunity to open up the whole scope of Federal jurisdiction in relation to unemployment." California Republican Bertrand Gearhart said that "the thing we have got to fight down is the crafty effort of so many groups to use the war for reorganization of the world after the war; to capitalize upon the war sentiment to accomplish their objectives which have to do with social uplift."[25]

Those suspicions made early 1944 committee hearings especially contentious. Support for aid was unanimous but many disagreed on how much and what kind of assistance veterans needed, much less who should provide it. Rankin, for example, sought a lump sum payment to keep millions off "Federal relief, which we call unemployment compensation," and prevent the need for "a swarm of bureaucrats that would almost equal the locusts of Egypt." Senate Finance Committee chairman Wiley also opposed giving a "toe-hold to federalizers," a sentiment akin to Ohio Republican Senator Robert Taft's opposition to anything that smacked of "utopian" planning. Illinois Republican Representative Everett Dirksen also lacked patience for any sort of social engineering since "Gabriel had blown his fiscal horn." Such remonstrations did not deter liberals. North Carolina Democratic Representative Graham Barden joined liberal Republican Wisconsin Senator Robert LaFollette in introducing a suggestion that FSA, not the VA, oversee benefits to any "war service person," not just GIs. Liberal Democrat Robert Wagner boldly demanded that the US Employment Service oversee job placement for veterans, a suggestion in line with the New Yorker's hope for a comprehensive, far-reaching unemployment compensation bill for the entire country. But Rankin threatened to abandon the bill over VA control, considering the decentralized agency much better suited to administering the help for which only veterans would qualify.[26]

Education proved equally divisive even though many doubted GIs would enroll. War Department surveys suggested that only 7 to 12 percent of combatants planned to go back to school. An even smaller number of officers and enlistees seemed likely to apply. Commanders testified that GIs eagerly kept up with correspondence courses but most lawmakers, including liberals, still doubted returnees would have any interest in additional learning. Junior Arizona Senator and Legionnaire Ernest McFarland even tried to quell concerns about the cost of his suggested schooling entitlements by predicting that few troops would want to or be able to take advantage of such generous support for all four years.[27]

Such reasoning helped liberals like Senator Claude Pepper of Florida, who wanted more robust postsecondary benefits. In Senate hearings, he scolded leaders of the committee Roosevelt had formed to design the education benefit because they proposed a selection process that would keep the number of eligible GIs down to a level based on total college enrollments before the war. Many back then, Pepper pointed out, had "dropped out because of financial demands and financial difficulties." He feared that if more was not done to enable "the boys and girls who come out of the armed services" to pursue vocational and higher education, and then to keep them from dropping out, "we will find them in the penitentiary or in the bread lines." How much better to give them "a practical example of democracy here and show them that you do not have to have money to go to college . . . in this country."[28]

In the same hearing, Pepper rebuked the chair of Roosevelt's committee, Major General Frederick Osborn, for proposing to pay student veterans just $50 per month to cover their living expenses on top of tuition and other educational costs. Pepper declared such paltry help "beneath the dignity and the responsibility of the United States Government." He himself had enjoyed only an "ordinary standard of living" on a $100 monthly allowance when he attended Harvard Law School in the early 1920s. Indignant at Osborn's suggestion that a higher amount might attract "men who preferred to have a comfortable education rather than to go to work," Pepper retorted that, "on the contrary, we should make it so high that it would lure a lot of men into going to school." As long as the standard was upheld that students must do "creditable work," their time would be better spent furthering their education. "That is not shirking anything. That is following the course that is of the greatest benefit to society."[29]

Those arguments hardly swayed congressional conservatives, who feared and opposed anything smacking of federal largesse. Rogers, the celebrated Angel of Walter Reed, opposed any schooling entitlements. Many of her colleagues shared Legionnaires' concerns that military service had put GIs at a disadvantage on the job market against the civilian war production workers who had received specialized training (sometimes from NYA). She and others also feared college help would actually deter troops from seeking gainful employment. "I want to give every boy that has been in the Army, the Navy, or the Marine Corps all possible opportunities," Clark vowed, but without encouraging "the idea of a kid living off the Government and going to school instead of going to work." Rankin shared that concern. He also worried that GIs would graduate overeducated and undertrained for the blue-collar work he presumed suited most veterans. Working-class warriors hardly needed exposure to the rarified world of academia where they would be "subject to the tainted theories of sociologists." VA head General Frank Hines also had no interest in leaving GIs beholden to "crackpots, long-haired professors, and radicals." The Spanish-American War veteran shared Rankin's and the Legion leadership's strident opposition to entrusting veterans' educational guarantees to the still tiny, relatively powerless Office of Education then housed under FSA. Hines promised to "utilize existing educational facilities to the fullest extent and to execute the law intelligently and economically." Privately he guaranteed Rankin the VA would exercise exclusive power over any education benefits.[30]

Educators helped liberals fight conservative proposals to lend soldiers the money to enroll. Such suggestions, like those for homes and small businesses, exemplified how government-brokered financial products had become more common and even accepted. But the president of the American Association of Teachers Colleges dissuaded lawmakers from dabbling in student loans. He testified that collecting on these risky financial products had always been a challenge. Better, he said, to let schools that still lent to undergraduates manage their existing programs than have the government get involved. Former Education Office director and American Council on Education head George Zook likewise disdained borrowing. He emphasized that his staff had found widespread enthusiasm for the tuition reimbursement plan the Legion and administration suggested but still cautioned "that there are usually differences of opinion among educators."[31]

Relations between parts of the academy and the federal government had improved. The war effort had nurtured partnerships that had continued after work-study's sudden end. Collaborations included the Manhattan Project, which built the atom bombs, as well as an agreement between the federal government and over four hundred colleges and universities to provide a wide range of educational opportunities (including correspondence programs) that military leaders considered vital for both morale and victory. That cooperation had been lucrative, even lifesaving, for many campuses, including the six hundred public and private affiliates of the Association of American Colleges, whose executive director testified that members were "in general sympathetic" with the administration's recommendations. Colleges and universities needed veterans by the end of the fall 1944 semester, when nearly all the Army and Navy trainees left campuses. The student body shrank to a third of what it had been in 1939. Veterans, the University of Cincinnati's president admitted to reporters, were "the chief hope of American colleges and universities for rescue from the present dearth of men students." The National Education Association's leader, the kind of person Roosevelt insiders would have dismissed as a part of the "school crowd," did not mention that calculation when he called the pending bill "one of the wisest pieces of legislation" to prevent "the loss of a single generation."[32]

But some leading academics brazenly denounced Title II. "The power to subsidize," historian Bernard DeVoto warned in a 1943 *Harper's Magazine* article, "is the power to destroy." Even indirect aid might lead to a vast federal education bureaucracy that could rob schools of "their autonomy" in matters of curricula, admissions, and faculty hiring. Like many professors and lawmakers, Harvard president Conant also assumed the military had drafted only a small number of young people talented enough to learn more. The academy, he still insisted, was best suited for the nation's "natural aristocracy." He doubted that flinging open the door to the Ivory Tower would prevent postwar political unrest. Only "a carefully selected number of returned veterans" should receive temporary aid to make up for "the national educational deficit caused by the war."[33]

These and other strident objections made the bill's passage tense and dramatic. Title II was only one hurdle. In early May, representatives spent but four days debating educational provisions. They could agree that Congress should pay for veterans' schooling but fought bitterly over how to ensure colleges would not find themselves under the federal control educators and many congressional conservatives feared. Rankin openly prioritized "maintaining the rights of the States and keeping as many bureaucrats out as possible" to "be dead sure" GIs could choose where they enrolled and what they studied. The chairman's efforts still did not satisfy lawmakers who trembled at the power the VA might have over higher education. Fighting continued throughout the summer and fall over the unemployment compensation that Rankin and another representative insisted "will discriminate against the men who go right back to work."[34]

Insiders knew racism was driving the frustrating House delays. Clark rebuked Rankin and his supporters on the Senate floor for being "so unwilling to let the Negro troops have the unemployment insurance to which they are entitled that they would be willing to withhold the benefits from all our troops." That recalcitrance also enraged the *Nation*'s leftwing editors, who berated Rankin for trying to ensure that "the sweatshoppers whom he represents . . . have an ample supply of cheap labor after war." Equality hardly concerned Legion commander Atherton, who reprimanded Rankin for opposing the unemployment compensation holding up the entire House bill for four months after the senators passed their version of the GI Bill. "The American Legion," he told reporters, "intend to fight him right down the line and take the issue to every voter in the country." The armed forces were already ready to join him. An *Army Times* editorial concluded "it's time to quit stalling." The GI Bill of Rights was not charity, it insisted, and veterans "deserve a little assistance in making their readjustments."[35]

Rankin's intransigence produced a limited bill that would be difficult to reconcile with the more generous Senate version. During tense conference committee deliberations, he trimmed the final legislation's level of unemployment compensation and continued to warn of radicalism when delegates discussed schooling. The deadlock frustrated Legionnaires, who "weren't going to let it die." New York Representative Pat Kearney warned that there would be one final meeting to try and reach an agreement, otherwise "the bill will be lost." The Republican knew that the ailing Representative John Gibson could "save the bill" if he could make it back from Georgia in time. A telephone operator helped a local Legionnaire track down the Democrat and was eager to do it because "My husband just landed in Normandy. We've got to pass that GI Bill for him." A frantic drive to a waiting plane in Jacksonville, Florida, barely got Gibson to the House in time. "I'm going to hold a press conference after this meeting," he reportedly warned as he strode into the conference committee, "I'm going to expose anyone who doesn't vote for the GI Bill of Rights." Both houses quickly approved the conference report. With little fanfare, some newspaper coverage, and limited editorial comment, the president signed the Servicemen's Readjustment Act on June 22, 1944.[36]

Administering Rights

The $500 million temporary program intended, as the act's official name indicated, to adjust servicemen as Legionnaries desired, not the economy as White House insiders had hoped. Public Law 346 provided a lot of help through the kind of government-guaranteed financial products with which New Dealers had experimented. It included fifty-two weeks of $20-a-week unemployment compensation and farm, home, and small business loans, which were far less generous than Legionnaires had wanted. The federal government only backed 50 percent of loans capped at $2,000 and 4 percent interest. Lawmakers had provided more substantial education benefits than in Colmery's initial proposal. On paper, ninety days of service qualified those GIs who had been drafted or had enlisted before turning twenty-five. The age restriction represented a compromise of sorts since it presumed younger veterans had had their schooling interrupted, but it effectively walled off older returnees from the program, thus keeping postsecondary schooling the purview of youth, even though New Dealers had once hoped to extend work-study eligibility to everyone under thirty. The US Employment Service, as liberals wanted, handled job placement services. Everything else fell under the purview of the VA, which, due to congressional conservatives' insistence, turned a lot of the oversight over to state boards and authorities.[37]

Title II's educational benefits still served as the kind of entering wedge conservatives feared and liberals wanted. The financing was, nonetheless, as creative and complicated as work-study's underwriting. New Deal experiments and wartime programs had helped repair campuses, improve facilities, and vastly expand top institutions' science departments. The entire academy still needed to grow substantially to meet citizen demands then and national needs in the future. Work-study, the short-lived loan program, and WWII educational partnerships had hardly laid the political or legal groundwork for directly funding colleges and universities, whose faculty and staff still often feared that hands-off aid, let alone direct support, would lead to government control. Fee reimbursements, though still controversial, had been far more politically palatable. Unlike work-study or the wartime loan program, campus staff did not bill soldiers for tuition. Administrators sent those invoices to the VA for payment. That agency also mailed purposefully meager subsistence checks directly to enrolled GIs. Congress had been far more generous to campuses than returnees to ensure price would not stop any talented veterans from going to top universities. Lawmakers set the maximum reimbursement at $500 for all fees, supplies, and services, a limit higher (as noted in hearings) than Harvard charged for tuition at the time. Public and private college presidents had urged lawmakers to reimburse campuses for the actual cost of instructing GIs, historically more than the educational fees charged. Lawmakers nevertheless were determined that the VA should be billed for the "customary tuition." Roosevelt's advisors had included that suggestion in their preliminary reports to Congress because that support, coupled with the subsistence allowance, would be much higher than most scholarships offered, including at expensive Ivy League schools that still expected recipients to work part time.[38]

Administrators demanded the VA do more for campuses immediately after the legislation's passage. The reimbursement restrictions, they claimed, would make it impossible to accommodate even the small number of veterans then expected to enroll. They particularly pressured the VA to provide additional reimbursement under the bill's promise of "fair and reasonable compensation," arguing in many cases that tuition rates were "inadequate." VA staff buckled. State institutions could bill the government for nonresident fees for all GIs, regardless of where they were from. Every institution, including private colleges and for-profit schools, was guaranteed to receive at least an additional $10 a month, $30 a quarter, or $40 a semester for each veteran, regardless of what it charged civilians.[39]

That kind of hidden, politically crafty maneuvering hardly endeared Public Law 346 to the public. "Why don't you," an irate citizen asked Rankin in May 1945, "just confiscate everything and hand it over to the veterans, including your seat in Congress?" The press also considered lawmakers to have been overly generous. Some reporters predicted that unemployment compensation would encourage lazy veterans to avoid looking for work. Title II seemed especially wasteful and unnecessary. An American Veterans Committee leader publicly called it "the best provision" that "will never be useful to the great majority of veterans." Some soldiers openly doubted the GI Bill would be of much help. "Several men in my crew," an ensign explained to *Los Angeles Times* readers in July 1945, "are young, some have never held a real job and they want to know what is going to be done toward giving them a chance." He added: "Many never finished high school [but] are old enough to have known the last depression."[40]

But faculty and staff remained divided about the relatively small number of GIs predicted to matriculate. New York University's chancellor warned in his 1944 annual report that every school would have to choose between "either greatly expanding, or increasing the selectivity of admissions." NYU would certainly welcome returnees but could not expand the student body much more than it had been before the war. But the president of the Teachers Union's college chapter publicly dismissed his fears. Quotas and strict admission standards, Sarah Riedman feared, would "carry us back to pre-war days, when thousands of capable students were denied admission." She predicted "a more productive post-war economy and of increased leisure will encourage a tremendous back-to-school movement" that would inaugurate "an era of greater governmental responsibility for financing of education" benefiting educators if they "assume responsibility for leadership."[41]

Few elite academics shared such sentiments, including those with Democratic Party ties. University of Chicago president Robert Hutchins, still regarded as a great educational reformer, defender of the humanities, public intellectual, civil libertarian, and masterful fundraiser, hardly admired fellow Yankee Roosevelt. "He was not a very good administrator, and I have some doubts about his claims to statesmanship," the legal theorist later explained. "But nobody can deny that he was a tremendous showman." Disregard did not stop Roosevelt's top aides from trying to convince the president to appoint Hutchins to high-ranking positions, including on the Supreme Court. Hutchins's strident opposition to entering the war before Pearl Harbor as well as his dedication to academic freedom also did not stop him from turning the University of Chicago into "an essential part of the American military machine." He even admitted in 1943, "I see no reason to suppose that education by contract will end with the war." Armistice posed many threats to his elite sensibilities. He feared the sciences and engineering would overwhelm the rest of the university at a moment when "the horrors of peace are likely to be worse than those of war." Hutchins warned trustees in 1946 that "A people who only a few years ago worked ten hours a day will not easily stand the shock of being reduced to four or five." He felt that "we Americans must discover some rational notion of leisure or degenerate into a nation of alcoholics, movie fans, and pulp-magazine consumers, a nation, in short, of morons and lunatics."[42]

Hutchins still recoiled at opening up higher education to the masses, including war heroes. Just months after FDR signed the bill, Hutchins publicly castigated Congress for using Title II to keep "veterans off the bread line" and making higher education "a substitute for the dole or for a national program of public works." As he put it, "Education is not a device for coping with mass unemployment." That misguided intention represented "the threat to American Education." Instead of "making a 50 per cent loan," the government gave "a 100 per cent gift," what Hutchins labeled "an open invitation to any entrepreneur . . . to buy up the charters of half a dozen bankrupt colleges and make his fortune." Title II, after all, was based on the unworkable "principle that there must be no relation between the education of a citizen and the income of his parents." Rather, he presumed that "sentimental pressures and financial temptation" guaranteed that "the least capable among the war generation, instead of the most capable, flood the facilities for advanced education in the United States." Since college and university admissions officers "cannot resist money," schools would be "converted into educational hobo jungles."[43]

The first GIs, according to Columbia professor Willard Waller, already proved themselves unworthy. Some "are aimless drifters with no purpose in life." The others seemed "pitifully in earnest and try tragically hard, wearing shabby clothes, living in somebody's basement, eating a few cents worth of bread and milk and sometimes growing hungry while they beat their brains out trying to master college algebra or English."[44]

Many reporters disagreed. *New York Times* correspondent Edith Efron considered the 1,957 GIs enrolled at NYU "a thing of beauty." No one could tell them apart from the other undergraduates, "save for the small golden eagle on their civilian lapels and a few tell-tale crow's feet around the eyes." Reporter Stephen Thompson praised Title II as "one of the most remarkable milestones in public education" because it "not only paves, it literally carpets the way for every G.I. Joe and G.I. Jane."[45]

But veterans were not thrilled with the stark difference between what they had been promised and what they received. A disappointed soldier wrote to the *Chicago Tribune* in support of a cash bonus to "let G.I. Joe make his own adjustments." He described the GI Bill as "the most confusing ball of red tape ever manufactured." Its home loan offer was "no better than a credit reference," he noted, and the "only concrete advantage is the college education . . . and this is practical only to the younger men." Disabled American Veterans spokesman Cicero Hogan openly labeled Title II "bunk" and the entire bill a fraud. No one seemed to qualify for loans or four years of schooling. "What the boys will get is a year or 18 months," he fumed, unless the government tried "to slip them a term in a business college," the kind of for-profit school elite academics had accused of bilking the striving Americans long unwelcome on elite campuses, like Hutchins's Chicago.[46]

Frustrated returnees found allies among journalists outside Hearst's media empire. Reporters doggedly highlighted that the legislation Hearst and the Legion championed already seemed incapable of helping the small number discharged, much less the thousands more to come. *New York Times, Saturday Evening Post,* and *Collier's* writers discovered that subsistence stipends failed to cover basic living expenses, that almost all eligible GIs struggled to make use of Title II, and that veterans fell victim to "racketeering landlords" in a "land of rundown dwellings." Mortgages barely helped veterans buy even a modest home, then averaging $10,000, during a nationwide housing shortage. Journalists also uncovered that soldiers did not know much about the law. Job-placement services were especially perplexing because Congress had split that duty between the VA and US Employment Service. Many veterans were unsure whom to approach for help, which already seemed woefully inadequate. Reporters also tugged at readers' hearts and purses. C. S. Forester profiled former colonel Philip Gray for *Ladies' Home Journal,* whose readers learned that many veterans were "willing to try anything," as Gray's wife explained, to stay in school. He could only afford to rent one room in a "shabby yellow rooming house" for his pregnant wife and toddler. They shared a two-bedroom bungalow with seven other people but still had to borrow $250 from a bank because his first subsistence check arrived more than two months late. He rarely had more than an hour a day to study since he picked up odd jobs to put food on the table. "We can get through seven more semesters," his wife guessed, "we always manage to eat somehow."[47]

Outrage from the public and the American Legion prompted Congress to act. Lawmakers first investigated the VA, a fifteen-year-old agency ill-suited to administering the GI Bill. They uncovered squabbling over authority between US Employment Service and VA heads, who only had 72,000 employees staffing thirteen branch and seventy regional offices to aid eleven million WWII veterans. Both Congress and the president worked to overhaul the agency. FDR's successor, Harry Truman, turned it over to General Omar Bradley in fall 1945, who oversaw a restructuring that created regional office divisions dedicated to education training; registration and research; adjustment and guidance; and training and facilities. These bureaus coordinated with state agencies as well as postsecondary schools, which needed to settle tuition rates, to set reimbursement procedures, and to prove they met Title II eligibility requirements.[48]

Public pressure also forced lawmakers to amend the GI Bill. Plentiful postwar jobs, the looming 1946 midterms, and the legislation's well-known shortcomings did not make the summer and fall 1945 hearings any less contentious than earlier debates, when many had feared another depression and Bonus March. Congress just tweaked or ignored the small farm and business loans, job placement services, unemployment provisions, and mortgage guarantees, in which veterans had shown far less interest than originally predicted. Soldiers, after all, qualified for the government-guaranteed financial products New Dealers had passed in the 1930s. Work-study's abrupt end had made Title II far more valuable and appealing to GIs but no less controversial among conservatives who still feared soldiers would take advantage of a program that seemed the definition of federal overreach. Senators and representatives easily agreed to extend how long a student had to begin and complete a degree program. They also quickly lifted the age restriction, since a contingent still remained convinced that those over twenty-five (roughly half of all returnees) had no interest in college.[49]

Fighting over eligible schools, tuition reimbursement rates, and stipends nevertheless dragged on. Educators knew that both veterans and campuses needed far more support. National Education Association (NEA) experts considered raising subsistence pay of the utmost importance. Expecting veterans "to do odd jobs" to afford basic necessities, one emphasized, "takes too much precious time from the veteran's delayed education." Just an extra $15 a month, advocates eventually convinced lawmakers, would help, while still ensuring students would not "have any money left over for movies or luxuries." GIs also needed far more housing options than colleges could provide.

Federal compensation was simply inadequate to fund expansions, particularly at state institutions. "People," an NEA official noted, "have been given the impression that the Federal Government is paying for the education of veterans, thus preventing many public schools from getting the necessary funds from State and local governments." Fee reimbursement still remained capped at $500. But campuses could charge the VA the actual cost of instruction, which enabled public universities to charge more for out-of-state students. Politicians also reluctantly agreed to extend eligibility to all accredited schools and correspondence programs.[50]

Those revisions helped GIs make a once controversial law into a now-lionized success. Hundreds of thousands of veterans defied the predictions they would be uninterested in and incapable of going to college. During the 1947–1948 school year, more than a million GIs matriculated, making veterans 49 percent of the country's student body and almost 70 percent of the men enrolled. They applied to Ivy League institutions, state universities, liberal arts colleges, and technical schools but only enrolled in junior and teacher colleges as a last resort, since, as *Time* journalists quipped, "why go to Podunk College when the Government will send you to Yale?" More importantly, they excelled, like work-studiers before them, often frustrating their civilian peers. Stanford students even labeled GIs "Damn Average Raisers," or "D.A.R.'s."[51]

Numerous studies revealed that former GIs earned higher grades than other undergraduates but also better marks than their abilities might otherwise predict. Experts marveled at how little difference there was between Americans who could afford college on their own and the many GIs who could not. Despite the assumptions of Hutchins and other academics, reports indicated no significant differences between the degree programs chosen. Results instead showed that even older GIs defied predictions, including the 20 percent that doubted or openly admitted that they would have not pursued college without Title II help. That group, roughly 445,000, represented a significant portion of the student body after World War II, when the total number of college students numbered just 2.3 million.[52]

Researchers discovered that undergraduates were far more likely to worry about money if they were veterans. That fact perplexed researchers trying to ascertain whether GIs were in fact outperforming their civilian counterparts. Even though lawmakers had increased subsistence stipends in 1945, a 1946 survey revealed that most enrolled soldiers had to work part time. Only a small percentage of single GIs reported subsistence checks covering their living expenses. Most of them lived at home and carefully budgeted their stipends. Those problems persisted. Approximately 70 percent of soldiers and roughly 40 percent of noncombatants surveyed in a 1951 Educational Testing Service study admitted that they feared "making ends meet financially." Indeed, a sizeable number of GIs (like 75 percent of Wayne State enrollees) continued to hold down jobs to afford to take classes.[53]

Those results captured what many Americans have forgotten: even the revised GI Bill's schooling provisions were not generous enough. Returnees certainly gushed about the opportunity to enroll but they also fought to ensure they actually got the rights promised them. Some veterans, their wives, and even their parents wrote directly to the White House to complain that the VA had failed to send subsistence checks or cover textbooks. Veterans and their wives also joined college staff in demanding Congress raise subsistence allowances again. Some telegraphed or wrote their representatives, others testified in person. University of Wisconsin undergraduate John Hunter reminded lawmakers that no GI "wants to get something for nothing from the Government." But his peers "are . . . dropping out of school." Instead of seeing his wife and children in West Virginia, he felt compelled to come "down here on my spring vacation" to hand representatives a petition that five thousand had signed in support of a raise. "The money I came down here on allotted me only a loaf of bread to eat since yesterday," he noted, "and a cup of coffee this morning."[54]

Many GIs unable to make it to Capitol Hill joined chapters of Operation Subsistence, a national organization that partnered with other veterans organizations to advocate for returnees' needs. Michigan stalwarts collaborated with the American Veterans Committee to survey how student-soldiers were subsisting at the University of Michigan. They publicized the startling 1947 findings in widely distributed pamphlets aimed at encouraging citizens to act before Title II "becomes an empty promise." By January 1948, a million GIs had joined Operation Subsistence chapters across the country. Their leaders demanded a meeting with Truman to discuss the paltry subsistence checks and skyrocketing consumer costs that had forced more than a million veterans to drop out. But the thirty-two delegates, representing fifteen states and the District of Columbia, got to meet with only one White House aide.[55]

Such frustrations did not stop GIs from talking to journalists, who documented crowded classrooms, decrepit dorms, and understocked libraries. A University of California undergraduate reported only being able to rent a bedroom for his wife and child. He still worked part-time jobs because subsistence payments barely covered basic living expenses and $10 rent in a boarding house accommodating nineteen other families. They all shared a kitchen that had one sink and a stove but lacked a refrigerator and icebox. LA-area college staff sent married veterans to homes defense workers once occupied. Shipyard surplus only made a dent in their waitlists. One GI ended up living in a trailer with his young family in the parking lot of the Hollywood Bowl, where he worked part time. *Ladies' Home Journal* reporters nevertheless marveled at the trailer park, affectionately dubbed "Hawkeye Village," for married University of Iowa veterans. One child contracted measles in the mud-filled camp, where couples "had to haul eight or nine buckets of water a day and to trek back and forth along the boardwalk to the toilets and showers—where little boys insisted on playing peekaboo." Parents "really enjoy trailer life," which helped them "make friends in a hurry." Rose Lee Jay gave *Ladies' Home Journal* readers a far different perspective when she wrote about her "Battle for Subsistence." She, like other young mothers married to studying veterans, valiantly scrimped to stop their husbands from dropping out. Coupon clipping simply could not stretch $90 far enough after the end of wartime price controls ushered in a period of inflation. Neither veterans nor their spouses could "earn enough with a part-time job to make up the difference." Such stories increasingly angered civilians, like Wicks, whose telegram to Truman had compared University of Missouri dorms to concentration camps.[56]

Lawmakers and VA officials did little to address the squalor making headlines. VA staff had tried to assess the quality and capacity of the country's colleges but few administrators had kept good records of their growth and resources. Many VA surveys were unanswered, incomplete, or poorly filled out. Washington insiders admitted by 1946 that they had not realized how unprepared colleges and universities were to accommodate the enormous number of GIs eager to study, a third of whom had families. In fairness, reporters noted that colleges had ignored ongoing VA requests for enrollment data (only in November 1947 had all but twenty-one schools supplied crucial information about their needs). Senator James Mead still publicly urged fellow lawmakers not to wait because veterans want "to go to college now—not 2 or

FIG 3.1 The quality of student housing for veterans enraged reporters across the country. The cramped, single-student housing at the University of Missouri pictured here was common during the fitful rollout of the GI Bill, used by 2.2 million former soldiers. Collection C:1 / 81 / 1, Box 6, University Archives, University of Missouri.

3 years from now." Government-paid tuition simply could not cover the expansions needed to accommodate veterans, much less the growth required for future generations of high-school graduates who would enroll. President Harry Truman subsequently pressured his staff to do everything to ensure GIs could take advantage of Title II. But Office of War Mobilization and Reconversion personnel nevertheless warned that "all education remains the primary concern of our free academic system" in their comprehensive, publicized report of housing, classroom, staff, and textbook shortages.[57]

Lawmakers did not try to revise the GI Bill again but episodically increased allocations to meet demand and quell outrage. That spending meagerly raised living allowances and directly funded some limited campus expansions. Lawmakers also amended wartime legislation to empower the National Housing Agency to help quarter soldiers in rentals and temporary units and to transfer a lot of surplus government property to campuses that used former mess tents, prefabricated steel barracks, and even landing ship tanks for accommodations. Subsequent amendments allocated wartime surpluses to create and outfit classrooms, labs, and offices. Congress and the VA initially expected colleges and universities to return these leftovers to the government because they assumed, unlike Roosevelt's aides, that the surge in applications and enrollments would be small and temporary. Lawmakers only made permanent the land and building donations, including the ramshackle housing widely publicized in the news, after tuition reimbursement rules failed to pay for essential campus improvements.[58]

State governments had far more authority to better conditions for GIs, but few legislatures acted. Some passed additional assistance to help cover veterans' college costs; Montana especially stood out for waiving tuition at its flagship university. Some assemblies also helped underwrite campus growth since tuition hikes did not do nearly enough to cover the expense of improvements at existing colleges, much less the costs of starting new ones in underserved areas. Illinois lawmakers came up with a creative solution, repurposing a military training center on the city's Navy Pier into a two-year college called the Chicago Undergraduate Center. Years before the so-called "Harvard on the Rocks" was moved and expanded into the University of Illinois Chicago, the campus was a godsend for many working-class Chicagoans who could not imagine leaving their neighborhoods for the University of Illinois at Urbana-Champaign, a public school already struggling to accommodate veterans. The city's small Catholic colleges were inundated with applications from the many Jewish, African American, and Catholic veterans who did not expect to get into nearby elite Northwestern, much less the University of Chicago. The building on Navy Pier could accommodate some four thousand soldiers, albeit in cramped classrooms.[59]

Expanding facilities, paying tuition bills, and donating surplus barracks did little to challenge the quota system that had kept Jews, Catholics, immigrants, and African Americans out. Federal policies, like a lot of those implemented under Roosevelt, left the fight for equality up to politicians, reporters, veterans, and concerned citizens. Elite educators still felt no reason to hide how selective they were or to apologize for wanting to keep the masses out of their rarified, overwhelmingly white institutions. They even shared application requirements, selection criteria, and enrollment statistics with

FIG 3.2 Separate registration lines for former soldiers and noncombatants at the Chicago Undergraduate Center in 1946, formerly the abandoned Navy Pier. The unintended consequences of the GI Bill limited opportunities for civilians, particularly women. Many Americans found themselves priced out of higher education after administrators across the country raised fees to take advantage of tuition reimbursements from the Veterans Administration. UA_96_033_017, Navy Pier Negatives and Prints, Special Collections & University Archives, University of Illinois Chicago.

investigators connected to New York mayor William O'Dwyer's Committee on Unity, whose report made the front page of the *New York Times* on January 22, 1946. Its revelations outraged the American Jewish Congress and the New York State Teachers Guild, which immediately demanded that private colleges lose their tax-exempt status. State legislators representing Catholics in Manhattan and Jews in Brooklyn quickly filed suits to create a state university to serve excluded students. There was real need behind that demand. Army officials had already warned state education officials to expect thousands of veterans to apply (military leaders raised estimates to 100,000 in June). Leaders of ten religious, civic, and veteran organizations jointly demanded that the New York City Council investigate admissions practices. The multi-ethnic, multiracial coalition pointed out that citizens had provided "a gift of millions of dollars in real estate tax exemptions" to nonprofit, secular public and private schools that illegally discriminated. Revoking culpable colleges' exemptions seemed the only way to end quotas bound to "poison the intellectual and moral atmosphere of educational institutions and prevent gifted students from making their fullest scientific and intellectual contributions." Both politicians and journalists condemned the state's private colleges and their quotas. *New York Post* columnist Max Lerner even pointedly castigated those colleges and professional schools that seemed happy to "judge their applicants for admission on the principles of Hitler's racist state."[60]

Outrage over rampant, unapologetic discrimination could be found across the country. Veteran James Burwell considered himself "just another disgusted GI," who found promises to be "hot air." He wrote to the *Chicago Tribune*: "The last straw is discovering that even the colleges have a priority system which works against students who were in the lower half or lower third of their high school class." Grades earned in the past "made no difference," he fumed, "when it came to selecting blood to spill on the battlefield, but as soon as we are home, discrimination sets in." The Supreme Court heard numerous challenges to segregation in higher education during the GI Bill's rollout. *Amicus curiae* briefs even asserted that discrimination had to end in order to give all GIs access to the law's benefits. Certain academics railed against the quotas that Alfonso Myers, a NYU education professor, openly called a "Nazi practice," toward which educators had turned a blind eye. In February 1945, he joined other faculty, including high-ranking NEA members, in demanding that FDR create an agency akin to the wartime Fair Employment Practices Commission for higher education. A National Fair Education Practice Committee would end "quotas and other forms of racial and religious discriminations in the nation's colleges." They nonetheless considered legislation unnecessary. In lieu of the federal oversight many academics continued to fear, they wanted a "capable and distinguished national" group to harness public outrage in order to ensure that GIs will no longer "be thwarted." Myers made his position clear: "Every college should adopt and announce a forthright policy against discrimination."[61]

Colleges and universities, despite the fears of academics and conservative lawmakers, never lost their discretion over who received education benefits.

As with work-study, such a shift would have abruptly broken a long-standing tradition and been uncharacteristic of Roosevelt-era experimentation. Staff continued to control admissions and ultimately determined how equal opportunities for more schooling would be. Some elite institutions, including the University of Chicago and Harvard, embraced entrance exams and standardized tests, like the SAT, to ferret out those with high IQs. Some campuses, including Syracuse, let military service stand in lieu of the required high-school diploma. Other colleges admitted those with just a GED. Some institutions even gave veterans course credit both for service as well as the education programs offered through the military's partnership with universities to provide opportunities to learn in foxholes.[62]

The institutions that adjusted to GIs' needs and demands transformed college life for subsequent generations of students. A 1946 survey indicated that even though the majority of veterans liked college, "it was 50-50 on the teaching methods and college systems." Respondents generally claimed "that the teaching staff was not up to the standards expected; that the lecture material was poorly organized [and] that colleges, on the whole, seemed to be uninterested in improving their standards and methods of instruction." Almost all wished for the kind of small discussion groups that Hilda Smith wanted as a part of the New Deal's Workers Education Project. Even though those questioned did "not expect the whole college system to be revamped to suit" them, faculty hired graduate students to run discussion sections for greatly expanded lecture classes. Demand was so high that registrars often scheduled these breakout sessions from morning to night, often at the same time. Some universities even began summer programs and issued numbered ID cards. Faculty size also swelled. New hires included academics fleeing wartorn Europe as well as high school teachers. The latter often taught the first-ever evening classes at large institutions, including Penn State. Urgent campus expansions forced administrators to turn to endowments, donors, and state legislatures. Cornell, for example, used state money to lease a nearby hotel to house GIs. But Notre Dame and Penn State built new facilities since they expected more Americans to apply after GI benefits expired.[63]

Title II also revolutionized how colleges shepherded students through degree programs and readied them to apply for jobs. University of Illinois officials provided free counseling and aptitude testing to veterans. But the VA also had the authority to set up vocational guidance centers for veterans. Administrators across the country lobbied officials to pick their campuses to house these programs. Schools received additional funding for hosting them, which many recognized (as the VA feared) as a resource that might convince GIs to use their benefits there. The agency ended up running sixty-three centers at big schools (such as the University of Pennsylvania, Rutgers, and City University of New York) as well as smaller institutions (including Fresno Junior College and Utah's Weber College). All these offices served veterans at nearby campuses, which enabled them to help over one million GIs navigate college life and find work after graduation. These short-lived bureaus set an important precedent for guidance and career services that parents and students would eventually come to expect.[64]

Campuses willing to cater to such careerism further enraged Title II's most strident academic critics. Hutchins disliked veterans' preference for engineering and the social sciences over the humanities, which smacked of the kind of vocational training this champion of the liberal arts disdained. Some faculty also resisted efforts to make education, particularly the humanities, more practical. Such "aggressive forces of commercialism," one professor complained in *The Journal of Higher Education,* would only "distract and debase" colleges, which other scholars worried might become mere "supply depots for industry and business." Such fears fed concerns that the GI Bill's emphasis on labor needs created unrealistic expectations for unemployment at a moment when the public still feared another depression. "We are training about three times as many engineers as the market can absorb," a UCLA admissions director reported in 1948. "There are two-and-one half times as many students in our College of Business Administration now as there were in 1940. Along with this, there are now 65,000 unemployed veterans . . . in Los Angeles County, alone, now! What will we do with these people when they reach the senior year?"[65]

Such questions fed festering fears of reporters, lawmakers, citizens, and VA officials over fraud, abuse, and corruption. Reports of the original and amended law's shortcomings did not vanquish suspicions that veterans would take advantage of Congress's generosity. *Ladies' Home Journal* staff even warned benefits were "making a bum out of G.I. Joe" in September 1946. The worries were somewhat justified. State unemployment compensation boards varied widely in how much they scrutinized GIs' aid applications. Some soldiers collected far more than they were entitled to by moving. Businesses also profited when they hired returnees, because they would be generously compensated for on-the-job training. State education boards bore some responsibility for that benefit's misuse. Even though VA higher-ups had asked agencies for a list of acceptable institutions immediately after FDR signed the GI Bill, many dithered, suggested unsuitable schools, or did not respond at all. The short-staffed VA subsequently scrambled to assess and approve GIs' applications, including for programs officials feared state agencies had just rubberstamped. The most egregious examples made headlines, including the Jackson, Mississippi, soldiers who wanted to be compensated for learning to be basketball players on the job.[66]

Lawmakers also received numerous complaints that schools, particularly vocational ones, were not offering veterans an education. Congress had expressed concerns about allowing veterans to use their benefits at for-profit schools during fights over the original law. Those proprietary institutions had declined in number during the Depression when they were ineligible for work-study and their reputations remained tarnished decades after elite college administrators had first declared war on them. Only thirty-five had state-education-board approval in 1944. By November 1947, 150,000 veterans had enrolled in the country's twelve hundred proprietary business schools, many of which did not fall under the purview of state education boards. The executive secretary of the National Council of Business Schools said that veterans probably felt that "intensive training offered by business schools gives them a better chance for good jobs." Those schools had also welcomed the many Americans excluded from nonprofit institutions, whose discriminatory practices may have unintentionally helped boost the number of for-profits to ten thousand by 1949. Classified ads for "GI Approved" proprietary schools appeared in papers, giving rise to much ridicule of charm courses, ballroom dancing lessons, and "chicken-sexing" classes. Journalists especially delighted in reporting the range of training programs the VA covered. Alongside the aspiring midwives, morticians, and cabinet makers were such curiosities as an Arkansas GI learning to raise quail and a former private taking judo lessons in Miami. Less covered were the trade schools that continued to offer the practical curricula that had given white-collar credentials to many women, immigrants, Jews, Catholics, and African Americans since the early twentieth century.[67]

The for-profits struggled to defend themselves against lawmakers. Illinois Democratic Senator Paul Douglas accused many of starting up just "to milk the system," as Hutchins had feared. VA officials struggled to police proprietary institutions, which eventually had to send the agency financial reports. Almost 60 percent charged far more than the nonprofits. VA staff still wanted to do more than force established for-profits to justify tuition hikes of more than 25 percent. H. V. Stirling, the VA's assistant administrator, warned that "taxpayers are going to be bled white" unless they stopped unemployed veterans from "course-hopping" between the new "fly-by-night" for-profits. Some of those schools had no financial history to help VA staff assess whether charges were exorbitant for the questionable courses on house painting and wallpapering marketed to GIs. Congress only agreed to impose stiffer restrictions in 1950. Proprietary schools still appealed, sometimes directly to the president's inner circle, when VA officials refused to fully reimburse the tuition charges that kept them open.[68]

Nonprofits did not receive the same scrutiny. VA staff never asked elite schools (including Harvard and the University of Chicago) to justify hiking tuition even though their fees jumped, on average, by a third. In hearings, lawmakers wondered whether the many campuses that had raised tuition had also improved services. Reports also surfaced of colleges and universities keeping fee reimbursements after students had either dropped out or their benefits had expired. College officials blamed the government for not providing enough money to actually cover the cost of educating students, particularly since the numbers enrolling far exceeded what anyone had anticipated.[69]

That defense failed to satisfy some lawmakers after the General Accounting Office completed a study of the GI Bill's actual costs in 1952. An estimated third of the $14.5 billion spent on Title II had gone to on-the-job training scams and sham institutions. Two-thirds of the schools investigated had "overcharged the government." Charles Eckert emphasized on the House floor that "It cannot be said that any particular type of institution . . . did not participate in this 'open season' on the Treasury." Nonprofits had "jumped" their fees after the bill's passage but trade schools had also "padded" costs. The findings enraged Texas Democratic Representative Olin Teague. "We wasted millions and millions of dollars on the thing," he fumed.[70]

But enthusiasm for Title II overshadowed the regrets, frustrations, and denunciations. Some reporters had predicted GIs "will not remember anything" about the terrible living conditions, delayed checks, and meager stipends. Such memories faded just a year after Harold Anderson finished his University of Nebraska electrical engineering degree and immediately received job offers from three top firms. When this family man thanked Truman for Public Law 346, he marveled at the financial assistance that "afforded me opportunities far above those ever anticipated." Anderson was not the only one who felt he owed "a great debt to my countrymen." Over time, graduates tended to forget how difficult getting their benefits had been. "We had to apply. It was processed through some regional offices," George Jotsen later recalled, "then we simply got a check. I got a check for $75 and the school was paid directly. It was an extremely convenient arrangement." Ross Flint remembered getting his "books at one counter, and the G.I. Bill at another" at Ohio State, where "the G.I. Bill paid for the whole [degree]."Ann Sharp recalled having "to bring your discharge papers to an office where they check them through, make copies, and certify that you were eligible for your $90 a month."[71]

Many beneficiaries, who had already served their country, still had the feeling that they owed the government for the tuition assistance provided to them. John Dee, like so many others, considered his education to be a "great gift" that he should work to repay. This Chicagoan promised to use the law degree he was earning "for government work in the future." New Yorker William Whittemore expressed his gratitude to the president and "The People of the United States" for the "magnificent training" he got at Cornell, and vowed to reciprocate by "teaching their children." Many veterans considered their educational opportunity precious even decades after they graduated. One woman celebrated the legislation because it "provided the foundation for a very successful teaching career." Another said it had flung open the doors "to a liberal education and a quest for more knowledge and the ability to weigh values and think through problems."[72]

Such enthusiasm, as with NYA's work-study program, helped change many educators' opinions regarding federal tuition assistance and opening the doors to the academy to the many Americans long assumed incapable of higher learning. Curtis Avery actually admitted he had been among the academics standing "somewhat bewildered . . . and expressing fear for the future of education" as he found himself "in the face of the horde of veterans which has descended on . . . campuses." Only about a thousand GIs had matriculated at the University of Minnesota in the program's first year. Four years later, nine thousand had enrolled. By then, Avery praised veterans' eagerness, maturity, and seriousness, which had forced him and his colleagues to finally adjust how they taught, guided, and served students. University of Wisconsin president E. B. Fred went so far as to call returnees a "stabilizing influence on Wisconsin student life." Yale higher-ups actually deemed the GI Bill to be "an extremely worth-while investment for the country and for higher education." Even James Conant admitted by summer 1946 that GIs had already proven to be "the most mature and promising students Harvard has ever had."[73]

Unequally Untapped Potential

The 2.2 million GIs who went to college were likely to succeed. The Army had turned away illiterate or physically unfit Americans until need pushed it to find a way to both educate and treat them. As such, an unprecedented 71 percent of service personnel had more than a grammar school education. World War II combatants also had the chance to continue their studies while serving through educational partnerships between universities and the armed forces. As a result, roughly 80 percent of the soldiers who took advantage of Title II had some vocational or postsecondary instruction. Most of them also indicated that they intended to return to college after being discharged. Indeed, the 25 percent of GIs who dropped out did not leave because they were ill-prepared or unsuited for college life, as experts and critics often presumed. Exit interviews instead revealed that most did not finish their degrees because they could not support their families on paltry, often-delayed stipends or find jobs to supplement those subsistence payments.[74]

Most soldiers, despite the GI Bill's mythos, also did not enroll in the country's most rarified schools. As with other iconic Roosevelt-era programs, the law as written and enforced never did enough to guarantee genuinely equal access. Syracuse stood out among top private institutions for its willingness to expand the student body and adapt to veteran needs in the wake of the New York admissions scandal. Public outcry barely dented the status quo at most elite universities, which generally admitted applicants whose profiles matched their existing student bodies. Conant, for example, while celebrating the 1946 entering class for its unprecedented level of economic and ethnic diversity, also described it as not unlike "a normal Harvard population." Just under half were soldiers, 75 percent of whom had left or deferred enrollment before service. The rest had wealthy families. This cohort also proved something of a blip; only 11 percent of subsequent classes were GIs. Most students also continued to come from prep schools as opposed to urban high schools, whose Jewish alumni continued to be denied admission. Yale also barely increased the percentage of Jews admitted, despite outrage over the quota system.[75]

The fact that African American GIs struggled to use their educational entitlements is a lesson in how liberal experiments have often managed to exacerbate inequality. Many Black soldiers had high hopes for what Army officer Campbell Johnson considered an unprecedentedly "inclusive program . . . for national heroes." He was confident he would be an "unforgotten man." More than half of African American GIs reported that family and friends encouraged them to take advantage of Title II (compared to just under a third of white GIs). But few of the million Black returnees could really use a benefit that, like federal and veterans' mortgage programs, would actually exacerbate what are now understood as historic racial wealth gaps. The VA was never headed by someone as dedicated to fighting racial inequality as the NYA's Aubrey Williams had been. Even if someone as radical as that southerner had been at the helm of administering the GI Bill, Congress had placed real limits on a supposedly universal program. Campus staff, as with workstudy, controlled admission. Qualifying for Title II eligibility did not hinge on guaranteeing the equal opportunity few faculty publicly demanded. Many eligible African American GIs also hailed from southern or border states with limited options for African American veterans, who tended to find themselves in underfunded Black colleges and universities. These struggling schools received some federal assistance to make room for applicants, but more than fifteen thousand found themselves turned away. African Americans in the North were also shut out of overcrowded colleges. Those admitted were often excluded from campus life. Northwestern's president brazenly defied demands that African American veterans be allowed to live in the dorms. He insisted the university would stick with the policy of requiring all undergraduates of color to live off campus—an act of intransigence that forced four veterans to sleep on cots in the dining room of Evanston's Black YMCA.[76]

Discrimination was just one reason that 7.8 million veterans never took advantage of Title II's education benefits, which included more than the well-known college program. Disabled soldiers generally struggled to enroll. VA officials instinctually directed them to vocational training, while college admissions officers refused to admit applicants they assumed were unsuited or physically unable to complete rigorous degree programs. Not everyone qualified for help. Some gay and lesbian returnees lost their benefits if officials learned about their sexuality. Over three million eligible soldiers gave a variety of other reasons for not using any of their newfound schooling rights. Some did not know about them or did not think they could use them; others opposed such government largesse.[77]

The relatively few women taking advantage of the program highlights how written laws did not necessarily yield rights in practice for soldiers or citizens. Unlike NYA offerings, women soldiers were not necessarily guaranteed entitlements. Officials only eventually extended coverage to women in the nursing corps and other branches of service but never included female air pilots. Yet newly eligible women still did not enroll. "We viewed it as a policy for the men," a former Army nurse explained decades later, "I mean, they really created it with the men in mind didn't they?" She, like other RNs, had, after all, completed the schooling necessary to care for soldiers. Indeed, women GIs tended to have gone further in their educations and come from more affluent families. Yet, in surveys, eligible women tended to cite familial obligations to explain why they did not take advantage of the GI Bill. "Mother passed away [and I] took care of Dad until I married," one explained. Another helped her new "husband operate a bakery," whereas many others simply just wrote in "married and moved" or "raising a family." Women enrollees tended to want to increase their skills through advanced nursing classes, secretarial courses, business colleges, and teaching programs. Some applied to universities, including a woman who proudly finished her degree, "which was my mother's dream for me." That desire reflected how women's eagerness and ability to enroll had increased during World War II but would be thwarted afterward. Coeds accounted for almost 60 percent of the student body in 1944 but broke the record for women enrollees in fall 1947, when more than 600,000 studied. Reporters still noted that many more applicants had been "elbowed out by veterans and held down by quotas." Education Office personnel admitted that "Girls are having to meet a higher standard than the men," but then joked about the "curious philosophy that if there are more than 40 per cent of women on the campus the school won't have a good football team."[78]

Who benefited the most from the GI Bill in general and Title II in particular underscored how this legislation, like so many other iconic laws Roosevelt signed, did the most for white men. That cohort already had an easier time enrolling in the colleges hellbent on keeping the academy overwhelmingly white, male, and nonprofit, a sharp contrast to the proprietary schools that dared offer far more citizens and immigrants the credentials increasingly required for white-collar work. Veteran alumni enjoyed better educational opportunities, had better living standards, and saved more over the course of their lifetimes than the civilians who did not have access to these entitlements or the veterans who could not take advantage of them. As such, Title II further ensconced higher education as a surefire way to enter the middle and professional classes or, as University of New Hampshire president Harold Stoke complained, "unwittingly imposed compulsory education on the nation." Veterans' eagerness to enroll led to a historic number of degrees being conferred in 1950, the year before schooling benefits expired. The record 496,000 sheepskins stood firm until the early 1960s, when colleges continued to struggle to provide spots for the growing number of Americans who wanted to continue their studies.[79]

Using tuition reimbursement to send GIs to college ensured that urgent expansions slowly reified the inequalities that many increasingly assumed higher education would lessen. The $500 tuition reimbursement maximum incentivized schools to admit GIs but also raised rates for everyone, not just the veterans whom the law singled out as uniquely deserving of this support. The number of schools charging more than the reimbursement maximum had substantially increased by 1947. When the GI Bill expired a few years later, tuition had risen by 65 percent since 1940 and 100 percent since the Depression. *Better Homes and Gardens* reporters warned young parents that increases would likely continue before their babies would start applying. Neither citizens nor soldiers would get much help paying those bills. Price-gouging charges made many lawmakers leery of generously supporting educational benefits in the GI Bill for Korean War veterans. Among other matters, there were disagreements over how tightly to regulate for-profit schools' eligibility to participate in the federal tuition assistance programs that continued to provide the fees upon which postsecondary institutions depended, regardless of their status as public, private, or nonprofit.[80]

Declining veteran enrollment put many schools in danger of operating in the red. A number of college administrators still hesitated to embrace government support even though many feared the GI Bill's end. Some academics, such as Algo Henderson, had become convinced that "the danger to this country lies in having too little—not too much—education." Speaking to the American Council on Education in 1949, he told its members: "There is no prospective lack of students," but colleges had tended to "deteriorate steadily during the prolonged depression and war periods" and had only been "supplemented with temporary shacks and barracks to carry the postwar load." Fundraising and expanding enrollments would not cover rising construction and operating costs. He instead held out hope for "a controversial subject," a shift to direct "Federal and State financial aid." Such a government handout appalled members of the Association of American Colleges and American Conference of Academic Deans. They had far more interest in scholarships, modeled on the GI Bill, that would help Americans afford the tuition hikes many staff feared might already have made higher education unaffordable for many. But leaders of the Association of American Universities warned against a reliance on federal grants and tuition assistance programs to brighten schools' financial futures in 1952, when the first GI Bill expired. Support from businesses, churches, unions, alumni, foundations, and local communities seemed far more likely to provide revenue without the control many professors and administrators still feared.[81]

Lawmakers, academics, and citizens continued to battle over how to help citizens afford degrees for years. The GI Bill's success had done even more than NYA's short-lived work-study program to show that mass higher education was beneficial and desirable for both individuals and the nation as a whole. But this storied legislation's success had hardly resolved the ongoing disagreements within both parties about federal authority, academic freedom, and equal opportunity. Those fights shaped Cold War conflicts between liberals and conservatives, which eventually birthed a student loan industry that would disproportionately hurt Americans who found themselves long shut out of the Ivory Tower. A financial sector built around such risky loans had been unimaginable in the 1930s and 1940s, when the Roosevelt administration had experimented with a number of government-guaranteed financial products that bolstered the private sector but did not assure economic security or reduce inequality in the long run.

4

The Fizzled Response to Sputnik

"My family could not have sent me to college without this loan," an undergraduate testified during tense, mid-1960s congressional negotiations to end the lending program central to the 1958 National Defense Education Act (NDEA). Another desperate student called this tuition assistance "one of the finest things that has happened to educational assistance." A Yale undergraduate explained in a letter to lawmakers involved in ongoing tuition assistance debates that his ability to enroll depended on this credit, which he much preferred "to the 'GI Bill' benefits that I will receive next year." Iowa parents also wrote in to ask for the opportunity to borrow, not "a federal hand out." It would be for the "good of our country as well as . . . young people," like the Clarkson College engineering student "grateful that I was born in a country where the government shows such a true interest in its citizens." Defense loans survived those fights to become what a senior Office of Education official later compared to a "little red wagon" that "you could load almost anything on . . . and get Congress to pass it because they were charmed by the National Defense Student Loan Program."[1]

That beloved lending scheme, like work-study and the GI Bill, had been a hard-fought, imperfect compromise over the issues that would continue to energize conservative movements across the country, and bedevil those trying to carry out liberal policies. Widespread deadlock over taxing, spending, federal power, inequality, and segregation steadily realigned the Democratic and Republican parties but did nothing to make college more affordable for many Americans during the early Cold War. Education experts already considered there to be a cost crisis. Yet citizens, politicians, and policymakers demanding more spots at lower prices did not talk as starkly about the labor market as they had during the Depression, World War II, and demobilization. They instead emphasized higher learning's importance to individual job opportunities and business innovations. But that reasoning failed to break up political logjams in state capitals and DC.

The October 1957 launch of Sputnik also did not resolve the larger ideological fights imperiling what remained of Roosevelt-era experiments. Contrary to popular lore, schools and students did not immediately receive substantial federal aid due to concern over Russian scientific superiority. Disagreements between southern Democrats, liberal Yankees, moderate Republicans, and conservative firebrands caused negotiations to drag on for almost a year within Congress and between lawmakers and White House aides. Like the GI Bill, NDEA was far less generous than most Americans remember. This legislation is often and wrongly credited with ushering in unprecedented federal support for schools and students (particularly those in college). Its temporary aid funded only specific departments, programs, and laboratories. The money usually went to well-established campuses that had eyed federal support with skepticism and resisted public outcry against the quota system that had long privileged the country's white, Protestant, male elite.[2]

The law's greatest legacy was, in retrospect, the small, hastily adopted undergraduate loan program. The National Defense Student Loan Program maintained the tradition of directly helping students to indirectly enable colleges to expand, a strategy that continued to reinforce the systemic inequality many social welfare policies and government-guaranteed financial products exacerbated. This kind of costly, inherently risky tuition assistance was hardly new. But lawmakers had never seriously considered loans in the 1930s, only briefly offered them during World War II, and ultimately rejected them during fraught GI Bill negotiations. All accredited nonprofit institutions, including segregated universities and those clinging to quotas, could apply for the opportunity to offer students an additional way to creatively finance their studies. NDEA loans, like earlier federally backed borrowing opportunities, masqueraded as genuine tuition assistance. Most academics did not consider this help a threat to their institutions' autonomy.

Financial aid personnel decided who received these loans and Office of Education officials lacked the power to channel funds to needy undergraduates and students of color, as some National Youth Administration staffers had done. Applicants only had to indicate on college forms that they intended to study math, science, or foreign languages, subjects which tended to attract more men than women. As with work-study and the GI Bill, campus staff could never offer enough government help to cover all college costs. Lawmakers kept maximums small because they expected students and parents to continue to cobble together the money to afford fees, books, and living expenses.

Educational Ambitions

More than a decade before the Soviets launched Sputnik, some citizens had demanded the Truman Administration do more to aid education than Aubrey Williams and other New Dealers ever considered. "A Secretary of Education in your Cabinet is a pertinent and immediate need," wrote Mabel Arleigh, an expert in primary grade mathematics instruction, in an August 1945 letter. "Just as social security is becoming nationalized," she explained, "so should Education be a national rather than a local project." A Puerto Rican housewife wanted the Office of Education's director to have the power to "watch over our sons and daughters and see that each state takes the best care possible of its young citizens, whether they be white or black." She hoped the new secretary would ensure "a more liberal use of scholarships" but also offer "a complete watch . . . on all schools and colleges." Oakland resident Burr Van Hoosean suggested Truman create an entire Department of Education and Information for "the welfare of every citizen now and those of the future" since the country's many teachers "should have a center—at the center of our government."[3]

A schooling overhaul was then on the Truman administration's agenda. War Mobilization and Reconversion officials had warned the president in May 1946 that efforts to ensure GIs could get an education must force the country "to re-examine the whole structure of higher education" because the GI Bill had shown how many more Americans could and should be educated. Title II had also revealed the problems of how to pay for desperately needed expansion. Advisers hoped the president might create a National Commission on Higher Education.[4]

That suggestion suited Harry S Truman in the mid-1940s, when Capitol Hill continued to be a war zone after the GOP dramatically retook Congress in the 1946 midterms. The Missourian had struggled to afford college in the early 1920s and, unlike fellow striver LBJ, had dropped out to help his family, who needed him to work. Truman never finished his degree and has remained the last American president without one. But he still tried to help other Americans finish their studies before he became president. Senator Truman's 1943 amendment to provide $48 million for defense training survived floor debates over the budget but not the final votes in the House or Senate that killed the National Youth Administration and many New Deal agencies. The newly sworn-in president had also signed the 1945 revisions to the Servicemen's Readjustment Act as well as subsequent bills for higher stipends, additional classrooms, and more living spaces.[5]

Only some of the education experts Truman asked to serve on the blue-ribbon Presidential Commission on Higher Education in July 1946 shared that concern. Its roster included religious leaders, business types, labor organizers, and journalists. But university presidents and administrators far outnumbered them. Among them were the heads of women's colleges, Black institutions, community colleges, Catholic universities, and state higher-education systems. Many of these administrators were far more enlightened than the "school crowd" FDR and Williams distrusted, including the twenty-eight-person commission's head, former Cornell professor George Zook. After leaving the administration during Roosevelt's first term, the Kansan had presided over the American Council on Education (ACE), which had partnered with the federal government to offer troops correspondence programs and other educational opportunities during World War II. Yet federal officials did not realize how much Zook, like many other academics, had changed his thinking on federal aid until he delivered the annual Inglis Lecture in Secondary Education at Harvard in 1945. Those comments made clear his desire for far more than limited student assistance, and impatience with "patchwork and piecemeal legislation" that would yield "a distorted and disjointed national policy in education." He called instead for comprehensive federal involvement at all levels of schooling, which would still respect the historic roles and authority of states, churches, and teachers. This expansive vision surprised a Bureau of the Budget official in the audience, E. C. Wine, who wrote to a friend afterward that had not expected such an "advance in the thinking" of the long-time ACE leader.[6]

The Zook Commission's six-volume 1948 report offered bold predictions about the country's projected needs in 1960. By then, the first wave of the many Americans born after WWII (the so-called Baby Boomers) would be in high school. The report warned of "formal education" becoming "a prerequisite to occupational and social advance" at a time when "the ladder of educational opportunity rises high at the doors of some youth and scarcely rises at the doors of others." Another troubling possibility: "Education may become the means, not of eliminating race and class distinctions, but deepening and solidifying them." Zook's team based their policy prescriptions on the assumption that work-study and the GI Bill had proven that 49 percent of Americans were capable of advanced learning. The extensive list of recommendations for primary, secondary, and postsecondary schooling laid out in *Higher Education for American Democracy* has been seen since as setting the stage for mid-1960s and early 1970s educational overhauls. Yet most of the Zook Commission's specific suggestions have never been adopted, including its call for a $120 million competitive scholarship program and full funding for the first two years of college for every citizen.[7]

Such proposals provoked furious debate among university and faculty staff across the country over federal control, the price of admission, and mass higher education's feasibility. The head of the Office of Education's Higher Education Division celebrated the massive report's determination to "break new ground" while ensuring "its premises are based on the solid ground of solid facts and accepted principles." John Russell told ACE stalwarts that, based on this report's findings, "we ought to be educating twice as many as are attending in the unexpectedly swollen enrollments of 1947." It proved, he emphasized, that many Americans "have ability to pursue courses beyond the high-school level." Not all were so impressed. Edward Elliott said of "the main conclusions" of the report that they might be "satisfying to the social and educational idealists," but they were not wholly convincing: "Many hard-headed realists are not so sure. Education skeptics are certain to have a field day." Even the esteemed African American historian Carter Woodson was not fully supportive of the report, despite its welcome recommendations to abandon "segregation as between Negroes and whites requiring duplicate school systems" and abolish the quota system that had pushed African Americans, Jews, Catholics, and immigrant strivers to enroll in the for-profits that nonprofits had tried to put out of business. It was the inclusion of a dissenting perspective in the report that sorely disappointed him. "Some of the educators from the backward area," he noted, "had not the courage to endorse the abolition of the segregation of whites and Negroes in colleges." The result was that "these would-be-liberal-educators" published a report containing a serious affront to the democracy held up in its very title.[8]

Enthusiasm, criticism, and the twenty thousand copies the White House distributed did nothing to spur either Truman or Congress to turn those ideas into actual policies. The president certainly publicly endorsed the Zook Report, as it became known. At his behest, Office of Education staffers drafted a recommendation to elevate the Department of Health, Education, and Welfare, which then housed the Office of Education, to become part of the cabinet. The president also recommended (but never vociferously advocated for) a federal scholarship program to aid education in 1950 and 1952.[9]

Those proposals reveal how divided the academy remained about federal aid, including tuition assistance, during the first GI Bill's final years. Association of American Colleges executive director Guy Snavely denounced the suggestion in Truman's 1950 budget message, suggesting it would lead to federal control and a "welfare state." Snavely warned, "Young people will get the notion" that "the Government will not only guarantee a college education but furnish suitable and good paying positions thereafter." He reminded the members that "regulation of schools and colleges has ever been concomitant with dictatorships." Many affiliates openly disagreed with Snavely and other officials who labeled Truman's suggestions "undemocratic and class legislation." But the president's limited plans failed to excite senators and representatives, including the relatively few then interested in helping more Americans enroll in college.[10]

Patchwork and Piecemeal

Despite popular memory and academic assertions, higher education's expansion (like the rest of the country's public-private social safety net) occurred as fitfully and haphazardly as Zook feared it would. Educators considered themselves facing a real crisis in the mid-1950s. National Education Association higher-ups warned members in 1954 to expect more than 4.5 million applicants by 1970, nearly double the number taking classes at the GI Bill's high watermark. Such rapid growth concerned many members. A few even warned that fees had already increased so much that undergraduates could not expect to work their ways through college even though campuses had begun to increase aid. Across the country, legislators still remained divided or even uninterested in earmarking money to meet this public need and desire, much less fulfill the Zook Commission's broader ambitions. Direct state and local expenditures for education certainly seemed to rise in the 1950s. In the 1951–1952 academic year, states devoted anywhere from $44 to $128 for every resident between the ages of eighteen and twenty-four. Data collected by Teachers College administrator Thad Hungate showed that "a few states now are demonstrating a pattern of substantial public support for higher education," but that "great inequality among the states remains." By 1956, the range had expanded to $70 to $356.[11]

That span masked the vast regional differences in spending starting to change during the rapid industrialization and political transformation of southern and western states. Many commentators at the time did not notice that the steel belt had begun to rust after World War II, while the South and West began to blossom into a conservative, Republican-dominated Sunbelt built on the era's most lucrative industries: high-tech electronics and aerospace. That kind of outside investment required good schools for the research, development, and workforce training that the Northeast and Midwest's leading universities (many of them private) had long been providing to manufacturers. Across the country, university administrators, some of them liberals, appealed to state policymakers eager to increase schooling opportunities and attract outside corporate investors. Together, educators and politicians courted rightwing local business leaders and high-ranking CEOs for the political and financial support needed to expand campuses fueling the economic engines of postwar prosperity.[12]

These seemingly strange bedfellows started to transform southern and western higher education, which had far fewer and less well-developed private and public colleges. Only the California legislature and liberal Republican governor Earl Warren began the kind of rigorous overhaul the Zook Commission recommended. Comprehensive studies of educational needs laid the groundwork for the storied 1960 Master Plan as well as the legislation supporting its ambitious three-tiered system of community colleges, state schools, and research universities that would set a new standard for American higher education, particularly since students did not have to pay tuition. College administrators in other parts of the emerging Sunbelt struggled to convince legislatures that schools needed to offer more than the agricultural research and mechanical training privileged by the Morrill Act. For example, despite the postwar dynamism of Arizona and North Carolina, leading local businessmen, top CEOs, and some high-profile college administrators worked to persuade hidebound legislators to invest in Phoenix's small Arizona State Teacher's College and to see the potential of the University of North Carolina's science programs. Only with the conservative business elite's growing political power and liberal academics' persistence during the 1950s was Arizona State University able to become a school that would fuel the state's economic fortunes and did UNC come to play an important role in the emergence of the Raleigh–Durham–Cary Research Triangle.[13]

Northeastern and midwestern legislators and governors proved equally uninterested in public school investments. Higher education in these parts of the country had historically been an overwhelmingly private affair. Elite universities and religious institutions jealously guarded their control of the market in these regions even though admissions officers often could not keep up with demand and faculty did not necessarily want to welcome more enrollees. Such reactionary educators had help from conservative lawmakers who chafed at expanding public schooling options, including New York governor Thomas Dewey during the GI Bill's rollout. The Republican took months to respond to public outcry over the quota system in the state's private schools and legislators' demands for a state university. At that time, only New York, which had some public options, lacked either a state research university or anything approximating a state higher education system. Dewey finally created a Temporary Commission on the Need for a State University, in July 1946, but gave the group of politicians, businessmen, educators, and civic leaders only a year to make its recommendations. General Electric executive and former National Youth Administration advisory committee member Owen Young chaired the group but because he did not manage to assemble a full research team until January 1947, lawmakers felt obliged to extend the commission's deadline by a year. This glacial pace suited the governor, who favored some kind of measure to ban the quota system but (like many conservatives in the Empire State) had no real interest in increasing public postsecondary options—particularly after hearing the commission's estimate that one university would cost at least $100 million to construct.[14]

Only politics spurred Dewey to move faster in early 1948. When he campaigned to unseat Truman, the Republican needed to prove he too cared about bolstering higher education, an issue important to a growing number of voters even before Zook delivered his report. Dewey embraced his temporary commission's suggestion that New York create a state university system composed of two-year community colleges around the state as well as a medical and dental school. Albany would cover construction and half the yearly operating expenses; local governments would have to make up the difference. The governor and his aides abandoned such stinginess after the public learned of the Zook Commission's proposals and instead endorsed allocating money to found a state university and medical college as well as front half the cost of a network of community colleges (leaving counties to cover the rest). That proposal pleased neither elite college administrators, who feared the growth of public schooling, nor liberal Democrats, who wanted more state options. Political wrangling ended with a ban on discrimination as well as the creation of the State University of New York system. Dewey dramatically left the campaign trail to sign the law on April 4, 1948. Yet his signature produced a university that largely existed on paper, since allocations were never enough to match citizens' demands, students' expectations, or Ivy League administrators' fears.[15]

Dewey's policy jujitsu did not ease the concerns of some of the country's leading executives, men who had been part of efforts since the 1930s to undermine the Roosevelt administration's reform agenda. These tycoons yearned to protect their vision of American free enterprise against government regulation, which they (like some academics) considered the same as control. Such CEOs increasingly called themselves conservatives during the early Cold War, when they funded many of the movements and politicians endeavoring to destroy the liberal social welfare programs that had survived the end of World War II.[16]

Some of the money went to charitable causes that spoke to the magnates' larger political ambitions. Donations, for example, helped campuses struggling to expand and stay solvent. Companies had certainly made such gifts in the past, usually to support technical training and ad hoc research projects to benefit a company's needs. Largesse took on additional importance during and after the Roosevelt era, when liberal lawmakers fought to offer citizens a lot of immediate relief and long-term promises for economic security. Many of those public-private social welfare pledges and government-guaranteed financial products required substantial taxes on business revenue. Deductions subsequently became a way to undermine New Deal experimentation. For example, 1935 tax code changes permitted a significant write-off for charitable giving that enabled entrepreneurs to reduce the funds available for government programs, shrink firms' tax bills, and improve CEOs' reputations at a moment when many business leaders greatly feared the public had turned against the corporate elite.[17]

Executives also worried about the academy's finances, particularly after World War II. Universities had always been expensive to run. Even the decidedly temporary work-study and GI Bill programs could not provide enough indirect tuition assistance to maintain or expand colleges in the long run. Plus, tycoons recognized that they, like other wealthy Americans, had less money to fund philanthropies, like the Rockefeller and Carnegie foundations, because their tax rates (despite write-offs) had gone up exponentially during the 1930s and 1940s. Those organizations had also begun to shy away from a broad effort to police and improve college finances and operations to more targeted involvement during the Cold War, particularly in Ivy League international studies programs as well as the social sciences. Concerned entrepreneurs subsequently predicted the kind of tuition increases that would deter the students needed to keep private colleges open but also to learn the skills firms expected universities to provide.[18]

Many, but not all, of the postwar, business-driven efforts to underwrite private universities became part of the general protracted war over regulation, taxation, social welfare, and federal authority that had already begun to realign the two parties. Business interests had an early victory in 1953 when plans were underway to amend the tax code and increase the limit of tax-deductible charitable giving, but only for donations in certain categories. Business leaders fought to ensure that this increase would apply to gifts to educational institutions as well as churches and hospitals. The Zook Commission had warned that this added incentive would not yield a level of giving sufficient to keep private schools open and tuition rates affordable.

Meanwhile, an important 1953 case before the New Jersey Supreme Court tested whether a corporation was within its rights to make a donation to a university when its shareholders did not regard that kind of charity as relevant to the success of the business. The unanimous decision in *AP Smith Manufacturing Co. v. Barlow* was that the firm should be allowed to do so. The size of the donation in this case was not great, at $1,500 to Princeton, but the court underscored the importance of the precedent. By enabling many more philanthropic contributions to private institutions of higher learning, its ruling would save these schools from being replaced by governmental institutions—which would be a fateful step toward dismantling the American system of capitalism and free enterprise. "The only hope for the survival of the privately supported American college and university," jurists held, "lies in the willingness of corporate wealth to furnish in moderation some support to institutions which are so essential to public welfare and therefore of necessity, to corporate welfare." The complaining shareholders had been thinking too narrowly, in other words, about AP Smith's business interests, because in fact there was no "greater benefit to corporations in this country . . . than to build and continue to build, respect for and adherence to a system of free enterprise and democratic government, the serious impairment of either of which may well spell the destruction of all corporate enterprise."[19]

The mixed reaction that followed reflected the complicated, uncertain public-private financing of American social welfare in general and higher education in particular. Legislatures across the country quickly amended their tax codes in light of the New Jersey court's judgment, which many journalists praised and many business leaders ignored. Some ardent champions of gifts to private colleges were delighted that by making donations that were tax-deductible they also deprived the federal government of funds to spend on higher education. For the most part, however, their business brethren were not so motivated by politics. Most executives remained uninterested in giving to colleges unless there was some clear connection to an improved bottom line (as in the case of developing Sunbelt schools, like Arizona State and UNC Chapel Hill, to improve regional workforces). Fears of a slippery slope to state control did inspire some to give generously to individual institutions. Other champions of business involvement in postsecondary schooling allocated money for statewide efforts.[20]

Interested donors found university staffs more than amenable to speaking their language. Two college presidents, for example, founded the Associated Colleges of Indiana in 1948 to appeal to executives' sensibilities and profit motives. This group raised almost $4 million in just nine years, more than similar rival associations in Michigan and Ohio. Fundraisers emphasized that firms could give up to 5 percent of their net income to help the liberal arts colleges that safeguarded freedom and produced the well-trained workers companies would continue to need.[21]

The country's great philanthropic organizations did far more to help executives and academics take advantage of the tax code's incentives. At the forefront stood the Ford Foundation, which xenophobic, isolationist automaker Henry Ford and his son Edsel had started as a means to evade taxes under Roosevelt. Both had died by 1946, when the small organization had mainly done work in the Detroit area, despite the fact that the foundation held 90 percent of company stock, worth roughly $2 billion. Trustees ordered staff to write a public report of how the money might be spent. One recommendation included using higher education to solve societal ills. That idea appealed to the foundation's new president, Paul Hoffman, a former Studebaker executive who also used his business expertise to oversee the Truman administration's Marshall Plan. This suggestion also complemented the thinking of associate director Robert Hutchins. The University of Chicago president had resigned in 1951 in order to join the still-fledgling philanthropy. This eminent legal scholar imagined using its resources to experiment with new ways of funding higher education, which harkened back to his remarkable ability to fundraise for the University of Chicago in the depths of the Depression. Hoffman and Hutchins steadily expanded this philanthropy's reach outside Michigan. New initiatives included the Fund for the Advancement of Education as well as collaborative projects like the Fund for Adult Education. That experiment tapped government, university, and telecommunication industry experts to use television for an updated version of the discussion-based study in Hilda Smith's Workers Education Program and the breakout sessions universities used for large lecture classes during the GI Bill's rollout.[22]

Ford Foundation leaders had to cajole their Carnegie Commission and Rockefeller Foundation counterparts to coordinate collegiate fundraising efforts among CEOs. The massive Zook Report had only spurred Rockefeller and Carnegie trustees to pledge a respective $400,000 and $50,000 to support the Commission on College and Industry of the Association of American Universities in 1949. That group included lawyers, manufacturers, and presidents of mostly private colleges, who produced nine studies of educational financing. It also held a 1951 dinner in New York for leading businessmen interested in channeling corporate donations to schools.[23]

Ford, Rockefeller, and Carnegie staff achieved far more through the Council on Financial Aid to Education. These three foundations, along with the Alfred P. Sloan Foundation, initially started CFAE in 1952 to fund studies of private postsecondary education's precarious financing. They intended CFAE to be a clearinghouse for information about and advice on privately underwriting the academy, to keep enrollment affordable for the growing number of Americans wanting to matriculate.[24]

Alfred Sloan, the long-serving head of General Motors, had established his eponymous foundation in 1934. The MIT alum, benefactor, and board member wanted to support economic education and research, a mission that was later broadened to include medicine, the physical sciences, and eventually an undergraduate scholarship program. Sloan openly bemoaned other CEOs' reluctance to invest in higher education in order to safeguard free enterprise, a frustration that fueled his efforts to redirect CFAE's energies toward undermining liberal efforts to increase state and federal spending on higher education.[25]

Sloan was not the only business executive shaping CFAE's agenda. The board included sixteen titans of industry as well as twelve university presidents. Some of the college administrators themselves had business experience, as well. CFAE's first president, for example, was Wilson Compton, whose 1944 appointment to the presidency of the State College of Washington had followed a quarter of a century as head of a trade lobbying group, the National Lumber Manufacturers Association. All the executives involved also had deep connections to top private universities and leading philanthropies. Standard Oil Company board chairman Frank Abrams, for example, was a veteran trustee, having served Syracuse University, the Sloan Foundation, and the Ford Foundation in that capacity, and he had long advocated for more corporate college aid. As early as 1947, he would later recall, he shared the view in a luncheon speech that "business was a kind of absentee stockholder in education and ought to pay some attention to its investment."[26]

Abrams liked to joke that he was "just an ordinary business guy that got shoved into . . . a Billy Sunday meeting." The hint of evangelism was intentional—CFAE needed fervor on par with budding conservative movements. Surveys showed that most executives and stockholders felt it was not rational for a business to donate money to higher education unless the business benefits were clear. CFAE leaders, philanthropists, executives, and academics discussed that challenge at annual meetings and tried to counter it with professional mass media campaigns. CFAE's widely circulated pamphlets and well-informed spokesmen emphasized the bottom-line returns of gifts that would reduce companies' taxable revenues and also, ideally, allow the government to scale back taxation for social programs. In that case, a GE executive explained, corporate donations would also serve to protect "the whole spectrum of voluntary associations," those vital institutions of civic society whose work could potentially be overtaken by government agencies. Benefactors also had the chance to stave off current and future tenured radicals, Abrams suggested. That money would help strengthen faculty's "belief in the American system of democratic capitalism," which seemed to have been weakening since the Depression. "Capitalism and free enterprise owe their survival to the existence of our private, independent universities," observed CFAE leader and US Steel chief executive Irving Olds. "We are through if the day ever comes when our tax-supported competitors can offer the youth of America a better education," he warned, "and at a lower price."[27]

Colleges had a mixed reaction to the CEOs' efforts. Many private schools celebrated donors and even shared CFAE crusaders' political convictions. The *Harvard Alumni Bulletin*, for example, told graduates that corporate giving might curtail increased taxing and spending. Editors wrote that Washington "should not be saddled with the task of raising tax money for the benefit of the privately supported colleges and universities which historically have proved such important counterpoises to our public institutions." Administrators of state schools, on the other hand, such as University of Vermont staff, considered both their Ivy League counterparts and their CEO allies to "have been carried away by their zeal to the extent that they have invoked the blessings of God, Country, and Private Enterprise."[28]

Such convictions produced the decidedly mixed results that have been endemic to the country's public-private approach to handling citizens' basic needs. CFAE personnel noted that 207 companies' donations rose from almost $34 million in 1956 to just over $50 million in 1960. The average annual contribution jumped from roughly $164,000 in 1956 to just over $234,000 in 1960. Yet only a slice of the country's business community donated, mostly firms in the transportation equipment, chemicals, oil, electronics, and primary metals sectors. But more giving did not substantially increase the number of schools helped. In the 1954–1955 academic year, corporations gave $40 million to 728 institutions. Individual alumni bequeathed $52 million at a moment when companies started to offer programs to match contributions. Less than a decade later, executives gave three times as much (more than $147 million) but only extended this generosity to an additional three hundred schools. That incremental growth in many ways reflected how executives explained their donations. Most, a 1960 CFAE survey revealed, privileged "meeting community responsibilities" or "creation of education manpower." Next on the short list included "insuring free enterprise system," followed by "public relations," then "aiding higher education." Even lower down were "fostering new knowledge" and "research," and finally (at the bottom), "tax savings."[29]

Those priorities reflected education experts' doubts that philanthropists could be a "sustaining force in . . . the education of youth," particularly ones who needed tuition assistance. CEOs had never given generously to help students afford fees, even before tuition rates started to soar during the rollouts of work-study and the GI Bill. Before 1952, corporate benefactors tended to give money for employees' children, particularly if they studied the sciences. Donations to campus scholarship funds did increase in the mid-1950s, the kind of gifts CFAE researchers considered a start to a corporation's investment in higher education. Staff still recognized "there are far from enough scholarships now available in our colleges, and the average is too small." Various restrictions, staff noted in 1955, "reduce the value . . . and even make it difficult or impossible to find recipients." A year later, personnel lamented that only half the estimated $80 million corporations donated went to student aid. Such reluctance inspired the Ford Foundation, aided with Carnegie Corporation money, to create the National Merit Scholarship Corporation in 1955 to both reward talented students with small scholarships and encourage businesses to donate for such grants. Such gifts remained so exceptional that GM made headlines in May 1956, when president Harlow Curtice announced the company would double its program of financial aid to education. The $5 million gave undergraduates anywhere from $200 to $2,000 in support at 350 eligible campuses, which could collect an additional $500 to $800 a year from the automaker.[30]

College admissions officers still had the power to decide who would be helped by tuition assistance funds. By and large, as Columbia's Thad Hungate wrote, "the major burden of support of higher education often [fell] heavily upon the student and his family," and they usually shouldered "the full responsibility for student cost of living." Few undergraduates, studies revealed, were given a free ride. Most received a mix of campus scholarships, work opportunities, and loans, continuing a tradition that neither work-study nor the GI Bill had ended. Lending, as CFAE researchers discovered, was somewhat uncommon across the country and unpopular among undergraduates. An Office of Education study noted that while $26 million was available, students used only half that amount, and usually for small, short-term, emergency credit. Borrowing was still the dominant form of financial assistance offered by elite schools. Between 1948 and 1956, for example, Harvard mostly loaned students money, giving out on average $500,000 in loans annually but only $10,000 in fellowships. MIT also had a thriving lending program befitting its relationship with Alfred Sloan, the CFAE founding member, whose donations helped to build its medical and business schools. And Rensselaer Polytechnic Institute, less well-funded and more dependent on students willing to borrow, made arrangements with New York's Marine Midland Bank to provide loans.[31]

Campus control over lending continued to keep educational opportunities unequal. Staff did not necessarily award support based on need, as the federal work-study program had mandated. Even though there had been uproar over the quota system after World War II, nothing forced personnel to ensure equal opportunities to the many immigrants and citizens who still struggled to gain admittance to, let alone to afford, higher education. As applicants were required to submit detailed financial records, the decisions may have appeared to be based purely on need, but reporters' and other investigations brought to light that colleges were in the habit of "bidding on brains" or athletic talent with financial assistance offers. For example, an internal evaluation by Western Conference Athletics, known by most as the Big Ten, produced a 1956 report calling the work-aid program "an invitation to hypocrisy and deceit," having uncovered many instances where there was not "full work for compensation received." Students generally got an average of $260 in job aid in 1955, which had soared from $47 in 1948; across the same years total sports scholarships rose from $56,694 to $348,688. Coaches spent in a range of $5,000 to $13,600 a year to entertain prospects visiting campuses, and admissions officers admitted the schools also "scouted and recruited" students of superior academic ability. Staff interviewed about the long-standing practice in 1958 complained that while they were "not against scholarship or student assistant programs," it was damaging to have "practices that pit institutions against each other in an all-out financial competition." Savvy students were learning to finagle more money than they needed from "prestigious institutions, which have no trouble attracting qualified candidates." Part of the problem, one administrator divulged, was that "each college is afraid that another will outbid it." In one such case, two schools had decided that a particularly promising boy needed only $400 in aid, but in the end he received $1,000 from the campus more eager to have him.[32]

Colleges took steps to control such fierce, costly bidding. New England and mid-Atlantic institutions had long relied on the College Entrance Examination Board's tests for admissions decisions but more than 150 of those schools beseeched that institution to help standardize the financial aid process. That agency's higher-ups subsequently created the College Scholarship Service in 1954, whose services included a standard financial aid form to help determine need. Years later, a financial aid insider said the questionnaire "came into being in response to a laudable and idealistic desire to apportion meager resources more justly and rationally." He added: "There is no doubt either that it was regarded as a device to restrain, or at least reduce, cutthroat competition for students through price cutting."[33]

As in decades past, relatively few campuses could afford to substantially help the many in need. The majority of private liberal arts colleges operated in the red in 1956, when overall enrollment jumped from 2,500,000 to 3,000,000. Such rapid expansion strained campuses, which continued to charge far less than the cost of instruction, a difference for which the VA had only begrudgingly reimbursed schools eligible for the GI Bill. In the 1950s, state universities asked for 20 percent of those expenses, whereas private colleges billed anywhere from 40 to 60 percent. Staff still needed to increase tuition. Ivy League institutions expected between $800 and $1,000 as well as additional fees. State schools also raised rates. Between 1952 and 1956, levies climbed by

25 to 30 percent, even though public colleges' expenses soared at rates from 44 to 85 percent. Undergraduates living on campus subsequently had to pay $1,500 to $2,500 a year. Those numbers alarmed many, including an assistant dean at Columbia University Teachers College, whose research indicated that 100,000 qualified applicants every year found themselves priced out of college.[34]

Those numbers inspired new ideas for helping undergraduates creatively finance their degrees. Administrators largely ignored University of Chicago economist Milton Friedman's theoretical suggestion that investors might "buy" shares in "an individual's earning prospects," in the same way they invested in promising businesses trying to get off the ground. It was a concept that would become known as an "Income Share Arrangement" decades after the economist included it in a 1955 article later collected in his 1962 bestseller *Capitalism and Freedom*. Like the CFAE's founding members, Friedman was dismayed by the federal government's growing power, which he saw as a "trend toward collectivism." A strong proponent of free markets, he detested the idea of an academy directly funded and controlled by government and instead suggested a kind of national voucher system for higher education, modeled on the GI Bill. He also suggested that a needy undergraduate might simply apply for "the funds needed to finance his training" from an investor, and be granted them "on condition that he agree to pay back the lender." A speculator might even "get back more than his initial investment from relatively successful individuals, which would compensate for the failure to recoup his original investment from the unsuccessful." Friedman saw "no legal obstacle" to such arrangements but knew there was little chance of their being embraced, as many would regard them as "economically equivalent to the purchase of a share in an individual's earning capacity and thus partial slavery." Still, as an economist he found it interesting to wrestle with what might go into enforcing and administering such indentures.[35]

Harvard financial aid officer John Munro encouraged administrators to "take advantage" of another, much older strategy for "financial strength and revenue": student loans. His advice highlighted how increasingly comfortable Americans had become with using financial products, including those without a government guarantee, to manage everyday expenses. "Our businessmen," he stressed in 1956, "have taught American consumers to use time payments to buy virtually anything that costs over 10 dollars." Munro admitted campus staff had struggled to collect repayment during the Depression, hardly needed to extend credit when soldiers could use GI Bill benefits, and reflexively used scholarships to compete for applicants in the "post-veteran" years, when no one really cared about "financial need." College Board staff had shown that only 40 percent of members advertised borrowing opportunities but all promoted the grants available. Munro figured colleges and universities had plenty of resources to construct attractive loan programs. The then-defunct Harmon Foundation's lending experiments had taught financial aid officers "businesslike methods" to assess need and likely repayment on these risky financial products in the 1920s. During the 1930s and 1940s, MIT, Yale, and Harvard reaped enormous returns on this "long-term student loan business." Munro admitted Harvard had a private trust set up solely for the purpose of extending credit to students, which stopped the university from having to borrow against its resources in order to extend credit. Nevertheless, Harvard's revamped lending scheme had been so successful that Munro and his staff were planning to let parents borrow, an experiment he considered especially important to schools admitting women. Coeds, after all, "expect to be married" and "hesitate to take a loan which might burden the prospective husband—or worse still, scare him away." Munro still encouraged women's and coeducational colleges to start "shaking off the old-fashioned idea of 'student' loans and begin thinking of the interest parents may have in liberal credit arrangements." He offered a personal perspective to his fellow financial aid officers: "As the father of two daughters, I myself am quite prepared to help pay their way with loans if I can get them."[36]

Few expressed such public enthusiasm for borrowing as Munro. A handful of leading educators had far more interest in a federal scholarship program that had a lot in common with earlier forms of government tuition assistance. American Council on Education higher-ups, for example, suggested $200 million to help undergraduates in 1956. By then, Truman's former Commissioner of Education, Earl McGrath, wanted $400 million. As the University of Kansas City's president, he could not imagine any other way Americans could afford colleges hiking rates by 50 percent, the kind of increase necessary to keep campuses solvent and expanding. "Our democratic philosophy," he insisted at a 1956 Conference on Education, should not underwrite "the boys and girls [who] park their fancy cars on the campuses while the state pays three-quarters of the cost of their college education." Even Ivy League bills, he claimed, were far from cost prohibitive.[37]

Sputtered Congressional Efforts

Lawmakers seemed as unlikely to pass tuition assistance in 1956 as they had been after the Zook Report. Scholars have continually noted that the kind of robust federal K-12 and higher education aid Zook wanted perpetually foundered on the same incendiary issues that had limited New Deal experiments, thwarted postwar efforts to expand social welfare programs, and energized conservative insurgencies. A deeply divided Congress, despite the fears of CFAE stalwarts and Ivy League faculties, doled out little more than targeted support to campuses and students after the GI Bill's passage. For example, Congress allocated money for the National Institutes of Health (NIH) as well as the National Science Foundation (NSF), which Harvard president James Conant had championed. NIH and NSF did offer some scholarships but applicants faced fierce competition for the limited federal support to study medicine, science, or engineering. Earmarks also funded research individuals or groups conducted. That money helped build and improve medical schools, science departments, and engineering labs. But this revenue really only expanded programs at the well-established public and private research universities best able to compete for federal support. But all institutions needed to grow in order to meet a steady stream of applicants struggling to afford fees. Bills for directly funding higher education's expansion had been introduced since the late 1930s. But only in the 1950s did congressional support grow. Some kind of national education policy seemed increasingly necessary to Democrats and Republicans worried about booming birth rates, overcrowded schools, teacher shortages, and widely circulated studies indicating that Soviet universities graduated more scientists and engineers than American campuses.[38]

Proposals repeatedly faltered on political divides since the New Deal. Republicans, for example, bitterly disagreed over whether education should remain the sole purview of schools, states, religious institutions, and private organizations. Ardent defenders of this deep-rooted tradition, like conservative Arizona Senator Barry Goldwater, suggested federal tax breaks for tuition payments would be more than enough to help Americans pursue advanced degrees. Liberal and moderate Republicans, including President Dwight Eisenhower and his advisers, flatly rejected the idea as continuing to make colleges the sole purview of elites. In contrast, liberal Democrats from northeastern, midwestern, and western districts had been pushing for federal assistance since the 1940s. Yankees still could not agree on whether or not private schools (particularly Catholic colleges) should be eligible for support. Many of these liberal Democrats also recoiled at the southern Democrats' insistence that segregated institutions be eligible for federal aid, particularly as African Americans began to attack segregation in the courts and attempt to integrate K-12 schools and college campuses.[39]

Few southern Democrats championed federal college aid but the two most outspoken had the power to break a congressional logjam that had as much to do with education as the ideological divisions transforming the two parties. Unapologetic Jim Crow defenders Lister Hill and Carl Elliott had little in common with fellow Alabaman Aubrey Williams. Montgomery native Hill did not have to worry about affording his degrees from the University of Alabama or Columbia's law school. The doctor's son still championed legislation to improve the basic infrastructure and respond to health and other needs of rural communities after he joined the House in 1923 and the Senate in 1938. He also wanted to do something to provide national support for all levels of schooling. The senator favored assistance that would prevent federal control, a conviction that very much shaped the segregationist stances for which he and Elliott became infamous. Elliott, unlike Hill, did not hail from their state's prosperous classes. He, like Williams, had worked his way out of poverty and through school. A variety of odd jobs (not ministry work) helped him afford finishing his University of Alabama degree two years before FDR established NYA. Work-study did not help Elliott finish his law degree there. The lawyer still dedicated himself to expanding educational opportunities after his surprising 1948 victory over a long-serving incumbent. Every session, he introduced a scholarship bill. Those efforts went nowhere until February 1957, when representatives reorganized the Education and Labor Committee and made him chairman of a permanent Subcommittee on Special Education, two years after Hill had taken the helm of the Senate Labor and Public Welfare Committee.[40]

Those leadership positions gave Hill and Elliott tremendous power over the schooling bills that continued to divide lawmakers, academics, and citizens. Elliott convened hearings on the federal role in education after high school with an emphasis on aiding college students in the summer and fall of 1957. Those Capitol Hill convenings and subsequent forums across the country unearthed a range of information about and opinions on funding higher education.[41]

Witnesses, including educators, overwhelmingly focused on undergraduate needs and desires. Education Office personnel, for example, shared surveys indicating that "capable" young people overwhelmingly cited "expense" when surveyed about decisions not to apply. Current students also swore they and many of their peers struggled to afford fees, including those receiving small scholarships or holding down part-time jobs. Studies showed colleges spent far more money on undergraduate scholarship and work options, which greatly outnumbered the loans made in the mid-1950s. Undergraduates reported they and their classmates would, by and large, be willing to borrow. Yet many speakers emphasized that few students took advantage of lending programs. Campuses often charged 4 to 5 percent interest on credit that had to be repaid within six months or two years, like the option Wisconsin's public welfare department had intermittently offered to talented, needy undergraduates since 1933. The University of Minnesota's director of student financial aid reported that, despite long-standing problems collecting those debts, their "students are a good investment." Undergraduates, he noted, certainly did not like to borrow for degrees, even though they used credit "for cars, and televisions, radios, everything under the sun." Students became far more amenable to loans after staff fundraised for a sizeable student aid fund, lowered the interest rate to 2 percent, set the minimum monthly repayment to $10, restricted the amount students could take out, and allowed alumni to consolidate debts.[42]

Such generous terms piqued Hill's interest but neither he nor his foes in both parties could count on support from Dwight Eisenhower. Unlike CFAE's outspoken business conservatives, the president did not want to dismantle the New Deal. This moderate Republican was far more interested in limiting the regulations, taxes, and social welfare guarantees that liberals had struggled to enact in the 1930s and 1940s, an inclination that irritated fellow Republicans, among them up-and-comer Barry Goldwater. The latter, an outspoken Arizonan, opposed the president's moderate stances on a range of issues, including education policies he and others saw as undermining free enterprise and states' rights. Ike, however, countered that his administration's ideas were preferable by far to the more expansive bills the liberal Democrats introduced. Those proposals often explicitly or implicitly left funding contingent on desegregation. The president hardly prioritized integration. He only begrudgingly enforced the 1954 *Brown v. Board of Education* decision, which he disliked as much as he regretted nominating Chief Justice Earl Warren, who wrote that unanimous opinion.[43]

Eisenhower also did not champion higher education with the energy the liberals did. The former general knew Americans needed more schooling. He had served as Supreme Allied Commander in Europe during World War II when the military had extended extraordinary means to offer troops the basic literacy, specialized study, and advanced education many wanted. After retiring from the military, he had hoped to head a small liberal arts college and did promptly join a prestigious group advising the National Education Association. Nonetheless, people who knew him at the time later remembered that Eisenhower had been surprised by and hesitant to accept Columbia University's presidency, perhaps not relishing the prospect of spending much of his time on fundraising for the school. Aides later maintained that the experience shaped Eisenhower's attitude toward federal education aid. As president, he personally wrote to public university administrators to share his fear that aid invited "a kind of Federal influence and domination that could have very bad effects." Eisenhower had more faith in the market than the state to produce top talent. When a CBS journalist questioned him in a 1954 press conference about the "output of science students," he began his response by reminding the group, "if you get few enough scientists, they can command prices that you will have a rush to the scientific colleges." He admitted, however, that "we can't wait for that, so I believe the Federal Government could establish scholarships." It would be some years until the president pursued grants or created educational advisory committees—and his blue-ribbon panels, well marbled with business executives, reached far different conclusions than the faculty-dominated Zook Commission.[44]

Eisenhower left Marion Folsom, Secretary of Health, Education, and Welfare, in charge of turning those teams' suggestions into legislative proposals. Folsom had a long-standing interest in offering public-private support to Americans. The former Eastman Kodak executive had not been among the businessmen trying to thwart the entire New Deal during the 1930s. This Harvard alum instead helped construct the Social Security Act to ensure real limits on how much the federal government would underwrite social welfare, a tactic he and others considered a better way to manage the costs of privately providing good wages and benefits, including financial products, like health insurance. That strategy also subtly and purposefully undermined unionization efforts while also keeping employees beholden to employers (not government agencies) for their overall standard of living. Folsom also understood the many needs and demands on colleges since his firm depended on institutions, like the University of Rochester, for its research and workforce needs.[45]

Those experiences and convictions shaped how Folsom and his staff responded to fears of and demands for federal education aid. He turned much of the work over to a young Massachusetts Republican lawyer who joined HEW in 1957. Elliot Richardson became far more famous as one of Richard Nixon's appointees, but the Harvard graduate began his government service crafting the Eisenhower administration's education proposals. They included increasing the number of teachers and professors, offering young people pre-college counseling and testing, providing tuition assistance, and financing school construction through need-based and temporary loan and grant programs. The latter also included, as Ike emphasized, "various kinds of protective devices" to prevent "control by the Federal Government."[46]

Sputnik orbited the earth after lawmakers and HEW staffers had started drafting legislative proposals from the ideas that had been percolating in Washington and around the country. But that small satellite, not their strategizing, made the headlines. A *New York Times* piece declared the October 4 launch a "spur to education." The *Los Angeles Times* began a series exploring the "Crisis Ahead in Education," while the editors of the *Wall Street Journal* examined the challenge Sputnik posed to "survival." A *Washington Post* dispatch noted a scholarly perspective that the Russians' breakthrough could serve as a "salutary jolt" for America, and "may save us."[47]

Sputnik did little to rattle the deep political fault lines in Washington but it did light a fire under lawmakers interested in aiding education. The Eisenhower administration responded first but hardly expeditiously. HEW higher-ups, for example, had been working on a scholarship program but, just days after the satellite circled the globe, they added more support for graduate studies, which included fellowships as well as matching grants to broadly expand many degree programs (not just support math and science). Eisenhower still waited a month to call a formal meeting on the issue with Folsom, Richardson, and other top aides in order to ask them for "something new and in the present public mood." The president had no interest in a rash, expansive, and costly effort to immediately overhaul American schooling. Intelligence reports clearly indicated the United States remained far more advanced technologically and militarily than the Soviets. The former general considered the many conflicts overseas far more pressing and remained skeptical of the bold ideas Richardson had compiled and Folsom presented. HEW staff still spent November canvassing educators and December conferring with federal education aid's congressional champions to get a sense of their needs and wants. Yet White House proposals actually became less generous, especially in comparison to what many educators, lawmakers, and HEW stalwarts desired. Eisenhower placed far more trust in his cabinet, some of whom outright opposed federal education intervention even after Sputnik's launch. The Bureau of the Budget staff trimmed an already temporary bill's allocations for labs, supplies, and buildings. The president certainly appreciated thrift but still feared too many limitations on who received support. "The American people," he told Folsom, must "understand that a football player is no more important than a person who does well in mathematics or a good well balanced student." He just "can't understand the United States being quite as panicky as they are." The president told his HEW secretary, "Anything you could hook on the defense situation would get by."[48]

Lawmakers eager to invest in education shared that assumption. They nevertheless waited far longer than the administration to craft proposals. Former Texas NYA director and current Senate majority leader Lyndon Baines Johnson held preparedness discussions on November 25, almost two months after Sputnik's launch and a few weeks after Eisenhower first sat down with aides. Congressional studies, conferences, and proposals followed, which White House staff tracked and considered as they crafted their suggestions. But Ike and congressional leaders did not meet to discuss possibilities until two months after the Soviets' scientific breakthrough.[49]

Neither Hill nor Elliott liked the administration's proposals for a temporary influx of money. Such earmarks could never substantially expand campuses or assist aspiring college students. But they rightly feared nothing else would pass. More hearings and constituent pleas seemed unlikely to persuade conservative Republicans and southern Democrats steadfastly opposed to federally funding education. Skeptics on either side of the aisle seemed likely to support an education bill only if the White House continued to press for such support. Elliott doubted enough liberals and moderates would back a plan that was so limited it would keep Eisenhower from issuing a veto—which a divided Congress would never override.[50]

Elliott and Hill also worried that leading academics would convince the president to back only limited help. After all, Eisenhower's brother Milton opposed government scholarships. He had presided over Kansas State University, Pennsylvania State University, and Johns Hopkins in the 1940s and 1950s, when neither work-study nor the GI Bill had covered the full costs of educating additional students. The federal supplements suggested for science and math teachers, Milton told his brother, also seemed likely to "throw the entire school system into turmoil." Conant also predicted chaos in a lengthy November telegram he sent to his close friend Eisenhower, who had appointed him ambassador to West Germany. The celebrated chemist and former Harvard president had become far more interested in secondary education in the late 1950s but still warned against "drastic reforms and crash programs." He remained of the opinion that young people did not necessarily need to go to college. Instead, high school graduates would be better served by better guidance on their options of what to do next. Higher-ups in the NSF, Conant's pet project, also opposed an expansive scholarship program since defense-related fields hardly seemed to have a "manpower shortage." They also rejected any drastic measures that might leave universities as overrun as the GI Bill's education guarantees had. They especially feared leaving such initiatives to Office of Education staffers who might try and claim some authority over NSF's programs.[51]

Such larger ideological divisions forced Elliott and Hill to strategize for the "education breakthrough" Elliott thought possible once Congress reconvened in early 1958. There seemed finally to be an opportunity to "move education closer to becoming a recognized national interest, along with highways, hospitals, old-age assistance, social security, and other fields." Both men had closely monitored the proposals that had eventually appeared in Sputnik's wake. They subsequently spent the holidays crafting omnibus legislation that national defense could justify in the hope it might survive the legislative process and win over the academy. The Hill-Elliott bill asked for less money than the White House's plan but allocated far more to help students. The southern Democrats hoped to encourage more young people to go to college through permanent testing and counseling programs, work-study opportunities, graduate school fellowships, and merit-based scholarships for undergraduates who would receive special consideration for expressing interest in math, science, or foreign languages. These lawmakers envisioned helping forty thousand undergraduates, but none of them, like work-studiers and GIs, would receive enough to cover all college costs. Recipients had six years to finish their studies on the $1,000 provided annually. During the initiative's first year, one thousand graduate students would receive a $2,000 stipend, which would remain the same over the subsequent five years when the support could go to fifteen hundred graduate students annually. Anything more generous would have broken with the limited nature of the country's public-private social welfare policies.[52]

Lawmakers still spent seven months wrangling over the Hill-Elliott bill and the White House's preferred legislation. Hearings occurred in the labor committees on which Hill and Elliott served but also in others that dealt with issues included in both proposals. Fights in both houses, across partisan divides, and within parties often swirled around the political issues unresolved during the Depression, World War II, and demobilization. Some lawmakers, for example, insisted that neither bill had anything to do with national defense. Both proposals instead seemed to be the kind of entering wedge into education erstwhile New Dealers had hoped (and reactionary Legionnaires had feared) the GI Bill would be. South Carolina Senator Strom Thurmond, for example, was indignant about a bill that "purports to be for the specific purpose of promoting the nation defense" but "is, in actuality, general Federal aid to education." Goldwater had even graver concerns that revealed how he and other Sunbelt Republicans and Democrats had already begun to find common cause. "If adopted," Goldwater predicted, "the legislation will mark the inception of aid, supervision, and ultimately control of education in this country by Federal authorities."[53]

Upsetting the historic balance of power between schools, local leaders, state legislatures, and the federal government remained a barrier to the kind of breakthrough Hill and Elliott wanted. During hearings, lawmakers heard proposals for severe limits on federal oversight or demands that the government impose standards set by independent scholars and scientists (not bureaucrats). US Chamber of Commerce representatives had little faith in such precautions. One insisted there was "no justification for a sudden intervention of the Federal Government into State school systems" or the "direct Federal scholarships [that] make the recipient wards of the State and invite untold political manipulations." Lawmakers, he contended, should amend the tax code only to encourage donations and to allow students and their parents to write off schooling costs. National Association of Manufacturers witnesses likewise shuddered at "Federal grant programs," as one of those kinds of "misuse of taxpayers' money" that, "once started, snowball." The question voiced by one executive was a simple one: "What will this do to industry and other private support of education?"[54]

That puzzle did not concern advocates of federal aid for schools and students. Oregon Senator Wayne Morse more emphatically declared government control fears to be "pure nonsense." Emphatically, the Democrat declared that "Timid politicians too frequently are following this propaganda line . . . denying to American boys and girls the educational opportunities that I think are their heritage." Such reasoning spoke to Students for Democratic Action members. States simply could not devote the money to "overcrowded and understaffed public schools" or stop colleges if they tended to "become again the exclusive privilege of the very wealthy." Those undergraduates, some of the few young people testifying, accordingly joined older witnesses in presuming that federal aid would encourage state and local governments to increase educational earmarks, not lessen allocations.[55]

National funding was bound up in other, larger issues that had long roiled national politics and kept Americans unequal: maintaining separation of church and state and segregating the races. Religious leaders (particularly Catholic clergy) disliked the very suggestion of subsidizing public schooling, particularly colleges. Catholics had matriculated at a greater rate than any other group during the 1930s. But the laity had increasingly been choosing secular postsecondary options, which threatened the finances of Catholic institutions originally founded because there had been little room for Catholics in the largely Protestant Ivory Tower. Jesuits subsequently made headlines when they testified in favor of federal education aid so long as their universities were eligible for construction aid and tuition assistance. That demand enraged Protestants United for the Separation of Church and State, whose leaders feared that such access might jeopardize an integral part of the First Amendment. Those testifying pointed out that Catholic academics had already begun labeling the GI Bill as the kind of precedent they feared might very well lead to "other forms of aid to sectarian institutions." Such a slippery slope also terrified *Washington Post* editorialists, who feared for both religious colleges and the many "independent educational institutions" that had "functioned outside governmental control."[56]

Equal opportunity guarantees proved just as divisive. Lawmakers did not consider the education barriers women had encountered, especially during and after the GI Bill's rollout. Many liberal Democrats instead recoiled at taxpayer dollars going to institutions that considered race, religion, or ethnicity as a part of the admissions process. Senators bucked a school construction provision that would have forced them to debate desegregation or, as Thurmond warned during deliberations, "further irritate race relations." Nevertheless, New York Democrat Adam Clayton Powell, Jr. publicly claimed he had the votes to ensure that the House bill's scholarship program would be open to all. The Harlem pastor's threat suited the National Student Association representatives appearing before lawmakers. The million-member organization called for any tuition assistance program to be open to every American, regardless of race, religion, country of origin, or sex. NAACP leaders made similar demands when they railed against the continued segregation both Elliott and Hill openly championed. The public disagreements frustrated White House Republicans, who had hoped to tackle federal aid separately from desegregation. They had even submitted charts of the available tuition assistance without any breakdown of how much aid was available to or received by people of color or women.[57]

The strategy did not help lawmakers reach an agreement on the student assistance that remained almost as controversial as directly supporting colleges and universities. Very few outright rejected any help for undergraduates. Three House Republicans made the claim that "ample evidence" existed "that able young people who wish to go to college find ways." Like CEOs disdainful of federal intervention, some ardent opponents (including Senator Goldwater), considered a tax credit or deduction to be more than enough support. When Folsom warned Eisenhower and his cabinet there would be a fight over such exemptions, the president reiterated that such write-offs "would in effect be of great advantage to the wealthy but of little advantage to the man of moderate means." Folsom and Richardson still struggled to convince lawmakers how breaks benefited those with the least need. Ike's aides had help from many witnesses who opposed an approach as regressive and revenue-reducing as the loopholes CFAE stalwarts exploited. Treasury Department officials warned lawmakers the government would lose $250 to $300 million yearly. National Student Association representatives repeatedly told skeptical lawmakers that the many undergraduates surveyed wanted scholarships since the existing opportunities were "inadequate and ineffective" and "far too small." They would only welcome tax credits alongside a federal grant program but had no interest in loans or work-study opportunities, unless they too were a part of a broad array of tuition assistance options.[58]

Subsidizing campuses enough to keep them from charging tuition remained completely off the table. Representatives from the AFL-CIO, American Council on Education, and National Education Association joined land-grant and state school officials in testifying for some direct aid. Such support, they emphasized, would help colleges expand without the fee increases pricing many Americans out of the academy. "One of the most dangerous tendencies," a state university staffer warned, was to "throw more and more of the cost of education on the student and, of course, on their families." Such arguments failed to persuade most lawmakers decades after New Dealers had used a lot of government-guaranteed financial products and limited public-private programs to creatively underwrite social welfare. Democrat John F. Kennedy, for example, was one of the few insisting on the school construction labor leaders also wanted. But the Bostonian did not make the suggestion in order to control costs. "There are quite adequate funds for any student to get either a scholarship or an education in the State University," the junior senator reasoned; as such, "Federal efforts should be directed toward providing funds so that the colleges can expand their facilities and the schools can expand their school buildings rather than in the area of scholarships."[59]

But fellowships also divided lawmakers and witnesses debating tuition assistance suggestions. They discussed the mix of options campuses had offered for more than a century. Most lawmakers wanting federal scholarships did not want to end the tradition. They envisioned a limited number of small grants that, like those in the competing Hill-Elliott and White House bills, could never cover all expenses. Labor leaders shared their view that more generous help would be "a long step forward toward a stronger democracy" that would stop "the monumental waste of talent." Professors, including those from elite institutions historically hostile to federal assistance, also demanded robust undergraduate aid. But American Council on Education representatives reported members far more interested in reviving work-study or offering loans than providing grants. They still urged lawmakers to open up scholarships to all majors, not just those subjects considered vital for defense. Campuses, they noted, needed funding to cover the cost of instruction for any option since all would likely increase enrollments. Representatives of state schools made similar arguments when they explained their hesitancy to endorse grants. Student aid could never be a substitute for directly supporting campuses. They considered work-study far more beneficial to colleges and students than the GI Bill, which had never provided enough support to make up for the expense of admitting more students. "Unless it is carefully devised," one higher-up predicted, "a Federal scholarship program is likely to have the effect of bringing pressure to bear on institutions to increase their charges . . . , thus making college attendance more difficult for nonscholarship students and requiring additional scholarship aid."[60]

Not everyone shared those concerns about increased costs and enrollments. Folsom constantly emphasized to concerned voters that the White House did not intend the small number of grants in the White House's plan to help the American student body grow dramatically. Philanthropists also doubted much would change. "Many institutions have selective admission standards," the Ford Foundation's Philip Coombs noted. "What a competitive scholarship program might do, what is already happening in many places, is simply to upgrade the average quality of students who attend college."[61]

But limited help, even if temporary, still irritated those who resented the persistence of New Deal public-private social welfare programs long past the war's end. Conservative lawmakers in both parties resisted anything that seemed like a federal free ride. "A boy or girl who feels that he must make some sacrifice," Texas Democrat Representative W. R. Poage reasoned, "is going to . . . put that education to much better use than somebody who has it handed to him." Representatives of the National Association of Manufacturers, US Chamber of Commerce, American Farm Bureau Federation, and even American Legion joined him and other politicians in denouncing even the small scholarships in the White House and Hill-Elliott bills. Like his counterparts at the CFAE, the head of the independent National Merit Scholarship Corporation feared that any government support would lessen the amount of private help available. The very suggestion of federal underwriting, a leading Chicago science researcher reported, had already led corporate benefactors and state officials to adopt a "let's wait and see" approach to student assistance offerings, which they even considered eliminating.[62]

Scholarship proposals forced lawmakers to answer a question that had long bedeviled social welfare policymaking: who was worthy of federal help? Many lawmakers worried that grants would not go to those who needed them. Among them was Democrat Edith Starrett Green, a former Oregon schoolteacher turned House representative, who was not opposed to a grant program but wanted to gather information before crafting one. She (like many Ivy League professors) contended that talent, not need, should determine who received assistance. She shared the view of many who implicitly wanted to protect the white Americans who had benefited the most from the New Deal's government-guaranteed financial products (like FHA mortgages). "I am particularly concerned about the middle class," she explained, "the people of no income, the government takes care of; but the people . . . who have the day to day struggle of sending their youngsters to college, that is the group that I think tremendous consideration should be given." After all, as she told a constituent, "any program undertaken by the Federal Government must have for its sole purpose the education of that half of the upper 25 percent of the high school graduates who do not enter college primarily for financial reasons."[63]

Green had a lot more faith in lending, an option that divided lawmakers and witnesses even though credit had become an increasingly common way to finance basic needs. Borrowing proposals came from northeastern and southern Democrats as well as Republicans, who did not serve on any of the committees conducting hearings on the Hill-Elliott and White House bills. They, like many witnesses, shared Republican Kentucky Senator John Cooper's sense that borrowing was "more in conformity with the American tradition." Academics did not make such arguments when politicians asked them about historically risky, difficult-to-collect student loans. National Education Association officials reported that their constituents were open to lending but far more in favor of the scholarships undergraduates overwhelmingly preferred. "They are actually showing their maturity," one delegate explained, "in being afraid of encumbering themselves with indebtedness before they see any chance of earning money." One spokesperson from a state school explained that "Attitudes are mixed among our people." Many understood how low-interest loans "would help many young people finance an education." Yet they also feared "influential people . . . who advocate that the cost of education be financed entirely by charges to students." Those educators "opposed any tendency to make it more costly to the student, so far as public higher education is concerned."[64]

Eisenhower and his top aides were skeptical. None of these moderate Republicans wanted loans to be a substitute for grants. Folsom and Richardson often explained to constituents and lawmakers eager for a robust federal borrowing program that the administration feared credit would just increase the size, not improve the quality, of the student body. This tuition assistance also seemed likely to be detrimental to women students and undergraduates eager to pursue less-lucrative careers, like teaching. Folsom begged leading Republican lawmakers to consider lending "a supplement" since credit was "a means of greater expansion of educational opportunity rather than of encouraging achievement." Richardson also explained to the president's science adviser, former MIT president James Killian, that loans "tend to enlarge enrollments" but did nothing to guarantee students excelled. Eisenhower also questioned borrowing since, as Columbia's president, he had witnessed the medical school's loan fund largely go untapped. Yet none of these men could ignore lending's popularity in Congress and among the public, who already expected campuses to offer needy students financing options. Killian also helped weaken the president's resolve when he explained how popular MIT's lending program was. Unlike Columbia, MIT set standards favorable to students who used the loan fund "right up to the hilt."[65]

Congressional and White House debates about such seemingly small issues touching on much bigger ideological differences dragged on for seven months. Amendments to add, modify, and delete loans, fellowships, and tax credits from bills left much unresolved by summer 1958 when public panic over Sputnik had greatly subsided. Senators still could not agree on who deserved scholarships, whether aid should be made available to private (particularly parochial) schools, how much money should be allotted for any part of the program, whether math and science should be privileged, and how best to support graduate programs and students. Of the utmost importance to Hill and other southern Democrats was how to "avoid the question of integration," a fitful, violent process that had quickly ended for Autherine Lucy at the University of Alabama in 1956, a year before the Little Rock Nine enrolled in Central High. Hill wanted to channel funding indirectly through students, which had once been a means for the Roosevelt administration to sidestep charges of federal overreach. But, in 1958, leaving the choice up to students helped lawmakers avoid controversies over desegregating colleges and funding religious institutions. Church and state's separation and integration also permeated House fights over emphasizing science education, underwriting school construction, establishing need as a condition of student assistance, reducing the number of years federal support would be available, and offering various forms of financial assistance (including lending and work-study programs).[66]

Ike, his staff, and lawmakers struggled to reach an agreement. The then-ailing president was focused on foreign policy. Only House delays drove him to bring the issue up to his trusted cabinet, which had been deeply divided on federal education aid. Eisenhower insisted on a limited, temporary bill during a high-level, contentious, summer 1958 meeting on a range of issues vexing his administration. But Folsom contended that such legislation should not include tax breaks or loans. Ike, too, doubted that either would stop "the loss of a student with real ability," noting that preventing such losses was "the real purpose behind legislation such as this." Yet he still only wanted ten thousand scholarships available in any given year. He subsequently ordered HEW officials to make his demands clear to Congress. Less than two weeks later, the House finally settled on a bill. Top officials shared the White House's disappointment with the press; representatives had offered undergraduates loans, not scholarships. Elliott, however, was relieved that his colleagues had not "bound" recipients "to stay in" a math, science, or foreign language major, which gave students "the freedom to change courses."[67]

Insiders still feared that entrenched political divisions would stop anything, no matter how limited and temporary, from being enacted. "In its present form the Committee bill is so close to the Administration's proposal, except for inclusion of the loan title," Richardson admitted, "I don't see how the Administration could make serious objection to it." Nevertheless, passage hinged on "vigorous, all-out, whole-hearted support from the Administration." Ike finally agreed to the borrowing scheme after a July meeting with Folsom, a member of the Bureau of the Budget, and several leading Republican lawmakers. The president held the line on limiting the scholarships available to graduate students, but acquiesced to letting undergraduates of "high scholastic competence and good standing" borrow. Ike seemed to backpedal, however, during a press conference when he reiterated the importance of small grants as well as limits on federal power that would help lawmakers sidestep ongoing desegregation fights.[68]

HEW appointees still had to do a lot to secure passage when the Rules Committee permitted hours of open debate in the House. They scrambled to include assurances that integration would not be a precondition of eligibility for any school or college support in the legislation. Lawmakers nevertheless repeated the same remonstrations and denunciations they had voiced even before Sputnik orbited the earth in fall 1957. Only public pressure, both from individual citizens as well as organizations like the AFL-CIO and the NEA, helped bring the contentious August 1958 discussions to a close. But tensions persisted. Graduate fellowships and undergraduate loans survived the fraught conference committee negotiations to reconcile the House and Senate bills. Undergraduate grants did not. Lawmakers instead agreed to make "Loans to Students in Institutions of Higher Education" the second title, which symbolized that section's importance to the entire plan to aid education and expand the opportunity to go to college. Eisenhower still reminded everyone the legislation was simply "an emergency undertaking to be terminated after four years" when he signed the National Defense Education Act on September 2 along with more than a hundred other bills.[69]

Failure to Launch

Americans nevertheless remember Public Law 864 as sweeping legislation that transformed schooling at all levels. Just two years later, Temple University staff assured lawmakers that loans went to talented undergraduates, many of whom had previously dropped out when they could no longer afford to study. Some parents also wrote to thank the president for the tuition assistance that enabled their hardworking children to stay in school.[70]

Pundits, politicians, and educators had far more mixed reactions. "With the ice broken with this aid-to-education legislation," Folsom cautiously hoped, "perhaps it will not be so difficult to have other measures enacted in the future." *Time,* in fact, lauded NDEA as a "sore defeat for hard-rock States'-righters," who had thwarted earlier federal efforts to aid education. Ardent segregationist Elliott disagreed. He celebrated that the law promised "to aid America's school system at what my committee thought were its weakest points." He even predicted the law "will take its place alongside the Northwest Ordinance, and the acts creating our land grant colleges." LBJ, like National Education Association heads, considered the legislation just a start, a beginning that one *Los Angeles Times* editorial deemed "a $900,000,000 Trojan horse." Yet Milton Eisenhower just dismissed NDEA as a "hodge-podge."[71]

The legislation, in many ways, epitomized the kind of piecemeal policy Zook had feared. It had shortcomings lawmakers only exacerbated by refusing to fully fund its many components. For example, Congress did not generously support all programs of study. It instead appropriated $32 million for improving language instruction and area studies, denoting research into and teaching about countries and regions outside the industrialized West. Another $20 million could help improve technology in the classrooms (especially television and radio). But Congress earmarked only $15 million for vocational education and $5 million for graduate fellowships to study math, science, and foreign languages, the subjects considered most vital to national defense. The first year of this grant program only provided 1,000 opportunities split across 272 separate degree programs at 123 campuses.[72]

Lawmakers did not fully fund but still devoted the most money to Title II's National Defense Student Loan Program (NDSLP), a decision reflecting how minimal tuition assistance had become fundamental to federal higher education policies. Work-study and the GI Bill had already offered indirect, temporary aid for colleges and universities, which had and still needed far more direct, sustained support. Yet lawmakers remained unwilling to guarantee anything as risky as lending money for degrees they could never repossess. This section instead directed the Office of Education to set up campus loan funds for a limited, self-perpetuating program. Campuses had to annually apply for their share. Under the law, $47.5 million was available for the first fiscal year (1959), a sum that grew to $90 million by 1962, the program's final year. A for-profit educator had testified in favor of making tuition assistance available to the proprietary schools' "training secretaries, clerks, accountants, and technicians who can assist the engineers and scientists." But only nonprofit accredited institutions, public or private, could receive a maximum of $250,000. Eligibility for this tuition assistance required two- and four-year campuses to only admit high school graduates and offer state-certified degree programs. But at colleges and universities, out of the money made available to lend out, financial aid officers had to front just 10 percent, to later be collected back for a pot of money, similar to the trust used by Harvard. Campuses unable to afford that buy-in could borrow money from the government's Institutional Matching Fund and negotiate a repayment plan. That cash seemed easy to recoup. This financial product's fixed 3 percent interest rate seemed guaranteed to increase the amount available to lend to future cohorts. This assistance also preferably went to accomplished, needy undergraduates who expressed an interest in science, math, engineering, or foreign languages—majors that would allow them to step into much-needed teaching roles and other well-paying jobs, and theoretically pay off those debts easily.[73]

This program, like the loan funds campuses had struggled to run for more than a century, quickly proved anything but self-perpetuating. Title II limited individual loans to $1,000 a year and restricted total support to $5,000 over the course of an undergraduate's time in school. Pupils did not accrue interest while enrolled. They also did not start repayment until a year after graduation. Borrowers had ten years to pay off the relatively small amounts, and if they went back to school or joined the military, they could also apply for deferments. Public schoolteachers could also have 10 percent of their principal and interest obligations canceled every year. They did, however, have to pay back at least 50 percent of what they took out.[74]

Office of Education staff quickly learned what others slowly realized: like so many federal, public-private social welfare initiatives, NDEA on paper and in practice did not offer colleges or students nearly enough support. Even if Congress had generously funded all the law's higher education programs, lawmakers would not have helped universities hire enough faculty to meet demand, particularly for the required subjects outside the privileged math, science, and foreign language departments. The legislation also could not underwrite the array of facilities, such as dormitories and cafeterias, needed for colleges to truly grow. Rules also did nothing to ensure that race, religion, or sex did not keep talented men and women from finding a spot in private schools or public universities. Even if they had, Education Office staff found themselves unable to force financial aid officers to award loans on the basis of talent and need, much less ensure recipients sign loyalty oaths as lawmakers had stipulated.[75]

Education Office appointees reported schools' eagerness to apply to have been "overwhelming." Lawmakers had assumed, based on undergraduates' reported disinterest in lending, that only eleven thousand students would receive $600 in credit for the first year. Fall 1958 questionnaires had also suggested that only eight hundred eligible institutions had any interest in participating. More than twelve hundred campuses applied after passage and then complained to their representatives when they received far less than requested. Within the first six months, colleges asked for $62 million in total, far more than Congress had earmarked for immediate use and the first fiscal year. A small private California community college actually requested five times what the entire University of California system wanted. Administrators were both disappointed and outraged. Bowdoin College president James Coles asked Office of Education higher-ups "what the hell he was supposed to do with" the $79 allocated to start the lending program. He and other university heads could theoretically appeal but, as appointees later remembered, "few did." Educators instead complained to their representatives, who grilled Education Office personnel. Staff testified during hearings that "we are administering the act in the manner in which it is written." Guidelines had not prepared anyone for campuses' eagerness to lend and students' willingness to borrow, which one Education Office higher-up considered "astonishing." At the start of the 1959–1960 academic year, $60 million could be loaned for the next two years. But the money had been given out or allocated before the fall semester's end.[76]

That shortfall epitomized the challenge of implementing NDEA, what one expert deemed in 1959 to be "one of the most complex education laws ever enacted." These loans were as complicated as other government-guaranteed financial products. Defense loan rules vexed the officials in charge of them. One joked decades later that "the basic federal loan program was written by members of Congress who did not really believe in loans, enacted by a Congress the majority of whose members did not believe in federal aid to education, and administered by a Secretary of Health, Education, and Welfare who, at the outset at least, did not believe that students would borrow." Crafting the loan program was a formidable task. "The original legislation defies comprehension in reading," a staffer overseeing fiscal operations lamented. Lawmakers had, after all, been so divided on whether or not to give students grants or loans that Education Office staff and consultants had to come up with a name for the program after passage. They also had to guess what Congress had wanted. One unpaid expert explained that they presumed "the goal was to draw into higher education students who would not otherwise get there—students whom [politicians] often described as 'high-risk,' without defining the term." Such convolutedness confounded many involved in the rollout, one of whom later admitted, "I never did understand the system and I don't believe others understood it." He just left the matter to staff who "worked it out and I just signed it."[77]

Education Office personnel also had to speculate about repayment, a crucial matter bound up in larger fears about government control and the dreaded free ride. "Obviously no federal effort was expected," one adviser later explained. The law, after all, forbade students from signing promissory notes, although there were some exceptions if campuses insisted. Colleges could (but did not have to) take alumni to court to collect the government-provided funds that institutions could avoid having to match. Consultants applied similar logic to loan forgiveness for public school teachers. It seemed "an acknowledgement of the wall between church and state" as well as the kind of grants program "the House would buy" since "it could be defended by pointing to the shortage of teachers." In this expert's view, NDEA's authors "could scarcely have believed that the forgiveness of a few hundred dollars in loans, spread over a five-year period, would draw many into teaching who would otherwise have entered more lucrative professions."[78]

The Education Office lacked the experienced personnel to put the $295 million Congress allocated for every NDEA program to use. Personnel, after all, had long been relegated to gathering data. The bureau's small Division of Higher Education had to quickly expand to oversee many titles, not just the second pertaining to loans. Staff had little support. Six months after passage, top personnel pointed out to frustrated lawmakers investigating their progress that "we are doing a 288-men job with about 101 people." The director of financial aid remembered his first office in DC having "a desk from government surplus and three or four orange crates."[79]

Officials looked to campuses to help staff the new Financial Aid Branch. The recruitment strategy continued the age-old practice of turning to outside experts to implement government programs. Education Office heads convinced some high-ranking administrators to take leaves of absence to join the four divisions (only one of which handled loans). Others, including Harvard's dean of financial aid and the University of Minnesota's director of financial aid, drafted regulations and guidelines as unpaid consultants, who (as one later recalled) "met, often for several days at a time, for the first year or two, hammering away at each problem as it arose." Education Office bureaucrats did not really interfere in deliberations. Only one top official dictated at the start of the complicated process that "the government should not, could not, and would not devise its own system of measuring need." The College Scholarship Service seemed, in his estimation, to have already created a far better system than bureaucrats ever could.[80]

That diktat eventually led to the creation of a form parents and students would come to dread by the 1990s, the Free Application for Federal Student Aid. The FAFSA exemplified how the private sector had long helped shape public social welfare policies. Defense-lending's complexity encouraged campuses across the country to hire financial aid officers. They generally turned to the standard financial aid form the College Scholarship Service had created for New England and mid-Atlantic institutions tired of bidding on brains and athletes. CSS staff did much to help college personnel new to lending. Of the utmost importance was mastering "aid-packaging," how experts described the complex mix of work, loans, and fellowships to fulfill "un-met need," a phrase denoting the money an applicant required beyond what, financial aid staff decided, his or her family could be expected to provide. Campus personnel could only offer undergraduates a defense act loan if their school was accredited by an organization the government deemed reputable. Those rules did not bother one of the first directors of the loan program until years later, when he wondered "how two private clubs (for that is what they were) were accepted so readily in the loan process." He recalled the result with dismay: "To be eligible to receive funds an institution had to be accredited or have its credits accepted by the anointed. To disburse funds, actually though not technically, they had to subscribe to the College Scholarship Service . . . principles of need analysis."[81]

Those involved in the loan program's start considered the real obstacle to be "the great ineptitude of the colleges themselves." Harvard's top financial aid officer had wrongly assumed campus staff across the country had the necessary experience to lend to students. Many institutions had participated in the work-study and GI Bill programs but, of the almost 1,400 schools applying in the first year, most, a consultant later remembered, "had never made or collected a loan before, had had no experience with need analysis, and indeed had no person, trained or untrained, vested with the responsibility to administer student aid." A regional director lamented that "In many small church related schools . . . willing and eager to participate in this new source of revenue, the Business Manager was a retired or incompetent man of the cloth who was ill-prepared to the task." The situation hardly improved after students actually started borrowing. "New colleges were entering the Program each year," one top official remembered. "Most were ill equipped to assume the responsibilities of a small loans business. . . . Collections were poor because timely, adequate and correct billing was not being performed. Failure to collect led to delinquency."[82]

Education Office personnel struggled to offer guidance as they wrote policy on the fly. The Ford Foundation tried to help by giving them two thousand copies of a handbook to distribute to campuses struggling to run the borrowing program. Almost half the institutions given loan funds still turned in incomplete, unacceptable, and unintelligible reports. College personnel continued to struggle to assess ability, need, and special talent in math, science, engineering, and foreign languages. Thirty schools desperately in need of the indirect aid actually forgot to reapply for the second year of funding. Nothing could be done for these struggling institutions because, as federal officials explained, "allocations had already been made."[83]

Government staffers and regulations really frustrated experienced business and financial aid officers. Seasoned pros disliked making a loan without a credit check or collateral. Neither likely would have helped the complex work of recouping payments from alumni, particularly with constant changes to cancellation and deferment rules. One campus administrator, who later joined the Education Office to direct the lending program, considered the first set of stipulations, "at the working level of the college, impossible." He also could not believe appointees refused to ask Congress for more money during and after the rollout. They had presumed students "would not borrow money and therefore large appropriations would not be needed."[84]

Loyalty oaths also vexed campuses. Indignant professors and students had been fighting such pledges for more than a decade. Some colleges, like Bennington, refused to participate in the lending program because of this rule. Others, including Harvard, took the capital for their loan fund but did not contribute to it or use it until the faculty approved. Yale, a former head of the government program remembered, "was in the absurd position of having loaned all its federal funds before deciding to withdraw." Faculty and staff complaints did not convince lawmakers to rescind the edict, which Congress quietly removed without any debate in 1962. The rule, an Education Office insider remembered, had nevertheless required a lot of staff and resources to enforce. He had assigned two clerks to check and file the sworn allegiances to the United States every time a student borrowed. Even in the late 1970s, he was "sure there are warehouses somewhere in Virginia still bulging with that paper."[85]

The loan program had far worse, long-term consequences. NDEA's Title II, unlike that section of the GI Bill, put many more campuses in the business of making and managing loans. More colleges and universities had credit funds in 1957 than in the early 1930s, when administrators had scrambled to shore up those reserves to find some way to keep students enrolled. Donations had done much to expand such options at individual campuses before Sputnik's launch. Almost 800 loaned $13 million to 80,000 students. Just three years after NDEA's passage, 1,400 gave 115,000 undergraduates roughly $52 million. By 1969, more than 1.5 million students had borrowed.[86]

Americans became increasingly comfortable with a financial product epitomizing the risk that 1930s banking legislation and government-guaranteed financial products, particularly mortgages, had tried to reduce. A small North Carolina bank and Presbyterian women's college had captured *Wall Street Journal* and *American Banker* reporters' attention in 1956 when they partnered to offer what campus staff labeled "installment buying" for diplomas. Just months before the Soviets launched Sputnik, the Massachusetts Bankers Association and Bay State lawmakers created a nonprofit that guaranteed bank loans to students. Fourteen months later, when Congress remained bogged down in debates over federal education aid, the Massachusetts Higher Education Assistance Corporation had approved two thousand loans on terms far more generous than most consumer credit lines at the time. Applicants had to meet with a loan officer at a bank near their hometowns. Colleges only certified the information provided. Afterward, students could borrow up to $500 a year (but not more than $1,500 in total) even if they were under the legal age to sign such a contract. Banks, however, often sought parental consent or made spouses co-sign. Interest stayed at 4.5 percent, most of which went to the bank. Only .5 percent covered the corporation's operating costs. The 36-month repayment plan started six months after graduation or immediately after a student dropped out. The $910,000 the agency loaned in 1958 quickly inspired Maine and New York legislators to set up similar guarantee agencies. More states entertained this option during and after NDEA's rollout, when few states funded higher education as generously as California. Yet the Empire State's nonprofit still stood out for using public appropriations to supplement the private capital financiers offered. That money helped liberal Republican Governor Nelson Rockefeller creatively finance SUNY's transformation into the public system Dewey had never wanted.[87]

Aspiring students in those states and others did not get much more help from the federal government. Congress allocated more money for the borrowing program in subsequent years, which enabled the Office of Education to expand and better handle NDEA's many components. Yet officials knew the funding did "not keep pace with need." Lawmakers had heeded the advice of Education Office personnel, who thought their recommended increase was as much as schools could possibly absorb. Yet, by the start of the spring 1960 academic term, complaints came from undergraduates about loan funds that were quickly exhausted, forcing them to drop out. Their grievances did not stop Eisenhower from trying to halve the budget for the loan program before he left office. But Education Office staffers predicted they would need $3 million more. College administrators submitted evidence to lawmakers that undergraduates needed more help, not less, leading to a temporary bill reauthorization in 1961 and an allocation of $30 million for the 1962 fiscal year. Yet when Congress extended the legislation, it only tinkered with lending maximums, loan cancellations, deferments, repayment rules, eligibility provisions, distribution mechanisms, and government contributions. There were cosmetic changes after NDEA's higher-education provisions were folded into the Higher Education Act, a legislative maneuver that did not stop cost-cutting presidents from trying to destroy this beloved "Little Red Wagon." Representative Carl Perkins, a Kentucky Democrat devoted to expanding educational opportunities, led the fight to keep this lending option available—the loan program that was eventually named after him and rededicated to helping impoverished students, without the rationale of defense needs.[88]

This cherished lending scheme did little in the long or short run to help more young people pay fees, particularly those historically excluded from the academy. Like work-study, the GI Bill, and other public-private social welfare programs, defense lending did not confront systemic inequities. Reporters quickly uncovered that colleges across the country still tended to award financial aid to students from so-called middle-income families, who remained far more likely to be admitted to segregated schools or institutions still operating under the quota system. No one really received the much-feared free ride. Students continued to cobble together help even if they were lucky enough to receive a package including work, loan, and scholarship offers. Only applicants indicating an interest in math, science, engineering, or foreign languages were eligible for the small federal loans that could be included in that basket of support. Women had barely increased their numbers in those majors, which feminist academics still considered the purview of men decades after NDEA's passage. Those subjects were largely absent from the curricula of for-profit schools ineligible for the tuition assistance program and still welcoming to citizens of color and immigrants, particularly women. CSS director Rexford Moon, Jr. insisted few nonprofits still bid on brains after

NDEA's passage but nevertheless guessed that colleges overlooked at least 150,000 gifted young people a year. Admissions officers feared the number would grow alongside steadily increasing fees. University of Illinois president David Henry in fact warned in 1959 that there was "desperate need" for more than what was available for the campus's twenty thousand students.[89]

Demand sparked another political firestorm that year, when fees were once again projected to rise at both public and private colleges. Harvard University economist Seymour Harris boldly suggested a $1.5 billion loan industry could help all aspiring students. He hoped either the government or the banking industry would boost a financial sector, which would likely need to grow to $2.5 billion by 1970. That suggestion outraged a leading figure in the American Association of Land Grant Colleges and State Universities. "It is almost inconceivable . . . in this day and age that the student should pay the [full] cost of his education," Russell Thackrey asserted. "I thought Thomas Jefferson had long since demolished that philosophy." After all, Thackrey added, the Soviets educated every child for free. The National Merit Scholarship Corporation's head also worried such widespread borrowing would start a "never-ending chase up the stairs, with the student following costs upward and always finding another flight ahead."[90]

That scramble had already started. Undergraduates and their parents had been scrounging to cover soaring college costs since the 1920s. Fees had risen a little when the work-study program assisted needy youth but rapidly increased during the GI Bill's rollout. The larger ideological struggles steadily remaking both parties and undermining what remained of the New Deal contributed to the escalating expense of pursuing the advanced degrees individuals needed and employers expected in the Cold War's early years. Politicians, like Dewey, and corporate executives, including CFAE stalwarts, desperately wanted to halt public higher education's already slow growth. Such hostility to more affordable, taxpayer-supported state options could also be found among lawmakers, who continually fought over and only managed to pass the piecemeal legislation Zook feared. NDEA's hastily approved, temporary loan program, like many patchwork federal policies and government-guaranteed financial products, neither offered generous support nor tackled discrimination. The slim (but beloved) lifeline largely aided white, middle-class, male students.

But this "Congressional accident," as lending director John Morse would later call it, helped change how many Americans thought higher education could or should be financed. The supposedly "revolutionary" idea steadily became far more popular with students, academics, and lawmakers. Borrowing seemed like a natural component of increasing state and federal aid to colleges and universities straining to accommodate the Baby Boomers applying in record numbers in the 1960s. Neither former Texas NYA director Lyndon Baines Johnson nor his congressional allies wanted to experiment with a novel approach to college financing. They instead modeled a student borrowing initiative on new state experiments and the New Deal's celebrated mortgage program—which, researchers later discovered, had actually exacerbated the inequality Johnson had declared war on as president.[91]

5

Federally Guaranteed Students

Weeks before the fall 1968 semester was supposed to begin, desperate under-graduates planned a bazaar with a kissing booth to raise money to keep John F. Kennedy College in Wahoo, Nebraska, solvent. The Save Our School Committee got some help from locals who considered the three-year-old college to be "the biggest industry in Saunders County." The secular, self-supporting liberal arts college also meant a lot to the eight hundred students who paid $900 a semester for room and board, tuition, and other fees. Those revenues, president Theodore Dillow explained to reporters, hardly covered operating costs, much less the capital required for new facilities and scholar-ships. Dillow had already warned twenty-six professors he could no longer pay their salaries. The entire campus would close unless he could quickly raise $207,000.[1]

A group of seven students piled into a beat-up station wagon and drove all day and all night on their way to New York City and Washington, DC, to try to raise money from donors. Hubert Humphrey wrote them a letter of support, shared with the press by the vice president's staff. Other than a short piece in *Newsweek* a month later, however, the story went uncovered. Paul Boyajian, a Virginia resident working as director of the Office of Equal Opportunity in the Department of the Interior, found that intensely frus-trating. He wrote angry letters to congressional education subcommittees and major media outlets, complaining that "not one Washington area newspaper or television station" considered these "young, clean, unbearded, simply but appropriately-dressed students . . . newsworthy." Especially given "the hue and cry for still more institutions of higher learning," it seemed preposterous to him that this rural college named after the recently slain president might be lost. "What purpose does student aid serve," he asked, "when there is no college to attend?" Something had to be done, he insisted, about "the unrealistic gap that separates small needy private colleges from the well-endowed massive State and Private institutions." Yes, JFK College was "in fairly serious temporary financial trouble due primarily to lack of long range planning," but Boyajian believed that saving it would go over well with "the great number of non political JFK followers, the large ethnic groups." He received only one reply, from a close friend in the Johnson White House, who wrote that the administration had "concluded that there was no way that we could be of help." After all, "the Eisenhower College in New York is in a similar predicament."[2]

That admission reflected how the Johnson White House and the Eighty-Ninth Congress attempted to complete the New Deal in the name of building a Great Society. Liberals had an agenda in this affluent era that was as expansive as their predecessors' during the Great Depression, if not more so. Scholars have likewise drawn attention to the health care and schooling breakthroughs many consider signature Sixties achievements. But those victories highlighted how much past policies and ongoing ideological fights had shaped reforms amid the continued realignment of the Democratic and Republican parties. Medicare, Medicaid, and the Guaranteed Student Loan Program extended the tradition of offering citizens government-guaranteed financial products (like unemployment insurance and long-term mortgages) instead of robust support. That public-private strategy neither defeated poverty nor built a more equitable America in the long run. Rather, the story of the celebrated 1965 Higher Education Act (HEA) was not unlike other ambitious Johnson White House initiatives. It was, in the words of historian Hugh Davis Graham, "a mixed story of initial failure and frustration, of political brilliance and luck, of partial success, of unintended consequences, and ultimately of being overwhelmed, even in triumph, by stronger forces."[3]

As with the National Youth Administration (NYA), the GI Bill, the National Defense Education Act (NDEA), and other federal social welfare programs, compromises on seemingly small details resulted in a complicated law with an equally fraught legacy. Lawmakers spent months wrangling over directly funding universities, offering tax breaks, and assisting students through work-study, scholarship, or borrowing programs. The 1964 Civil Rights Act ended the need to fight over funding segregated campuses. Healthy economic growth, rising prosperity, and scientific advances across the decade also eased concerns about national defense and employment levels. Politicians instead battled over the best way to guarantee equal educational opportunities. At first, it appeared that the White House and an overwhelmingly Democratic Congress had agreed on the need to provide generous support directly to all nonprofit campuses, including small colleges like the one in Wahoo. As it turned out, lawmakers and White House staffers opted again for tuition assistance to students, mostly in the form of loans not expected to cover all college costs.

The 1960s liberals did take a step further than their predecessors who had also shown preference for such indirect financing. They intended borrowing to jumpstart a new, permanent student loan industry, which in the years before Sputnik's launch only a handful of economists had considered a viable way to underwrite the academy's much-needed expansion. Even though leading bankers denounced this federally assured lending scheme as an overreach, a majority of Republicans and Democrats considered the approach feasible, politically palatable, and cost-effective. By the mid-1960s, government-guaranteed financial products had seemed to give middle-class standards of living to the white working class, recognized to be an important Democratic constituency. Just as federal mortgages had seemed a cheaper way to turn the country into a nation of homeowners and save the banking industry in the 1930s, student loans seemed capable of aiding undergraduates and the academy while lawmakers spent considerable money on other domestic and foreign policy imperatives, including the ongoing Vietnam War.

Such calculations did not consider the risk student loans still posed to young people and campuses. Lawmakers promised that financiers would be repaid, but interest-paying students would pay more for their degrees over time. Graduates seemed overwhelmingly likely to land the kind of jobs that would make repayment within a decade painless and exponentially increase what they would earn over their lifetimes. Yet, like the still-revered GI Bill, this federal help (supposedly open to all) trusted campus financial aid officers to dole it out equitably. To the extent that did not happen, federal tuition assistance, like so many public-private offerings, exacerbated historic inequities in subsequent decades, even as many colleges' finances remained shaky and tuition rates continued to soar.

Overcrowded Campuses and Underfunded Students

Even before Dwight Eisenhower left the White House, many academics, journalists, and citizens recognized that the country's K-12 and postsecondary schools and students needed far more support than what the government had been willing or able to provide. Public and private colleges had to increase rates to hire more professors, build additional classrooms, construct new dormitories, or just keep campuses running. Top northeastern institutions still charged the most, even though many of them had substantial endowments and more success in procuring federal grants to fund research in the sciences and medicine. State universities also raised fees, even though legislatures earmarked more for education. Early 1960s allocations still varied wildly from place to place. School administrators continued the age-old tradition of cobbling together money from a range of income sources, including endowments, donors, federal grants, and student fees.[4]

Campuses needed revenues to prepare for the predicted tidal wave of Baby Boomer applicants, including African Americans and other citizens of color bravely challenging segregated universities. Many college hopefuls were also the children of veterans who had taken advantage of the GI Bill and had enjoyed the affluence their advanced degrees made possible for them. Yet parents in the largely white middle and professional classes still needed to stretch their incomes and budgets to afford to send their children to college, as Congresswoman Edith Green had mentioned in NDEA hearings. Blue-collar families, regardless of race or religion, struggled more, since tuition had risen moderately but steadily before and after that law's laborious passage.[5]

Borrowing became more commonplace and accepted after NDEA's enactment. Congress steadily increased support for defense loans and borrowing options for would-be nurses, doctors, and optometrists. But state experiments to broker credit for undergraduates also piqued the interest of some financiers. The Massachusetts Higher Education Assistance Corporation had already inspired other legislatures to encourage bankers to lend to students before a self-described "small group of far-seeing men" founded the nonprofit United States Aid Funds in 1960. USAF arranged for colleges and universities to receive lines of credit from banks that did not demand repayment until five months after a student dropped out or graduated. The banks collected payments, at 6 percent annual interest, on loans that financial aid officers awarded based on their assessments of individual students' needs. Schools could participate only if they deposited money into USAF's guarantee funds. Those accounts' interest earnings covered the cost of administering the almost $40 million lent by 1965. The $30 million distributed annually by more than five thousand banks to roughly seven hundred colleges in forty-nine states remained far less than the credit generated from the public-private partnerships modeled on the Massachusetts Higher Education Assistance Corporation. By the mid-1960s, twelve additional northeastern, midwestern, and southern states used similar arrangements, demonstrating how comfortable policymakers, bankers, and citizens had become with relying on government-guaranteed financial products to fund important needs like the fee revenues on which campuses depended.[6]

More opportunities to borrow hardly stopped demands for federal higher education aid. By 1960, a survey by the Council on Financial Aid to Education, whose big-business benefactors had once challenged the need for expansion of public higher education, revealed a distinct change in corporate donors' attitudes toward state assistance. Asked what impact a federal education program would have on their giving, most executives gave an answer of none or unknown—a finding that undercut arguments made just two years before against NDEA's passage. CEOs were found to have continued their charitable giving during and after defense lending's rollout. A 1962 analysis by the National Industrial Conference Board, for example, showed that firms gifted more to education than to either health or welfare causes. Postsecondary schooling received 42 percent of the total $154 million contributed by 420 businesses that year.[7]

Neither those donations nor new sources of student loans stopped college and university administrators from seeking direct support from the federal government. Twenty-six major institutions made headlines in July 1963 when a Carnegie Foundation for the Advancement of Teaching study indicated that higher-ups considered federal aid "highly beneficial." Many administrators hated that only 5 percent of campuses benefited from federally funded research grants, fellowships, construction projects, educational initiatives, and training opportunities. Staff also disliked the inequities that targeted support created between departments not deemed vital for health, scientific advancement, or national defense. Respondents did not fear federal support would come at the expense of their academic freedom. By the 1960s, paltry funding seemed far more dangerous to both the academy and the country.[8]

The Carnegie investigation highlighted an important thirty-year sea change in academic attitudes epitomized by James Conant's about-face on federal aid and mass higher education. Harvard's former president trusted the Ivy League to sift out the country's natural aristocracy but, by the mid-1960s, the noted chemist also recognized that America would benefit from having a far more educated citizenry. His 1964 *Shaping Educational Policy* slammed the "educational establishment" for standing in the way of creating a national policy, even though he himself had once been a member of the "school crowd" that New Dealers had derided. Conant now envisioned state educational agencies cooperating to arrive at rigorous standards and high principles that would, by default, create a new, better national norm, particularly for high schools. He also remained frustrated with the fraught politics of government spending, especially in steel belt states. Illinois, Indiana, and Pennsylvania educators seemed to routinely trade political favors for allocations. Conant noted with approval the aggressive effort that Governor Nelson Rockefeller was making to expand SUNY and also expressed hope that other state officials across the country would emulate California's ambitious Master Plan.[9]

Conant was among the many heaping praise on the University of California (UC) in the early 1960s. By then, that three-tiered system and its president Clark Kerr had seemed to eclipse the power and authority of hidebound institutions like Harvard and their retrograde administrators, who had, like Conant, decried work-study and the GI Bill. Kerr has remained famous for students protesting him for being too backward-looking and Governor Ronald Reagan firing him for being too lenient. This Pennsylvania coal-country native also had a broad vision for mass higher education that Harvard's former president had spent much of his life fighting and young radicals would spend much of the 1960s decrying. Kerr's mother had married a part-time schoolteacher and farmer but refused to have children until she had earned enough as a milliner to ensure, as he later explained, that they "would have the chance of an education which she'd never had." It was in part because "she had worked so hard and sacrificed so much" to save for his education at Swarthmore that Kerr had a lifelong "sense of obligation."[10]

The Depression also shaped how he managed a state higher education system designed to meet the increasingly popular goal of additional learning for anyone interested. The Berkeley PhD arguably received his real education outside the classroom when he traveled with radical economist Paul Taylor into the impoverished California farmlands. Celebrated antifascist lawyer and journalist Carey McWilliams famously warned those "factories in the fields" were the seedbeds of the American fascism Roosevelt insiders hoped work-study might help uproot. Kerr observed firsthand the threat inequality posed to democracy. The best defense seemed to be New Dealers' efforts to negotiate a truce between labor and capitalism. Kerr, in fact, put his training in labor economics to work on Roosevelt's National War Labor Board. That service honed his faith and expertise in technocratic planning and industrial pluralism, shaping his thinking about the larger economy and the specific task of running a university. He did not assume Berkeley's chancellorship until 1952, when work had already begun to create the higher education infrastructure that liberal Republican governor Earl Warren had envisioned and UC president Robert Sproul resisted.[11]

Kerr proved much keener than his predecessor to fulfill national needs and public demands. By the mid-1950s, he foresaw a newly post-industrial America needing the knowledge produced in sprawling research universities. He set out to construct such campuses after he took control of the entire UC system in 1958. By then, politicians and educators across the country had noticed the West Coast experiment in mass higher education. That notoriety served as a pulpit for Kerr's conception of what universities were and what they could be, a vision fully outlined in his 1963 *Uses of the University*. Kerr foresaw what he called "multiversities" that, like postwar UC campuses, were centuries removed from the European "academic cloister . . . with its intellectual oligarchy." Such institutions would instead serve undergraduates, graduates, humanists, social scientists, engineers, professionals, administrators, farmers, industrialists, and politicians.[12]

That lofty mission hinged on generous direct federal support, which seemed unlikely even after John F. Kennedy prevailed in the 1960 presidential election. Historians have continually debated this Massachusetts Democrat's commitment to education, particularly public institutions. He had largely been taught at top private schools. As a representative, he had introduced legislation to benefit Catholic colleges that unceremoniously died, a bill that still pleased his Irish Catholic constituents, who did not seem to notice or care that he generally dodged later debates over aiding education. That topic frequently sparked discussion of civil rights and religious freedoms that the then-senator had wished to avoid because many voters and pundits eyed his ethnic heritage with suspicion amid ongoing struggles to desegregate all levels of American schooling. He nevertheless spoke in favor of direct, sustained funding for all postsecondary institutions over student financial assistance programs and tax cuts during NDEA deliberations. Yet neither he nor Vice President Richard Nixon divulged details about their preferred education policies in the 1960 presidential election, including how much of the federal budget they wanted to spend on college loans or scholarships.[13]

Kennedy lacked the expert advice and enthusiasm to do much for higher learning. He assembled a task force of elite educators and philanthropists before his inauguration who had grand but unattainable ambitions. All of them were white, none of them southern. "We came up with a report," one later admitted, that "would probably have broken the bank in no time at all." They wanted $9 billion (spread out over four-and-a-half years) to construct K-12 schools, raise teacher salaries, build dorms, expand campuses, and forgive NDEA loans for private school teachers. Kennedy aides reported the president-elect to be "quite annoyed, quite upset because [the report] contained what he thought was a very unrealistic program." JFK also had to face the press after his secretary released the seven-page study. Insiders remembered that "we had one or two [newspapers] delay headline, and we were attacked by the conservative press." The suggestions also enraged Catholics who feared their struggling colleges would be left out of the federal largesse. But however annoyed he was privately, Kennedy hedged in front of the public. He called the ideas of "great value" even if he did not "know whether we have the resources immediately to take on the whole program." He allowed that "we'll have to decide the degree of need and set up a list of priorities." Elementary and secondary education, in fact, ranked seventh on the list of the administration's top concerns, just two places above postsecondary instruction.[14]

JFK's narrow victory also left him without the coattails to get much through a still-divided Congress and Democratic Party. Liberals actually faced fierce opposition from some of the highest-ranking members of the education committees—notably, Senator Lister Hill, Representative Carl Elliott, and Oregon Congresswoman Edith Green.[15]

Green shared her senior colleagues' fears of the federal overreach that had once terrified academics, still angered southern Democrats, and continued to hamstring social welfare legislation for a range of issues, including education. Green's anxiety, along with her concerns for women's rights and inequality, stemmed from her years of teaching in Salem schools as well as her family's Populist Party roots. Her eagerness to improve Oregon classrooms brought her into politics after World War II. She became much more involved in the Oregon Education Association and turned her attention to building the state's Democratic Party in the early 1950s, when Republicans dominated the state. She routinely addressed teacher and civic groups to assail strident anti-Communists' attacks on progressive education. She won her seat in the House in 1954 by advocating for more government spending, supporting trade unionism, and toeing the liberal line on social issues. But Green was never quite comfortable in the party's liberal wing, particularly as the country's political terrain continued to shift. She fought for "the issues . . . closest to my heart," which, she explained to a reporter in 1957, "center around the education and welfare of the nation's children." She had been unsure during the 1958 NDEA debates whether loans or grants represented the best method to support undergraduates. She did know that federal support must come without the control many educators and conservatives had long feared. She eagerly headed up the Oregon effort to elect Kennedy, but equivocated over supporting his administration's early failed effort to provide all nonprofit colleges with construction loans and scholarships for talented, needy undergraduates. Lawmakers managed to agree to reauthorize NDEA only in 1961, which hardly resolved the conflicts that had made the temporary program little more than a legislative band-aid just three years earlier.[16]

The president had stressed continued unaffordability in his failed attempt to convince Congress to do more. "The average cost of higher education today," Kennedy emphasized in a special 1962 education message to Congress, was "up nearly 90 percent since 1950 and still rising." Students and parents paid more than $1,750 a year. The roughly $7,000 needed to pay for a four-year degree was not cheap in 1960, when, as JFK noted, half of American families had incomes below $5,600. "Industrious students can earn a part of this," he said, and "they or their families can borrow a part of it." But "they cannot be expected to borrow $4,000 for each talented son or daughter that deserves to go to college." Even undergraduate defense loans, the president emphasized, could only "fill part of this gap."[17]

Kennedy and his aides struggled to maneuver around continued congressional deadlock on aid connected to so many larger ideological issues. Staff tried to cajole lawmakers into transforming NDEA loans into de facto grants by substantially changing the repayment requirements. Green liked that July 1962 suggestion, but Republican Ohio Congressman John Ashbrook called the "nonreimbursable loan . . . semantic doubletalk." That defeat and others, Kennedy aide and former Harvard dean McGeorge Bundy contended, led both Education Commissioner Sterling McMurrin and Health Education and Welfare Director Abraham Ribicoff to resign in fall 1962. But their departures gave the president a chance to recruit Cleveland mayor Anthony Celebrezze and Francis Keppel to help navigate DC's deep divisions.[18]

Kennedy's close friend Keppel seemed a natural pick to head the Office of Education. The Harvard alum straddled the elite Ivy League and a new generation of educators who embraced Clark Kerr's enthusiasm for mass higher education. Keppel had served fourteen years as the Harvard Graduate School of Education's dean without ever having even attempted a PhD. He had nevertheless been comfortable among academics. His father had been dean of Columbia College and later president of the Carnegie Corporation, which gave him the opportunity to work closely with Conant. Young Francis left for Rome in 1938 to pursue sculpting but quickly gave up on that dream. He instead returned to Cambridge, where he first served as his alma mater's assistant dean of freshmen and then as secretary of the Joint Army and Navy Committee on Welfare and Recreation. He eventually enlisted but did not use his GI Bill benefits for an advanced degree. He instead accepted the deanship of Harvard's Graduate School of Education in 1948, when Conant had an acute need for someone to oversee its expansion. Keppel quickly proved far less reactionary than his boss and other faculty. He had long feared that schools failed to meet poor children's educational needs. He encouraged experimental curriculum reform, educational television, programmed learning, and team teaching, all reminiscent of the innovative teaching in Hilda Smith's

Workers Education Program and the pedagogy GIs had demanded. Keppel also crafted a new opportunity for alumni to earn a Master of Arts in Teaching, which required a year of coursework as well as an internship to prepare them to be public school instructors.[19]

Keppel brought such forward-thinking sensibilities to an Office of Education better poised since NDEA's fitful rollout to craft K-12 and postsecondary policy. He eagerly strategized with Celebrezze and Bureau of the Budget staff, who suggested the administration pursue an omnibus bill that emphasized education's importance to "aiding people—from childhood to old age," instead of the need for better schools or more government programs. Citizens need to be reminded that education was "integrally connected with a person throughout his life, to his freedom, his individual social and economic welfare and in turn to the freedom, social, and economic wellbeing of the Nation." Only more schooling could prepare individuals and the country for future "technology, automation, leisure, urban, rural change, unemployment and population increase." These talking points very much echoed what many New Dealers had concluded in the 1930s, what Zook Commission members had emphasized in the wake of the GI Bill's rollout, and what a new cohort of academic leaders (like Kerr) had begun to assert. But Budget Bureau stalwarts did not share the loftiest of those ambitions. They wanted federal aid to provide only incentives and small breakthroughs that might eventually spark more sweeping change. After all, allocations seemed unlikely to ever match the $20 billion spent annually on just the country's public and private colleges. Keppel found that strategy appealing and embraced their omnibus proposal, which did the most for colleges and universities. "The best hope one could have would be to keep a program before Congress," he later explained, "and try to keep the lobbyists from killing each other." Celebrezze still dreaded "the religious question or the racial question" that invariably blocked education aid. "The thing we had to do," he remembered insisting in a cabinet meeting, was to get a "civil rights bill which would cover this."[20]

Kennedy's team first took on the seemingly easier task of passing the administration's preferred education legislation. That torturous process eventually severed K-12 and postsecondary federal aid but actually offered undergraduates and colleges something far better than loans. The proposed National Education Improvement Act only offered credit for college construction as well as, what Kennedy called, "selective stimulative and, where possible, transitional" aid designed to improve existing K-12 school systems in order to make them more independent. Keppel tasked himself with getting Catholic, private, and public college administrators "to shut up about things they didn't like and only talk about things they did like." The commissioner could not stop lawmakers from breaking up the proposal into four separate pieces of legislation they heavily amended during deliberations. The surviving bill offered no direct help for K-12 schools. The Higher Education Facilities Act (HEFA) allocated $1 billion over five years to build postsecondary facilities but also expanded opportunities for vocational programs, public libraries, teacher training opportunities, and national defense loans. The agreement lawmakers reached in their conference committee represented a breakthrough of sorts because religious institutions could receive funds as long as college staff did not use the money for buildings dedicated to spiritual purposes. Passage subsequently seemed likely in late fall, and a November 6 House vote registered 258 in favor and just 92 opposed. Many pundits considered Senate approval a given even before JFK's November 22 assassination. But national mourning did not produce a lopsided December 10 vote: only fifty-four supported the bill.[21]

Borrowing Breakthrough

When Lyndon Johnson signed the limited legislation into law just six days later, the Texan previewed his administration's determination to pass far more monumental social welfare legislation, particularly for K-12 and postsecondary schooling. Though the former NYA director lauded lawmakers for passing "the most significant education bill . . . in the history of the Republic," he still cautioned that "these new measures will still not do the whole job of extending educational opportunities to all who want and can benefit by them, nor in meeting our growing national needs." The act merely highlighted that government must "battle the ancient enemies of mankind, illiteracy and poverty and disease"—the evils that New Dealers had been unable to vanquish during the politically tumultuous 1930s and early 1940s, despite Democratic control of Congress and the White House.[22]

Scholars have long agreed that the word *ambitious* best described Johnson. But popular memory and historical assessments of the man, his mission, his record, and his legacy have remained mixed, particularly in regard to executive power, legislative strategy, social welfare policy, civil rights, and the Vietnam War. Many have likewise criticized his K-12 and postsecondary programs, even as they acknowledge his efforts in directing NYA's Texas offices and, as Aubrey Williams instructed, giving special consideration to young African Americans. Often overlooked is the young representative's defense of Williams on the House floor, where Johnson temporarily saved an agency so vital to youth, the academy, and the war effort. It has seemed more important, in retrospect, that he had already begun to learn how lucrative working with business owners could be as the Roosevelt administration steadily built the vaunted arsenal of democracy. Johnson did a lot for the Brown & Root executives contracting with the federal government, helping to turn that small construction firm into a powerful Houston-based defense enterprise. But his constituents, as well as business executives and Johnson himself, also profited from the federal pork he procured for the Lone Star State.[23]

Education Office staffers would later say they never suspected that the "Master of the Senate" they knew would go on to become known as the "Education President." As a congressman, Johnson had introduced proposals for a scholarship program, tuition tax credit, and government-insured student lending. Insiders remembered that he proposed two failed student loan bills only after defense lending proved wildly popular with the public. He even sent copies of his 1959 and 1960 suggestions to college officials for comments just before his 1960 presidential bid. The presidents of Yale, Harvard, Brandeis, Notre Dame, and Princeton all endorsed the purportedly self-supporting plan to provide private money for colleges to lend at a low interest rate. As with the federal mortgage program, the government only guaranteed that lenders would be repaid. That strategy failed to impress senators and the financial aid experts still working out the details of NDEA's complicated, underfunded campus loan funds. The Education Office appointees offered only faint praise during hearings, one guessing it "would not do much harm," but still considering it unfair to needy students. Undergraduates "who borrowed $4,000 would have to repay more than $5,700." And, he added, "Five percent interest seemed awfully high and $5,700 a lot of money."[24]

Passing something similar was hardly a foregone conclusion when Johnson signed the Higher Education Facilities Act in 1963. He understood, arguably better than anyone, that a substantial educational overhaul, prolonged war on poverty, and broad expansion of the social safety net would depend on a decisive victory for Democrats in the 1964 election. The incumbent had reason to doubt he would even win. Ongoing congressional stalemates over segregation, inequality, religious freedom, federal power, taxing, and spending hinted at the steadily building power and success of conservative insurgencies some Council on Financial Aid to Education powerbrokers funded. The Republican Party's right wing had already frustrated various agendas at local, state, and federal levels, stymied congressional efforts to expand on New Deal promises for economic security, and made political inroads in southern, western, and even steel belt suburbs. That gradual metropolitan, regional, and national party realignment threatened Johnson before his famous prediction that signing the 1964 Civil Rights Act had "delivered the South to the Republican Party for a long time to come." The Texan had already faced a formidable conservative Republican opponent for his Senate seat in 1960, the former southern Democrat John Tower, who lost the race but handily won the 1961 special election to fill the seat after Johnson assumed the vice presidency.[25]

That upset did not predict the outcome of the 1964 primary and general elections but still offered a glimpse of the future of American politics. Schooling figured prominently in the 1964 contests. Education had already become a minor feature of the 1964 War on Poverty, whose programs included work training, adult literacy, and a revival of work-study. But Johnson singled out K-12 classrooms as a central pillar of a much more education-focused Great Society in his famous 1964 Michigan commencement address.[26]

The president also waded into the fight over tuition tax breaks, a flashpoint in the larger ideological wars over taxing, spending, and government-guaranteed social welfare. Liberals and moderates had adamantly opposed college fee write-offs in the 1950s. After Senator Abraham Ribicoff, a freshman Democrat and former governor of Connecticut, introduced a proposal in early 1964, the idea gained traction in Congress but roiled the White House. Ribicoff had, after all, headed the Department of Health, Education, and Welfare (HEW) under Kennedy. Ribicoff's suggestion reflected his service as an ex officio member of the Yale Corporation and the demands of wealthy constituents, who generally enrolled their children in private colleges. An early but narrow defeat in February did not stop Republicans from including proposed write-offs in the GOP's 1964 platform instead of earmarks for campus construction projects, student loans, and undergraduate scholarships. Barry Goldwater tried to cash in on the loophole's increasing popularity as his presidential campaign sputtered, a political move that unintentionally helped the Johnson campaign. Even though the Democratic incumbent had made a similar proposal as a senator, he eagerly attacked Goldwater's motivations: the privileged heir to a chain of successful department stores was advocating a form of aid that would benefit wealthy families most. Notably, that attack reflected the argument made to convince Eisenhower and his aides to oppose Goldwater's idea of making such deductions central to the NDEA instead of grants or loans.[27]

Voters initially seemed overwhelmingly to reject Goldwater's conservatism. The senator only carried Arizona, Alabama, Louisiana, Georgia, Mississippi, and South Carolina. The returns also looked grim for Republicans: Johnson won more than 60 percent of the popular vote and Democrats secured 68-seat and 295-seat majorities in the Senate and the House. Many CEOs only backed and funded Johnson because even though they agreed with Goldwater politically they feared wasting their money on the obvious loser. None wanted to sacrifice their influence over Johnson, who had secretly promised to cut the budget and keep the business tax cuts Kennedy had signed. Those tycoons were a critical part of the new Republican base the Goldwater campaign had solidified in 1964, when South Carolina Senator Strom Thurmond dramatically changed his affiliation to the GOP. That switch foretold of a new Republican base that would help elect Ronald Reagan to the White House sixteen years later but, at the time, highlighted how the stark divides among Democrats had worsened since the New Deal.[28]

Johnson knew those political fault lines well and wasted no time pushing a domestic agenda that would, despite his political coattails, be hard to get through Congress. The Texan demanded both staffers and party stalwarts try to pass a lot before the upcoming 1966 midterms, when the party was sure to lose its congressional supermajority. Johnson even had aides preemptively create fourteen task forces in the midst of his 1964 presidential campaign. Staff wanted them to have reports and policy proposals ready just a week after Election Day, early into the president's predicted honeymoon period with Congress.[29]

Federal K-12 and higher education policy breakthroughs seemed possible then. Lawmakers had passed HEFA before Johnson and his aides spent much of 1964 pushing for poverty programs and civil rights guarantees. The former had included important schooling provisions, which had established education as a part of the White House's expansive social welfare agenda. As Kennedy aides recognized, the 1964 Civil Rights Act's anti-discrimination decrees had also done much to end the controversy over segregated schools' receiving federal funds, whether for dorms, classrooms, research projects, supplies, or student assistance.[30]

Better odds and looming deadlines did not help the education task force reach a consensus. Johnson's schooling workgroup looked nothing like his predecessor's. A former member of Kennedy's transition-period education task force, the liberal Republican John Gardner, chaired the group of K-12 and postsecondary educators from public universities, private postsecondary schools, parochial colleges, and Black postsecondary institutions. Gardner brought the group together only four times—and some of its most notable members, including Clark Kerr, missed every meeting. Despite those absences, there were plenty of bitter disagreements, previewing how raucous the congressional debate over White House proposals would be. Task force members rejected tuition tax credits, even though some Johnson insiders considered those regressive write-offs a good idea. Gardner's team also disagreed over whether the government should fund a vast network of education centers, research and development labs, urban education initiatives, and state education departments, whose appointees Keppel would later describe as "the feeblest bunch of second-rate, or fifth-rate, educators who combined educational incompetence with bureaucratic immovability." Gardner cobbled together many of the group's ideas, as well as suggestions for student assistance, in his eighty-three-page report. But it warned, as some academics had feared for years, that loans, scholarships, and work-study opportunities might "encourage schools to up the cost of education." Fees had already increased substantially during and after the GI Bill's rollout. Just as importantly, HEFA's recent passage had made directly funding campuses seem feasible enough that Gardner decided to call for federally funded campus improvements to avoid passing those costs on to students.[31]

The task force considered such support especially important for "developing institutions." That phrase was a euphemism befitting an era when politicians and policymakers wanted to appear color-blind and obscure attempts to thwart and support desegregation. The legislation actually defined what historically Black colleges and universities were; henceforth they increasingly became labeled HBCUs instead of Negro colleges. But White House staff purposefully chose a phrase for this section's title that could describe many institutions, including financially shaky nonprofits. Journalists occasionally noted that this "developing institutions" section could "particularly" strengthen "small Negro colleges in the South," but only years later did aides publicly admit they had wanted to hide their intent to assist HBCUs. Those campuses had done much to give African Americans the chance to pursue college degrees, but had struggled to accommodate the growing number of applicants since the GI Bill. Twenty years after the legislation's passage, HBCUs still lacked secure funding, top faculty, a solid curriculum, and respect from leading education associations. Kerr later explained to interviewers that task force participants had tacitly agreed that "half the money would go to historically black colleges, the other half would go to private white colleges." But "you couldn't" lay that out in the bill even though "it was intended that way."[32]

The administration's proposal to Congress included the seemingly universal effort to promote equal opportunity and the direct funding for which this legislation became most famous. Insiders especially wanted to strengthen public and private institutions in metropolitan areas. The generally remote land-grants had gained the most from the federal largesse meted out since the Morrill Act. By the 1960s, they seemed far removed from urban areas, which, as Kerr and other experts pointed out, had pressing needs for the many benefits of the modern university. White House insiders were also convinced by Keppel that education legislation must support campus libraries, as the 1963 law had done, and pushed for the creation of the Teacher Corps to address the staffing shortfall in K-12 schools.[33]

But the Johnson administration still continued the tradition of prioritizing student assistance. They envisioned funding the kind of financial aid packages colleges had offered for years. Undergraduates would not get a free ride but a mix of scholarships, work-study opportunities, and loans given out by campus financial aid officers.[34]

The president and Treasury staff particularly liked a loan program, which maintained the public-private tradition of offering government-guaranteed financial products in lieu of robust social welfare support. The administration's plan borrowed a lot from the federal mortgage and the National

Defense Student Loan programs as well as state higher education assistance corporation schemes. Credit opportunities for lower- and middle-income students would, like the already popular NDEA offerings, have a low interest rate that the government would subsidize. Undergraduates would not have to demonstrate need for credit they would pay back within ten years of leaving college, whether or not they graduated. Many policymakers, at the time, considered a decade to be a long-term loan, even though it was a third the length of the still popular federal mortgage program. Policymakers intentionally labeled the Guaranteed Student Loan Program (GSLP) "indirect" because, unlike the defense act program, private lenders put up the money in a way similar to Johnson's earlier failed bills and many state initiatives, including the Massachusetts experiment and the New York program helping to creatively finance the State University of New York's expansion. Bankers kept the money earned from interest instead of investing those returns back into the loan funds campuses ran, either on their own or with NDEA money. Like the federal mortgage program that had transformed homeownership in the 1930s, GSLP guaranteed that bankers would be repaid, an approach far different than allocating money for the defense loans that financial aid officers controlled. That choice reflected White House aides' hopes that this federally guaranteed loan program would nurture a student loan industry in the way that federally assured credit for homes had grown the mortgage sector since the Depression. Home buyers had to put at least 10 percent down, and their properties could be repossessed, yet the suggestions for guaranteed student lending in the 1960s included no such safeguards for a far riskier financial product. The fact that lenders could not ask for upfront deposits, much less take away a person's knowledge or degree, had always made the money students borrowed from colleges and philanthropies difficult to recover.[35]

Johnson insiders proceeded quickly, cautiously, and strategically to get congressional approval. Keppel remembered the president's demand to "get it done, get it done fast, or don't try it now." Keppel appreciated the emphasis on speed, which reflected Johnson's sense of how quickly he might, like FDR, lose the opportunity to pass substantial reforms. Johnson's staff swiftly and shrewdly divided the education suggestions for the 1965 legislative sessions into separate bills for K-12 and postsecondary instruction. This choice reflected the nuts-and-bolts differences in authority and structure of those schooling levels as well as the lessons learned from the Kennedy White

House's omnibus education legislation, which lawmakers had divided into four bills. Recalling that only HEFA had survived that 1963 brawl, Johnson aides pursued elementary and secondary schooling aid first; passage of the Elementary and Secondary Education Act in 1965 would represent the bigger political breakthrough.[36]

Securing K-12 funding hardly guaranteed that the White House's higher education proposals would sail through Congress in the summer of 1965. Lawmakers on both sides of the aisle remained far too divided on the seemingly small issues, with liberals and conservatives continuing to fight over what remained of the New Deal. Republicans, particularly the conservatives, outright opposed much of the bill. Johnson's staff also could not count on Democrats. Aides preemptively took Edith Green to lunch "simply to 'massage her ego.'" They warned that the Oregon representative "opposed . . . the idea of guaranteed loans because of potential abuses in the system." Green had also become more interested in tax credits but still preferred increasing the income limits on NDEA loans so that more middle-income families qualified. She still joined Oregon Senator Wayne Morse in submitting the White House bills to Congress. Their Democratic colleagues tended to demand both institutional financial aid and student assistance but remained divided on the proposal's details, as did the many witnesses from education, labor, and business circles. The AFL-CIO's director of education, Lawrence Rogin, testified before Congress that "the best way in which to assist young people to obtain a higher education is by providing tuition-free colleges, junior colleges, and universities within reasonable distance of the student's home." Academics, in contrast, were just excited for additional direct support and student assistance. None, including those from the major educational associations, raised fears of federal control. They instead lauded Title I's direct assistance, a CUNY dean even labeling it "additional muscle."[37]

Lawmakers and witnesses also wrangled over the "developing institutions" section that tried, however covertly, to address the historic inequities in both the academy and federal social welfare policy. Higher-ups from the Health, Education, and Welfare department and Office of Education liked to say the section had been inspired by a proposal Green had previously introduced. HEW Secretary Celebrezze described Title III as a response to the fact that "many of our developing institutions of higher education are striving for higher standards of quality but are short of the means to achieve them." They lacked the necessary credentials, research facilities, and instructors. "This bill should be open to all qualified young Americans," Education Office personnel reiterated under questioning. The administration, in fact, had "no position . . . on picking out particular categories of students, be they veterans or women or people of a given race." Aides also assured lawmakers they had no intention of assisting what Green called "degree-granting mills." By "developing institutions" they meant poorly endowed nonprofit colleges that had only a few donors, a handful of degree programs, poorly stocked library shelves, barely any labs, only a smattering of professors with PhDs, numerous dropouts resuming their studies, and significant numbers of transfer students. A representative of small Protestant, Catholic, secular and community colleges, Alfred Hill, testified that they would use earmarks to expand and continue "preserving the cherished American tradition of diversity and independence in education" that Green, wealthy donors, and many others prized. Some educators acknowledged that this section would help HBCUs even if they were happy to add, as Elvis Stahr of the American Council on Education did in Senate testimony, that "it will be equally helpful in strengthening other institutions who have predominantly white enrollment." Such predictions failed to satisfy hostile lawmakers, like Green, who bristled at hearing the Education Office say her ideas had inspired this plank. She and some of her colleagues grilled HBCU leaders, demanding to know how Title III would help the schools integrate white students into their student bodies. Yet no one made the same inquiries about whether Title III would enable more women to enroll. American Association of University Women leaders, for example, endorsed all the bill's titles and noted that scholarships had helped many notable women pursue their educational ambitions.[38]

Such arguments highlighted how much the debate over student assistance had shifted since the 1930s, when many New Dealers doubted most Americans would want, need, or be capable of pursuing advanced degrees. Policymakers no longer sought tuition help to stop young people from radicalizing, to keep them out of a saturated labor market, to remove them from welfare rolls, to bolster the academy's finances, or to improve the nation's defenses. Lawmakers instead sought ways to ensure that the majority of Americans would have the chance to enroll. That goal presumed mass higher education was feasible, desirable, and advantageous. It also assumed admission alone signaled a student's likelihood of success while studying and after graduation. Mass higher education had become a way to ensure upward mobility for a far bigger share of the citizenry since, by then, degrees generally guaranteed entry into or the ability to stay in the middle and professional classes. Those white-collar workers' skills seemed likely to become even more important to the kind of post-industrial utopia that Kerr and other social scientists considered imminent.

Left unsaid, in this era of color-blind politics on both sides of the aisle, was the assumption that more tuition assistance programs would actually guarantee equal opportunities to the many immigrants and citizens historically excluded from the academy. They had been left with few options but the long-reviled proprietary schools, which begged lawmakers to permit them to be eligible for Title IV's grants, loans, and work-study opportunities. Lawmakers had no interest in letting for-profits offer this help. Liberals particularly hoped tuition assistance might covertly hasten desegregation in the wake of the Civil Rights Act's passage. Offering financial aid officers more help to dole out funds seemed a politically safe way of improving the likelihood of African Americans, in particular, being able to get into and afford any non-profit postsecondary institution, not just the HBCUs Title III was supposed to covertly bolster.[39]

HEW officials testifying before Congress also shied away from explicitly discussing racial inequality when discussing how unaffordable higher education remained. They instead emphasized that many Americans struggled to finance degrees. Of the one million high school graduates who did not go to college in 1960, 42 percent reported that cost stopped them from applying. Those officials drew attention to the Americans whom Green most wanted to help: middle-income families making between $6,000 and $12,000 a year. Those parents might be able to afford to enroll one child but paying fees for siblings was unimaginable since their household incomes likely disqualified them from scholarship and loan programs. Even if parents could take out the roughly $5,000 needed to send two children to college, the interest rates were often prohibitively high.[40]

Campus administrators and financial aid officers helped HEW appointees make the case for the federal tuition assistance that academics had fitfully embraced since the New Deal's experiment with work-study. Many endorsed all of Title IV's tuition assistance options, including campus personnel who negotiated support through USAF and state-guarantee agencies. Those in the trenches assisting undergraduates hoped the defense loan program would continue, knowing it had already helped many students finish degrees. Current and future undergraduates, they underscored, needed the chance to work part-time, receive a small grant, and take out a federally guaranteed loan. Though campus staff discussed potentially burdensome administrative costs of this option, they still remained convinced these credit lines were far superior to what states and USAF offered. None feared the federal control that once terrified academics. Education association higher-ups instead lauded this provision for enabling college personnel to craft the support packages that had become increasingly popular since Eisenhower signed NDEA. "Experience tells us," one expert emphasized, "that no one form of student aid can be expected to do the trick." He had such faith in lending's role in financing degrees for all four years of college that he boldly suggested lawmakers add a guaranteed loan program for middle-income parents, who faced "educational costs too large to be met out of their current income."[41]

Lawmakers never really considered lending to parents, but they and many witnesses fought over offering them write-offs, an issue at the heart of the larger ongoing war over taxing and spending. Deductions remained popular with conservative Republicans (including Johnson's Senate successor, John Tower) but also a few Democrats, including Ribicoff and Vice President Hubert Humphrey. Leading liberals actually sponsored a bill that used deductions to lower college costs for the middle class. Administrators of private institutions, especially those at the helm of the Association of American Colleges and the Citizens Committee for Higher Education, liked the credits since parents could deduct any fee increases, as Barry Goldwater had emphasized during NDEA hearings and his failed presidential campaign. Top economists vehemently emphasized that hikes needed to be avoided. Students and parents would not necessarily get that money back after April 15. Instead, many Americans would likely find themselves priced out. Treasury officials also predicted this supposed benefit would cost $1.25 billion the first year alone. HEW officials emphasized that reduced revenue would do little to help the low- and middle-income students Title IV promised to assist. High-income earners would instead benefit. Those testifying did not explicitly mention that this cohort remained disproportionately white and could more easily gain admission to the expensive colleges that could basically ensure alumni remained in the middle, professional, and upper classes. Land-grant and state university higher-ups also only alluded to long-standing inequities when they declared deductions would effectively "discriminate against large groups of students." An American Council on Education representative foresaw "a genuine potential for encouraging both private and public institutions to raise their charges." He warned that "every time you raise a fee, you cut somebody off the bottom of the ladder." But such predictions did not frighten the majority of senators. More than half embraced write-offs.[42]

Such enthusiasm reflected what had by then become broad support for federal student assistance on Capitol Hill and across the country. Many lawmakers liked the idea of a support package that financial aid staff crafted for an individual student's needs. No one could expect a free ride from the federal government; like so many earlier young strivers, every student would have to cobble together the money to afford fees, books, and living expenses. That approach also kept with elite institutions' historic practice of offering a mix of help, which other institutions had started to embrace after the NDEA loan program's rollout. Education association lobbyists testified their recent survey had found that public and private university administrators overwhelmingly embraced combining aid as opposed to only offering students one means of assistance in the form of a government loan, tax credit, or federal scholarship.[43]

Yet academics and Johnson insiders still struggled to convince lawmakers that undergraduates needed many different sources of support. Many in Congress, HEW staff realized, were too young to remember the NYA. Aides emphasized its revival had already proven a formidable weapon in the War on Poverty, but, they reiterated, the $71 million spent had not even come close to meeting the need. More funds were required to provide jobs in the assistance packages Johnson's education task force had envisioned offering to every undergraduate, not just those enrolled in colleges with campus and NDEA loan funds. White House higher-ups also pushed for the scholarships many Democrats wanted. Yet congressional liberals sharply disagreed over whether merit or need should determine who received help. They also fought over whether campuses, state education boards, or federal officials should distribute that aid. Democrats only started to win over Republicans when they acquiesced to capping support to half of a student's predicted educational expenses. Yet liberal lawmakers still struggled to save the proposal. They ended up renaming it an "Educational Opportunity Grant" and emphasizing the provision as an anti-poverty measure, which, in the era's evolving color-blind rhetoric, hid the intention to help students of color, particularly African Americans. Keppel even agreed with lawmakers eager to label grants a "student incentive pattern" since "'scholarship' has a fuzzy meaning."[44]

But borrowing, despite the NDEA lending program's popularity, proved the most divisive Title IV provision. The inherent riskiness of student loans permeated the debates. The default rates on defense loans particularly alarmed dubious lawmakers. HEW officials admitted that borrowers had missed payments on roughly $3 million of the $18 million due since the program started. "Eventually we will recoup our losses," Celebrezze predicted, on the $443 million loaned. Education Office calculations still made NDEA repayment rules seem better than the commercial loans with higher interest rates, shorter repayment periods, and no opportunities for deferment or forgiveness. "These [defense loans] are not the best risks to begin with," the HEW secretary acknowledged, "they are not insured loans, they are not cosigned . . . , and there is no security put up for them." Many in danger of default simply seemed to have forgotten to apply for deferments after joining the military or becoming disabled. Johnson insiders also pointed out that Education Office personnel had been working with financial aid officers across the country to improve collections. Such assurances failed to satisfy senators and representatives leery of offering another opportunity to borrow. They grilled campus staffers in favor of defense and guaranteed loans, many of whom assured lawmakers that procedures had greatly improved. "Loss in the terms of ultimate nonrepayment would be very small," an Indiana University financial aid officer projected. "If the people live," another land-grant administrator assured lawmakers, "they repay it."[45]

White House staffers, witnesses, and lawmakers still went back and forth on whether the government should continue the NDEA option or experiment with guaranteed credit—or do both. For example, the Education Office's director of student loans shared an informal study showing how much more expensive it was than the NDEA scheme. Another senior staffer, Clarence Deakins, liked the White House's indirect offering but did not want it to replace defense loans, as Johnson hoped. Despite reports that at least some campuses continued to use this assistance to bid on brains, he emphasized that defense act campus loan funds had actually provided support for low-income students. He thus considered this new guaranteed offering necessary to provide "loans of convenience for middle and upper-income families" who needed "an opportunity to spread the cost of their children's education over a period of years." Deakins advocated for an interest subsidy, but raised no objection to loans having to be countersigned since "it is accepted practice in business to require an endorser." That stipulation did not concern the many university administrators and financial aid officers in favor of federally guaranteed loans. Keppel reminded hesitant senators that this option was intended "to educate the young, not set up a system under which somebody is going to make a killing off of them." That veiled warning against the private loans USAF offered did not satisfy lawmakers, who doubted the necessity of more federal tuition assistance options. Disagreements also remained among the Democrats and Republicans in favor of supporting more borrowing. They quarreled over whether credit should be extended to those with the most aptitude or to those with the most need, as well as about who should negotiate and give out these credit lines.[46]

Leading bankers vehemently opposed letting the federal government broker those deals. Even though a similar arrangement had transformed the mortgage industry in the 1930s, testifying financiers recoiled at offering a low-interest option even if repayment was guaranteed. USAF's president insisted that the nonprofit could handle student lending far better than the government. He refuted the evidence about defense loan debt collections that Education Office staffers and financial aid officers had presented. He hoped the program might eventually be phased out. "Rapid and continuing growth of State and private loan insurance programs," this CEO insisted, were already providing the credit necessary to supplement the savings, grants, and part-time jobs needed to pay for college. "A Federal guarantee," he predicted, "might have the entirely unintended effect of putting non-Federal loan guarantee plans out of business." If lawmakers insisted on keeping this assistance in the bill, this USAF executive demanded it be "a last resort" for colleges with no other state or private options for securing guaranteed credit for undergraduates. Still, no lender or state should be forced to follow the federal regulations for student borrowing laid out in Title IV. He brazenly suggested it would be far better for Congress to lend campuses the money needed to join USAF.[47]

Those arguments appalled many Washington powerbrokers. Such public-private arrangements had already become, like government-guaranteed financial products, a notable feature of American social welfare programs. Yet giving state and private institutions the money to contract with USAF still seemed a step too far for Johnson insiders and some lawmakers. "You are asking us to take quite a gamble in going along with you," Jacob Javits noted. The liberal New York Republican joined other senators in doubting the approach would guarantee equal opportunities. Alarmed lawmakers wondered if undergraduates would be able to easily obtain credit, if banks would be willing to participate, and if the loans would be far more lucrative to lenders than the young people who needed help.[48]

Financiers worked as hard to assuage dubious Democrats and Republicans as Council on Financial Aid to Education stalwarts had done to undermine public higher education's 1950s expansion. Like Marion Folsom and the other business executives who had carved out a place for private enterprise in 1930s social welfare legislation, American Banking Association (ABA) representatives begrudgingly supported Title IV's grants, work-study opportunities, and national defense loans. They presumed the Eisenhower-era program would become unnecessary if the federal government did not offer guaranteed loans. They insisted that demand would ensure state and private programs increased to meet needs. USAF also inundated the White House with proof that it was all students, parents, and colleges needed. Bankers also joined forces with ABA officials to aggressively lobby lawmakers, the organization even publicly demanding financiers extend more credit to students. This pressure made House fights especially contentious. Representatives eventually passed a bill without the loans Green had come to consider an unnecessary provision that would surely become a boondoggle.[49]

That omission terrified parents and students, who had been banking on an additional opportunity to borrow. Citizens had, after all, become accustomed to creatively financing basic needs. They wrote to the president asking about his promise of "incentives for those who wish to learn" throughout the Higher Education Act debates. A mother sought help to afford her daughter's training to become a special-needs teacher, but did not seem to qualify. Their "Hebrew" faith, despite the Civil Rights Act, remained "another barrier, we come across." A disabled veteran admitted he had never been able to get the kind of job to enable him to save for his children's college educations. His son had won a small scholarship to pursue his dreams of teaching music, but the dishonorably discharged GI still wondered: "Is there any way we can be assured our son . . . will be able to go to college?" Another parent explained that one of her four sons had a demanding job at a lumber mill that left him too exhausted to also study for a degree. She hoped "for any funds or loan" he could get to study full-time. Students wrote in, frightened they could not get advances. A young woman had spent the summer after her freshman year working and had desperately applied to a North Carolina bank for a loan to help her afford her second year. She was informed it was far too late, which made returning to Fayetteville State College unimaginable for a woman "willing to pay back any loans I might secure." A Missouri undergraduate also needed a $1,500 advance after medical bills and family needs had emptied her savings account of the money set aside for books, living expenses, and campus fees.[50]

The president and his staff dearly wanted them and millions of other young people to be able to finance at least some college costs. The administration's faith in the Guaranteed Student Loan Program was a part of complicated fiscal and political calculations rooted in thirty years of creatively underwriting, not generously funding, public-private social welfare guarantees. Commissioner of Education Harold Howe later explained that the guaranteed loan program appealed to the president as "a device which would make money available to students who wanted to go to higher education institutions, but would do so without impact on the federal budget, or as direct an impact as NDEA loans had." That inclination also reflected Johnson's memory of how borrowing had helped him finish his teacher's college degree in the 1920s, making his political coming of age during the Roosevelt administration possible. New Dealers had done much to tame capitalism by offering homebuyers well-regulated mortgages, not numerous public housing options. Johnson's education office appointees even publicly deemed the 1934 National Housing Act the "framework for revolutionary lending methods." They did not emphasize their hope to nurture a new industry by guaranteeing lenders would be paid. That federal assurance had been compelling to central bankers to offer well-regulated mortgages to the white working- and middle-class Americans whose payments had first revived and then sustained the housing industry. Such advances for higher education had been unimaginable in the 1930s when liberals first experimented with work-study and passed banking regulations limiting the kind of risk endemic to the student loans campuses and philanthropies had increasingly offered in the speculative

1920s. Those pools of money had a lot in common with loan funds NDEA helped start at campuses across the country thirty years later. Voters embraced those defense-targeted credit lines in the late 1950s, when the first state education assistance corporations had been making arrangements with bankers to provide tuition assistance. By 1964, New York's initiative alone had generated $80 million in loans to finance the rapid expansion of the State University of New York that Conant had considered promising. From the point of view of Johnson and his advisers, a federal partnership with the banking industry subsequently seemed likely to be as profitable and revolutionary for colleges, students, and lenders as the federal mortgage program had been for builders, financiers, and aspiring white, male homeowners. The money saved on building campuses for a Great Society could then theoretically be devoted to wars abroad against Communism and at home against inequality. Such spending would not require lawmakers to reverse the Kennedy tax cuts still popular with the conservative CEOs who had turned their backs on Goldwater and sided with Johnson in the 1964 election.[51]

Losing the loan program also seemed likely to stop some lawmakers from supporting the scholarship provisions. Many had only accepted grants as a part of a package of limited support. They still wanted students to borrow some of the money needed upfront and then pay back the debt after they graduated and presumably landed well-paying jobs. Sacrificing another form of assistance would likely leave undergraduates with little more than the regressive tax credits, which would go against the spirit of the Great Society, undercut the War on Poverty, and rob the federal government of the revenue the White House wanted to direct toward other parts of its expensive domestic and foreign agendas.[52]

The White House sought a détente with bankers in summer 1965. The president first tried to use his private connections to beseech ABA officials to stay out of congressional student loan fights. They refused. So insiders invited top financiers to the White House to hammer out an agreement. Lenders wanted a three-year trial program, more than what the House had proposed but less than the five years Senate enthusiasts wanted. This federal lending scheme had to include allocations for states and private lending options that had increased since Massachusetts legislators had first worked out such a public-private partnership. Moreover, campuses could only use the guaranteed federal program if the education commissioner considered those resources inadequate. That federal fail-safe seemed unlikely to be triggered, since USAF was so intent on building partnerships with postsecondary schools and donors.[53]

A Legacy of Lending

Those summits helped secure HEA's passage, with ABA officials telling the press in September 1965 that it fully endorsed a "stand-by" federally guaranteed student loan program. Earmarks to "assist state and private non-profit programs" seemed more than enough to entice "private lenders to take an active part" in assisting students. Conservative financiers' support helped conference committee negotiations and final votes in both chambers during a period that many historians have considered the highwater mark of postwar liberalism. A handful abstained, but 368 representatives and 79 senators voted in favor. Only twenty-two in the House and three in the Senate (all southern Democrats) objected.[54]

Response to the now lauded legislation was mixed. A *Chicago Tribune* piece reported that Illinois institutions would get almost $9 million in aid, far more than the amount allocated for DC, Virginia, and Maryland. The Golden State received an even larger allocation, although a University of California dean still considered Title I's direct support "very vague." A Stanford administrator dismissed the entire act as "a hodgepodge." A *Wall Street Journal* reporter noted the small Office of Education would need to hire "the right people" to oversee new or vastly expanded initiatives at a moment when the president seemed far more invested in the Vietnam War and other parts of the Great Society. Commentators especially doubted how much money would be available to the mysterious developing institutions that, *Los Angeles Times* reporters quipped, could describe a college that "pre-dated the discovery of fire." Only a few experts and journalists suggested Title III was actually intended to aid HBCUs.[55]

Those astute commentators, like many other reporters and educators, had far more faith in Title IV's assistance programs. A *New York Times* editorialist considered them proof that "Washington . . . is ready to help show the way, but not to defray the long-range travel costs," to the Great Society. On paper, journalists noted, Title IV provided more money for individual students than most public institutions charged and almost as much as undergraduates needed for the average private university. New income limits meant far more Americans were eligible for grants, work-study opportunities, national defense loans, and the seemingly revolutionary guaranteed loans. "We are attempting to use normal channels of credit" to provide unprecedented help for middle-income families, one Office of Education staffer enthusiastically explained, "instead of going to direct federal loans." He admitted that "the real question is whether the credit institutions will provide the credit." This aide still predicted Title IV "could hit a million kids pretty quickly." He added: "We just hope colleges won't use this as an excuse for runaway increases in tuition and other costs."[56]

Johnson never mentioned that possibility when he signed HEA on November 8 at his alma mater. The small teacher's college had already grown into the Southwest Texas State College. The president spoke about living above the college president's garage, showering in a nearby gym, and working an astounding array of odd jobs. "I was one of the lucky ones—and I knew it even then," the Texan claimed. As a sophomore, he had taught at the Welhausen Mexican School and later realized "that college was closed to practically every one of those children because they were too poor." The former NYA director did not draw attention to his pupils' racial backgrounds but instead celebrated that HEA meant "the path of knowledge is open to all that have the determination to walk it." The president barely mentioned the direct federal funding that would turn "the ivory towers of learning into the allies of a better life in our cities," guarantee "that college and university libraries will no longer be the anemic stepchildren of Federal assistance," assist "smaller, undernourished colleges," underwrite "first-class equipment in order to have first-class classrooms," and create a National Teacher Corps. Instead he spent half his time lauding the student assistance provisions, which guaranteed "a high school senior anywhere in this great land of ours can apply to any university in any of the fifty states and not be turned away because his family is poor." Higher learning would not only be an avenue out of poverty, Johnson assured his audience, but "a way to deeper personal fulfillment, greater personal productivity, and increased personal reward."[57]

This legislation certainly seemed to guarantee the education infrastructure a truly great society needed. It still gave states and campuses a lot of au-

FIG 5.1 Lyndon Baines Johnson returned to his alma mater, then Southwest Texas State College, to sign the 1965 Higher Education Act. After mentioning how poor he was when he tried to finish his degree in the 1920s, the president spoke about new opportunities to borrow through the guaranteed-loan program. Like the 1930s federal mortgage program, this tuition-assistance option promised bankers a return on a financial product designed to start a new industry. LBJ Library photo by Frank Wolfe, Serial Number: 852-4-WH65.

thority in a law that, like NDEA, had to come up for periodic reauthorization. Unlike the 1958 legislation, the new law carried no pretext of being temporary, despite the truce bankers and White House aides had negotiated. The first title promised direct support to underwrite programs to turn remote colleges into modern metropolitan multiversities that, as Kerr and his acolytes wanted, would serve a number of constituents (not just students and professors). Such sprawling research institutions needed better repositories and more librarians, both funded by the second section. Lawmakers allowed the money to go to all accredited, nonprofit institutions, even if they were private, public, or religious colleges. The third part also provided direct aid to "developing institutions," the politically palatable way Johnson insiders had used to try and quietly direct money to HBCUs.[58]

"Student Assistance" was sandwiched between those titles and the final four portions devoted to teacher training, undergraduate instruction, and amendments to earlier federal education legislation. Title IV outlined four basic forms of help to create the kind of individually tailored packages that had become more common since NDEA's passage. Campus financial aid officers would determine the mix of support from campus resources, state programs, and federal offerings that included grants, work-study opportunities, defense loans, and the new guaranteed loans that would ideally be brokered through state agencies partnered with lenders. If a state had not yet created such a public-private partnership to offer those financial products, the federal government would supply seed money to start one. Location did not determine students' eligibility. An undergraduate qualified for credit if financial aid officers determined that their family's adjusted income was less than $15,000, a calculation that only reinforced campus staff's dependence on the College Scholarship Service's Financial Aid Form. Personnel gave young people the documentation needed to prove admission and guaranteed loan eligibility, which aspiring students brought to participating lenders who decided whether or not to extend credit. That complicated process epitomized the lengths lawmakers went in the name of preserving federalism and supporting free enterprise. Congress had privileged the authority of states and private businesses and protected the power of campus staff to decide whom to admit and what tuition assistance a student would receive. Title IV (like NYA's work-study and the GI Bill) only stipulated that no undergraduate would receive the mythical free ride that had long seemed un-American to so many. Students would instead have to continue to cobble together money for fees, books, and living expenses.[59]

Campus administrators, state officials, and students instead got the opportunity to creatively finance educations. Lawmakers only generously funded parts of this promised pathway into the still largely white middle and upper classes, which reflected the hope of nurturing a student loan industry to underwrite mass higher education. Senators and representatives modestly funded the three sections devoted to directly aiding colleges and libraries for the 1966 through 1968 fiscal years even though influential academics, like Kerr, had continually emphasized such support would keep tuition costs down. Title I received only $25 million during the first fiscal year and $50 million for the subsequent two. Librarians could expect just $50 million for each of those fiscal periods. But HBCU administrators might get an additional $5 million because lawmakers wanted to spend far more money on student assistance. They allocated $70 million annually for the Equal Opportunity Grants, allowed $50 million a year for defense loans, and gradually raised the work-study earmarks from $129 million to $200 million over three years. Lawmakers placed a far different cap on the new Guaranteed Student Loan Program that relied on bankers to lend. Congress only allowed an undergraduate to borrow $1,500 a year through an initiative that could only extend $700 million in credit for the first fiscal year, a limit that rose to $1.4 billion by June 30, 1968. The government would cover the 6 percent interest charges on the loans but assumed the federal government would not have to pay back those hefty sums if undergraduates ever defaulted. Lawmakers had, after all, provided seed money to help legislatures set up state guarantee agencies similar to the ones first founded in Massachusetts and New York. This allocation reflected the hopes of conservative lawmakers and lenders, who wanted the federal government to be the guarantor of last resort.[60]

That desire seemed a pipe dream in the program's early years. The president, top aides, and ABA leaders hammered out the details of the complex lending scheme in closed, high-level meetings after the law's passage. Johnson, an aide later recounted, liked to "reminisce at considerable length about the very great advantage that had accrued to some banker in Texas through making a small loan . . . allowing him to continue his education." The president "kept a deposit in that bank," a fact he used to underscore that "even though [lenders] might not make an immediate big return on these federally guaranteed loans," they would "build up some future paying customers." Education Office personnel traveled the country to explain to state leaders, college personnel, financiers, and students that this legislation represented "a chance and a challenge" to help Americans afford college, "the largest investment that most families make apart from buying a home." Few legislators had any interest in contracting with USAF or setting up public-private partnerships, like those in New York and a handful of other states. As one insider remembered, "Nobody wanted to see the direct federal guarantee applied," but financiers ended up receiving far more reassurance from Washington than from states.[61]

Neither colleges nor undergraduates received anything close to the guaranteed tuition assistance the program's name implied. The ABA spent summer 1966 pushing fourteen thousand members to participate but beltway insiders deemed the results "dismal." Three DC-area banks dropped out of a program in which only two of the city's fifteen lenders participated. Eighteen months after passage, less than eleven thousand creditors had made 330,000 loans. The $294 million extended to students was far less than undergraduates, financial aid officers, Education Office staffers, and lawmakers had wanted. Two-thirds of campuses surveyed in 1967 reported that eligible students had been turned down. One skeptical financier explained that his compatriots were being asked for a lot of money up front but without "a nickel coming in" for five years. That complaint really reflected how much lenders detested the program's complicated paperwork, which they had to fill out quarterly in order to get government money to cover the interest accruing on loans while borrowers studied.[62]

Early setbacks did not shake White House insiders' faith in guaranteed lending. Aides spent much of 1966 and 1967 figuring out how to change the program to entice lenders to participate without sacrificing the support of lawmakers and college administrators. The president also tried to cajole Congress into allocating no money for campus defense loan funds for the 1966 fiscal year. Education Office staff remembered being "inundated with mail, both from the public and Congress." Lawmakers brazenly appropriated $181,550,000 for the National Defense Student Loan Program. This defeat did not stop Johnson from trying to pressure lawmakers to fund and run NDEA borrowing like the guaranteed loan offering. Top appointees disliked that suggestion, which would have reduced the budget but "would have been hard to make it work by the time the colleges opened the following September." Luckily lawmakers balked at dismantling this "very popular program . . . in which a lot of individual congressmen and senators take a great deal of pride," including Edith Green, who collected pleas from college presidents, financial aid officers, and fellow lawmakers to preserve defense lending.[63]

Those constituents expressed a lot of mistrust in the private sector and the complicated guaranteed loan program. They still had faith in defense lending. But undergraduates did not want to see "poor students and their families" subjected to "business-like scrutiny" or "at the tender mercy of our esteemed New York bankers." Parents complained they "couldn't obtain aid from a bank," that local creditors "were not interested in loans," and that their children would graduate "with a debt that is a mill stone around his neck." A Florida mother spoke for many when she concluded "the impersonal federal government is best" because "a small town bank can not be impartial."[64]

Johnson's eagerness to change the popular defense loan program's funding mechanism reflected his administration's infamous fiscal jujitsu. Scholars have noted that the White House often proposed new Great Society programs but sometimes underfunded older initiatives to support additional undertakings or relied on so-called off-budget devices to hide spending increases. The president particularly liked guaranteed lending because government accounting practices at the time hid, as an Education Office staffer had warned during hearings, how expensive this form of tuition assistance would be. Only interest subsidies and default payments appeared on the budget, which wrongly made the lending scheme seem far cheaper than directly underwriting institutions or offering indirect aid through other tuition assistance programs, such as NDEA campus loan funds, work-study opportunities, or scholarships. In contrast to all the hidden costs of running guaranteed loans, the executive branch had to plan and account for the money directed to those other Title IV offerings. Tricky bookkeeping made guaranteed credit even more important to the Johnson White House after the 1966 midterms, when (as the former Senate majority leader had predicted) Republicans made sizeable gains across the country and on Capitol Hill. Rightly fearing he would not be reelected in 1968, the unpopular incumbent approved personal and corporate tax increases, asked for more money to fight the war in Vietnam, and put a lid on domestic spending levels. "The President had to worry about budgets," a staffer later explained. Johnson, the former NYA director, boldly asked Congress to basically halve the previous year's education authorizations and declined to increase undergraduate assistance programs, which, unlike the guaranteed loan offering he favored, had to appear on budget spreadsheets.[65]

Yet "Congressional committees dealing with education," as an aide later explained, "are 'spenders.'" Lawmakers ignored Johnson's suggestions when they set out to reauthorize HEA in 1968, keeping the tradition of assisting students, not aiding campuses. The earmarks for college construction dropped from $817 million to $300 million. Congress easily agreed to maintain how defense act loans were funded, which kept that line item on the budget. Education earmarks also went up by $200 million, which included $53 million more for student aid. Congress also fought over a range of new programs. Still, they only added provisions for students to alternate between working and studying full time, funds for counseling and tutoring needy undergraduates, initiatives to encourage campuses to share resources, efforts to have law school curricula expand to include firsthand experience, and funds to improve graduate training. They even ordered a study of ways to ensure postsecondary options would be available to every qualified, interested young person, as Johnson had pledged in his signing statement.[66]

Johnson seemed likely to keep that promise before he dropped out of the 1968 election. Federal college aid between 1963 and 1966 more than doubled (rising from $1.4 billion to $3.7 billion). Historians have linked that jump to the exponential growth of the country's student body between 1955 and 1974. The number of students tripled, the percentage of 18- to 24-year-olds pursuing higher learning almost doubled, and the number of community colleges more than doubled. Almost every state started or developed a new public research university. Campuses even awarded almost five times as many master's degrees as well as almost quadruple the number of doctorates. More women and minorities also matriculated. Guaranteed lending seemed, as one historian insisted, "a small price to pay for the achievement of federal grants for needy students."[67]

Their enrollment had had little to do with the hidden efforts to bolster HBCUs or provide grants for low-income, presumably minority, students. Reporters noted in August 1968 that financial aid officers gave "too large a proportion of the [guaranteed] loans to students from affluent families," who had long received far more generous packages than genuinely needy applicants. That summer Education Office higher-ups did hire the former president of Bennett College, an HBCU, to implement Title III. Journalists noted that the "highly articulate" Willa Player wanted to bolster the small colleges "better geared to serve individual students, particularly those we are trying to help out of disadvantaged backgrounds." That section hardly ensured another option on par with the country's best state and private universities. "Name a Negro college and you'll probably be naming a developing institution," African American journalist Adolph Slaughter pointed out after lawmakers allocated less than a tenth of the $55 million HEA permitted for the 1966 fiscal year. HBCUs, he fumed, "ain't going to be developed this year and the education is going to be just as bad as it was last year." The money did some good at a handful of HBCUs. Slaughter's prediction still came true for a lot of them as well as other small colleges. Many little, largely white Catholic, Protestant, and secular institutions profusely thanked lawmakers for Title III. This enthusiasm quickly gave way to disappointment, particularly among HBCU administrators who asked lawmakers why they received so little aid. Green blamed her colleagues for making vague compromises during difficult negotiations. Such wrangling over Title III proved habitual. Many nonprofits qualified for the much-needed direct funding, which, unlike so many other federal earmarks, remained unconnected to the research, for which these colleges did not have the resources to compete.[68]

Such conflicts were far removed from ordinary Americans' struggle to receive the tuition assistance, like the supposed rights in the GI Bill, promised to everyone. Education Office officials admitted later that integration was slow and piecemeal. After all, "it was a very great act of courage for a Negro youngster to exercise the choice to go to a white school" even after the Civil Rights Act's passage. The protests and court challenges of young men and women of color pushed public and private institutions to comply with a law whose rules were far stricter than Title IV's standards for financial aid. Only later did researchers uncover that increasing enrollments and opportunities to borrow did not erase long-standing inequalities after graduation. Even if undergraduates successfully financed their degrees, they still struggled to land good jobs or be paid equally for the same work in order to pay back their debts or save as much as their wealthier peers, who had paid less over time for the same credentials.[69]

That reality highlighted the pitfalls of the public-private financing behind federal investment in education, in particular, and American social welfare, in general. More spending in the 1960s did not stop nonprofits, whether public or private, from relying on a mix of revenue sources (see Appendix, figure A1). Indeed, federal spending tabulations have historically separated the earmarks to assist students from the allocations to directly support campuses, whether for construction, research, or other needs. Such calculations have retrospectively revealed the historic importance of legislative support, philanthropy, and tuition. Washington directly supplied a greater amount of revenue than state and local governments only during World War II and the GI Bill rollout. In the mid-1960s, Congress contributed a greater share than it had during the previous fifteen years but still only approached what state and local governments were then bestowing. In those discrete moments, federal funding did provide more resources than tuition. Nevertheless, the fees, whether creatively financed through government programs or paid out of pocket, continued to supply more of the money needed to keep public and private universities open for much of the twentieth century.[70]

HEA hardly eased the complexity of paying for college or keeping the academy solvent. "We could scarcely . . . have devised a more confusing, more expensive, or less efficient program," one of guaranteed lending's architects lamented less than twenty years after enactment. Administering the many components of this legislation fell to federal officials, state education boards, and university administrators who exercised the kind of discretion over earmarks that did little to ensure the money would be fairly allocated. The Johnson administration's final years previewed how unpredictable direct federal support would be. HEA continually came up for reauthorization, which gave everyone invested in the business of postsecondary schooling a chance to lobby lawmakers. Yet no one could predict whether members of Congress or presidents would continue the status quo, provide additional help, or reduce aid. Any agreements (as always) only set new ceilings for, not guarantees of, how much Congress would annually earmark for various programs.[71]

As such, HEA hardly represented the kind of educational overhaul Americans still remember it as. This signature 1960s achievement only promised the academy new, but still unpredictable, revenue streams in a future that proved anything but prosperous for many campuses and citizens. Colleges still had to compete fiercely for the donations and earmarks needed to keep tuition rates down. Leading public and private institutions, which remained the purview of a largely white male elite in the 1970s and 1980s, tended to remain better able to vie for federal grants, donors, and fees. Tuition rates continued to rise everywhere, however, so that growing numbers of students felt the need to borrow to earn degrees—credentials that equipped them to compete for well-paying jobs, but offered steadily declining assurance of entry into the middle and professional classes.

Aspiring students steadily found themselves with fewer options. Some institutions could not expand enrollments or even remain open, like Wahoo's Kennedy College. The small Nebraska campus closed in 1975, just ten years after its founding, HEA's enactment, and a spike in campus closures and mergers nationwide.[72] The seven desperate Save Our Schools Committee undergraduates had arrived in DC in 1968, when both congressional and White House powerbrokers used the reauthorization process to bolster Title IV. Its loan provision was supposed to nurture a student loan industry capable of indirectly financing higher education's expansion and directly helping undergraduates pay for degrees expected in an increasingly knowledge-oriented labor market. But the academy's finances continued to weaken in the 1970s, when fees also soared. Amid economic stagnation and the political parties' continued realignment, lawmakers agreed on little else but doubling down on the Guaranteed Student Loan Program and making it even more attractive to financiers. That choice reflected the growing importance of financial and public-private solutions in subsequent decades, when additional opportunities to borrow did little to address the racial and gender disparities policymakers had assumed government-supported financial sectors would lessen.

6

Reauthorizing the Loan Industry

Unlike so many college students making headlines in the late 1960s and early 1970s, Andrew Pognany did not write to Richard Nixon denouncing the Vietnam War. The law student instead wrote to protest "the proposed curtailment by the federal government of the last major source of financial aid to students from middle income families, the federally subsidized guaranteed loan program." Pognany, who had campaigned for the president in 1968, considered the 1972 cutback "an inconceivable insensitivity to the hopes and dreams for ordinary Americans: to see their sons and daughters attend and graduate from college." Like "countless thousands who share our plight," the aspiring attorney explained, "I will not be able to show the hardship necessary to qualify under the new standards. I am equally certain that without these funds I will not be able to continue my legal education without pushing my parents into financial catastrophe."[1]

Mothers and fathers complained to the president about confusing amendments to a relatively new loan program that financiers had not embraced. "With the large amount that taxes takes out of our salaries along with trying to pay for our home, car, food, and clothing," a Wisconsin parent explained, "we find financing a college education a rather difficult task." Another, from Washington State, felt the same way. "We as a family have paid our taxes and conformed to all of the bureaucracies that now prevail and yet we find because of the present system we can't send our son to college." The experience left him indignant: "Why must the 'middle Class people' pay the major cost of all government services and yet derive the least benefit?"[2]

These letters, a Treasury Department staffer warned Nixon aides, represented "a brief sampling of grief mail" that followed the Higher Education Act's (HEA) 1972 reauthorization. Citizens had reason to be both irate and fearful. Lyndon Johnson had pledged that the 1965 legislation would ensure that every determined student could afford college, but fees, books, and living expenses remained too expensive for both blue- and white-collar Americans. Costs became only more prohibitive after the 1968 reauthorization. Industries stagnated, prices soared, employment opportunities declined, and social welfare guarantees fell short. State and federal lawmakers' eagerness to cut taxes and spending reduced the funds earmarked for education and left many administrators with little choice but to raise tuition rates for the legions of Baby Boomers still eagerly enrolling.[3]

That pervasive sense of crisis and rage has rarely been mentioned when scholars and journalists have celebrated the 1972 Education Amendments that inspired such "grief mail." New, controversial provisions seemed to provide unprecedented access to the academy for Americans long excluded because of sex, race, religion, and class. Title IX, for example, did far more than enable women to compete in college sports. Lawmakers passed this edict against sex discrimination during the highwater mark of political and public support for the Equal Rights Amendment. Title IX also accompanied another form of still-revered student aid intended to help the poor: Basic Educational Opportunity Grants. Basic grants or BEOGs, like HEA's support for "developing institutions," epitomized lawmakers' efforts to covertly assist students of color, who (like women) still struggled to afford college. Politicians eager for equal opportunities did not dare single out support for any minority group or describe the tuition assistance as a kind of affirmative action. Senator Claiborne Pell of Rhode Island instead promised that the scholarships later named after him would give *every* American the right to an education at a moment when policies intended to confront systemic discrimination infuriated many citizens. He and other lawmakers still assumed African Americans would be the main recipients of this color-blind help. But undergraduates only had to prove need in order to receive this direct financial assistance, which was distributed by federal officials, not college financial aid officers or lenders. The program also seemed capable of coercing and cajoling admissions staff to admit needy applicants of color. Lawmakers tied 45 percent of that direct assistance to the number of Pell recipients enrolled on any given campus, which theoretically empowered awardees (like GIs after World War II) to choose which institutions got this vital revenue.

Long-overlooked, expensive additions to the 1972 reauthorization instead left a growing number of students, particularly coeds and students of color, at the mercy of bankers. Senators, representatives, and White House aides spent months fighting over Pell's grant proposal, campus funding, and Title IX but easily reached agreement on expanding eligibility for federal student assistance to more schools, including for-profits, and creating the Student Loan Marketing Association, better known as SLMA or Sallie Mae.

Both battles and bipartisan endorsements reflected how much had and had not changed since the Depression. Major ideological divisions remained between and within the parties as their steady local, state, and national realignment continued in the 1970s, when some historians have asserted the country was "rightward bound." Voters and their elected representatives seemed far more interested in dismantling what remained of the public-private social safety net New Dealers had created. That effort included reducing revenue, cutting spending, limiting federal power, deregulating industries (such as banking), and forcing Americans to rely even more on financial products for basic needs. Finance and insurance, along with real estate, started building a far more regressive and unequal postindustrial America than the one Clark Kerr and other liberal social scientists had imagined in the 1960s. Yet other scholars have noted the stagnant 1970s seemed to be, as radical journalist Michael Harrington famously quipped, "vigorously left, right, and center." Conservatives and liberals continued to tangle over political, economic, and social policies that simultaneously tried to advance, limit, and rescind the social welfare and equal opportunity guarantees fought over for decades. Getting anything through Congress continued to be difficult in years when the Nixon administration sought to devolve more power onto the states and exercise more executive authority in the White House.[4]

HEA's hard-fought 1972 reauthorization exemplified how the past shaped a so-called "pivotal decade" that ushered in a new era of increasing inequality and precarity. How and how much the federal government directly funded higher education continued to be controversial even though many academics no longer worried that the support would mean a loss of academic freedom or campus autonomy. But lawmakers remained far more amenable to color-blind assistance to students, which indirectly helped the nonprofits that had historically counted on tuition revenue. Opening up Title IV programs to proprietary schools did not break previous precedents. The Roosevelt administration had never considered making for-profits eligible for work-study. But Congress and the Veterans Administration had permitted them to take advantage of the original GI Bill, which Roosevelt appointees had considered a way to ease unemployment and improve the country's workforce. Journalists and lawmakers had heaped scorn on for-profits, which had continued (despite the 1964 Civil Rights Act) to be more accessible to women, citizens of color, and immigrants than public and private nonprofit colleges. Extending federal financing opportunities to more postsecondary institutions appealed to lawmakers eager to help Americans pay for the kind of training needed in the 1970s, when many found themselves out of work and without the skills to compete in a rapidly changing labor market and economy.

Encouraging postsecondary institutions and students to use the Guaranteed Student Loan Program complemented enthusiasm, across the political spectrum, for creating SLMA. It both exemplified policymakers' preference, since the 1930s, to underwrite (not directly fund) public-private social welfare programs and previewed how finance would become even more important to American life. Lawmakers intended the government-sponsored enterprise, like the Federal National Mortgage Association included in the 1934 National Housing Act, to motivate more financiers to participate in a student loan industry still getting off the ground. Like Fannie Mae, the federal clearinghouse for student debt made buying, selling, and profiting off guaranteed loans easier. More undergraduates desperately needed this credit from bankers that federal officials incentivized because, even in the early years of 1970s stagflation, many Americans (including Pognany and his classmates of color) had already found themselves in the peculiar position of not being able to afford either skipping or attending college. Only a degree could ensure a person's ability to compete for (not necessarily get) a well-paying job. Such positions (despite the Civil Rights Act) still seemed out of reach for many white women and citizens of color, who continued to find themselves excluded from nonprofit schools and paying more over time for educations that did not guarantee that they would be paid equally—or even hired—after graduation.

A Right to Education, or Financing Floor for It?

Education experts, however, feared there would be no room for college hopefuls in the early 1970s, when top researchers warned of, as Berkeley professor Earl Cheit titled his landmark 1971 study, "The New Depression in Higher Education." Some scholars considered the Ford Foundation and Carnegie Commission on Higher Education–supported study to be "inaccurate and alarmist" but even Cheit's sharpest critics admitted college finances had long been shaky. New Dealers had little interest in directly bailing out universities decades before Kennedy College undergraduates struggled to get attention from reporters and lawmakers in the midst of HEA's 1968 reauthorization. Just three years later, Cheit noted, "accounts of the financial plight of schools are now front-page stories and the subject of concerned editorials." He cited seventy references to precarious academic finances published between 1967 and 1970, when some campuses closed, made cuts, reallocated resources, or even operated in the red. He uncovered that many institutions faced serious financial issues. In 1970, 42 percent seemed headed for trouble and another 19 percent already faced difficulties. Public institutions tended to have the surest financing: 50 percent were considered solvent. Private colleges and universities faced more dire circumstances. Only 28 percent were not currently in financial straits, slightly less than the proportion of solvent liberal arts institutions. Small colleges actually fared better than universities, only 19 percent of which were fiscally sound.[5]

Most blamed insolvency on not enough government, particularly federal, investment. Such accusations exemplified how much had changed since the elite "school crowd" fought the Roosevelt administration during the Great Depression. Expenditures had dramatically increased in the twenty years after Sputnik's 1957 launch; state appropriations had quadrupled in the 1960s. However, revenue streams rose far slower after 1967, which only exacerbated the feverish competition for research grants, donors, government allocations, and students. The number of college-age Americans leveled off in the early 1970s. Many administrators desperately needed their tuition payments because colleges and universities did not benefit equally from the seemingly substantial 207 percent increase in federal earmarks between 1968 and 1977. In those years, the portion of overall higher education revenue made up by federal allocations plummeted from its mid-1960s surge (see appendix, figure A1). That drop partly reflected government research support shrinking from $5 billion to $4.7 billion between 1968 and 1974. Even scholarships began to disappear. By 1974, 15 percent of doctoral students borrowed. Legislators contributed a larger share of the academy's revenue in these years but states continued to vary widely on how much they allocated. Legislators generally tended to direct more money toward community colleges and financial assistance programs while providing slightly less support to public colleges. Plus, the state boards and agencies overseeing higher education only received a little more money in years when public research universities saw a noticeable drop in support (from 54 percent to 46 percent). Such cuts left many institutions scrambling to live up to their varied uses and obligations, as former UC president, then Carnegie Commission on Higher Education head Clark Kerr pointed out in the early 1970s.[6]

Even though unaffordable colleges and poorly financed universities had been making headlines, Washington insiders had far more interest in overhauling programs for student assistance as they faced the deadline to once again reauthorize HEA. Claiborne Pell's enthusiasm particularly surprised many on Capitol Hill. The Kennedy family friend had not made a name for himself either in the field of education or in the Senate. Eight years had only shown that "Pell isn't at all a typical politician," a reporter noted, adding that "he thinks like a diplomat." That may have been the result of Pell's seven years in the Foreign Service, on top of his upbringing in a blue blood family. His wealth could be traced back to an eighteenth-century royal land charter and was vast enough that, as his *New York Times* obituary would note, "he could have *purchased* some of the educational institutions" that students used Pell grants to attend. The Princeton undergraduate and liberal Democrat had followed in the footsteps of five relatives who had served in the House and the Senate, but nonetheless prided himself on being someone who would "go up and down the halls trying to explain my ideas to the others." He considered that doing "my work quietly" but doubted "my record is known." Early in his career, colleagues mostly knew him for his support for metric conversion and desire to keep nuclear weapons off sea beds. A biographer noted that Pell became associated with "a mix of down-to-earth and pie-in-the-sky" causes, including driver safety, high-speed rail, universal health care, and daylight savings time year-round.[7]

Pell later insisted he had a long-standing commitment to social welfare in general and to increasing opportunities to go to college in particular. The GI Bill had paid for an international relations master's degree from Columbia, the kind of credentials needed for service in the State Department. The rich Coast Guard enlistee hardly needed to use that benefit but he embraced the idea that advanced learning should be "a matter of right" for all Americans, not just veterans. Indeed, in later interviews, Pell asserted that sixteen years of schooling, two more than the Zook Commission had demanded after World War II, should "be available to young people if they have the moxie and the intelligence and the drive."[8]

He constantly repeated that sentiment even though it struck some beltway insiders as disingenuous. Pell, as a member of the full Labor and Public Welfare Committee, had sponsored a two-volume statistical report in 1963 that experts have sometimes cited as an important first step in the eventual creation of the basic grant program that later bore the senator's name. Seniority ultimately gave him the chairmanship of the education subcommittee after the tumultuous 1968 elections. Pell's predecessor, Democratic Oregon Senator Wayne Morse, had already expressed interest in some kind of minimal federal aid to higher education. Pell first attempted to propose a new grant program in 1969. "When Pell sent us that piece of paper saying I want a bill," a subcommittee staffer later recounted, "I was surprised at how little he knew about higher education, student assistance, and what was in existence then. It was almost as if nothing had happened or that the federal government was not involved already." Pell's desire to create new legislation did not seem oppositional. "He had no antipathy for the existing programs," the aide believed, "he just didn't care about them because they weren't his." Another staffer also intimated that Pell might have had more interest in making a name for himself than helping students.[9]

Pell's aides nevertheless helped him cobble together a bill in keeping with the general spirit of limited, color-blind, direct assistance for those most in need and with the tradition of aiding students, not campuses. This proposal bore little resemblance to the full tuition assistance and stipends in the GI Bill or the generous support for two additional years of schooling in the Zook

Report. Pell's scheme augmented rather than replaced the existing patchwork system of Title IV, state, and campus tuition assistance with targeted support from the federal government. Every student would receive $1,000 to spend on the first two years of college. That support hardly would have made those semesters free, as the postwar Zook Commission had suggested doing through direct aid to campuses so as to avoid piecemeal federal higher education policies.[10]

The defeat of Pell's multi-billion-dollar motion hardly deterred a senator who prided himself on being an "idea man," leaving the details to aides. After the bill's demise, he went skiing in the Alps. At lunch one day he used a placemat to roughly outline "a new way of trying to secure entrants to college from the lowest income percentiles without subsidizing those who can afford it." He presumed, like Great Society liberals before him, that such color-blind aid would help African Americans, who still struggled, despite the Civil Rights and Higher Education Acts, to gain admittance to and pay for college. He demanded staff figure out how to transform his hastily written idea into a simple way to provide needy undergraduates with a set amount of assistance that would be reduced by how much their parents paid in yearly income taxes. He insisted this metric would be a reasonable, straightforward indicator of their overall wealth, even though aides repeatedly warned that suggestion would be so unpopular that it might doom passage.[11]

Still, Pell's assistants incorporated the income-based needs test into an amendment of Title IV's existing grant offering, the Equal Opportunity Grant (EOG), given out by campus financial aid officers. "The process of teaching Pell what was in existence already," a staffer later recounted, "was as difficult as figuring out how to fit his program with the then-existing programs." The final draft ended up retaining the other Title IV offerings, which would, as Pell explained in a letter to a skeptical colleague, "supplement the basic grants in cases where students had extraordinary need or were attending more expensive colleges." Indeed, the bill changed the name of the EOG to the Supplemental Education Opportunity Grants (SEOG) since the new Basic Educational Opportunity Grant initiative provided every student with, at most, $1,200 annually for four years of college. With that direct federal guarantee, everything else (to Pell at least) seemed to be an add-on.[12]

That plan highlighted how inseparable student assistance and campus support had become by the early 1970s. BEOGs, or basic grants, included a

FIG 6.1 Senator Claiborne Pell speaking to Rhode Island College undergraduates. Though on the Senate Education and Labor Committee, Pell had not yet made a name for himself as an advocate for college students, so his eagerness to pass the Basic Educational Opportunity Grants surprised many in Washington in the early 1970s. Congress passed the grant program later named after Pell in the 1972 Educational Amendments that included Title IX. Research Collection of the Senatorial Papers of Claiborne Pell, Photographs, Mss. Gr. 71.9, University of Rhode Island, Distinctive Collections and Archives.

"cost-of-instruction" allowance for colleges, which had continued the historic tradition of not charging the full expense of educating students. Since the federal government first started offering tuition assistance through work-study in the 1930s, schools had struggled to finance expansions because additional fee revenue rarely covered the cost of expanding their student bodies. That pricing convention had even forced federal and state authorities to offer limited direct support for universities during the GI Bill's rollout. Such help had not come with the defense loan program. Only Great Society liberals had recognized that institutional aid was needed as well as student assistance. But

Pell insisted on giving colleges additional money for any enrollee who qualified for the basic grants intended to help poor undergraduates. This carrot differed in important ways from the GI Bill's incentives. Under Pell's proposal, per-pupil support would be $1,000 minus the cost of tuition. His advisers considered that formula a means to encourage colleges to admit low-income students without rewarding expensive institutions or encouraging cheaper options to raise their rates, as nonprofit and for-profit schools had done during the heyday of the 1930s work-study program and the first GI Bill.[13]

Nixon aides had little interest in subsidizing instructional expenses when they fashioned White House plans for overhauling federal student assistance and reauthorizing HEA. "The existing student aid programs," insiders later explained, seemed to be "dealing only with the tip of the iceberg." Like Pell, Nixon insiders noticed that seemingly equitable Title IV, state, and campus offerings failed to assist many Americans. Staff particularly worried about "dropouts who left school because of the lack of financial aid, students from families who don't encourage the pursuit of a college education, as well as students from non-participating institutions," an allusion to the for-profits and other postsecondary options then ineligible for Title IV.[14]

Those concerns captured the complexity of the Nixon administration's approach to domestic policymaking in general and higher education funding in particular. Experts remain divided on whether the Whittier College and Duke Law School alum governed as a liberal or a conservative. He had viciously red-baited a liberal Democrat to become a representative in the 1940s, but was moderate Republican Dwight Eisenhower's second-in-command in the 1950s. He cast the tie-breaking vote against a teacher salary bill before his 1960 presidential run, told reporters he was "a nut on education" during the 1968 campaign, signed far reaching environmental legislation in 1970, briefly advocated a universal "basic income" provision, changed federal affirmative action policy to focus on goals instead of quotas, made coded racist appeals to a white silent majority, and promised a tough application of the law to restore order (particularly in inner cities and on college campuses). Many scholars contend that this seemingly quixotic record reflected the realities of running for office, climbing to the top of a fractious GOP, and presiding when the nation was undergoing tectonic political, economic, and cultural changes. Nixon also came into office with impressive Democratic majorities in Congress, constraining his administration's ability to cede substantial federal authority to states and municipalities, cut spending, deregulate industry, and reduce the size of government. He and his staff nevertheless made progress toward his stated goal of a "New Federalism" through revenue sharing and block grants. Both strategies started the process of decreasing national support for and oversight over state and local governments, a key sticking point in forty years of fighting over federal higher education funding.[15]

Many of the seemingly small issues and larger ideological battles that had forestalled federal education aid for years continued to divide members of Nixon's Working Group in Higher Education. The panel included staff from the White House; Health, Education, and Welfare Department (HEW); Office of Management and Budget; Office of Science and Technology; Labor Department; and Office of Education. The president's first HEW Secretary, Robert Finch, shared the same general disregard for the Office of Education as many of his predecessors. He did not, like New Dealers, malign them as the "school crowd" but instead dismissed them as Great Society holdovers with too many connections to what Finch labeled educational "trade associations." Many considered the lawyer and Ronald Reagan's former lieutenant governor a more moderate Republican but Finch, like members of HEW's Office of Legislation, wanted to keep spending down. He also supported seemingly less expensive indirect student assistance over direct spending either on campuses or defense loans. Everyone else in the working group also agreed federal higher education aid needed a more simplified, market-based approach that channeled any government aid primarily through students. Many also detested the tuition tax credits Democrats and Republicans continued to propose. Only Education Commissioner James Allen advocated keeping at least some of the meager direct support for colleges and universities that had been in the first three titles of the original act passed during the Johnson administration's heyday.[16]

Tuition assistance debates exemplified how HEA's passage had scarcely resolved long-standing differences. Advisers barely questioned the tradition of indirectly aiding the academy through student assistance, but they entertained cuts to the beloved defense loan program and discussed ways to expand the laggard guaranteed loan program that Great Society insiders had helped fashion. Nixon's aides considered it far more pivotal to and appropriate for financing higher education because "the financial returns in the form of higher earnings throughout one's life time seemed clear." Unfortunately, many students, parents, and campuses continued to scramble before the start of the academic year to get much-needed credit from lenders. The disarray reflected the loan program's guarantee that banks would be repaid, not that lenders would extend credit. Some Nixon advisers actually considered the Johnson administration's ideas to ensure credit availability, including creating a kind of education bank that could warehouse loans financiers would agree to extend well before classes started in order to end the unpredictability that frustrated financial aid officers, undergraduates, and parents. Some work group members even suggested such an institution could partner with the IRS to collect debts in order to ensure repayment did not burden low-income borrowers.[17]

Many Nixon stalwarts had far more faith in an older form of creative financing. They suggested starting another government-sponsored enterprise, like those liberals had used to nurture industries around the government-guaranteed financial products interwoven into the country's public-private social safety net. They wanted this new GSE to act as a secondary market for student debt, which aides started calling Sallie Mae in 1969. Like Fannie Mae and the other GSEs created in the 1910s and 1930s, it would be a privately owned, federally chartered financial institution supported by special tax exemptions and federally guaranteed debts. Such clearinghouses for government-guaranteed debts had enabled financiers to more easily buy and sell loans whose liquidity would theoretically make them more attractive. Fannie Mae, arguably the best known GSE, seemed like a particularly promising model in the early 1970s because, since the 1930s, it had nurtured a supposedly color-blind mortgage market many credited with turning the country into a nation of homeowners.[18]

Borrowing that decades-old progressive and liberal innovation did nothing to lessen the risk of lending to students or give them equal opportunities. Historians have painstakingly documented that federal policies and local practices actually made the federal mortgage program a tool to protect white supremacy. The vast majority of borrowers had been white men with the savings and salaries to qualify for notes on homes that met basic housing standards and were in white neighborhoods that real estate agents, bankers, and policymakers considered a better investment than communities of color, which were redlined. The secondary market for student loans did not include rigid rules to reduce the risk that had plagued student lending since campuses first extended credit in the early days of the republic. The proposed GSE just increased these financial products' liquidity and profitability. Any accredited institution willing to participate in the program could offer eligible undergraduates a loan to finance the fees campuses needed. Sallie Mae did not change the guaranteed loan program's implicit trust in school officers to vouch for an enrollee's ability to eventually pay back all they owed. This GSE did not threaten that guarantee to bankers, stop campus staff from using tuition assistance to compete for smart, athletic undergraduates, or compel financial aid officers and financiers to extend credit to coeds and applicants of color. But, unlike with mortgages, those taking on debt for education did not have to fear that any course credits and college degrees attained could be repossessed.[19]

HEW higher-ups certainly disliked continuing to let campus staff decide who received tuition assistance. Yet aides worried about persistent biases, not conflicting interests. Journalists had been running reports of admissions officers buying brains and jocks since the mid-1950s. A Nixon insider later explained that many still feared that "the existing programs failed to reach a lot of poor people." White House staff particularly worried about "those in community colleges and small institutions such as the Black colleges in the South that don't have the where with all to influence national policy to their advantage or are simply not aware of the existence of programs in which they could participate."[20]

Appointees had no interest in robustly funding what Title III had politely deemed "developing institutions," the color-blind term used by Great Society liberals to tackle the inequality built into the academy. Nixon insiders certainly praised HBCUs publicly. They also fretted privately that the institutions could not afford the matching funds necessary for federal low-cost construction loans intended to help them expand. Yet many workgroup members were convinced that ensuring HBCUs' eligibility for guaranteed loans would be enough support. Some nevertheless recoiled at "their use by students from poverty backgrounds," who seemed likely to be supporting "parents and siblings" and "should not start life saddled with this sort of burden."[21]

Yet, like their liberal opponents then and in the past, Nixon's aides never considered openly assisting the many Americans long excluded from higher education. They suggested something seemingly akin to Pell's color-blind basic grant idea. But their recommendation had far more in common with the administration's proposal for a federal Family Assistance Plan. FAP provided citizens with a minimum income, an idea embraced by the University of Chicago's Milton Friedman. The libertarian economist saw what he termed a negative income tax as a way to provide social welfare benefits directly to the needy and avoid the convoluted, expensive bureaucracy of the New Dealers' many agencies and government-guaranteed financial products. For higher education, HEW staffers envisioned directly guaranteeing all students at least some money to pay tuition at whatever postsecondary school they chose. As with Pell's plan, financial aid officers would not decide who received help. Applicants would theoretically become better shoppers and funds would flow toward the degree programs and institutions that really deserved tuition revenue. Moreover, unlike Pell's, this plan did away with complicated rubrics that allocated federal aid to campuses based on individual states' needs.[22]

Nixon appreciated these recommendations, which also represented a shrewd way to limit the funding for and authority of an academy that seemed far more liberal than it had been when New Dealers contemplated assisting students. The working group helped write a 1970 message to Congress, which promised, as LBJ and Pell had, that a person's lack of money would no longer keep them from enrolling in or finishing college. Nixon promised reform, innovation, and equal opportunity if Congress created a national student loan association that would "play substantially the same role in student loans that the Federal National Mortgage Association plays in home loans," and that would be sure to support a range of postsecondary options—because "community college or technical training . . . are far better suited to the interests of many young people" than "a four-year liberal arts diploma." He promised the accompanying bill would encourage "diversity . . . both between institutions and within each institution," strengthen campus autonomy, and empower every student "to choose the kind of quality education most suited to him." Guaranteed subsidized loans as well as grants would become a kind of "financing floor." Those and other forms of support, Nixon reasoned, "should complement rather than supplant additional and continuing help from all other sources."[23]

The bill sent over to Congress with that missive epitomized the tricky ways the Nixon administration sought to undermine what remained of the New

Deal and Great Society. The White House really wanted to restrict the already limited, direct spending on campuses and students. This proposal repealed funding for construction and continued support for developing institutions in favor of more student assistance. Unlike the amendments to Title IV that Pell introduced, the White House's changes and additions put even more emphasis on creatively financing tuition bills. The HEW secretary would have the ability to set eligibility rules, the government would no longer subsidize guaranteed loan interest payments while a borrower studied, Congress would cease capping the amounts loaned through the program, and banks (not government-provided campus loan funds) would indirectly finance the beloved Eisenhower-era defense loans. Nothing in the bill directly controlled, much less decreased, college expenses. In fact, these plans doubled the repayment period, which theoretically lessened the burden many felt immediately after graduation but really just increased what alumni paid over longer periods of time. Nixon's "financing floor" also, unlike Pell's idea of a "right" to an education, did nothing to subsidize instructional costs even though the baseline seemed somewhat more generous. Families earning more than $10,000 a year would be ineligible for this direct federal support. Everyone below that threshold would receive help to ensure a student had at least $1,400 in federal aid, the maximum for any undergraduate. Yet only parents earning less than $3,000 a year could expect their kids to receive full assistance, which was low enough to ensure that destitute undergraduates would have to borrow and work their way through college.[24]

Washington at War

Negotiations on a still-divided Capitol Hill dragged on for two years, twice as long as after Sputnik's 1957 launch. Lawmakers hated poorly formulated presidential plans. One openly scorned the 1970 proposal as forcing young people to "mortgage their future." One senator openly admonished Nixon aides during hearings for writing proposals in "secret and there was almost no consultation with members of the higher education community [who] I know are screaming their heads off." White House staffers blamed this furor on their approach. They had largely formulated ideas in-house in what a higher-up called a "cavalier fashion." In this man's words, "The Administration just did it, there was no consultation with members of Congress"—including Republicans on the education subcommittees and Treasury officials. At the time, insiders also recognized the "bill simply ignores political reality. The real pressure for expansion . . . comes from middle income families, much as we would like to think that near poverty-level families should be served first." Lawmakers interpreted that proposal as an attempt to "downgrade vocational schools," which was "contrary to the president's message."[25]

Uproar hardly eased congressional gridlock during pivotal years in the ongoing realignment of the Democratic and Republican parties. Edith Green had introduced an omnibus House bill to reauthorize HEA roughly a month before the president's message. Her proposal extended existing programs but also included titles to combat student unrest and create a Department of Education and Manpower, the kind of standalone bureaucracy some Americans had asked Truman to establish. Hearings nevertheless dragged on as representatives submitted additional bills for discussions. They subsequently scrambled in 1971 to ensure HEA could have an automatic one-year extension, which senators passed shortly before the law's expiration. They had also spent months holding hearings but, as Pell remembered, "the climate was not right; nothing jelled; there was no consensus for action either among the witnesses or the Subcommittee members."[26]

Dithering enabled Nixon appointees to change how they handled DC power-brokers. By early 1971, Finch and Allen had left the administration. New HEW Secretary Elliot Richardson prized both analysis and debate in order to divine ways to tame the bureaucracy he now oversaw. The Harvard Law School graduate was well suited to the task of shaping HEA's next congressional reauthorization. He had played an important role in reaching an agreement between Congress and President Eisenhower during the tense National Defense Education Act (NDEA) negotiations. Before Watergate wrecked this lifelong Republican's career, he collaborated with career Office of Education officials who had years of experience overseeing federal higher education assistance and working with academics. Richardson also met monthly with education associations, which so many of his liberal and conservative predecessors had detested.[27]

But Richardson only tweaked the White House's first recommendations into two new bills that reflected the guileful way the Nixon administration tried to undermine liberal social welfare policies and programs. The proposal that explicitly tackled campus financial aid and student assistance craftily retained grants and loans for construction but appropriated no money for either. It also kept with the general idea of directing support to a range of postsecondary institutions through student assistance, the preferred approach since the 1930s, despite what was outlined in the original HEA's first three titles. Richardson also offered to preserve the Title IV provisions, which campus financial aid officers handed out. He likewise sought, however, to add direct federal support for students, which seemed similar to the right to education that Pell envisioned. The White House wanted a sliding scale to determine how much of a financing floor an individual received. Richardson and other staff were adamant that this baseline should not be used to subsidize the middle class, who already heavily relied on guaranteed loans. Nixon appointees instead wanted to directly assist only the poorest undergraduates. But Green was against a system that would encourage "the neediest student to go to the most expensive school, courtesy of the taxes which the middle income people pay."[28]

She was not the only one in Congress who disliked the lightly revised White House suggestions; antipathy was widespread, making it difficult for lawmakers to reach a consensus on HEA's reauthorization. There were bitter fights in the House and Senate over what Pell and Green submitted as well as the many amendments their colleagues proposed. Lengthy hearings in both chambers covered a range of topics including student protests, precarious college finances, libraries, HBCU needs, language and area studies, better options for Native Americans, problems with federally guaranteed loans, basic grants, and women's rights. The college presidents, higher education association representatives, education experts, Nixon appointees, lenders, and financial aid officers who testified had a range of opinions on all these important issues. But lawmakers, as during NDEA and HEA deliberations, heard from very few undergraduates in the early 1970s. As historians have shown, liberal, left, and conservative student organizations were focused on other issues, including free speech, civil rights, feminism, the Vietnam War, and free enterprise. One of the handful of students who did appear took the few minutes allocated to him to rebuke lawmakers for asking if college was "a right or a privilege" when "today it's a necessity."[29]

That simple truth did not resolve the continuous fights over inequality, taxing, spending, and federal authority that had derailed federal higher education aid and other social welfare legislation for decades. Senators and representatives could finally agree the federal government would help underwrite higher education but still vehemently disagreed over how. Lawmakers fought, for example, over continuing the temporary guaranteed loan program, "the largest single source of financial aid," reporters noted. Pell recoiled at the administration's second proposal, which seemed to guarantee "that college tuitions are going to continue to increase, with the result that higher education will be almost completely financed by tuition." His prediction: "Students will pay that by borrowing large sums," which would "institutionalize the guaranteed student loan program that should be a temporary thing." He was quick to denounce White House suggestions and to defend basic grants and cost-of-instruction payments: "We should be seeking tuition-free higher education as a floor." Others shared his concerns. Lawmakers continually grilled bankers on already alarming national defense and guaranteed loan default rates. Yet many of Pell's colleagues still resisted the kind of direct support that would have freed the academy from its historic need for tuition revenue. They had far more faith in the historic practice of relying on the private sector and complicated government-backed financial products. Liberal Republican Jacob Javits even pushed the college presidents appearing before the Senate education subcommittee "to enlist the banking community as your allies . . . ; they are very ingenious when it comes to money."[30]

Most lawmakers were far more interested in tuition assistance than directly aiding the academy. They certainly heard arguments for funding specific programs (then called categorical support) or so-called untargeted money administrators could use as they wished. But Congress continued to prefer far more convoluted ways of spending money on higher education. Some lawmakers wanted to only support students, give block grants to states (then labeled revenue sharing), or indirectly help parents afford college through a variety of tax breaks. Write-off advocates pointed out that relief would make additional government support unnecessary and liberate colleges from federal red tape. Critics labeled that suggestion backdoor financing that would only benefit the wealthiest Americans at the expense of revenue needed for vital social welfare programs. Such warnings had come up when Senator Barry Goldwater had pushed for write-offs in the late 1950s, and again during the 1964 presidential election. Yet, like that conservative Republican, some early 1970s tax skeptics also chafed at increasing federal authority and power, wanting either states or campus financial aid officers to mete out both financial aid for campuses and assistance to students.[31]

Those small differences mattered in the larger debate over whether Americans would get a financing floor or deserved a right to an education, a question that epitomized the ongoing fights over the country's haphazard, incomplete, creatively financed, public versus private social safety net. Lawmakers had a mixed response to what Pell's staff had devised. Many of his colleagues prioritized student assistance and were open to the general idea but did not like the details the senator had left to assistants. Skeptics included Vermont Senator Winston Prouty, who had introduced the president's bill but only "for the sake of discussion." Offering a basic, predictable amount of direct aid for every student appealed to Prouty, who openly desired a "GI Bill for everybody someday." But this Republican had far more interest in other proposed forms of student assistance, including making loan repayment contingent on income.[32]

Prouty, like other lawmakers, also disliked Pell's insistence on an income-tax test. They did not question, as Pell had proposed, limiting help to a maximum of $1,200 or half the cost of enrolling full- or part-time. That rule, after all, reflected the larger ways policymakers had limited who would receive direct help from the federal government and stopped students from receiving a federal free ride. Yet, as Pell's staff had warned, many witnesses, politicians, and their aides rejected his formula as an accurate way to determine who could actually afford college and who really needed help. Most lawmakers favored a far more elaborate way of figuring out expected family contributions, which better fit the tradition of offering Americans complex, limited, public-private social welfare guarantees.[33]

Pell faced even more opposition over his $1,000 cost-of-education allowance. College presidents had had to beg the VA for such assistance during the GI Bill's helter-skelter rollout. The little help offered then, targeted to defense needs after Sputnik's launch, and earmarked in 1960s legislation did not help Pell make his case in the early 1970s. Subsidizing instructional costs put him at odds with both Republicans and Minnesota Democrat Walter Mondale, who had his staff draw up a separate bill emphasizing direct student aid. "The single most effective way to remove the financial obstacle to college attendance by needy and lower-middle-income students," Mondale contended, was distributing grants "on a national basis, regardless of where a student lives or where he wants to attend college." As with Pell's plan, applicants would have the ability to choose where they used this support but Mondale envisioned a sliding scale to determine cost-of-instruction allowances. He wanted to ensure that private colleges did not become the exclusive purview of the rich. He continually reminded Pell, a fellow liberal Democrat, that a graduated system would not privilege Ivy League schools since not all private institutions were that wealthy.[34]

But the politics surrounding such direct support had shifted substantially, particularly on college campuses, since Roosevelt had fought the "school crowd." Representatives from a range of nonprofit intuitions had far more interest in receiving direct support and improving existing Title IV offerings than in adding a new form of tuition assistance. Both Pell's and the Nixon administration's direct federal student aid proposals stripped campus staff of authority over who received help. Academics, unlike in decades past, did not try to defend their freedom or authority. College higher-ups vividly testified about the apparent new depression Cheit had painstakingly researched and discussed before the House education subcommittee. NYU's president blamed the widespread troubles on inflation as well as "the leveling off and cutbacks in Federal funding." He underscored that the individual and the states should both "play a part" but that "the time has come finally to face up to the issue of the Federal Government taking a part in maintenance of our colleges and universities." A junior college administrator confronted lawmakers for "tearing down" rather than building up, a hopelessly "squeezed academy" that was becoming a "luxury" for Americans who in fact saw it as a basic need. "The Federal Government must pick up some share of the load," a representative from multiple education associations testified, adding that "as fees go up . . . one automatically builds a need for greater and larger student aid programs." A president of a large, private university likewise emphasized that "direct student aid alone is not sufficient. Each institution spends more on educating the student than he pays."[35]

Academics still remained divided on what they wanted and feared. Private college heads reiterated that "there must be some way of bringing this widening gap between public and private costs," the kind of divergence that had terrified elite educators and wealthy CEOs who had feverishly fundraised throughout the 1950s to stop their lower-cost, state competitors' proliferation. Land-grant and state school representatives pointed out that their fees had risen, as well. They, too, needed robust support from the federal government. That demand actually put them at odds with representatives from the Carnegie Commission Clark Kerr then headed; some members still feared that too much reliance on federal financial aid might come at the expense of states' historic role over education, particularly public institutions.[36]

Academics' attitudes perplexed Pell. He considered his proposal "the first bill which clearly states that the United States has a responsibility to provide . . . a degree of institutional support." He complained to them "I need help" but "I haven't gotten a damn thing." Leading educators instead aligned themselves with the basic grant's most outspoken critic, Congresswoman Edith Green. "The powerful lady lawmaker could upstage the Nixon administration on this major issue," one reporter warned. The former Oregon schoolteacher had (unlike Pell) made a name for herself in demanding generous support for higher education. This descendant of Populist Party stalwarts had also earned a reputation as a liberal Democrat for her demands for equality, especially for women, and help for middle-income families, whom she had sought to assist since the incendiary fights over the Eisenhower-era defense loans. But she had antagonized members of her own party by siding with the racial justice activists of the Mississippi Freedom Delegation in their fight with the all-white Mississippi Democratic Party to be seated at the 1964 Democratic convention. She also advocated for women to have equal access during debates over education bills in the 1970 and 1971 legislative sessions, where she advanced a cogent argument that "the major government effort ought to be directed to decreasing all college tuitions, private and public, so that a choice, a choice of a college—large or small, public or private—is within the reach of more and more students rather than fewer and fewer."[37]

Noted in 1961 for never having worked with conservatives in Congress, by the early 1970s Green supported conservative initiatives 48 percent of the time. Those votes reflected the ongoing shifting political fault lines in the 1960s and 1970s and her changing personal beliefs about equality and opportunity. That discomfort was already apparent in the 1965 hearings, when she grilled HBCU officials about how they might use Title III's support. Like many older white Democrats in the early 1970s, personal unease had turned to outrage amid repeated inner-city uprisings, increased campus protests, and escalating demands for affirmative action.[38]

Green dismissed both the White House's financing floor and Pell's basic grant as threats to cherished education traditions—conventions that have since been reevaluated for their roles in perpetuating inequality. For example, she always insisted that help should go first to those with talent, which, according to elite institutions (like James Conant's Harvard) could be assessed scientifically. In reality, the metrics they used favored applicants who only added to the exclusive, all-white, masculine atmosphere that already prevailed on these campuses. Likewise, Green perpetually advocated for states' rights, local control, and institutional autonomy, not the expansion of federal power needed to fundamentally reconstruct the nation, much less the academy, during and after the New Deal. She continued her allegiance to those principles into the 1960s when hers was one of the loudest voices arguing for campus financial aid officers, not federal officials, to have authority over the money distributed through HEA's tuition assistance options.[39]

She considered those threats to academic autonomy to have instigated the campus unrest she found so repugnant in the late 1960s and early 1970s. She blamed overly generous financial assistance for enabling ungrateful young people to enroll. She alluded to white insurgents and radicals of color when she railed against the "disorder and disruption [that] threaten to rip the fabric binding our institutions of higher education." She also insinuated that these presumably poor, minority upstarts might be uninterested in going to class because they were unprepared for demanding coursework, a rebuke of the need-based support she had opposed since the lengthy defense act deliberations. Just five years after HEA had offered such aid, she assumed the scholarships had lowered both admission standards and the overall quality of campuses, now riddled with un-American zealots.[40]

Green sounded a lot like the conservative Americans that Nixon liked to call the silent majority—and that historians have considered the backbone of a white backlash. The former schoolteacher was hardly quiet when colleagues discussed the basic grant plan, the omnibus bill the president submitted to the Senate, and the White House's financing floor. Students were not "'entitled' as a matter of right to $1,400 of other taxpayers' money," she declared. Help had to remain "an educational program." She demanded that

"Financial aid supplied by the Federal Government should depend on the academic achievement and the motivation of the student." Anything else, she feared, would turn "student financial aid . . . into a welfare program."[41]

There was an ugly truth at the heart of Green's repugnant remonstrations that would not become clear for decades. Enrolling in, much less affording, higher education remained unimaginable for the many citizens and immigrants excluded from the Ivory Tower before and after HEA's passage. Yet many white middle- and working-class Americans (including those sending Nixon "grief mail") also struggled to afford higher education. Degrees had become necessary to stay in (much less enter) the middle or professional classes in the twentieth century's final decades, when well-paying work steadily disappeared and inequality soared. Those Americans' livelihoods had never really been all that secure. New Dealers had, after all, creatively financed what scholars later labeled affirmative action for white families headed by men. Government-guaranteed financial products and public-private support for housing, retirement, and unemployment had never included adequate education and health care from cradle to grave. By the early 1970s, Green had reason to fear that Nixon's financing floor and Pell's basic grant would lead to the "disenfranchisement of the middle class." She received letters from self-described "middle-income people" from around the country "at my wits end in trying to determine how I can survive this environment of taxes and costs." The writer, a frustrated, indebted father, could not "even take my wife out to dinner" after paying for the needs of his three children, sister-in-law, and senile father living in a nursing home.[42]

Green still did not want to break with the tradition of offering the most federal support for students. She nevertheless wanted a mix of tuition assistance for undergraduates and financial aid for campuses. She still shuddered at giving anyone the federal free ride lawmakers had despised since the GI Bill deliberations. She never considered making campus funding contingent on college admissions or financial aid policies. At hearings she accordingly pressed academics to offer concrete proposals but also worked with them privately to craft an approach to better allocate government resources between postsecondary institutions. Many education lobbyists discussed unrestricted support based on unmet instructional costs, graduation rates, and enrollment numbers but finally settled on grants based on the number of students and additional allowances for needy undergraduates.

Green could get behind basing funding on undergraduate enrollments but refused to champion tying aid to admitting needy applicants. Unlike Pell and Nixon aides, she wanted financial aid officers to have even more discretion over distributing federal tuition assistance. She envisioned reducing the importance of family income for scholarship eligibility, which undergraduates would no longer receive with a guarantee of funding for subsequent academic years. She expected students to prove themselves deserving of such help. She also wanted work-study to be offered on the basis of merit as well as financial need, not just family income, believing that promising young people, including middle-class and upper-income enrollees in expensive campuses, should have the opportunity to work their way through college. She even recommended eligibility for part-time students, so they would not be effectively punished for balancing work with study, as strivers had done to pay for their own educations for decades.[43]

Few lawmakers wanted as much robust, unconditional direct aid for campuses as Green did. They certainly discussed dire assessments of the academy's new depression, but some privately admitted it might be best to let underfunded institutions, like Nebraska's Wahoo College, close rather than intervene to keep them open. Yet some, including Minnesota Representative Albert Quie, had a particular fondness for and allegiance to small private institutions, like his own alma mater, St. Olaf College. He had dutifully submitted the president's overall proposal for consideration and hoped the idea for a financial assistance floor would become a substitute (rather than a supplement, as Pell proposed) for the federal grants that colleges allocated. Quie showed far more interest in a plan he introduced, along with fellow Republican Senator Peter Dominick, from Colorado, to provide institutional funding based on graduation rates. Both disliked the idea of basing funding on enrollments, which they feared might lower admission standards. Their suggestion found surprising support from Harvard alumnus John Brademas. The Indiana Democrat had spent a year teaching political science at St. Mary's College and also rejected the notion of basing federal support on the enrollment numbers that colleges submitted. Quie and Dominick's plan left enrollment determining just 15 percent of the funding for two-year institutions. But community colleges had a real champion in Senator Harrison Williams, a New Jersey Republican, who proposed broad support that was eventually folded into the omnibus bill that senators would spend months fighting over.[44]

Lawmakers also wrangled over Title IX, an addition that exemplified the complexity of 1970s politics. Well before some congresswomen called for laws to prohibit sex discrimination, in the 1971 and 1972 legislative sessions, feminists across the country had been publicly demanding that colleges genuinely open their doors to women. Neither they nor their allies, however, shared the same personal reasons for waging the political fight to add Title IX. Green, the former schoolteacher, had tried to include equal rights language in earlier legislation, a provision that also appealed to Representative Patsy Mink of Hawaii, who had joined the House after the overwhelming 1964 Democratic victories. Unlike Green, whose vocation as a teacher had long been dominated by women, Mink was an attorney—and one who had initially pursued law only because, despite her standout undergraduate record, no medical school would admit her. She graduated from the University of Chicago Law School and became the first Asian American woman admitted to the Aloha State's bar. Alas, no established firm would hire her, so she opened her own practice and, like Green, pursued a political career through Democrat circles. Both Mink and Green pushed for Title IX in the House, and Women's Equity League activists credit Green especially with ensuring its passage. These "determined women" had been, as Eric Wentworth wrote in the *Washington Post*, "bombarding both the Nixon Administration and Congress with demands" for educational equity. "Don't lobby for this bill," one feminist remembered Green insisting. "Leave it. The opposition is not there right now so don't call attention to it." But some House Republicans did fight the provision, mostly with an eye to protecting the traditions of the Ivy League, the majority of whose colleges were still single-sex. Mink and House Representative Shirley Chisholm, Democrat from New York, stopped them from omitting Title IX, although neither could prevent an Illinois Republican from adding an amendment that exempted admissions from Title IX's broad guarantees.[45]

Indiana Democrat Birch Bayh had a much tougher fight in the Senate, in which no woman served in 1972. American Association of University Women representatives, for example, had to assure his colleagues that equal opportunities to borrow for higher learning would not saddle young women with "the so-called negative dowry" that had come up in college-cost discussions since the 1950s. Bayh had both political and personal reasons for insisting sex discrimination be prohibited in the reauthorization. He considered the ban a backup in case the Equal Rights Amendment, despite recent momentum, was not ratified. Such federal assurances were important to a Hoosier who remembered his grandmother doing much to run the family farm. His wife, Marvella, had been denied admission to the University of Virginia, an elite public university the courts had forced to become completely coed in 1970. He later admitted he had been uncomfortable when she decided to use her teaching degree after their children had left home. "Her ability to do so many things," the senator later explained, "gave me an insight and I became familiar with some of the limitations that were placed on women that had that kind of talent."[46]

Bayh failed to convince his colleagues, despite citing statistics and hundreds of charges women made against universities in his February 1971 amendment to the Senate bill. University of Indiana, Notre Dame, and Purdue presidents continually pressured him to abandon Title IX. They, like many other administrators and parents complaining to lawmakers, feared it would ruin men's sports. Bayh's colleagues in a Senate colloquy barely discussed his bill. Colorado Republican Peter Dominick asked about quotas, military schools, dorms, and athletics. Bayh dismissed those concerns, despite his Rocky Mountain colleague's joke that he "would have had much more fun playing college football if it had been integrated." South Carolina's Strom Thurmond was able to kill the bill the day after Bayh introduced it. He warned of federal control over state systems that might threaten women's colleges and military academies, like his state's then men's-only Citadel. Nevada's Howard Cannon ruled that Bayh's proposal had nothing to do with the educational amendments being discussed, an assertion only thirty-two senators opposed.[47]

Lawmakers had a far easier time agreeing to create Sallie Mae, the government-sponsored enterprise that would become emblematic of the importance of government-guaranteed financial products to the country's public-private social safety net. A California representative had submitted a bill for an "FHA-type mechanism for education" months before Nixon's first education message. Such a mechanism had been one of the few presidential suggestions senators had shown any interest in during the hearings over the president's first education proposal. College administrators disliked making campuses the primary lender and turning defense loans over to a National Student Loan Association, but as one Nixon aide wrote in a 1970 memo, there seemed "to be unanimous support for the secondary market concept among lenders, state guarantee agencies, and educators" as long as bankers originated any guaranteed loans.[48]

Representatives, in fact, did not raise many objections when two Illinois Republicans sponsored House bills to create a secondary market for guaranteed loans in 1970 to end the "bitter money squeeze" making it impossible for lenders to "meet the demands for student loans." Green received letters from college presidents, students, and middle-income parents confident that creating a secondary market would encourage banks to make more loans. One Georgia mother wrote that she felt "discouraged when all around me the children of welfare recipients are enrolling in college and having their way 'paid' by the taxpayers." Other lawmakers shared correspondence from eager financiers and desperate undergraduates who had been urged to write their representatives. Financial aid officers and lenders testified forcefully in favor of a secondary market. One American Banking Association representative even reminded lawmakers that "there is one thing in the housing area that has been the salvation of housing in the past five years, and that has been the Federal National Mortgage Association, and that is exactly what we are asking for in the student loan area." Amid such widespread enthusiasm, the *Wall Street Journal* quipped during the contentious hearings that the "son of Fannie Mae is going to college" with ambitions "to buy student loans."[49]

Only Pell tried to stop Sallie Mae from showing up on campuses, although Green, too, had concerns about the secondary market. The latter privately asked Treasury officials to assess how "spiraling college costs" and "debt burdens" might affect alumni's "willingness . . . to marry and create families, to buy cars and homes." Pell's fear was that this GSE would encourage the federal government to only use guaranteed loans to fund higher education. "If we create a Federal agency," he explained, "I think [that program] will stay forever." He hated the idea of stockholders electing a board of directors, which would rob Congress and the executive branch of any real control. He instead suggested having the Treasury Department store a ready supply of guaranteed loans in the reauthorization bill, an idea similar to the Educational Development Bank that Johnson and Nixon staffers had considered. Pell desperately tried to get top educators to embrace this "warehousing account in the Treasury" during hearings, but they were inclined to defer to the Treasury and commercial lenders' judgment of what would ensure enough "liquidity . . . to keep the program going," stressing simply that "we see a need for the program." Richardson, meanwhile, along with other White House aides, dismissed the idea of just storing credit opportunities because the "authority to buy and sell student loans is also essential." Pell gave in to his Republican colleague Peter Dominick's insistence on including a secondary market only in the final months of wrangling, when Dominick came out in support of the general spirit of Pell's pet project, the basic grant.[50]

Lawmakers were divided far more by the basic grant, direct campus funding, and Title IX than they were by the idea of making more schools and degree programs eligible for federal tuition assistance. There was an important precedent for indirect federal support for a wider range of educational opportunities. Subsequent versions of the original GI Bill had allowed veterans to use their education benefits at a proprietary institution if civilians comprised at least 15 percent of the student body. More than twenty years after lawmakers had called out for-profits for their widespread abuse of the 1944 Servicemen's Adjustment Act, top academics continued to attack proprietary schools. Yet, a few education experts started to suggest in the late 1960s that those institutions should be eligible for guaranteed loans. For-profits, along with a surprising range of nonprofit public and private options, had been offering the kind of flexible technical training and certification that many students valued more than liberal arts degrees, particularly if they had dropped out or were looking for new or better jobs during the stagnant 1970s. States had even begun to certify and license more of the estimated ten thousand proprietary outfits providing technical, vocational, business, cosmetology, flight, and medical training to over three million students through short-term, two-year, four-year, and correspondence programs.[51]

Giving Americans alternatives appealed to many in Washington. Choice had always been a fundamental feature of federal higher education policies, which had always let campus administrators and students decide if they wanted to take advantage of government aid. That approach had helped lawmakers skirt thorny issues, like exercising federal control or supporting segregated institutions, since the 1930s. Such liberties became important in a new way in the 1970s, when some lawmakers raised concerns about the increased likelihood that alumni of for-profit schools would default. HEW officials insisted that helping Americans afford trade schools, community colleges, and other public, private, and for-profit schools would actually "diversify" the academy and ensure that "a student coming from a very poor family can receive sufficient assistance." Such "freedom of choice" would "preserve the pluralism that is inherent in higher education." Different types of schools combined to make up "a single great natural resource," whether "public or private." Those arguments appealed to Pell, who had benefited greatly from correspondence courses as an adult and valued those "privately owned institutions that serve a real need in their community" and in many cases had "gained fine reputations." When he met with academics, he also reiterated that the bill made no assumption that "everybody should go to college" but instead provided needed opportunities to enroll in "career training, junior and community colleges, branch campuses and proprietary business schools." American Association of University Women representatives also insisted that this change would be invaluable to the many older women in need of retraining or advanced skills "to enter or reenter the labor force"—the kind of classes that trade schools focused on offering. The American Vocational Association's president even insisted that "vocational education, not general education, is truly the mainstream of an education and manpower training program."[52]

Broad bipartisan agreement on increasing Title IV eligibility and creating Sallie Mae still did not ensure that a deeply divided Congress would actually reauthorize HEA before the hastily added one-year extension expired. The issue of busing almost derailed the entire legislative process in the final months of negotiations. During two years of wrangling over HEA, children, parents, and judges had grown impatient with the slow pace of integrating elementary and secondary schools. K-12 education policies had been severed from postsecondary aid since the early 1960s but this issue was timely and somewhat related to higher education since K-12 teachers prepared young people for the college educations they would need to even compete for decent jobs. Court-ordered busing had hardly pleased mothers, fathers, kids, and teachers who protested the mandate, found themselves in the middle of protests, or read extensive newspaper accounts of conflicts across the country. Representatives started offering amendments to the reauthorization legislation to curb busing in late 1971, all of which passed by a two-to-one margin. Senators did not join the legislative free-for-all until February 1972. They spent six hours a day for seven days debating twenty amendments pertaining to busing and desegregation, a delay that gave Bayh the opportunity to add back in a sex-discrimination ban stricken from the Senate's reauthorization legislation.[53]

Temporary Reconciliation

That massive bill still had to be reconciled with the equally sprawling House version, a formidable task for Representative Carl Perkins's conference committee. The quiet, often rumpled, former schoolteacher turned lawyer had more than enough experience. The Kentucky Democrat had assumed chairmanship of the House Education and Labor Committee in 1967. He had spent his almost twenty years in Congress supporting civil rights legislation, demanding money to aid his impoverished home district, and advocating for generous social welfare programs. "He smiles and clutches your arm, but watch out," a colleague once remarked. "He would do anything to get his way." Another remembered, "He just wears the opposition out." Indeed, Perkins constantly told 1972 conference delegates, "We're going to get a bill."[54]

One colleague remembered that he "handled the conference like [chess champion] Bobby Fischer." The process unfolded over two months, which included eighty hours of closed-door meetings. House and Senate delegates spent twenty-one sessions trying to come to agreement on the hundreds of differences between the chambers' two bills, which took four large volumes to enumerate. Some of the distinctions seemed trivial, like which formula to use to allocate support, but in fact signified important political differences that would have a major impact on campus financing and college affordability. Other dissimilarities were more obvious. For example, the House bill lacked a provision for the basic grant. There were also stark differences between the prohibitions against sex discrimination. Institutional aid also divided lawmakers, whose discussions nevertheless revolved around busing.[55]

The Conference Committee, under Perkins's direction, tackled issues in numerical order instead of dealing with items that might derail the entire process. They easily reached agreement on provisions like SLMA, which kept with the general spirit of how lawmakers had creatively financed higher education and social welfare. Perkins called for a vote only when a consensus seemed to have emerged. If debate persisted without any apparent reconciliation, he tabled discussion so hearings could move on. Members took just two weeks to make their way through the bills the first time. Lawmakers hammered out an accord on Sallie Mae on March 27, just eleven days after they first met. They also quickly concurred on Title IX, which still broadly forbade sex discrimination but exempted dorms, military schools, private colleges' admissions offices, and single-sex institutions. Lawmakers even waived rules for seven years for universities starting to become coed.[56]

Perkins had them tackle that difference after a particularly rancorous session over a serious sticking point, the basic grant. Such direct help for undergraduates was in some ways a break with past practices which either offered them defense or guaranteed loans or relied on campuses to award scholarships. Green still found herself hopelessly outnumbered whenever conferees debated the financing floor. Most supported the program, but fought over details of eligibility for the full amount and whether basic grants would come at the expense of existing federal financial aid offerings. Only in early May did conferees reach an agreement to fund this program provided that the other three forms of tuition assistance were also funded at set dollar amounts.[57]

Disagreements persisted over institutional support. That political logjam highlighted how decades of fighting over taxing, spending, and states' rights continued to thwart federal support for higher education, which many now recognized as a public good and an individual need, perhaps even as a right (as Pell insisted). But lawmakers hated Pell's method for allocating money for instructional costs. They could only agree to the "Mooney Cocktail," named after an aide who came up with it during intense, private negotiations that did not include Green. Those involved insisted only 10 percent of direct support for campuses would be based on enrollments. As such, this so-called capitation grant barely supplemented the 90 percent given out on the basis of the number of students using financial assistance. In order to incentivize and award institutions that admitted undergraduates whom federal officials deemed in need of support, half the cost of the instruction allowance would be based on the number of basic grant recipients. The other half (45 percent of the direct assistance available) would be determined by the number of students whom campus financial aid officers designated in need of help. This formula even included a bonus for small colleges that admitted low-income students.[58]

Rumors about the plan circulated but its announcement at the May 16 final session ambushed Green almost as dramatically as lawmakers had thwarted John Rankin in the final hours of GI Bill negotiations. Busing had bogged down the previous week's morning discussions. During the final afternoon session, conferees worked out details on easier items, including allocating state aid and guaranteed loan eligibility. Conferees only returned to busing in the early morning hours, when they brokered a complicated agreement that even necessitated frantic phone calls to those absent. Only at the very end of the drawn-out session did the members return to institutional aid. Pell dramatically proposed a 50/50 financial aid formula, which Brademas countered with the already agreed-upon Mooney Cocktail's 10-45-45 arrangement. This staged give-and-take lasted but five minutes. Neither idea thrilled Green, who chafed at making support contingent on tuition assistance. She tried to stop the session by claiming there was no longer a quorum, only to find her count off because someone had briefly left the room for a drink of water. She ended up leaving before the session's 5:13 A.M. end.[59]

Senate, House, or presidential approval of the conference report was hardly a given. Pell endeavored to convince his colleagues to ignore the busing restrictions tagged on since the bill, particularly through the basic grant, provided so much support for undergraduates and colleges. "The wealth of our nation lies in the education of its citizens," he reminded his colleagues when presenting the legislation he insisted "would invest much in that citizenry." Only fifteen senators ended up voting against the act, which sixty-three approved.[60]

Passage in the House seemed far less certain. Representatives remained bitterly divided over the busing issue and many disliked the complicated Mooney Cocktail. Green tried to exploit those frustrations by trying to get higher education lobbyists to denounce the legislation just weeks before the extension was set to expire. College and university higher-ups could hardly reject $21 million in support even if all of it did not go to them or would be given out as they wanted. "We felt she had done our bidding and now we had some obligation to help her and stick by her," one lobbyist explained. "However, the question really becomes, does one have some obligation to commit suicide?" Perkins and others involved in conference negotiations warned that academics could not expect anything better. "If higher education fails to back this now," one member warned, "cries of fiscal crisis in higher education will fall on deaf ears in the future." Perkins also tried to persuade educators and his colleagues. He had more resources than Green to do so. Staffers remembered "sending out poop sheets and summaries and analyses and counter summaries, and we were on the telephone with everyone we could think of." One recalled that "Perkins was talking to every member on the floor, and particularly cornering southerners," even calling them up "at home in the evening." The congressman, he said, "could dwell on whatever piece of the bill was most of interest to them." Perkins labored so hard, another assistant recalled, that "this bill practically killed the Chairman." He actually collapsed just days after the June 8 vote, when 218 representatives approved and 108 opposed the bill.[61]

That legislation also divided and vexed the Nixon administration. Some aides wanted the president to veto the entire bill. Others urged him to sign it but exploit the busing provision "to the hilt" in order for Nixon to "be credited with exposing a Congressional fraud and defending the common man." The busing add-on rankled many White House officials, who dismissed the bill as a costly "mixed bag." The White House had been signaling during months of congressional squabbling that both chambers' bills were too big and expensive. Yet, as a Senate aide pointed out, "the way the Basic Grant came out was philosophically so close to what the Administration had been thinking that they were stuck with it." Richardson agreed with that sentiment and urged Nixon to sign: "This is the issue over which we fought the entire higher education establishment in Washington, Mrs. Green, and won."[62]

The bill's details differed in important ways but generally fit with the basic idea of providing a financing floor for higher education, prioritizing student assistance over institutional aid, and theoretically empowering students to choose where they would use the money. Such direct federal tuition assistance spoke to the education workgroup's initial hope to use even more market mechanisms to fund, expand, and diversify higher education. Colleges would need to compete for needy students who would be empowered consumers with more choices thanks to basic grants and new Title IV eligibility rules. Richardson also emphasized that Congress had created SLMA. He even publicly deemed the final legislation "a major achievement" capturing "the heart of President Nixon's higher education initiatives." College heads from around the country begged the president to sign the bill but Nixon still told reporters that "it is one of the closest calls that I have had since being in this office." He had "mixed emotions" since "many of the education provisions . . . are recommendations of this Administration" and "very much in the public interest." Section 803, the busing provisions, still gave the president pause, because "from a legal standpoint it is so vague and so ambiguous that it totally fails to deal with this highly volatile issue." They made him hesitate, whereas "If they could be separated from the rest of the bill, there would not be any question about signing the bill."[63]

Busing in fact dominated the president's remarks when he sat down to sign the 1972 Education Amendments Act on June 23, 1972, just days before HEA would expire. Nixon warned that, despite the changes, "we will not be able to realize fully our principles of equity." He never explained why he reached that conclusion and never even mentioned Title IX or expanding Title IV eligibility. Instead, the self-appointed spokesman for the silent majority spent his time deriding the busing section, where he considered the reauthorization "most obviously deficient." He had, after all, "asked Congress to draw up new uniform national desegregation standards" in order "to resolve the spreading social crisis that has arisen . . . as a result of massive court-order busing." The president fumed that "Congress has not given us the answer," but only "rhetoric" and a temporary moratorium whose relief "is illusory."[64]

Pell and many others looked past Nixon's digs at lawmakers. "One of my desires on entering the Senate was to work on education," the senator told his colleagues the day the bill became law. To have the act "signed into law and know that in the future, higher education will be available to so many more people, is a most gratifying event." Some college presidents admitted relief because "it was this or nothing at all for the next year or two." Reporters quoted disgruntled administrators but paid far more attention to the controversial busing provisions when briefly summarizing key policy changes, which also included the new basic grant program, $900 million for college assistance, a slush fund to help financially strapped small colleges, a sizeable guaranteed loan expansion, and Sallie Mae. All seemed proof that "the federal government's prime objective is to equalize educational opportunities," both by subsidizing "needy students" and "schools to the extent they further equal opportunities." Economist Herbert Stein, writing in *Ladies' Home Journal*, declared Title IX to be part of a "second economic revolution" for women, who would "obtain freedom in the choice of occupations, and equality of pay and equal job opportunities." Most journalists, however, barely covered that addition or for-profits' eligibility in their glowing coverage of these amendments. *New Republic* editors did publish an education professor's fear that most young people would use federal tuition assistance at liberal arts colleges that needed fee revenue and the institutional aid tied to the basic grant. The result would be "an overcredentialed society . . . that too infrequently identifies real skills and talents and too often labels as failures those who don't have some kind of credential."[65]

Praise and reservation quickly gave way to rage after the Nixon administration started trying to carry out what lawmakers had passed. Implementing the Education Amendments was just as complicated as rolling out the GI Bill and NDEA. Education Commissioner Sidney Marland openly complained that the "hundreds of pieces in this mosaic of law" hardly clarified what Congress wanted the administration to do with the lengthy legislation. "It depends on whom you talk to," Marland noted, "as to what Congress meant." He and other Education Office personnel quickly realized that Congress and the president had agreed on a bill that almost derailed the guaranteed loan program SLMA was supposed to improve and for-profit schools were intended to use. The reauthorization had mandated that all students had to prove need in order to qualify for guaranteed lending. The Education Commissioner's staff considered themselves following the letter of the complex law when they issued new rules for a needs test just a month after Nixon signed the legislation.[66]

The ill-timed release derailed crucial summer negotiations with banks for the credit that so many Americans relied on to finance their tuition bills. The requirements confused and enraged thousands of Americans, who hardly questioned the use of complicated government guaranteed loans to cover basic needs. Some, like law student Andrew Pognany, fumed to Nixon about offering basic grants to the poor but not ensuring that the middle class continued to be able to borrow. Some applicants found themselves excluded from the federal help they desperately needed. Clearly qualified candidates also rightly worried that classes would start before they received funds to cover tuition. The new requirement also frustrated financial aid officers and lenders. The National Association of Student Financial Aid Administrators warned that the "burdensome new administrative requirements" had "increased red tape" and processing costs, which were already starting to discourage financiers from participating in a program many Americans considered vital. The American Banking Association added to the uproar when it publicly doubted all applications could be processed before fall classes began.[67]

Outrage prompted lawmakers to act far faster than they had when starting the complex reauthorization process. White House aides fought over how to respond since "the political ramifications" in an election year, as a Treasury official emphasized, "are very serious and could significantly damage the president's image and standing amongst students, parents of college-age students (especially in the middle-income and upper-lower ranges), educators, and some lenders." The administration ultimately asked Congress to pass emergency legislation delaying the rule's implementation in order to process pending loans and work out new qualification guidelines. Furious senators and representatives accused the administration of intentionally creating the logjam to cut spending and create regulations that were, as one Republican fumed, "so cumbersome and so troublesome that very few students have been able to get past the institution's financial aid officer and through the bank." Lawmakers nonetheless passed a bill just days after the president's request.[68]

That quick action hardly lessened the arduous, multifaceted task of implementing the 1972 legislation's changes. Education Office staff still had to figure out, for example, how to get basic grants to students, as the other assistance programs had always been channeled through campus financial aid offices. Appointees also struggled to determine basic grant eligibility rules since Congress had only broadly outlined how to determine need and family contribution. They could not easily ascertain, for example, whether lawmakers had agreed to help only low-income applicants or help any low- or moderate-income undergraduates who could demonstrate need. Aides endeavored to figure out all the details while simultaneously organizing and staffing SLMA.[69]

Those managerial headaches failed to stop the Nixon administration from (as some lawmakers feared) surreptitiously undercutting the legislation the president had just begrudgingly signed. Historians have only recently recognized how White House Republicans used their power over bureaucratic agencies to thwart the Democrats who controlled Congress—a strategy, one appointee later explained, that helped the Nixon administration make policy covertly because "operations is policy." Elaborating on that phrase, he said why: "Much of the day-to-day management of domestic programs—regulation-writing, grant approval, and budget apportionment" involved many substantive decisions that affected outcomes. "Getting control" of mundane tasks drove "the President's strategy for domestic government in his second term." This sly master plan involved a range of seemingly benign actions. Nixon, for example, replaced HEW Secretary Elliot Richardson in February 1973 with Caspar Weinberger, the fiscally conservative director of the Office of Management and Budget.[70]

That staffing change proved pivotal in budget battles that cost colleges and students dearly. Nixon aides sought to rein in spending and cut what they considered bureaucratic bloat from the many agencies created during and since the New Deal. The president threatened to override allocation bills and impound funds Congress had already earmarked. Chief executives (including Thomas Jefferson, Franklin Roosevelt, Harry Truman, John Kennedy, and LBJ) had received congressional permission to withdraw relatively small funding amounts if an agency no longer needed them. Nixon turned this fiscal tool into a political weapon when he demanded $12 billion impounded. Democratic senators successfully sued to protect congressional power over the purse in 1973, which did little to erase confusion over the White House's proposed dramatic cuts to social welfare programs. "I use to have fun," a HEW higher-up remembered in a later interview, "by pointing out that the Nixon Administration's budgets for education provided significant increases over the Johnson budgets." Neither president had requested Title IV's scholarships be fully funded, nor had lawmakers appropriated as much as the law permitted. The devil remained in the details, though. Nixon's 1973 proposal generously allotted almost $1 billion for the basic grant program but authorized no money for other new HEA initiatives and phased out the still beloved defense loans Johnson had unsuccessfully tried to vanquish.[71]

Many lawmakers and college administrators protested the surreptitious cuts, but both they and White House aides found themselves largely at Green's mercy. After the reauthorization's passage, she dramatically abandoned her senior position on the House education subcommittee in what would be her final two years in office. She chose instead to take a seemingly low-ranking position on the powerful Ways and Means and Appropriations committees, where, she predicted in her 1973 letter resigning from the education committee, "action this year is going to be . . . based on the Presidential vetoes of appropriations bills, the impoundment of so many billions of dollars' worth of funds, and the executive action to terminate programs." The former schoolteacher ended up on the subcommittee overseeing HEW, where her expertise in education actually gave her considerable clout in deliberations over funding for an agency that still housed the Office of Education. She first exercised this newfound power in spring 1973, less than a year after Congress had amended HEA. Funding needed to be decided for the upcoming academic year, and in hearings she made no secret of her dislike of the basic grants. Federal officials, she railed, would run "all of the kids through a computer" to determine their needs instead of letting financial aid officers "sit across the table from the student." Her warnings shaped what her colleagues allocated. Congress restored funds for campus-distributed assistance and equipment, as well as language and area studies. Money also incentivized states to offer scholarships and start educational agencies, the kind of devolution of federal power and authority both Green and Nixon sought. A longtime defender of talent over need, Green also convinced her colleagues to only devote $122 million to the basic grant that helped low-income students, not the middle-income families she had long privileged. But that direct help for the poor, lawmakers ruled, could only go to fully enrolled freshman, who could only receive a maximum of $300.[72]

Neglect proved just as damaging as political combat in that budget skirmish, the battle over higher education funding, and the larger war over what remained of the New Deal and Great Society. Lawmakers, including the fanciful Pell, had a lot on their dockets and difficulty keeping up with the status of and funding for pet projects. By the time Nixon resigned in August 1974, for example, occupational education, community college, and cost-of-instruction (except for veterans) received no money. There had also been many false starts and puny earmarks for older programs, new initiatives, and expanding state education commissions, which now had to include representatives from proprietary institutions if states wanted federal aid. Pell and his staff even struggled to keep tabs on the basic grant program because, as he fretted, Education Office appointees tended "to rewrite the law . . . to the point that we do not recognize it."[73]

SLMA also seemed to have had a false start. Financiers paid the most attention to a GSE that reporters described as "designed to backstop the $4.5-billion Student Loan Program by providing liquidity to lenders, both through 'warehousing' of loans and, later, through actual purchase of the loans." This agency had little in common with the education bank with which

Nixon and Johnson White House officials had toyed. SLMA's newly appointed president publicly promised to raise $1 billion in the agency's first year but was not able to raise money on the stock market to start buying loans until October 1973 when many students, parents, and financial aid officers still had a hard time securing guaranteed loans. Nevertheless, "Sallie Mae was a smash hit," which Lehman Brothers, Merrill Lynch, Morgan Stanley, and Salomon Brothers handled. A dealer still dismissed the $745 million in bids for the $100 million in 182-day notes as "the usual rush to put a new name on the portfolio books."[74]

Wall Street excitement at the time did not seem to foretell how finance would become even more important to American life than it had already been. Experts considered Sallie Mae's charter, purpose, operations, and future "clouded" in the mid-1970s. The infant agency appeared to have "had little impact on the student loan market" lawmakers had intended the debt clearinghouse to nurture. Insiders outlining SLMA's operations a few years later, when HEA again came up for renewal, still had to explain the government-sponsored enterprise "in layman's terms." Lawmakers did not seem to grasp the importance of SLMA buying existing loans, collecting those debts, and lending to banks whose "funds are no longer tied up in its student loan portfolio," so "the funds received from Sallie Mae can be turned into more student loans."[75]

Such seemingly mundane tasks enabled Sallie Mae appointees to eventually transform the nascent student loan industry into a powerful, lucrative financial sector to which Americans would find themselves overwhelmingly indebted. By the 1970–1971 academic year, one million had to borrow more than $1 billion just for two semesters or three quarters of college. That headline-making record was followed just a few months later by reports of the default rate reaching 4 percent and Education Office officials promising "to collect every dime that's been paid in claims" for the roughly $50 million owed when Congress finally passed the complicated Education Amendments that doubled down on lending.[76]

Those changes did little to make higher education more affordable as the parties continued to realign and lawmakers in and outside Washington steadily cut higher education spending in the decades that followed. The colloquial definition of federal education aid understandably shifted from direct government support for campuses to tuition assistance for students. Their fees had always been an important revenue source for nonprofit institutions but public and private campuses became even more reliant on tuition before experts finally recognized, decades later, that the 1970s stagflation had foretold a new era of political gridlock, insecurity, inequality, and decline. Increasing tuition rates and debt levels made it difficult for even college graduates to survive in a country ever more dependent on financial products and real estate transactions. More government-guaranteed credit, still masquerading as federal support for social welfare, helped students and parents creatively finance degrees that gave them only a chance to compete for decent jobs. By the millennium's turn, many citizens, including those from the shrinking middle class, proclaimed themselves trapped by the debt they owed for their educations. The most indentured were low-income enrollees, women, and borrowers of color. They had historically been excluded from many nonprofit institutions, had to fight for equal opportunities promised under the law, were unequally paid for the same jobs (no matter their credentials), and were supposed to benefit the most from the celebrated color-blind and gender-equity additions to HEA.

7

Bankers Lose Their Sweetheart Deal

"How much do I have to pay?" many Americans asked during a late-1990s study of what the public understood about college costs and financial assistance programs. University of Illinois chancellor Stanley Ikenberry and American Council on Education executive Terry Hartle painted a grim picture in their 1998 report on a nine-month investigation underwritten by the Lilly Endowment (a philanthropy) and USA Group Foundation (the nation's largest guarantor of student loans). The study had included sixteen parental focus groups and telephone interviews with two thousand randomly selected citizens across the country ranging in age from twenty-one to seventy. "Despite the high price tag" associated with higher education, Ikenberry and Hartle reported, "the public thinks that it represents a 'good value for the money' since it will 'lead to a good life.'" They went on to conclude: "The link between a college education and access to the American middle-class has never been more obvious."[1]

But respondents still worried about cost. They had no idea how expensive college was, did not understand why the price continued to rise, considered professors indifferent to the expense, and generally did not "know how much financial aid is available to help meet college bills, where it comes from, or how to get it." Ikenberry and Hartle reported that the firm hired to field their survey "had never seen a knowledge gap of such size or magnitude." A third of respondents blamed high salaries for faculty and administrators. Few named the reasons that college presidents gave for hiking fees, which included needs to keep up with technology, fund scientific research, make up for cuts in state support, provide in-house student aid, and comply with government regulations.[2]

Those surveyed knew even less about tuition assistance. Many thought businesses, corporations, and universities provided help. Others resented not knowing the answers. As Ikenberry and Hartle put it, "Some—especially low-income and minority parents—believe that high prices and the seeming absence of information about student aid are part of a deliberate effort to prevent their children from going to college." When participants were aware that the government did, in fact, provide help, they usually responded that both state and federal authorities offered such assistance. The majority also thought that the total aid available yearly amounted to just a few billion dollars. Most doubted researchers informing them that $50 billion could be tapped annually. One jokingly "asked where she could 'get in line.'" More than a third did not see loans as a "form of financial aid," despite the cost savings from the interest subsidy on many federal offerings, "because it comes with a string attached—it has to be repaid." The authors interpreted these findings with dismay: "The public's lack of understanding can only be viewed as a failure by those of us who pride ourselves as teachers and educators."[3]

Respondents had a better understanding of the status quo than the researchers realized. They may not have grasped how much campuses depended on them to enroll and make use of financial aid options, but their responses captured the complexity of student assistance. The industry around tuition programs exploded after the 1972 reauthorization created Sallie Mae (SLMA). By 2007, the sector included three thousand lenders, thirty guarantee agencies, seventy loan servicing companies, and several clearinghouses—totals that did not include the many paid consultants who charged students and parents for advice on financing degrees. The industry's size showed the extent to which families relied on the loans that bankers offered, financial aid officers gave out, and federal officials guaranteed. States also continued to offer tuition assistance, although far less was available than in decades past. Help could also be found from businesses, religious organizations, community groups, and nonprofits.[4]

Citizens were understandably confused about how much support was available. Caps, interest rates, and eligibility rules for Title IV programs had fluctuated since the passage of the Higher Education Act in 1965. Some cuts, as parents rightly sensed, had also been made to limit access, especially to the coeds and students of color that liberals had tried to help through Title IX and the basic grant program. Survey participants were correct in their hesitation to call lending, which represented the bulk of the billions available, a real form of financial assistance. The loans came with interest, which meant a needy student might spend more in the end than their wealthier classmates for the same education. Borrowers would spend even more if they took advantage of the extended repayment and temporary forbearance options intended to keep them from defaulting. The necessity of such alternatives reflected that defaults had only increased since the early 1960s, when lawmakers first noticed borrowers failing to pay back defense loans after dropping out or graduating. Remittance was even less certain after the 1970s, by which point a college degree had become a requirement just to compete for white-collar work. Ongoing political warfare had shredded even the Roosevelt administration's limited public-private provisions and government-guaranteed financial instruments for economic stability, individual opportunity, and social welfare. During that pivotal decade, college costs continued to increase while job standards, wages, and benefits stagnated.

That reality became increasingly undeniable in the new millennium. Politicians remained as starkly divided as ever after the 1972 reauthorization. But the country's tectonic political realignment had steadily left the real divisions between, not within, the two major parties. Democrats and Republicans fought over loans, tax breaks, interest rates, bankruptcy rules, for-profit eligibility guidelines, and a host of seemingly small (but still nefarious) rules and regulations. Seesawing control of and standoffs between the White House and Congress resulted in only fig-leaf reforms that promised to help the growing number of students facing fewer options after commencement. Citizens instead struggled to finance education costs, find good-paying jobs, and repay debts. Those from groups historically excluded from the academy received only marginal help from government-guaranteed financial products, color-blind policies, and targeted assurances of equity such as Title IX. Average household wealth grew much faster for white families than for families of color in this era of escalating inequality and precarity. Women, especially those of color, continued to borrow more and take longer to repay. Senators, representatives, and presidents nevertheless directed their energies toward doing more for the financial services sector, as finance and insurance came to play even more important and visible roles in American life. This, too, mostly benefited the wealthiest Americans, the demographics of which remained as they had always been—despite the fact that more women were becoming their families' main breadwinners and minorities were adding up to majorities in several sizeable states.[5]

Americans drowning in debt finally began to give voice to their heartbreaking stories in the new millennium. Prices and tuition assistance options had increased throughout the twentieth century but struggles to afford college bore a haunting resemblance to the student poverty of the 1920s, which President Johnson had recalled when he signed the 1965 Higher Education Act, and to hardships recounted in the letters that Nixon aides called "grief mail." Now Washington's power brokers heard new tales of woe, along with fraud prosecutions and fresh evidence of how student debt ensnared young people. Finally they were forced to confront, police, and even try to destroy the industry their predecessors had presumed could easily and cheaply expand higher education.

A New Era in Higher Education's Creative Financing

The student loan industry had thrived on the complicated, piecemeal federal policies that made up the American approach to underwriting postsecondary education. The 1972 amendments, it later became apparent, marked the end of congressional interest in direct funding for colleges and universities to ensure affordability. Thereafter, some administrators continued to beg for such support to keep costs down, but most Democrats and Republicans only entertained proposals for tinkering with the cost-of-instruction payments eventually included in the GI Bill's rollout and fought over in the 1972 reauthorization. Mere fiddling could not overcome the challenges to colleges hit by rising operational costs, new rules for hiring, employment benefits, and workplace safety, and aging facilities and equipment (including such mundane burdens as antiquated telephone systems). Educators nevertheless found themselves among many beleaguered public and nonprofit institutions competing for fewer resources in the 1970s, 1980s, and 1990s. These were decades that would later be associated with a triumph of conservatism in the United

States and of neoliberalism around the world. Lawmakers in both parties had little interest in taxing and spending more to support what remained of the New Deal's public-private social safety net.[6]

Legislatures across the country cut higher education earmarks in the 1970s and after. State and local officials provided a third of operating budgets nationwide in the 1970s and 1980s, while the federal government's share (excluding tuition assistance) continued to decline and the portion covered by fees steadily increased (see appendix, figure A1). Institutions covered 15 percent of their needs with funds from endowments and other internal sources, and just 6 percent with private gifts, donations, and contracts. This disinvestment by government coincided with state universities' long stretch of postwar growth. The percentage of students enrolled in private campuses dropped by 20 percent between 1950 and 1990, while the proportion of public options among all American postsecondary institutions jumped from 35 percent to 55 percent. Yet, by the 1990–1991 academic year, postsecondary earmarks accounted for just 14.1 percent of state budgets, and by a decade later, that figure had fallen to 11.5 percent. Even though the number and percentage of college-aged Americans soared in and after the 1990s, public institutions went from receiving 38.3 percent of their revenue from states to just 24.4 percent. The federal government contributed just 13 percent (a figure that reflects cuts to research support and direct funds, but does not factor in federal funds allocated to the tuition assistance programs accessed by students individually).[7]

By the turn of the millennium, the trend seemed irreversible. As one consultancy to higher education institutions flatly stated, its clients would have to face "the fact that higher education is a discretionary state expenditure, and every public official knows that colleges and universities can raise tuition to compensate for state cutbacks." Tuition rates rose far faster than consumer prices and average disposable incomes after the 1972 reauthorization. For much of the twentieth century, tuition had accounted for 20 percent to 25 percent of the academy's revenue. By 2000, enrollees and their families covered 28 percent of private campuses' operating costs and 19 percent of public institutions' needs. Average tuition rates rose by 47 percent at public universities and 42 percent at private institutions between the 1993–1994 and 2003–2004 academic years.[8]

Cuts undermined lawmakers' promises and federal guarantees of equal, expanded educational opportunities. A few Ivy League schools used endowments to assist talented, needy students. Many admissions officers admitted that spending reductions had reversed the steady inclusion of women, minorities, and first-generation undergraduates, even as they should have had a better chance of enrolling. After the 1972 reauthorization, the number of college-age Americans leveled off and then shrank after the last of the Baby Boomers graduated. Campuses needed more applicants to fill empty spots but higher education still remained disproportionately unaffordable for families of color (see appendix, figure A2). The 1964 Civil Rights Act, Title IX, and color-blind policies like the basic grants did not end systemic racial and gender inequality. Only white and Asian American households earned more than the median household income, which never kept pace with escalating living costs during and after the stagnant 1970s. But private colleges still raised rates in the early 1980s. Experts predicted fewer applications but young people instead clamored to be admitted. Students conflated higher price tags with the prestige necessary for landing lucrative positions and being accepted into top professional and graduate programs. Tax cuts in the 1980s also enabled wealthy families to pay out of pocket for the air of exclusivity these institutions had earnestly cultivated in the early twentieth century. Less prestigious colleges, in contrast, feverishly competed for the next, smaller generation of college-age Americans. Their admissions officers encouraged older Americans, women, immigrants, and citizens of color to apply for full- or part-time programs that promised the skills, alumni connections, and degrees needed to compete for good jobs in years when factories were downsizing or closing, unions were accepting wage and benefit concessions, and better opportunities seemed to be found in the white-collar service sector. For-profits still remained an attractive option for nontraditional students, particularly after Congress eased federal financial aid eligibility requirements. Only .2 percent of students enrolled in proprietary schools in the 1970s, a percentage that rose to 1.6 percent by 1993.[9]

Inequality continued to persist despite the hopes of lawmakers who had crafted the original Higher Education Act (HEA), Title IX, and basic grant program. By 1980, the number of men and women enrolled was about the same. Thereafter, women steadily became a larger share of the country's student body, accompanied by a growing number of students of color. The fourteen million enrolled at the turn of the millennium included less than a million Asian Americans, roughly 1.4 million Latinx students, and fewer than two million African Americans. By 1991, more than twenty-five years after Congress passed the Civil Rights Act, a quarter of white men had finished four years of college, a greater percentage than men of color and women of any race. Yet white middle-income undergraduates were increasingly missing from universities, which reflected rising costs as well as the simultaneous shrinking of the middle class. Degrees still generally guaranteed higher incomes for men. But Title IX did nothing to help coeds find a job or receive equal pay after graduation; even in 1991, women degree holders still generally earned less than men without sheepskins.[10]

Also steadily increasing was enrollees' risk of finding themselves on a pathway into poverty instead of the disappearing middle class. Student loan defaults remained below 10 percent throughout the 1970s but reached 15 percent by 1990. The cost of the government's guarantee to lenders subsequently soared from $166 million in 1981 to $3.245 billion a decade later. "The system is completely flawed," an Education Department official admitted to reporters in 1991. "There isn't anyone who really loses with higher defaults except the federal government."[11]

But students, parents, and campuses really paid the price of the political warfare that continued long after the 1972 reauthorization. Standoffs over Title IV programs and tax deductions became habitual. College administrators and education experts successfully pushed lawmakers to provide genuine help through grant and work-study programs in the mid-1970s, when scholarships accounted for 75 percent of support, loans made up 21 percent, and work-study jobs accounted for the rest. At the time, basic grants covered 46 percent of college costs. But ever-rising fees intensified demands for tax breaks. Polls overwhelmingly indicated voters wanted such write-offs, and Congress feared what one called an "impending tax revolt by middle income taxpayers." Lawmakers decided to use deductions to nurture state investment in the student loan industry in the mid-1970s but still could not agree on whether students and parents deserved write-offs.[12]

A bitter standoff between the Carter White House and Congress over such breaks ended with passage of the 1978 Middle Income Student Assistance Act. MISAA expanded eligibility for student assistance through all federal programs but did not provide for write-offs. This truce ensured that working- and middle-class Americans would receive the most help from the guaranteed loan program instead of other Title IV options. As such, MISAA only intensified the importance of government-guaranteed financial products as the country's social safety net frayed and the financial, insurance, and real estate sectors expanded.[13]

Lawmakers did even more to boost the already robust student loan industry after MISAA's passage. Escalating fees forced basic grant recipients and more affluent students to borrow. Loan volume rose from less than $2 billion for the 1978 fiscal year to $5 billion in 1980, when the HEA reauthorization also increased the opportunity to borrow. That revamp more famously renamed the basic grants after Claiborne Pell and created the Department of Education, which a growing number of citizens and lawmakers had been asking for since the GI Bill. It also included a guaranteed loan program for parents, who (unlike their children) incurred interest charges on and had to begin repaying the PLUS loans immediately after taking them out. Families could also count on having access to these new financial products. Congress authorized Sallie Mae to act as a guarantor in states where demand for loans surpassed supply, to offer credit in areas of the country where bankers were not participating in the program, and to let borrowers consolidate all the loans they had taken out in order to have lower monthly payments and more time to repay, which upped the amount owed.[14]

Students and parents had to borrow more during Ronald Reagan's presidency. Conservatives at the time lauded his 1980 victory as winning the larger war, after the battle that Barry Goldwater had lost in 1964. Historians have nonetheless noted that the former Democrat, actor, and Republican governor of California did not bring forth the instantaneous revolution many Americans have associated with his administration. Continual assaults on the New Deal order did not guarantee that Reagan and the conservatives then dominating the GOP could immediately turn the country or its academy right side up. The conservative movement that had transformed the Republican Party had been an uneasy coalition whose different social, economic, and foreign policy agendas made setting policy and governing a challenge on par with managing the divisions within the Democratic Party during the Roosevelt era. But the Reagan White House also faced substantial opposition from Democratic lawmakers, who thwarted Republicans' plans for an even greater reversal of liberal 1930s and 1960s achievements.[15]

Yet Reaganites arguably did more to destroy an already frayed public-private social safety net, particularly in higher education, than previous

Republican presidents had. Education spending dropped by 25 percent during the Gipper's first term. Earmarks for Title IV programs that campuses distributed fell by $594 million and Pell grants by $338 million. By the 1984–1985 academic year, government-guaranteed credit accounted for almost two-thirds of assistance, work-study had risen to 5 percent, and grants accounted for just under a third, while the already intentionally paltry Pell grants covered only about 30 percent of college costs. Families earning more than $30,000 a year also had to prove they needed guaranteed loans, which included a new origination fee the government kept along with the interest accrued on this added cost. More than 250,000 freshmen found themselves ineligible for federal aid between 1980 and 1986, when borrowing nevertheless increased by 25 percent. Even though lawmakers had limited eligibility for guaranteed loans, the credit extended dramatically rose from $1.8 billion in 1977 to $12 billion in 1989.[16]

That jump showed the degree to which a still deeply divided Congress enabled the Reagan administration to cultivate the student loan industry. The 1986 reauthorization allowed borrowers to consolidate the guaranteed loans they took out on a yearly basis at a lower interest rate but for a longer repayment period, which again increased how much students had to pay over time. Lawmakers also permitted trust companies, stock savings banks, and the Rural Rehabilitation Corporation to participate in this rapidly growing financial sector. Sallie Mae powerbrokers also gained authority to securitize and trade debt for building educational and training facilities, which only multiplied its size and influence over higher education's still precarious financing.[17]

The Reagan administration went to great lengths to ensure that borrowers, not the federal government, paid lenders. Like Nixon, Reagan put aides on the frontlines of the battles over tuition assistance and the larger war on liberal policies. He named Education Department secretaries who detested student aid and the brand new agency's very existence. His second appointee, William Bennett, even publicly insisted that undergraduates receiving Title IV help were no different than welfare cheats. The self-identified "recovering" Democrat's grandstanding symbolized how the new Education Department sought to undermine the equal access and opportunity that had shaped the Kennedy and Johnson administrations' color-blind approach to securing federal education aid. The Government Accounting Office discovered in the mid-1980s that 45 percent of this lightning-rod agency's appointees were political (far greater than any other government bureaucracy). Staff used their power to slash personnel by more than a third by 1986, particularly in the division devoted to civil rights. The department's Office of the Inspector General grew in size, authority, and funding in order to do more than just collect complaints. It launched full-blown investigations into fraud and abuse of student aid. Investigators, with help from other agencies, went after alumni struggling to pay, not the financial aid officers encouraging them to borrow. Most defaulters had dropped out of for-profit vocational or technical schools, which generally only received a warning in the mail. Federal marshals invaded the homes of former pupils. A Reagan official crowed about confiscating $116 million from 217,000 former students in just six months. "Our success," he insisted, is "good news for all those young Americans who . . . will find that they to wish to seek" a government-guaranteed loan.[18]

Raids, investigations, and cuts served a variety of conservative goals in the larger effort to roll back liberal equal opportunity and social welfare guarantees. Slashing support and ensuring that students (not taxpayers) repaid loans meant less government spending, a smaller deficit, and more limited federal power over not only campuses but also households. Parents, many family-values conservatives insisted, should be the ones making decisions about their children's educations. Some on the right, like Office of Management and Budget Director David Stockman, rejected "the notion that the federal government has an obligation to fund generous grants to anybody that wants to go to college." In debate before the US House budget committee, he continued: "If people wanted to go to college bad enough, then there is opportunity and responsibility on their part to finance their way through the best way they can." To some, undergraduates using financial aid already seemed no better than food-stamp recipients or the welfare queens Reagan and other conservatives frequently demonized.[19]

Such analogies reflected how tinkering with student aid seemed a way for Republicans to undermine the Civil Rights Act, Title IX, and Pell program. Justice and Education Department officials, for example, debated ideas to "exclude federal student assistance from coverage under the Civil Rights statutes" and give "some women's and other 'civil rights' groups . . . a political victory" in the courts "without any political advantage to the President." Education cuts would also force needy students to borrow without any guarantee they would have the same access to federal assistance. Reagan appointees and future Supreme Court justices Clarence Thomas and John Roberts even crafted a more restricted aid offering to help the few small liberal arts colleges that were avowedly conservative circumvent Title IX. But some Reaganites hated this idea, including the president's first education secretary, who considered subsidizing higher education far better than financing "cancer-causing tobacco."[20]

Government policies since the 1972 reauthorization had benefited the student loan industry, not the academy. Experts later emphasized that Sallie Mae had turned this sector into "a gold mine." American financiers needed the government-backed financial products and the secondary market to trade them in the 1970s and 1980s, when lawmakers began to tear apart the rules and regulations that had made banking safe for consumers and boring for bankers since the 1930s. Finance, insurance, and real estate only became more lucrative in decades scholars have associated with the country's financialization. The new student loan program modeled on older federal mortgage assistance just offered financiers another way to increase customers and profits at a time when they faced more competition from across state lines and international borders as a new multipolar global economic order emerged. The promised rate of return on guaranteed student loans was relatively low but federal and state governments still assured some profit in decades when such certainty was rare. The expected earnings enticed more lenders, state and private guarantee agencies, loan servicers, collection agencies, and secondary markets to actively participate in a financial sector increasingly offering once rare private student loans. Those liens came with no assurance of repayment from state, federal, or university officials, unlike the credit state higher education assistance corporations, United States Aid Funds, and federal authorities began offering just before and soon after Sputnik's 1957 launch. Bankers had plenty of customers for the risky financial products after 1972. Real wages stagnated, inequality rose, and congressional fighting reduced education spending, limited tuition assistance, and kept federal borrowing maximums far less than what colleges charged to make up for rising operating costs and less state investment. Loans and the debts incurred from state, federal, and private programs could be easily bought and sold through Sallie Mae, the government-sponsored enterprise whose 1983 public stock market debut raised $357 million, half the amount collected in 1973 to start the program.[21]

Lawmakers doubled down on creative financing and reduced spending despite pleas for help from students, parents, and college administrators to congressional representatives throughout the 1970s and 1980s. "Colleges and universities are struggling to keep costs down," a beleaguered Montana State University official warned. Less funding caused enrollment reductions that in turn "demand further increases in tuition and costs," making for "an unending cycle" that, she believed, was quickly turning higher education into "a commodity for the financial elite." A mother of three worried about the effect on her eldest son, who "doesn't need the tension of wondering how to meet expenses and keep up his grades, too." Prospective students were already concerned "about going to college next year," a high school senior explained. A coed worried that neither she nor her sister would be able to finish college, even though "if I left school my chances of finding a job is almost out of the question." She wondered "how anybody really expects students to survive," emphasizing that "students have no where to turn financially," and "the stress students go through just to stay here academically is hard enough." Another undergraduate felt compelled to speak for "millions of others across the nation," whose parents' savings had fallen short "due to economic hardship and inflation in the price of a college education." And another predicted that the expense would deter young people from applying, resulting "in an overabundance of unskilled labor, that would increase the number of unemployed." He feared "a separation of classes where the rich would control the professional decision making ranks and the less affluent would . . . fall behind in the areas of economic standing and social growth and development."[22]

That outcry, which lacked the rage in the letters Nixon staffers had labeled "grief mail," foretold what experts later deemed a new era in higher education financing. By 1990, minorities, particularly women, remained far more burdened by student debt, but all poor, working-class, and middle-class enrollees struggled to afford fees, finish degrees, and repay loans. Most undergraduates could no longer choose between paying out of pocket, borrowing, or working their way through college as Great Society liberals had intended. Students and their families usually had to do all three. The caps on the money students could receive from government grants and loans often did not make up the chasm between what financial aid formulas indicated a family could pay and what they actually might be able to spare in an era when decades of stagnant household incomes ended with an actual decline in the 2000s. That drop failed to erase the stark gaps between what white families and families of color earned. As such, the disparity between what families could actually pay and what help they could receive particularly hurt low-income, minority students who qualified for paltry federal grants and work-study opportunities. Offsite part-time jobs were more readily available since work-study did not receive much money even before lending supplanted loans as the preeminent source of support. Off-campus jobs rarely paid enough or had schedules suitable for undergraduates studying full time (a prerequisite for maximum state, federal, and often private assistance). Many subsequently turned to private financing. Their parents might also take out risky financial products or unsubsidized federal loans because enrollment and borrowing were no longer a choice but an imperative.[23]

This status quo saddened those who had helped construct the student loan industry decades before. Francis Keppel, a principal architect of the original HEA, admitted after the 1986 reauthorization that they had "conceived of a package of grants, loans, and work-study reasonably balanced so as to leave students and their families with a manageable debt at the end of higher education." They "did not expect the amounts disbursed as loans to increase so rapidly, or to take so large a part in each student's financial aid 'package.'" They had also intended Title IV "to provide equal opportunity for the poor," whom he and other Johnson aides had presumed to be only citizens of color. Such careful, color-blind plans had seemed possible, one Education Office insider later explained, when "the fund-eating dragon we have today was little more than a salamander."[24]

Directly Cutting Out the Middlemen

That monster piqued the interest of unapologetic third-term Senator Sam Nunn in 1989. The Georgian's independent streak made him stand out among southern Democrats who had never switched their affiliation as the parties had gradually realigned. He remained a wild card on deploying troops, cutting taxes, and slashing earmarks. Nunn also openly feared that both Democrats and Republicans were more interested in policing budgets than evaluating programs. He prioritized such assessments when he chaired the Senate Permanent Subcommittee on Investigations, the so-called Nunn Committee, designated one of his top priorities. He could pick and choose what he wanted to inspect but did not prioritize higher education, even though he considered science and engineering of the utmost importance to the country's defense, labor, and economic needs. Only default rates, particularly among for-profit alumni, led him to call for hearings, which began in fall 1989 and continued for a year.[25]

Investigators found trade schools, lenders, guarantee agencies, and for-profits egregiously misusing the Guaranteed Student Loan Program at the expense of students, parents, and taxpayers. Dropouts and graduates movingly testified about worthless courses and aggressive recruiters. One had convinced an unemployed Florida woman to finance "tuition through the school . . . leaving me with the impression that I was guaranteed to get the loan. I was never told that this was a Federally guaranteed loan" until a collections firm started calling her parents. By then, numerous employers had told her the travel agent program at her for-profit institution was useless, a judgment its former employees corroborated when they appeared before senators.[26]

Such revelations enraged Nunn. He praised the "many trade and proprietary schools . . . helping many Americans become able and productive members of the job force" but denounced "unscrupulous schools" luring "unwary Americans" with "sophisticated sales pitches" and "promises of bright futures, high paying jobs and Federal loans for financing." Lawmakers, he fumed, "did not hear of even a single part of the guaranteed student loan program that is working efficiently or effectively." The bipartisan subcommittee's devastating report cataloged rampant abuse by five hundred trade schools and made twenty-seven specific recommendations to police for-profits, which included Title IV eligibility limits, uniform accreditation standards, state licensing procedures, and stricter regulation of lenders. Many of his colleagues either ignored or dismissed those suggestions, which went against the current political mood of regulating businesses less and encouraging more private financial solutions to meet individual and public needs. Skeptics included high-ranking members of congressional education committees, like Michigan House Democrat William Ford, who had attended an automotive trade school before pursuing his law degree. He did not even bother to read the findings before publicly insisting that "the government has no business telling one type of school is better than another."[27]

Naysayers could not stop the uproar when the Higher Education Assistance Foundation collapsed during Nunn's investigations. Kansas-based HEAF was the largest of the more than fifty private and state-run guarantors of student loans. The private firm's portfolio epitomized the risk historically endemic in student lending yet prized in the decades when banking stopped being boring. HEAF's founders had, since its 1976 founding, done business across the country, not in a single state like the original higher education associations. CEOs decided in the 1980s to invest more in banks specializing in trade school loans. Those institutions' abysmal completion rates, questionable credentials, and sometimes worthless degrees had increasingly left borrowers unable to find the jobs they needed to pay off high-interest debts in years when even four-year nonprofit university alumni struggled to find well-paying work.[28]

Investing in such risky loans initially seemed to pay off. By 1990, HEAF had expanded operations to eighteen states and held $9.6 billion in credit, half of which had been funneled through for-profit colleges. Banks with HEAF-guaranteed loans had already been struggling to sell those debts. HEAF posted a $44 million loss in the 1989 fiscal year and a $40 million deficit just ten months into the following year. Top personnel subsequently found themselves borrowing $1 billion from Sallie Mae before the Education Department dissolved HEAF, whose operations SLMA staff wound down.[29]

More scrutiny of federal financial aid programs followed. Insiders had known that the purposefully diffuse program had operated haphazardly for years. Jimmy Carter's Secretary of Health, Education, and Welfare, Joseph Califano, later recalled that his staff had discovered poorly kept borrowing records, sometimes even on "index cards in shoeboxes; in others, what little computer training existed was woefully inadequate to the task of collection." Investigators spent three years working through the disarray, which had continued into the 1980s, when the drive to cut costs and regulations had given more power to creditors, guarantee agencies, investors, state officials, SLMA employees, and campus officials. Only HEAF's bankruptcy led the Education Department to take a much closer look at the student loan program, which was "a mess," one staffer recalled. "People had the wrong incentives and nobody was policing it," he lamented, and "it was abundantly clear that the Department of Education's higher education operation was a joke and nobody had any clue."[30]

Investigators also discovered that government accounting practices had hidden how costly the guaranteed loan program had always been. Only interest subsidies and default payments had appeared on federal ledgers, which did not begin to capture the expense. The Johnson administration had purposefully exploited such creative bookkeeping in order to evade charges that it spent too much and collected too little revenue. Johnson had also tried to end the popular defense loans, whose full costs appeared on budgets. Great Society Education Office personnel intent on saving that aid had accordingly taken it upon themselves to show just how much more cost effective the federal campus assistance program was than guaranteed loans. That internal study had done nothing to dampen enthusiasm for guaranteed student lending in the 1970s when lawmakers embraced finance to meet social needs even more than their predecessors had. Guaranteed loans seemed like the only option as state and federal educational expenditures shrank, college costs rose, and other forms of student aid failed to cover the bills. A lawyer in the newly created Congressional Budget Office still tried to caution policymakers on relying on these financial products in 1979, insisting "higher costs" were not for "the benefit of student borrowers, but rather to the benefit of the financial institutions that make the loans." He ultimately concluded that "the program has gone through piecemeal alterations that have transformed it into a system much more costly than a direct federal loan program."[31]

His warning was ignored until the early 1990s, when many education experts and lawmakers began to embrace what then seemed like a sea change in college lending: direct loans. These financial products were not revolutionary, as they kept with the tradition of providing more assistance to students than the campuses dependent on their tuition payments. But direct lending did represent a significant shift away from the complicated government-guaranteed financial products that had been a part of the country's public-private social safety net for decades. The direct lending label had once been applied to the defense loan program in order to differentiate it from the Guaranteed Student Loan Program. The federal government had, after all, directly supplied a substantial amount of the money to start and maintain the defense loan funds that campus personnel administered and student interest charges somewhat replenished. The program continued to give out millions to mostly low-income students, as later HEA reauthorizations had dictated.[32]

Lawmakers and educators intent on reform began to use "direct lending" to describe credit coming straight from state and federal governments. For example, bankers' initial refusal to participate in and willingness to drop out of the guaranteed loan program had left Johnson aides to wonder in 1966, "How about a program of direct government loans to college students?" Johnson and Nixon advisers had also considered various ideas for federal education banks, including one suggestion that would have loaned everything students needed to cover college expenses. Some aides had even incorporated economist Milton Friedman's suggestion that the IRS help collect repayment of thirty-year student loans that would be contingent on the income reported when citizens filed their taxes. Academics and administrators became increasingly interested in similar proposals throughout the 1970s, when lawmakers introduced a few failed bills and Carnegie Commission leaders warned that "further tinkering with the [guaranteed loan] program is unlikely to solve the problems and also to increase costs—borne, in the main, by federal taxpayers." Oklahoma, North Carolina, Wisconsin, Florida, Kentucky, Minnesota, New Mexico, and Texas legislators were far more amenable to such an overhaul than their DC counterparts. By the late 1970s, those states' direct loan programs acted as lenders of last resort or were the main source of credit for state loan programs. Unlike the New York and Massachusetts education associations created in the 1950s, these states turned to private lenders, tax revenues, or selling tax-exempt bonds to raise the capital necessary to lend directly to students.[33]

Capitol Hill insiders remember an industry blindsided by the threats posed by state experiments, Nunn's investigations, and HEAF's collapse. Danger increased after a deeply divided Congress passed the 1990 Federal Credit Reform Act, which required far more accurate accounting of federal loan debt. Ledgers, for example, had to include all yearly costs for the guaranteed loan program. The law also mandated that the costs of any direct loans be calculated based on the amount of capital loaned, money spent on future administrative costs, and the expense of collecting debts. This bookkeeping change intensified interest in direct lending during 1991 discussions of reauthorizing HEA. That year, the Government Accounting Office issued a report showing a federal direct loan program could save $1 billion, an estimate on par with the Congressional Budget Office's estimate of $900 million savings in the first year alone. These findings excited the many educators, financial aid officers, federal officials, and lawmakers eager to experiment with direct lending. But the idea divided the George H. W. Bush administration. That discord reflected how conservatives had continued to disagree about their agenda since Reagan's historic 1980 victory. This particular quarrel pitted cost-cutting against increasing federal power and aiding bankers.[34]

Education Department staffers embraced direct lending in 1990 and wanted it to be a part of the upcoming HEA amendments. Enthusiasts even leaked findings about cost savings to the press in early 1991, which accompanied reports the White House might even be interested in substituting direct lending for the guaranteed loan program instead of just offering undergraduates another financing option. Office of Management and Budget director Richard Darman called both ideas, according to sources close to him, "insane." He questioned "taking a system of taking private capital and delivering it through banks and turning it into a public system that is going to be run by the federal government. We should be going the other way. We should take federal loan programs and turn them into guarantee programs. Make sure they are run right." One insider hypothesized that Darman really considered "the education department . . . not capable of managing direct loans." The White House sided with Darman, whose thinking aligned with incoming Secretary of Education Lamar Alexander's views. The Tennessee Republican, one congressional aide later explained, seemed to be against direct lending because "he felt that there was major spadework that needed to be done in the departments, getting the departments better organized." Alexander testified against any kind of direct lending program when he appeared before the House. Yet the administration only submitted a proposal reflecting that view for both chambers to entertain in June 1991, when the Senate had almost completed its reauthorization hearings.[35]

This delay hardly mattered. Democrats controlled the two principal committees overseeing HEA's reauthorization and Congress. Hearings were numerous and lengthy, which reflected how big and complex the business of higher education had gotten as it had become more fully interwoven in American life. Lawmakers heard testimony from six hundred K-12 teachers, HBCU administrators, trade school operators, liberal arts college presidents, religious college leaders, community college officials, financial aid officers, Education Department officials, bankers, and more. Lengthy sessions covered such wide-ranging topics as flailing teacher training programs, Pell grant increases, Title IX procedures, fraud investigations, veterans' needs, for-profit eligibility requirements, accreditation guidelines, foreign-study programs, new repayment options, stagnant household incomes, declining enrollments, and the loss of faith in higher education. Fifty students also testified during the House subcommittees' forty-four hearings, far more than ever before.[36]

But lawmakers really broke precedent by asking the United States Student Association, one of the country's largest student groups, to organize a March 1991 afternoon hearing so both chambers' education committees could hear from undergraduates. The ten witnesses included African American, Latino, indigenous, and first-generation South Asian undergraduates from across the country. These men and women boldly shared "how inadequate aid had forced them to eat food donated by friends, to sell blood for cash, and to take out large loans"—the kind of scrounging Lyndon Johnson had recalled when he promised HEA would make college affordable. Democrats seemed particularly taken aback by their accounts. Senator Chris Dodd of Connecticut called the students' testimony "about as eloquent as any one of us has heard, regardless of how long we've served." In the House, William Ford asked them to keep speaking out and protesting. He even alluded to the kind of tactics 1960s campus radicals had used when demonstrating against segregation, sexism, and the Vietnam War. "I'm not advocating burning any campuses or shutting them down," the Michigan Democrat emphasized, "but if it's necessary, I'm not telling you you shouldn't." The two hundred students jammed into the hearing room immediately erupted in cheers, startling journalists and lawmakers.[37]

Eagerness and need for reform could not guarantee that lawmakers would experiment with direct lending. The six largest higher education lobbying groups all wanted it as an additional option for students—one they hoped might make the guaranteed loan program and the larger industry it supported wither away, just as 1960s USAF executives had hoped private loans might make the defense lending program wilt. Others, including students, advocated a range of plans, from a limited pilot program to immediate replacement of the guaranteed program with direct lending (the latter a dream of the University of Michigan administrator and Harvard financial aid coordinator, who persuaded Democrat Rob Andrew to propose such a switch). The freshman New Jersey representative emphasized throughout the hearings how much direct lending would save the government. He hoped to counter Republican reluctance, as Representative Tom Coleman of Missouri later put it, to "fool with the system that has performed well." Democratic congressional staffers remembered being surprised that "Republicans talked about opposing it but never really did." They "basically worked off the Andrew bill." Education Department personnel credit this tacit bipartisanship to the fact that "the numbers got out showing the department's own cost estimates about the savings." A staffer later explained why these calculations mattered. "I knew that those estimates existed because I had done them," he recalled. "Once those numbers became public there was a lot of interest. Some Republicans and some Democrats said this is not a bad idea. We can get some deficit reduction out of it. Other Democrats said, hey, with 4 or 5 billion worth of savings, we could apply it to other activities." The aging Senator Pell, in fact, stood out for opposing direct lending, which he feared might come at the cost of the grants named after him. He sounded like a man from an earlier and different political era, however, warning that direct lending would subsequently "do something for well-off families at the expense of needy and deserving families." He especially did not like "favoring loans over grants."[38]

Leading liberal skeptics also had far more faith in expanding the Pell grant program and tinkering with repayment than experimenting with direct lending. Some, for example, advocated having the IRS collect payments that would be contingent on income reported. But House Subcommittee on Postsecondary Education chairman William Ford had more faith in adjusting the Pell grant program to fix the "convoluted mass that has grown by accretion." His staff had spent more than twenty years logging thousands of letters from desperate students, parents, and college administrators describing the loan industry's malignant expansion. But evidence of "more and more low income people . . . borrowing more and more money" concerned Ford in the early 1990s, even as he remained grateful for the help the GI Bill had provided to him. He wanted, like other older representatives, to make the Pell program a genuine entitlement, an idea harking back to Pell's initial hope of using the grants to provide the right to an education. Ford decided not to put forth any bills of his own during reauthorization hearings. He and his aides instead strove to ensure the House's legislation included a provision giving freshmen and sophomores a legal right to the full amount for which they were eligible, not the free ride George Zook had proposed decades before. The estimated $10 to $12 billion cost, Ford recognized, might be "either the glue that holds this whole thing together or the Plastique that blows the thing apart." His dogged insistence on vastly expanding eligibility for this help concerned many within his own party. No leaders from the major higher education associations testified in favor of this proposal, which struck a Senate staffer as proof the academics had chosen to "represent the interest of institutions over the interest of poor kids." One Capitol Hill insider, Barmak Nassirian, instead shared the opinion that Ford was "losing touch with reality on this one."[39]

Ford had, in fact, been slow to recognize the real danger that for-profits posed just twenty years after the 1972 reauthorization. Proprietary outfits' share of federal tuition assistance steadily rose in the 1970s and 1980s. By the end of the latter decade, their students used 30 percent of Pell allocations and 22 percent of guaranteed loans. This increase reflected the fact that, for women, immigrants, citizens of color, and returning students, these institutions remained more accessible than nonprofits, even including the less prestigious colleges scrambling to fill seats as the last of the Baby Boomers graduated. But proprietary schools had also begun charging more than many public and private institutions in the 1980s, giving rise to news reports of "diploma mills" all too eagerly "skimming benefits from financial aid programs." Such charges had dogged proprietary schools since the GI Bill. But these accusations alarmed White House Republicans as well as some congressional Democrats, who managed to agree on new minor restrictions on for-profits' use of tuition assistance in 1989. Lobbyists representing the for-profits frustrated additional bipartisan efforts in 1990, when Nunn's committee began investigating the proprietary outfits before HEAF's dramatic collapse.[40]

Ford had dismissed the Nunn committee's findings then but not during the 1992 reauthorization. He could not ignore the liberal and southern Democrats as well as the Republicans working together to introduce amendments to police the for-profit sector, whose institutions educated 1.6 percent of postsecondary students in 1993 but accounted for a substantial amount of the money defaulted on through the guaranteed-lending program. California Representative Maxine Waters stood out among the strange bedfellows, who could agree on saving money even if it meant the federal government would police recruitment techniques and cut off aid to institutions upon which many residents unable to enroll in nonprofits relied. She proposed that proprietary schools could only earn 85 percent of their revenue from federal tuition assistance programs in order to remain eligible for the indirect aid. The so-called 85/15 rule had been used since the Korean War GI Bill to determine if veterans could use their benefits at the for-profit institutions that she and other Congressional Black Caucus stalwarts considered "a rip-off." They were more concerned about how the for-profits had harmed "our communities," as Waters later explained, than controlling spending. "The jobs that were promised were never forthcoming," she emphasized, but alumni still had "to pay back those government loans."[41]

Direct lending and the Pell program's expansion, not the Waters amendment, almost thwarted the reconciliation process. That near-miss foretold how gridlock would persist despite the two parties' dramatic, decades-long transformation. President Bush threatened to veto any legislation that included either measure. The many lenders, who had initially dismissed the threat that direct lending posed, were relieved when congressional Republicans dutifully lined up with the administration on both issues. A few GOP lawmakers and White House aides continued to favor direct lending but Democrats caved on making the direct loan program permanent and turning Pell grants into an entitlement. Republicans and Democrats still struggled to reach agreement during conference committee deliberations that started in May and stretched into the summer. "I had already decided," a Republican House conferee admitted, that "my mission in life was to try to get that [direct-lending] pilot project as small as possible." Bush, meanwhile, seemed to many Republicans in the months before the 1992 elections to be a "no man" or an "I don't know man," out of step with the party and the country. A Democratic staffer later shared his sense of the conferees' attitude: "since the administration was continuing to threaten to veto the bill, because the pilot was too big and out of control and all this . . . to hell with them."[42]

Republicans and twenty of the fifty conferees ended up visiting the White House to persuade Bush not to veto a hard-fought bill. The legislation included bipartisan restrictions on for-profits' Title IV eligibility and allocated 95 percent of the $21.5 billion authorized for all federal student assistance. The president eventually acquiesced to allowing $500 million to be spent on a direct lending tester instead of capping the number of campuses allowed to participate. After all, the law he signed on July 23, 1992, potentially earmarked $13.7 billion for guaranteed loans (then called the Federal Family Education Loans). It only authorized $5.5 billion on a Pell program limited to providing a quarter of a recipient's college costs. This reauthorization also devoted a substantial amount of money for a new federally guaranteed financial product whose interest the government did not subsidize, an add-on that pleased Republicans focused on cutting costs and buoying bankers. Financiers seemed likely to have even more customers because the reauthorization required students and parents to fill out the new Free Application for Federal Student Aid. Families came to dread the complicated, lengthy FAFSA, which had evolved out of the paperwork the College Scholarship Service had first developed in the 1950s and campus financial aid officers had increasingly relied on since the defense loan program's fitful rollout.[43]

A Republican involved in the 1992 reauthorization admitted, "We probably weren't going to be revolutionary," but Bill Clinton still hoped to overthrow the loan industry when he moved to Washington just a few months later. Education was important to the Arkansan, who had graduated from Georgetown just three years after LBJ promised that the door to college would never be shut to someone as poor as "the man from Hope." Clinton, in fact, relied on part-time jobs and financial aid to finance his remarkable rags-to-riches story. Budgeting himself to live on $25 a week in college did not keep him from academia's most rarified realms. The former Rhodes Scholar unsurprisingly included a promise to fundamentally overhaul American higher education in his campaign to unseat Bush, then launched into a grudge match with Democrats over direct lending. Clinton never considered something as pathbreaking as robustly funding campuses to lessen reliance on the tuition parents and students struggled to pay. His wish list instead included a new financial product to help parents save as well as a national service program that would forgive some of the money owed. Clinton, a JFK admirer, sometimes likened that pet project to the Peace Corps and occasionally called it a Domestic GI Bill. Some of his advisers laughed at the idea. "Every candidate has one of those things," salty southerner James Carville quipped. "You humor him and move on."[44]

Clinton's eagerness to permanently replace the guaranteed loan program with direct lending was no joke. The former 1960s radical and his aides embraced many of the suggestions floated in the reauthorization hearings, including rapidly but incrementally increasing the amount of new loans coming directly from the government. By the 1997–1998 academic year, students and parents would not go through the complicated, costly program that relied on bankers and financial aid officers to issue loans. The more streamlined approach also cut out all middlemen from the repayment process. There would no longer be a set payment due each month. Instead, the IRS would use reported income to determine how much to collect, ensuring that borrowers paid what they could actually afford. That approach would stop the defaults that cost both borrowers and the federal government guaranteeing the loans. Estimates projected that, by 1996, the government would need to earmark at least $1.9 billion less for higher education.[45]

"No sooner had I even mentioned this system," the newly elected president complained, "than Congress was deluged with lobbyists." Even though the White House's three-pronged higher education reforms kept with the tradition of helping citizens creatively finance basic needs, those proposals still represented a serious threat to the student loan industry—and to the Republicans' cost-cutting, tax-slashing, and government-shrinking agenda. A coordinated effort by some fifty student loan enterprises, many represented by lobbyists with deep ties to the Democratic Party then controlling both Congress and the White House, managed to defeat the proposed National Service Act and the Student Loan Reform Act. Executives at Sallie Mae, it was later revealed, tried to recruit two University of Wisconsin undergraduates to start an on-campus group to campaign against direct lending. They envisioned the same kind of orchestrated "grassroots" rebellion the Student Loan Funding Corporation bankrolled at the University of Cincinnati. Financiers also had help from Republicans. Bill Goodling, a Pennsylvania representative on Ford's higher education subcommittee, hated direct lending, national service debt forgiveness, and empowering the IRS to collect student loan payments. His fierce opposition reflected how much the Republican Party had changed as conservatives' power had steadily increased. Democrats and Republicans had once been open to tasking the IRS with collecting student debt, but its tax collection duties made it a favorite target of right-wing Republicans like Goodling. He still couched his opposition to pardoning even a portion of what alumni owed as a measure that would rob the academy of much-needed resources. Forgiveness, he insisted, would help a few at the expense of the many. Such arguments resonated with many college administrators who worried about precarious finances and feared anything more than a direct loan tester.[46]

Ford and Pell played outsized, unexpected roles in turning the pilot into a permanent program that still bears the Michigan representative's name. Both senior Democrats had been far more interested in expanding the Pell grant program in 1992. A year later, Ford actually introduced the White House's direct lending bill. "I was surprised that he was willing," a colleague admitted, as the Reform Act could end up "destroying a system which he should have some pride of authorship on and has defended and protected for 20-some years." An insider later said the chairman remained unconvinced "that this was really a good policy change." But Ford still used the projected savings to win over representatives on both sides of the aisle. Democrats nevertheless abandoned having the IRS collect loan repayments to get the votes for the bill that created AmeriCorps, Clinton's domestic Peace Corps.[47]

The IRS recoupment strategy was a crucial feature of direct lending's threat to the student loan industry, which senators also balked at upending. Senator Nancy Kassebaum of Kansas feared "an enormous change" but allowed that "if it can be shown to be successful, then no, I wouldn't have a problem." Fellow Republican Jim Jeffords also worried about replacing the guaranteed loan program with something that had only recently been added as a tester. Even Democrats shared the Vermont senator's doubts. Pell feared that the executive bureaucracies could not handle the gargantuan task of directly lending to students and parents. The many college presidents, financial aid officers, and higher education association lobbyists writing to Pell shared that concern but still hoped to get, at least, a permanent program. However, when the direct lending amendment to the Senate's budget bill failed fifty-one to forty-seven, Pell nonetheless endeavored to reach some kind of agreement with financiers, who refused to compromise.[48]

Pell's staff subsequently crafted a plan to phase in direct lending. Congress would only consider expanding the program once 30 percent of campuses participated. His colleagues accepted that tradeoff, but it did not satisfy everyone on the conference committee. Ford insisted that direct lending must replace the old Guaranteed Student Loan Program but even pressure from the White House could not get the Senate to back the president's plans. A week of what insiders called "combative, frustrating, and tedious" meetings ended with an agreement close to what Pell had proposed.[49]

"The cost-saving provisions may drive us out of the program," USA Group's chairman warned after Democrats resorted to the budget reconciliation process to pass the 1993 Student Loan Reform Act. This maneuver reflected how Capitol Hill budget battles had become more important to resolving legislative stalemates since the Nixon era. Reconciliation only became more crucial but this law did little to thwart the student loan industry. The theoretically permanent William D. Ford Direct Lending Program, much like the pilot, broke with lawmakers' historic preference for government-guaranteed financial products but still reflected a continued faith in lending, instead of direct funding, to respond to public needs. This experiment also retained the tradition of offering better options for a lucky few of the students enrolled in colleges opting for this tuition assistance. Choice had been a feature of federal tuition assistance programs since the New Deal. The custom of limited aid also persisted because Republicans had forced Democrats to cap the offering at 40 percent of total federal loan volume. But aspects of this legislation also drew from earlier efforts to save borrowers money and protect them from unscrupulous lenders. Education Department officials, for example, picked the lenders that financial aid officers could work with through the guaranteed loan program. The law also included four repayment options, including one contingent on income, even though congressional staffers had warned that these alternatives might leave 52 percent of borrowers paying significantly more over longer periods of time, though they could get some of their balances forgiven if they worked in the public sector. Lawmakers looked on these less lucrative jobs as a form of national service that needed to be rewarded, as teaching had been under the original National Defense Loan Program.[50]

Many still considered direct lending "a hit," as a University of Illinois financial aid director enthusiastically described it. It was far less complex than the government-guaranteed financial products lawmakers had been using for decades. More than a hundred institutions tried direct lending during its inaugural year as a permanent program, which a postsecondary expert declared "a great start in a remarkably short period of time." University of California administrators reminded reporters that guaranteed lending "has been brutal for the kids and their parents." The streamlined option, a Colorado State University staffer enthused, "helps us provide better students with better service, period." (This financial aid officer went so far as to call working directly with the federal government a "spiritual experience.") Students filled out simpler paperwork and received their credit within weeks, not months. The CSU staffer was not the only administrator to publicly give the initiative high marks. "The lines are gone," an Iowa State staffer celebrated. University of Florida personnel actually threatened to leave if top brass even considered going back to the guaranteed loan program. Direct lending was much easier for students too. A Colorado State journalism major even deemed direct lending "the best thing since microwave brownies." Far more campuses applied to use the program for the next academic year; 800 ended up on a waitlist for the Ford program's third year. By then, private and even quasi-public financiers (most notably Sallie Mae) had lost a third of their business and Clinton aides were intent on increasing the number of colleges participating from 1,500 to 1,641.[51]

Republicans made that incremental step a pipe dream after the 1994 elections gave Republicans control of both the House and Senate. Georgia's Newt Gingrich stood at the forefront of the so-called Republican Revolution, which many scholars have labeled the start of a new era in partisan gridlock. Early fights over destroying the newly permanent direct loan program highlighted how much old battle lines shaped the fights over the GOP's cost-cutting, tax-slashing Contract with America. A few Republicans brought up the money direct lending saved but their colleagues were far more concerned about shrinking the government and protecting the loan industry. Republicans' numerous 1995 proposals subsequently included an outright repeal of the Student Loan Reform Act and capping the volume of direct loans to 10 percent of available credit. The latter sailed through Congress in a bill that also would have privatized Sallie Mae. Clinton vetoed that legislation but, to end this particular Washington showdown, his administration agreed to no longer promote the direct Ford loans as a more desirable alternative to the guaranteed program.[52]

This olive branch did not shield direct lending from Republicans' and financiers' assaults. High-ranking Republicans, like House Budget Committee chairman John Kasich, dismissed the many expert reports documenting how direct lending cost students, parents, campuses, and taxpayers less than guaranteed borrowing. Outside Washington, student lenders shamelessly courted financial aid officers with free concert tickets, first-class retreats, and other posh perks one financial aid director considered "quite comical at times." There was nothing funny about how beholden campuses were to powerful bankers, who determined whether or not students would get the credit to enroll so institutions could stay open. Small, underfunded colleges especially needed the help lenders were more than willing to provide. For example, Tuskegee, a poorly endowed HBCU, needed far more aid than it could ever get from Title III's color-blind assistance for developing institutions. Administrators could hardly turn away a lender willing to provide the computer upgrades and temporary employees needed to process the complicated guaranteed loan paperwork. Much larger universities also needed to cash in on the opportunities offered by financiers in the 1990s. Some bankers provided a line of credit to colleges and universities, money that enabled them to make loans to graduate and professional students enrolled in increasingly expensive programs with few fellowship opportunities. Staff did not put interest toward replenishing campus loan funds as the defense loan program had required them to do. Financial aid officers instead sold those liens to their creditors, who handsomely rewarded these campuses. Wayne State higher-ups admitted that they expected to make more than $1 million a year. Such windfalls embarrassed a University of Florida financial aid officer, who worried "it ruins our credibility" to "make more money by making loans."[53]

Fighting Over Fig-Leaf Reforms

Those buy-offs reflected how finance would become even more interwoven in American life as the war between the Clinton White House and the Republican-controlled Congress dragged on, a conflict that damaged the reputation of both sides in the long run. Many on the left hoped Clinton would halt the country's rightward drift but he instead remained infamous for his affair with Monica Lewinsky, subsequent impeachment, and signing a lot of bills that arguably did far more to dismantle what remained of the New Deal than Carter, Reagan, or Bush had done. Clinton pushed for welfare reform and crime control, what many at the time and decades after considered both insult and injury to communities of color, particularly the many women at the head of low-income families who never qualified for the middle-class tax cuts he signed into law. Experts have linked some of that legislation, like the repeal of already weakened New Deal banking regulations, to the Great Recession that left many Americans nostalgic for the booming 1990s. Hindsight also forced Americans to remember that the Democratic president, as many supporters pointed out in the 2010s, had little leeway when Republicans retook Congress in 1994. Conservatives still did not get everything they wanted. Clinton's obstinacy on some issues led to two dramatic government shutdowns over budget allocations that would further eviscerate the country's public-private social welfare programs. The 1995 budget standoff also ended with the public siding with the president, much to the outrage of his Capitol Hill opponents. Clinton soon perfected ripping off popular GOP ideas that his staff rebranded as coming from a new kind of Democrat desperately seeking a third way between liberals and conservatives.[54]

Compromising on higher education policies was hard in 1990s Washington. Fights over writing off tuition, tinkering with the interest rate, revising the bankruptcy provision, increasing for-profit schools' eligibility, and privatizing Sallie Mae were really skirmishes in the larger battle over direct lending. The Ford program's fate suggested that the "era of big government" might not really be over, as Clinton had proclaimed it to be in his 1996 State of the Union address. This creative financing option's survival was also symbolic of how much more of the country's threadbare, public-private social safety net would be turned over to financiers, who offered financial products far more complex and risky than the 1930s government-guaranteed experiments that had provided the white working and middle classes with limited pensions, long-term mortgages, and unemployment provisions. But, as banking became more profitable for lenders, it became far less safe for residents, particularly the many women, immigrants, and citizens of color who had long struggled to enroll in college, get loans, and finish degrees.[55]

White Americans remained far more likely to benefit from the tax breaks, such as the tuition write-offs, that Clinton promised to pass during his 1996 reelection campaign. His pledges epitomized how much the politics of social welfare in general and higher education policy in particular had changed since the New Deal. Both moderate Republicans, like Eisenhower, and Democrats, including Carter, had warned that less revenue would mean less government support for public needs, including postsecondary schooling. But years of both tax and spending cuts had made write-offs increasingly popular among politicians and their constituents, who seemed to have grown as accustomed to receiving deductions as they had to using financial products for basic necessities like housing, health care, and education. Indeed, higher education association leaders, parents, and students had begged newly inaugurated Clinton to revive the deduction for interest paid on student loans which had been eliminated in the 1986 HEA reauthorization, included in the 1992 conference committee bill, and opposed by Bush. Desperate constituents, including an African American mother emphasizing that her family had "never been on welfare," considered the break "the same" as mortgage write-offs, an ostensibly color-blind deduction that experts have linked to ever-widening racial wealth gaps. Aides flagged such mail but focused far more on Georgia's 1993 lottery-funded Hope Scholarship program. By 1995, that initiative had expanded to give high-school seniors graduating with a B average free in-state tuition or $3,000 that could be used at the state's private colleges and universities. Even before Kentucky, Louisiana, Maryland, and South Carolina legislatures passed similar benefits, this tax credit proved popular with white middle-class Georgians, who eagerly reelected Democrat Zell Miller in 1994, when voters also chose to send Clinton's Capitol Hill nemesis, Newt Gingrich, back to Washington.[56]

Many pundits and reporters immediately realized that Clinton's 1996 campaign proposal had little in common with the Peach State scholarships. He promised to "make the 13th and 14th year of education as universal as the first 12 are today." But his plan to expand access to higher education scarcely resembled what the Zook Commission had suggested and Eisenhower had reluctantly signed. Americans would receive a $1,500 tax credit for the first two years of college, which theoretically ensured everyone could at least go to a community college. At the time, the average cost of a two-year California college was still $363. Ivy League schools were, of course, much more. Thus the write-offs posed little threat to the student loan industry then trying to undermine direct lending. Undergraduates, after all, would still have to borrow to pay tuition bills due much earlier than April 15, as opponents to deductions had emphasized since the 1950s. Such write-offs still polled well with voters even though Clinton promised to offset the revenue reduction by raising fees on foreign travel and limiting tax credits for firms that sold goods overseas. A Republican strategist fumed that rebranding such tax chicanery as a scholarship was "classic Clinton. . . . He says, 'I have in my hand two apples,' and you have to say, 'No, sir, you have an apple and an orange,' and then it comes down to, 'Is so. Is not. Is so. Is not.'" An education policy expert was equally unimpressed. "If there's $25 billion to invest in addressing this problem," he explained, "I would put it into student aid programs, direct expenditure programs."[57]

That kind of targeted spending had been off the table for years, but Clinton still struggled to win over academics, economists, and Republicans after his 1996 reelection. He outlined the Helping Outstanding Pupils Educationally (HOPE) Scholarship Tax Credit in his 1997 State of the Union address, which also mentioned a substantial Pell grant increase as well as tax cuts (not just for higher education) to help the middle class. Lawmakers on both sides of the aisle disliked these suggestions. Republicans countered White House proposals with interest payment deductions, incentives to save for college, and education subsidies for which, like so many other social welfare programs, relatively few Americans could qualify. Republican ideas frustrated Democrats and educators as much as Clinton's plans. Academics feared a new set of complicated negotiations with the government, this time with the IRS, in order to prove students had the grades to qualify. These ideas also seemed more likely to decrease, not increase, the money states earmarked for postsecondary education. Reporters noted that Georgia's in-state fees had actually skyrocketed soon after the supposed scholarship program started. Doubling down on deductions also seemed a threat to the existing, poorly underfunded programs, most notably the Pell grants that actually lessened what Americans had to borrow. These tax subsidies, as critics had emphasized since the 1950s, also seemed far more likely to benefit young people already destined for college instead of encouraging those who considered the expense insurmountable.[58]

The Clinton administration in many ways prevailed in bitter fights over write-offs and college-savings incentives. The 1997 Balanced Budget Act and corresponding reconciliation legislation, the Taxpayer Relief Act, together aimed to reduce government revenue by $41 billion over five years through a smorgasbord of reductions for taxpayers. They included child tax credits, incentives to save for retirement in new financial products, breaks to encourage business investment in urban and rural areas, benefits for employers who hired Americans through the administration's Welfare-to-Work program, capital gains reductions, and exemptions that lowered estate taxes. They also included a lot of higher education write-offs. Congress ended the tax on loans forgiven for public service, created the HOPE Scholarship credits for first- and second-year students, passed the Lifetime Learning Tax Credit for subsequent semesters, and resurrected the popular interest deduction. Republicans and Democrats also agreed on tax incentives to encourage parents to contribute money to state-based college savings plans and other complicated financial products, which could be used to pay for increasingly expensive educations. Clinton, in fact, praised Congress for a "tax-cut package" that he considered "fiscally responsible" because it avoided "an explosion in revenue costs," while being designed to "provide a fair balance of benefits for working Americans." He also expected it to "encourage economic growth" through its "significant expansion of opportunities for higher education for Americans of all ages."[59]

Clinton insisted the write-offs were "the largest investment in higher education since the G.I. Bill," but the deductions were nothing like that celebrated legislation or a scholarship, as the HOPE write-off's name implied. Almost all the 1997 breaks required undergraduates, or their parents, to earn enough to itemize. This supposedly color-blind help continued the tradition of disproportionately helping the white middle- and upper-classes since sharp differences in household income had persisted since the passage of the Civil Rights Act and Higher Education Act (see appendix, figure A2). Some Americans immediately recognized how useless these write-offs were. "There's no way that I could have come up with $1,500 to begin with," Albany Technical Institute student Audrey Dismuke complained. "Most people without money," the Georgia mother of three predicted, "aren't going to understand what a tax credit will do for them." Better-off Americans did not get it either, even though the reductions seemed to disproportionately help the white middle class. Most beneficiaries received less credit than permitted (the 2000 average was $731). The deductions, as college tax-cut critics had feared since the 1950s, gave wealthier pupils bigger breaks since they generally attended more expensive institutions, subsequently had to borrow more, and would pay far less in taxes. Their families also seemed more likely to benefit from the tax-incentivized financial products intended to encourage parents to save for their children's education. Richer parents tended to be able to set money aside and more often participated in state programs to pay college costs in advance.

Even so, financial planners called the benefits of these educational financial products "much ado about nothing"; they would not yield enough to fully cover a year of postsecondary schooling.[60]

Usage nevertheless fell well below the dire projections made by education experts after Clinton signed the legislation. Analysts feared that "once all the credits, incentives, and deductions are fully used," taxpayers could "approximately equal the cost of *all other existing federal financial aid programs combined*." Yet only a third of eligible students claimed credits in the program's second year. The subsidies also did not drastically change college revenue sources. The federal government still spent far more money underwriting research and assisting students than businesses, philanthropies, and states, which researchers correctly predicted would continue to reduce education earmarks and force colleges to raise fees. Lending (whether private, indirect, or direct) remained a critical source of support for individuals, families, and campuses. Complex, confusing tax subsidies just lessened the costs for some students and parents by later reducing their tax bills.[61]

Ending Sallie Mae's status as a government-sponsored enterprise helped extend the tradition of creatively financing higher education into the new millennium. Scholars have noted that privatization was part of the cuts to the public-private social safety net that made poorly regulated financial products increasingly important in day-to-day living since the 1970s. By the time of the 1997 write-offs, SLMA's tax exemptions, federal debt guarantees, low-interest Treasury funds, and increased responsibilities had made it enormous, profitable, and powerful. This public-private secondary market's federal charter nevertheless restricted its ability to compete with other industry rivals, who could more easily diversify and peddle their financial aid products and services. For example, USA Group, which had helped underwrite Ikenberry and Hartle's study, managed an $11.6 billion loan portfolio for 150 bankers, operated a secondary market, included a consulting firm that helped campuses navigate financial aid, and guaranteed 1.5 million loans worth roughly $6 billion. Sallie Mae's loan portfolio still dwarfed USA Group and other industry competitors, which, SLMA executives hoped, might allow them to continue to undercut their competition after privatization.[62]

That process took on new importance in the early 1990s. Reagan-era banking scandals and HEAF's startling collapse pushed Treasury officials and lawmakers to scrutinize GSEs in general and Sallie Mae in particular. SLMA's fate seemed unclear after the Clinton administration set out to replace the guaranteed loan program lawmakers had designed to nurture a student loan industry. Top brass unsuccessfully lobbied the administration to include privatization in its direct lending plan. The Wall Street "darling," reporters noted, was "off the buy lists" by August 1993. Before and immediately after the 1994 midterm elections, Education Department officials covertly tried to use their regulatory powers to hinder the GSE's ability to compete with direct lending. Industry insiders warned Clinton that Republicans "would have a field day" if word got out. SLMA officers could hardly expect a GOP rescue after the 1995 showdown failed to destroy direct lending in its infancy.[63]

Sallie Mae's leaders prevailed just weeks before Clinton signed off on the 1997 tax cuts. They had sent Representative Ford bills for two different privatization strategies after direct lending was made permanent. He subsequently joined other congressional Democrats in asking the administration to explore options. A year later, SLMA representatives assured Clinton that the GSE "has successfully accomplished its mission" and sought "new ways and means to better serve students, the education community, taxpayers, and our shareholders." By 1996, many in Washington favored taking away the special status hated by rival lenders, like USA Group. Only Senator Claiborne Pell, Clinton aides reported, seemed "a possible problem." Sallie Mae higher-ups nevertheless vigorously argued in lengthy hearings that the Fortune 100 company no longer required its special status, must be allowed to freely compete, and needed to increase its line of financial products. Some even suggested the entire process might show policymakers how to privatize the ten other GSEs. Administration officials constantly fretted that "Sallie Mae has won every round of the 'negotiations'" on timing and oversight, which seemed threatening "to the government's right to set public policy." Clinton's self-appointed "eyes and ears" on the board had to beg him to keep supporting privatization in the final months of the 1996 campaign, when "Wall Street reaction . . . will be swift and disastrous" and "you need to take yet another Republican position / value from [Republicans]."[64]

That year's Student Loan Marketing Association Reorganization Act still left the GSE's future unclear. It permitted officials to create a holding company that could dally in services not listed in SLMA's federal charter. The change nevertheless hinged on shareholders agreeing on a privatization plan. White House insiders watched but did not intervene in the bitter fights between stakeholders and president-appointed board members. Self-described dissidents insisted the company should focus on making student loans and recoiled at the board's plan to expand into other financial markets. The battle ended with a close vote on July 31, 1997, that entrusted the company's reorganization to mutineers. SLMA's new heads quickly created the SLMA Holding Corporation, which housed SLMA and a new, non-GSE firm simply called Sallie Mae. SLMA remained a secondary-market servicer as its managers slowly restructured operations for its eventual dissolution. But Sallie Mae, like so many other financial behemoths in this era of universal banking and less government oversight, could experiment with new business activities to expand. Such ventures included originating guaranteed loans, creating unique credit options, financing campus infrastructure, securitizing more assets, and consulting.[65]

Democrats and Republicans also bolstered for-profits, which began to experiment with lending during SLMA's seven-year privatization. Professors protective of the starkly white Ivory Tower had scorned proprietary schools decades before VA staffers had singled out for-profits in the entire academy's abuse of the GI Bill. But the Clinton administration largely ignored the extent to which proprietary outfits were harnessing the internet's reach, convenience, and profit potential in the mid-1990s. Institutions that were soon to become notorious, like the University of Phoenix, were using their escalating earnings to spend millions lobbying both Democrats and Republicans. Such for-profits, Apollo and University of Phoenix founder John Sperling later recalled, would not "exist without the ability to protect them from regulatory and political attack." He was unapologetic about his company's campaign contributions: "Yes, we use money to get their attention—our American system of campaign finance gives us no other alternative. Sadly, it's the only way to do it when you are from out-of-state and the forces against you have money, votes, and even football tickets!" The for-profits' business model gave them a foothold in congressional districts across the country as campaigning for reelection became increasingly more expensive. "When it comes down to an institution that happens to be in their general jurisdiction," an Education Department aide pointedly reminded senators in 1994, most politicians balked at shutting a for-profit down, even though "every Congressman I have talked to wants us to manage this program more tightly."[66]

Reporters noted lawmakers nervously laughed in response, which hardly made their willingness to sign off on the 1998 HEA reauthorization surprising. Revisions once again benefited for-profits and bankers at the expense of borrowers and taxpayers. Parts of the sprawling legislation certainly seemed beneficial to students and parents, as lawmakers earmarked funds to improve distance learning, train K-12 teachers, and reach out to disadvantaged young people to prepare them for college. The bill also promised to improve delivery of financial aid funds. Congress also cut the interest rate on student loans from 8.25 to 7.46 percent and gave debtors four months to refinance, which, federal officials predicted, would reduce the amount paid by $11 billion. House Committee on Education and the Workplace chairman John Boehner, other Republicans, and a few Congressional Black Caucus Democrats also led the charge to weaken the 1992 for-profit eligibility regulations. Afterward, for-profits could earn 90 percent of their revenue from federal tuition assistance programs. Boehner dismissed the General Accounting Office reports showing that proprietary schools had abysmal completion rates, terrible job placement records, and numerous students defaulting. The Ohio representative instead emphasized that "statistics show proprietary schools tend to serve larger populations of needy, high-risk, minority students," the "most in need of federal assistance." Conservatives, like Boehner, especially liked the for-profits' focus on job training, which complemented the GOP's cost-cutting, government-shrinking, welfare-ending agenda. The reauthorization's new bankruptcy rules, arguably its most infamous provision, complemented that mission. Federal officials and lawmakers had been steadily making it harder for borrowers to escape repayment since the 1972 reauthorization. Twenty-five years later, Congress just tightened the screws when lawmakers prohibited federal loans from being discharged during bankruptcy.[67]

Republicans controlling Congress continued to push through reforms that did more for banks than for students, parents, and campuses after George W. Bush assumed the presidency. The 2005 Bankruptcy Abuse Prevention and Consumer Protection Act, for example, made the bankruptcy restriction Clinton had signed into law even stricter. The 2006 budget also further loosened restrictions on for-profits' Title IV eligibility. More than half the student body could now be enrolled in correspondence courses, including those conducted online. Enrollments surged in existing and new for-profits, but they faced stiff competition from the many nonprofit colleges, including venerable public universities, offsetting the cost of their brick-and-mortar operations with cheap, profitable online options.[68]

Executive appointees arguably did the most to further the conservative agenda, the reach of the student loan sector, and the profits of proprietary schools. Operations had always been a stealth approach to policymaking, as Nixon insiders had noted, but staffing decisions arguably became more important in this particular era of partisan gridlock. Bush named a top for-profit college lobbyist as Assistant Secretary of Postsecondary Education, which university administrators, education experts, or business leaders had always filled previously. Sally Stroup joined other financial aid heavy hitters in restaffing an Education Department that opposed policing for-profits, financiers, or campus financial aid officers. The University of Phoenix's John Sperling recognized a windfall in the making. At his 2001 birthday party, the octogenarian proclaimed his intent to raise enrollments to more than 470,000 students (more than tripling the school's far-flung student body). The institution's owner, the Apollo Group, soon announced a snappier goal: "Five Years, Five Million Students, and Five Billion Dollars." That target seemed reachable after the Education Department decided for-profits would only be fined (not lose access to Title IV programs) if they rewarded staff for recruiting enrollees with excessive compensation. Thereafter, aggressive call-center tactics handsomely rewarded employees who got "asses in classes," as *60 Minutes* and *Frontline* exposés later revealed. Staff in nonprofit institutions (ranging from community colleges to Ivy League universities) also received even better perks than they had in the 1990s. Lenders desperately competing with each other to extend credit to students and parents plied personnel with cupcakes, shopping sprees, all-expense-paid trips, revenue shares, and stock options.[69]

Competition, not the direct loan program, was the financiers' greatest threat. The Bush administration doubled down on dismantling what remained of liberals' public-private social welfare programs. Hostile Education Department staffers, additional restrictions, and declining budget allocations dramatically decreased the amount of loans the government made directly to students between 1999 and 2006. Bush appointees still failed to fully destroy the program by selling off the government's direct loan portfolio to a private investor. Thereafter, officials still managed to reduce the credit offered through the Ford program to a negligible percentage of the total student loan volume between 2005 and 2007.[70]

State authorities started to investigate the student loan industry. Iowa officials looked into the nonprofit Iowa Student Loan Liquidity Corporation to figure out why the Hawkeye State had the second-highest debt burden per student. Its 2007 reports indicated that lax oversight and "an aggressive, offensive strategy" had been responsible for the kind of "hypergrowth" that had left a company of four hundred employees holding $3.3 billion in outstanding debts. Other states, including Pennsylvania and Missouri, had similar outfits that had become far more lucrative than anyone had imagined when Massachusetts and New York lawmakers first experimented with higher education assistance corporations in the late 1950s. Five decades later, New York attorney general Andrew Cuomo uncovered rampant abuse of perks and revenue-sharing arrangements by both campuses and lenders. He also discovered that financiers charged HBCU students higher fees and interest rates.[71]

That revelation repulsed many inside and outside Washington. One top Democrat compared such blatant discrimination to the redlining that had prevented so many African Americans from buying homes and enjoying the fruits of postwar prosperity. Participants in the sprawling student loan industry openly shared their doubts about the salamander that had evolved into a 1980s revenue-sucking dragon, and then into a millennial many-headed hydra. "When a student signs the paper for these loans," a top college admissions officer lamented to reporters, "they are basically signing an indenture." Some, he knew, would never shake off that burden: "We're indebting these kids for life."[72]

Congressional Democrats only managed to ease the plight of students and parents facing a mountain of debt in the Bush administration's final years. Lenders had already started to extend less credit in the months before Democrats won control of both congressional houses in 2006. With presidential primaries rapidly approaching, and investigations underway of abuses in student lending, the president fired industry insiders from a purposely lax Education Department. Republicans fumed that they subsequently had no role in shaping the 2007 College Reform and Access Act and reauthorizing HEA in 2008, five years overdue. The 2007 legislation significantly bolstered the

Pell grant program, substantially cut the guaranteed loan lender subsidy, halved the Stafford loan program's interest rate, added four new income-based repayment options, and forgave balances after ten years of public service or twenty-five years of payments. But lawmakers really broke precedent when they abandoned the color-blind help for developing institutions, earmarking far more than what Aubrey Williams, director of the National Youth Administration back in the New Deal era, had openly set aside for HBCUs and students of color. The 2007 law explicitly allocated $500 million to bolster HBCUs, institutions predominantly serving Latinos, and other minority-majority colleges.[73]

The 2008 reauthorization attempted to better oversee financiers, states, and college administrators. Lawmakers compelled the Education Department to collect far more data on the loan industry and student debt but federalism continued to constrain what Congress could do to oversee higher education. Lawmakers could end legislatures' access to federal higher education support if assemblies cut higher education spending and student assistance too much. But lawmakers did the most, as many academics of Harvard president James Conant's generation had feared, to scrutinize what campus staff did. This legislation included new measures, intended to be strictly enforced, for improving campus safety, limiting file sharing among students (particularly of copyrighted material), reining in textbook costs, protecting student free-speech rights, bettering teacher training programs, and encouraging international education curricula. The law importantly stipulated that states, colleges, and financiers had to submit detailed information to the Education Department, which had to publish charts of college prices, expense estimates, and tuition increases in order to enable students and parents to make informed choices. Any institution hiking fees had to include a substantial report justifying the raise and offering a plan to reduce undergraduate expenses. Every postsecondary school offering federal tuition assistance or working with preferred private lenders also had to establish and publicize a code of conduct. Lawmakers even tackled accreditation, finally agreeing on a definition of the long-dreaded diploma mills, whose business strategies and educational approaches set enrollees up to go into debt, drop out, and likely fail to repay loans.[74]

Great Recession Hail Mary

Staff and faculty at for-profit and nonprofit colleges felt far more immediate effects from the Great Recession than the 2008 reauthorization. Experts quickly linked the housing and banking crises to the kind of risky financing anathema to New Deal banking reforms and the government-guaranteed financial products interwoven into the country's public-private social safety net. The global financial catastrophe was far worse than the 1970s stagflation that had inaugurated higher education's so-called New Depression. The 2008 crisis was still not as dire as the Great Depression of the 1930s, which had threatened to shutter many campuses. But once again, state budgets shrank, higher education allocations fell, and tuition rates soared. Those trends were deeply interrelated. States generally earmarked the most for K-12 education and health care because there remained, despite the 2008 reauthorization, far fewer federal funding mandates or matching requirements for postsecondary schooling. College applications nevertheless increased (as did unemployment rates, particularly for young people). Enrollees certainly benefited from the recent expansion of the Pell program, but they continued to receive the most money from loans. Several years after economists declared the Great Recession over, most campus personnel doubted the seemingly new status quo would change anytime soon. "In the past, economic downturns were followed by periods of economic boom and losses were recovered relatively quickly," a Maryland university system official admitted. "I know no one who predicts that will be the case with our current fiscal decline."[75]

More borrowers stopped suffering in silence in the months leading up to and during the Great Recession. Household debt had steadily climbed since the 1930s. Edith Green had constantly brought up her constituents' struggles to afford and borrow for basic needs—frustrations also brought up in the "grief mail" sent to Nixon and pleas for help mailed to Ford. But only at the millennium's turn was the data collected and available to differentiate between what Americans owed for cars, homes, medical expenses, and college courses (see appendix, figure A3). Student loans had already become one of the largest burdens before Tacoma resident Alan Collinge started StudentLoanJustice.org, which he considered a "sort of complaint box for the industry." The website nonetheless made headlines, and Collinge soon appeared on *60 Minutes* to damn Sallie Mae, the nation's largest lender. Reporters also interviewed defaulters who told all-too-familiar stories of falling behind on, feeling embarrassed about, and even ending relationships over seemingly unpayable debts. Teacher, dancer, and choreographer Garrett Mockler had been particularly stung to have emerged from filing for bankruptcy in 2004 only to find himself still owing for his college degrees. Others expressed sadness about the paths they could not take. First-generation American Lucia DiPoi asked herself, "How bad could it be?" when she took out private loans to make up what federal student aid had not covered. Just a few years after graduation, she found herself almost $90,000 in debt. Her $900 monthly payments upended her dreams of working in an overseas refugee camp, as the salary "would have been enough for me but not for Sallie Mae." Others could not find jobs during the Great Recession. "You often hear the quote that you can't put a price on ignorance," Winona State University graduate Ezra Kazee noted, "but . . . ignorance is looking more and more affordable every day." It certainly looked that way to twenty-seven-year-old Gregory Westby, who had not found a full-time job since graduating New York's School of Visual Arts. He deferred his payments, which only bought time: "I'm surviving, but who knows when I'll be able to start paying my loans back?" Some graduates found debts limited employment opportunities to repay their burdens. Forty-seven-year-old Robert Bowman, for example, overcame two horrible accidents before he worked and borrowed his way through college, graduate school, and law school. His scrupulous records showed Sallie Mae had overcharged him, forbade him from deferring payments, and threatened to prevent him from getting his law license. Five state appellate judges still ruled after he passed the bar exam that his $400,000 balance proved that Bowman "has not presently established the character and general fitness requisite for an attorney."[76]

Barack Obama stood out on the 2008 campaign trail for knowing exactly how burdensome that kind of debt could be. In his 2006 memoir, *The Audacity of Hope*, he wrote that education was "at the heart of a bargain this nation makes with its citizens: If you work hard and take responsibility, you'll have a chance for a better life." Seventeen years earlier, he had taken out more than $40,000 to attend Harvard Law School. His wife, Michelle, had borrowed as well. Despite their high salaries, it had taken until January 2004 for the couple to retire their education debts. Much as his opponents liked to paint them as elitist, he told reporters in Indianapolis that "in fact, our lives, when you look over the last two decades, more closely approximate the lives of the average voter than any of the other candidates." Elaborating, he said, "we've struggled with paying student loans. We've tried to figure out whether we have adequate daycare. I've actually filled up my own gas tank." His wife more pointedly rejected the idea that her Ivy League education had shaped her outlook on life. "I am the product of a middle class upbringing," she told Pennsylvania voters gathered at Haverford College. "I grew up on the South Side of Chicago in a working-class community," which she did not have to remind anyone was predominantly African American. As for her husband, she asked: "When is the last time you've seen a president of the United States who just paid off his loan debt?" Obama also reminded voters of how much he understood such burdens in the presidential election against Republican John McCain, who had graduated from the Naval Academy with an obligation to serve but no requirement to pay back Sallie Mae. Student loans were just one of the issues the senators sparred over, however, as voters were also focused on the economy, Iraq War, health care, immigration, and climate change.[77]

The Obama administration prioritized student aid even though fights over health care, financial regulation, and economic recovery dominated headlines after the senator's historic victory. Just weeks after taking office, he signed the 2009 American Reinvestment and Recovery Act, which included billions to bolster Title IV student assistance offerings. Officials hoped the relief would reach seven million struggling undergraduates. Many critics still feared that Democrats had once again done more for the wealthiest Americans, as more than a third of the relief in the $787 billion stimulus took the form of tax credits. Those breaks included the American Opportunity Tax Credit that replaced the HOPE Scholarship write-off. More Americans could benefit from this deduction but, as tuition tax-cut opponents had emphasized since the 1950s, tax refunds came late for families who had to pay tuition bills up front. This change would also reduce the revenue that could be directly spent on real relief for residents.[78]

The Obama administration also used the budget to get bankers out of the business of student lending. The president called his 2009 budget proposal "a threat to the status quo in Washington." Among the provisions for health care and a tax-code overhaul was swapping direct lending for the guaranteed loan program. Campuses had been trying to build support for such a switch since the mid-1990s. Clinton aides had retreated after the 1994 midterms but Obama's staff now sought to win that fight. "We want to help more students," Education Secretary Arne Duncan insisted, "rather than continuing to subsidize banks." Estimates suggested that ending guaranteed lending could free up money that could be directed toward community colleges and legis-latures supporting college-readiness and degree-completion programs. Savings could also be used to finally make Pell grants an entitlement, like the pension in the New Deal's Social Security legislation. These suggestions thrilled higher education lobbyists, with one boldly labeling the postsec-ondary provisions "the biggest proposed change in federal student aid pro-grams since the Higher Education Act was created in 1965."[79]

Democratic congressional leaders braced themselves for the kind of fight that had punctuated decades of warfare over taxing, spending, regulating, and ensuring equal opportunity. Both chambers' budget committees pre-pared plans in April 2009 to include the direct lending switch through budget reconciliation, to avoid the need for a three-fifths majority vote, the threshold by then basically required to pass laws. Obama went on the offensive amid the covert planning, fuming publicly that "lenders get a big government subsidy with every loan they make," but "that's a premium we cannot afford—not when we could be investing the same money in our students, in our economy, and in our country." He knew that those lenders had already "mo-bilized an army of lobbyists," but intended to thwart them: "They are gearing up for battle. So am I."[80]

Obama had ample support for that declaration of war. Sallie Mae execu-tives spent $4 million lobbying Congress in 2009, and encouraged employees across the country to rally in support of the jobs they might lose if direct lending replaced the guaranteed loan system. But the United States Student Association, US Public Interest Research Group, AFL-CIO, SEIU, NAACP, La Raza, and other organizations galvanized Americans nationwide to fight for reform. Students bravely shared how much they borrowed. Many also signed petitions, joined social-networking sites, participated in call-ins, and even used fax-ins to demand lawmakers act.[81]

Victory was hardly assured. Republicans doggedly defended guaranteed lending. Lamar Alexander, a senator from Tennessee and George H. W. Bush's Secretary of Education, assailed direct loans as "another Washington take-over." His rebuke failed to answer California Democrat George Miller's pointed questions about the costs of outsourcing federal student aid. "Why are we paying people to lend the government's money," the House Labor and Education Committee chairman asked, "and then the government guaran-tees the loan and the government takes back the loan?" His Democratic col-leagues nevertheless retreated quietly and quickly from bills to turn Pell grants into the basic right the Zook Committee had hoped for and Claiborne Pell had promised. They, along with many Republicans, had no interest in another entitlement that reduced congressional control of the budget. Liberals still openly derided Sallie Mae and other large lenders for offering a plan they promised would offer the same savings as what the administration wanted. Miller boldly attacked financiers for "using legislative gimmicks to mask the fact that their proposal would divert $15 billion into their own pockets at the expense of students." He brazenly introduced a bill similar to the White House plan. "We can either keep sending these subsidies to banks or we can start sending them directly to students," Miller emphasized. Action took much longer in the Senate, but most of Miller's House colleagues were convinced. "We are absolutely moving in the right direction," New York Representative Timothy Bishop enthused. The former campus financial aid officer assured reporters that "students are going to benefit." In mid-September, he and 252 other representatives approved legislation that looked remarkably similar to what Obama had outlined.[82]

Republican Scott Brown's surprise special-election victory in Massachusetts ended up imperiling reform of both health care and student aid, the costly items New Dealers had not integrated into the social safety net. Democrats lost their sixty-seat majority, which forced both issues onto a budget reconciliation bill. Senate Budget Committee chair Kent Conrad balked at including student lending in the legislation. Shocked and outraged Democrats considered the North Dakotan too beholden to the Bank of North Dakota, which provided jobs to his constituents and hardly championed direct loans. Six other senators warned party leaders they feared job losses in their states. Prominent among the direct loan opponents was Nebraska Democrat Ben Nelson, whom many critics considered far too protective of the massive student lender Nelnet, headquartered in his state. Neither he nor Conrad really capitulated. Conrad included student loan changes but used far more conservative budget estimates that provided significantly less money for community colleges, degree-completion programs, and Pell grant increases.[83]

Neither senator voted for the budget reconciliation legislation. An insider still lauded the narrow March 2010 margin of victory because it would take "money from a vested interest and give it to some of the most low income people in our country. We don't do that very often." The president was far more celebratory when he traveled to the same community college where George Bush had signed the 1992 reauthorization creating the direct loan pilot. "That's two major victories in one week," Obama emphasized when signing the 2010 Health Care and Education Reconciliation Act. The first was, of course, health care. The second was the end of the once revered Guaranteed Student Loan Program LBJ had signed into law, Pell had feared would never be ended, and Obama labeled "a sweetheart deal . . . that essentially gave billions of dollars to banks."[84]

The many compromises in making federal loan programs profitable enabled a number of the largest lenders to survive what Democrats had hoped would be their death knell. Lawmakers had never allowed the IRS to collect debts despite decades of bipartisan interest. Financiers could no longer originate government loans but could still service them for a price. That outsourcing, so common in the decades-long push to turn more government services fully over to the private sector, preserved a portion of student lenders' lucrative trade. USA Group, the guarantor that had partly underwritten Ikenberry and Hartle's survey, joined other lenders in transferring guaranteed loan holdings to the Great Lakes Higher Education Corporation, which solely serviced federal loans. That nonprofit was one of four preferred government contractors. Another was Navient, a company that Sallie Mae officials spun off in 2014 to get rid of student loan operations and focus on consumer lending. Financial aid behemoths also made a lot of money on private loans to students and parents.[85]

These financial products remained offers many aspiring undergraduates could not refuse. The 2010 reconciliation bill, unlike the 2008 reforms, had done nothing to squarely address federal higher education and tuition assistance policies that had helped worsen racial and gender inequality over time. Expensive for-profits still seemed cheaper and more accessible to nontraditional students, immigrants, and low-income Americans. Federal aid limits on grants, loans, and work-study opportunities also left many families, including those paying for nonprofit colleges and universities, with little choice but to hold multiple jobs and take out private loans.[86]

After the 2010 midterm elections, Democrats were not in a position to help the millions struggling with student debt. Fees continued to climb despite the Great Recession's supposed end in June 2009. It hardly restored the limited public-private social welfare provisions enacted in the New Deal, rectified the inequities built into supposedly color-blind tuition assistance programs, lessened the importance of finance to cover basic needs, or heralded the return of the kind of well-paying work borrowers needed to repay debts. Such change,

FIG 7.1 Lawmakers and Northern Virginia Community College professors and students surrounded President Barack Obama as he signed the 2010 Health Care and Education Reconciliation Act. Though most known for enacting the Affordable Care Act, the legislation also ended the guaranteed-loan program that LBJ had championed but that Obama, who only recently had paid off his student loans, considered a sweetheart deal for banks. Pat Benic / UPI / Newscom.

despite Obama's campaign promises, seemed impossible after the party lost the congressional seats that had enabled them to tackle college lending, health care, consumer protection, and financial oversight. Republicans flexed their muscles in Congress, turning themselves into the "Party of No," which prevented their rivals from passing laws or even holding hearings on a Supreme Court nominee. Washington gridlock, by then between—not within—the parties, also led to a government shutdown over the budget. Costly closures remained a constant threat because lawmakers continued to operate under short-term agreements that did little to address the country's many pressing needs, including a fundamental overhaul of higher education financing. But alumni, students, and parents only became more indignant about the financial risks of pursuing degrees that were ultimately unaffordable—except perhaps to the people who, in 2011, Wall Street protesters started calling "the one percent."[87]

Epilogue

A Brave New World of Indentured Students

"Many of us who attended Corinthian are in worse financial condition than before we started school," complained a Florida-based member of a group calling itself the Corinthian 15. These former students announced in March 2015 that they would no longer be paying off their student loans. Their declaration came several years after Corinthian Colleges, a collection of many for-profit trade schools across the country, had begun fighting class-action lawsuits, state investigations, and federal inquiries. Just months earlier, the company had agreed to shut down or sell off most of its schools. Weeks earlier, Ontario policymakers had suspended its license to operate in Canada, and the US Consumer Financial Protection Bureau had negotiated $480 million in debt relief for American students who had taken out loans directly from Corinthian. Federal investigators declared its in-house lending to be an illegal, predatory scheme. The settlement made headlines but for the beneficiaries it meant that only 40 percent of their debt was erased. That amount was hardly enough to make up for worthless degrees and time wasted in programs students now could not finish—and not every borrower qualified for forgiveness. "Corinthian and the investors who funded it should be paying our debts," the Florida student insisted, "and they should pay for us to get an education from a reputable college that is not-for-profit and that is regionally accredited."[1]

The Corinthian 15 caught the media's attention because they were among many Americans increasingly "coming out" about their student loan burdens in the wake of the Great Recession. Many expressed a sense that their debt had trapped or indentured them, since they believed they had really had no choice but to pursue degrees to get good jobs, which turned out not to be guaranteed or sufficient to pay the loans off quickly. Reporters profiled some of these frustrated Americans in eye-opening reports on the growing number of defaults, dollars owed, bankruptcies declared, and repayment periods extended. Their stories featured both former students and aging parents, some of whom had funds garnished from their Social Security checks. Others who struggled to repay shared their stories at the "debtor assemblies" convened by the Occupy Student Debt campaign, an offshoot of the amorphous Occupy movement—more famous for its encampments of activists railing against government bank bailouts after the 2008 financial crisis and the runaway wealth of society's richest 1 percent.[2]

Occupy Student Debt activists had early victories on the West Coast. Organizers rallied campus union members, faculty associations, and some ten thousand students from community colleges, California State University, and the University of California, who participated in walkouts and sit-ins throughout the fall 2011 and winter 2012 terms. They helped to energize a broader coalition of organizations under the banner of ReFund California, which pushed Governor Jerry Brown to endorse Proposition 30, which stopped fee hikes and education cuts. That 2012 referendum passed at a moment when similar alliances of student-faculty unions were forming across the country. By 2014, the American Federation of Teachers, Center for American Progress, Jobs with Justice, and the United States Student Association had partnered to launch "Higher Ed, Not Debt," a campaign pushing for change at the federal level.[3]

The Higher Ed, Not Debt coalition got some attention, but not nearly as much as Strike Debt, the subsequent name of the Occupy Student Debt campaign. Strike Debt piqued the interest of reporters around the world, as governments were increasingly using student lending to fund higher education and sparking student and parent outrage in other nations. Strike Debt's innovative, US-based Rolling Jubilee also caught the attention of American journalists. This fundraiser had initially focused on those with unpaid medical bills, drumming up small, grassroots donations to buy debts and forgive

FIG E.1 Part of a national day of action on March 4, 2010, protesters in Berkeley, California, decried education funding cuts and tuition increases, which had become all too common since the 1970s. Current and former students as well as parents had grown far more outspoken about the burden of student debt following the 2008 Great Recession. Photo by Justin Sullivan / Getty Images.

them. Soon it expanded its mission to pay off student loans in default, too. Lapsed credit can be bought for pennies on the dollar through secondary markets. By the time the Corinthian 15 were publicly announcing their refusal to pay, Strike Debt had already purchased and erased $27 million worth of delinquent medical and student loans for less than $400,000. "It's really a crowdsourced project," one participant enthused. By 2015, small donors had given more than $700,000. "I just thought that the concept of mutually buying discounted debt and abolishing it was really clever," another donor told a *Guardian* reporter, even if "the debt market is too big for Rolling Jubilee to make a difference." Another marveled at how the arrangement offered "bang for your buck. Rather than straight paying $50 worth of someone's bill, that $50 gets so much more done the way Strike Debt did it." She also liked it from "a theoretical perspective," because "it shows that debt is . . . kind of not real, you know?" One of the borrowers whose debt was relieved, twenty-four-year-old Courtney Brown, told the *Washington Post* she "thought it was a joke," when she got a letter from Rolling Jubilee in August 2014. But the work the activists were doing to free her and thousands of others from delinquent loans made a serious difference.[4]

Debt erasure by charity was only the attention-getting start of Strike Debt. Its leaders soon shifted to a larger vision of organizing the millions of people saddled with student loans into a substantial resistance movement. "We wanted to get past the donate button," Strike Debt's Ann Larson told *The Atlantic*, "and build a membership organization—something that people can actually join and provide a platform of political engagement that would unite people across party lines." Cofounder Thomas Gokey told the *Post* the group would move to "larger, more aggressive tactics" because "we want to make all public higher education completely free—that's a practical, achievable goal. We can't wait for Congress to do it."[5]

Strike Debt activists were rightly skeptical that any relief would come out of a deeply divided Washington. Democrats had barely managed, in 2010, to replace the original program of guaranteed loans through banks with direct lending by the federal government, and the culmination of that twenty-year effort would do little to stop students and parents from taking on more debt. The number of annual Pell grant recipients was increasing but, after Republicans retook Congress in the 2010 midterms, Democrats had little hope of delivering the kind of sweeping change Barack Obama had promised in 2008. Budget battles, like those that had felled the National Youth Administration in the 1940s and later imperiled direct federal lending, continued to chip away at the financial assistance students and campuses needed. One Obama-era showdown destroyed the federal Perkins loan program, a financial aid option for low-income students that had evolved out of the old National Defense Student Loan program. Thwarted by Capitol Hill Republicans, Obama and his aides resorted to the kind of executive-branch actions that other twentieth-century presidents had used to circumvent Washington gridlock: issuing executive orders and tinkering with department rules to achieve more under existing policies relating to public health, workplace safety, consumer protection, and the environment.[6]

Obama issued slightly fewer executive orders than many of his predecessors but the actions he took had impact. The Education Department was directed to do more to publicize income-driven repayment options, simplify enrollment in such programs, and draft rights for borrowers. Staffers also engaged with the state attorneys general who were best positioned to crack down on abuses by for-profit colleges and lenders. This cooperation brought an end to Corinthian Colleges and put pressure on the University of Phoenix, whose enrollments plummeted during these years, reportedly from a peak of 470,000 students in 2010 to 130,000 in 2016. By the end of the Obama administration, the Education Department even published a lengthy list of degree programs that did not pay off for their graduates in terms of income gains that exceeded their costs. These tended to be the institutions whose students struggled most to pay off what they had borrowed: top offenders included trade schools and online for-profits. Even at Harvard, however, a small, two-year graduate program to study the dramatic arts made the list; the A.R.T. Institute temporarily suspended enrollments amid the negative news coverage, including a *New York Times* piece noting that "even the most prestigious colleges may not be paying enough attention to whether their degrees are worth the price of admission."[7]

That was just one of many attention-getting revelations that came with the additional data disclosure called for in the 2008 reauthorization of the Higher Education Act, and the fuller information gained by the federal government after it ended the provision of guaranteed loans through private banks. Only after the Education Department became the sole provider of federal loans did staffers notice that direct lending required more stringent credit checks. They may have believed that applying a stricter standard would have little impact on students, parents, and nonprofit campuses, but by the summer of 2012 it was evident to federal officials and financial aid officers that an unusually large number of student loan applications had been denied because would-be borrowers presented unacceptable levels of default risk. Most of the four hundred thousand rejected applicants were low-income parents of color, the population historically lacking the income and savings to pay large bills out of pocket. Turning these families down not only derailed education dreams; it also wreaked budgetary havoc on institutions that enrolled large numbers of students of color. Chronically underfunded HBCUs had seen twenty-eight thousand of their enrollees denied, and therefore lost fees sorely needed to keep their doors open. After lobbying and pressure from the Congressional Black Caucus, the Education Department changed the rules so that low-income parents with bad credit could borrow again.[8]

Education Department data, especially in combination with Internal Revenue Service statistics, helped reveal the inequalities built into and sustained by the American system of higher education. Analysis exposed, for example, that education borrowing had in fact only added to the wealth gaps between men and women and between whites and people of color. Other startling trends also became evident: growing numbers of Americans were borrowing far more than in decades past, owed more than they took out for years after graduation, and were headed for likely default, even if they graduated from reputable two- and four-year colleges. In 2020, a watchdog group even discovered a data-driven private lender offering higher interest rates to debt holders who had attended HBCUs or predominantly Latinx institutions.[9]

These startling reports did not convince everyone that American higher education's precarious, regressive financing needed a fundamental overhaul. Economists who did not see the student loan situation as a catastrophe prescribed only incremental changes. One esteemed higher education analyst, Sandy Baum, outlined a policy agenda including more guidance for students, stricter borrowing limits, tougher eligibility rules to exclude institutions that do not serve students well, improving on income-driven repayment options, making repayments easier by, for example, allowing payroll deductions for student loan payments, offering variable interest rates, and allowing some forgiveness for student debt during bankruptcy proceedings. Specialists who worry about a future crisis have made similar suggestions, on the assumption that disaster can be averted. Beth Akers and Matthew Chingos, for example, advocate more consumer protection for students and parents, arming them with better information about degree programs, likely earnings, income-contingent payback options, and choices available in times of health crisis or financial hardship.[10]

A smattering of economists, journalists, and policymakers have championed nongovernmental solutions, such as the "no loan" options that some universities offer. These financial aid packages, typically awarded by prestigious schools with healthy endowments, combine generous scholarships with reasonable expectations of what students can contribute from part-time or summer jobs. A handful of medical schools have created major scholarship programs for low-income students with money from private donors, in part to enable more graduates to choose the medical career that is most meaningful to them, rather than the most lucrative specialization to allow them to pay back loans. (The hope is that more will become the general practitioners that so many communities desperately need.) A growing number of businesses now include assistance in student loan repayment in the employee benefits packages that they use to attract and retain talent.[11]

One idea that has cropped up at different points has been to treat education like other forms of investment by allowing a party with capital to fund a student's studies and then see returns on that outlay in the form of some percentage of the student's later earnings. Economics Nobel laureate Milton Friedman first outlined the possibility of such contracts in the mid-1950s, while cautioning that they would be "economically equivalent to the purchase of a share in an individual's earning capacity and thus to partial slavery." That concern did not dissuade some colleges, universities, and states from exploring so-called income-contingent loans in the early 1970s, when the Guaranteed Student Loan Program was in its infancy. Yale and Duke stood out for launching programs that allowed students to join cohorts of borrowers, each of which would pay the same percentage of their individual earnings until their whole cohort's debt was paid back.[12]

The idea went dormant as government-guaranteed and private loans became far more common and well known—yet public outcry over student debt and lending in the new millennium has sparked new interest in what are now called income-share agreements. Purdue University, for example, assembled a group of corporate and individual donors to provide the money for "Back a Boiler," a financial aid option it first offered in the 2016–2017 academic year. President Mitch Daniels, who came to Purdue after eight years as Indiana's Republican governor, called it "true 'debt-free' college" because select students could sign a contract to hand over a percentage of their income for ten years after graduation, regardless of whether that added up to more or less than the cost of their education. "If the graduate earns less than expected," Daniels emphasized, "it is the investors who are disappointed." The experiment caught the attention of economists, journalists, and Silicon Valley venture capitalists. Soon, Bay Area speculators (along with actor Ashton Kutcher) were putting money into a venture called Lambda School, an online company focused on teaching people to code at no cost upfront, instead using an income-share model for payment later. And in 2018, a billionaire from the private-equity industry joined forces with the former chief operating officer of Federal Student Aid to launch the Education Finance Institute, a nonprofit organization to help traditional colleges start income-share agreements and other experimental programs. Clearly the enthusiasm is infectious, even as higher education researchers voice concerns that many young people will not understand this venture capital style of financing or recognize its onerous terms. Harking back to Milton Friedman's logic, some have called these complicated agreements a new version of indentured servitude.[13]

Many student debt scholars, particularly those on the left, have little faith that what they consider a true national emergency can be resolved by such private and nonprofit easures. Sociologist Sara Goldrick-Rab, founder of Temple's Hope Center for College, Community, and Justice, suggests a fundamental overhaul of the Higher Education Act, whose most recent reauthorization expired in 2014. Her ideas include a dramatic expansion of the law's work-study provisions, which are currently underfunded and difficult to use, and rules forcing states to use federal expenditures to supplement, not supplant, state earmarks. She even suggests regulations to ensure that money is equitably distributed among campuses rather than spent mostly on flagship schools. Other experts have outlined ways to make public colleges and universities tuition free. David Deming, director of Harvard's Malcolm Wiener Center for Social Policy, points out that the federal government has spent $12 billion more on higher education annually than state institutions have collected in student fees. It would not be so great a change, then, to redirect federal funds and eliminate state institutions' need to charge tuition completely. More than a third of the $91 billion earmarked annually, he notes, has taken the form of tax breaks to tuition payers, and that money could instead be channeled directly into aid programs of greater relevance to poorer students. After all, it is the nature of tax deductions that they benefit only those with higher incomes and therefore larger tax burdens. Federal expenditures on tuition assistance programs for low-income and military enrollees could also be redirected if public campuses did not charge tuition, perhaps to help the neediest enrollees with living expenses. Anthropologist Caitlin Zaloom, having spent four years closely studying how and why middle-class families manage to pay exorbitant college bills, is also convinced that government should do more to achieve "free or lower tuition." Part of the problem is that, when families take on heavy financial burdens, they focus on whether the investment will pay off in narrow financial terms. When the government foots more of the bill, it "represents an investment in the nation's future." It also "generates common experiences and social solidarity between the people it serves" and, as New Dealers realized in the 1930s, "it can also foster stronger moral bonds between citizens and the state."[14]

Legislators and city leaders in fact experimented with a range of ways to ease the student debt crisis. A majority of states relied on tuition revenue to fund public higher education by 2017 but forty-five states and the District of Columbia nevertheless offered a range of debt forgiveness programs. Shoddy accounting and missing paperwork, which reminded journalists of the subprime mortgage crisis, also prompted judges across the country to throw out lenders' lawsuits against borrowers in the 2010s. But some policymakers were already endeavoring to stop Americans from having to borrow large sums, or any money at all. San Francisco city and county officials worked with the local school district to start automatically contributing to college savings accounts started for every kindergartner, an idea adopted in St. Louis, Oakland, and a few other cities. Tennessee and Oregon legislators crafted programs to help cover community college expenses that inspired other states to try to guarantee an additional two years of schooling, decades after the Zook Commission first made that suggestion. New York governor Andrew Cuomo boldly promised to make two- and four-year public institutions free for families earning less than $125,000 a year. Experts expressed skepticism and noted many flaws with the 2017 plan, but New Mexico legislators still announced a 2019 initiative to make college at any state campus free, regardless of a resident's income.[15]

Many of these initiatives had been discussed and even rolled out before the 2016 presidential election, when voters expressed great enthusiasm for actual reform, if not the eventual end, of the student loan industry. Vermont Senator Bernie Sanders promised free college—to the thrill of many students and more than a few parents who disregarded the conservative and liberal pundits scoffing at the idea. Hillary Clinton could not ignore public enthusiasm. The former First Lady, senator, and secretary of state announced that summer that she would eventually make going to college debt-free for some citizens. Families making less than $125,000 would not be paying any tuition at four-year state schools. And, for those who had already had to borrow, she also promised an immediate three-month repayment holiday to give them a chance to refinance their loans and enroll in income-based repayment plans, though indebted alumni already had such payback options. She did, however, pledge to open up public-sector loan forgiveness to entrepreneurs and make it easier for employers to offer student loan repayment benefits.[16]

Neither relief, reform, nor wholesale change seemed likely after the general election. During the primaries, Donald Trump had made only a smattering of vague statements about getting universities to cut costs, forgiving loans after fifteen years, and capping monthly payments at 12.5 percent of monthly income (without mentioning that the federal government already offered a repayment option with a 10 percent cap). Even though the student loan industry received barely a mention in his plans to "Make America Great Again," Trump seemed inclined to expand that still-sizeable financial sector after he took office. His first budget proposal called for the end of the Public Sector Loan Forgiveness Program, by which any employee of a federal, state, local, or tribal government agency can have their student debt balance erased after making 120 payments. He also outraged many by nominating wealthy Republican donor Betsy DeVos as Education Secretary. The Amway heiress had never worked in an educational institution, K–12 or postsecondary, but had founded and run nonprofit organizations to support and advocate for school choice. Democrats grilled her on her lack of experience during confirmation hearings but she was never formally asked to defend her financial ties to the student loan industry, which had already lobbied the Trump transition team to permit private lenders to once again be involved in federal loan programs.[17]

DeVos did not manage to destroy direct lending but did a lot to protect for-profit schools as well as the industry the guaranteed-loan program had created and Sallie Mae had nurtured. Senator Elizabeth Warren of Massachusetts openly questioned DeVos's decision to hire two men with deep ties to the for-profit college industry. Early into the education secretary's term, she also halted Obama-era efforts to streamline and standardize loan servicing. Numerous complaints to the Consumer Financial Protection Bureau also did not stop DeVos from lessening accountability for firms contracted to manage federal loans. The Education Department also permitted those companies to charge higher fees on borrowers behind on their payments. She also ordered the dismantlement of the gainful employment regulations threatening proprietary institutions' eligibility for the federal tuition assistance programs that legally could supply 90 percent of their revenue. She called the rules "a muddled process that's unfair to students and schools" even though the protections had proven successful in putting some predatory institutions, like Corinthian, out of business. The education secretary also froze Obama-era procedures to help borrowers, like the Corinthian 15, erase debts incurred through practices deemed fraudulent.[18]

State attorneys general and judges did the most to stop the Education Department from undoing what the Obama administration had achieved. Illinois and Washington state attorneys general filed lawsuits against Sallie Mae spinoff Navient just days into the new Trump administration. Their complaints echoed the charges the Consumer Financial Protection Bureau had filed against the loan servicer before Obama left office. Those prosecutors made headlines months later for suing Navient for loans that attorneys insisted "were designed to fail."[19]

Eighteen states also sued DeVos and the Education Department to have Obama-era debt-relief protocols restored, an effort one Education appointee deemed "ideologically driven." Those cases did little to expedite approval of the thousands of relief applications borrowers filed at the end of Obama's presidency. Not a single one was approved during Trump's first six months in office, when the Education Department received fifteen thousand more applications. A federal judge deemed freezing the rules "arbitrary and capricious" in an October 2018 ruling, but that did not stop Education Department staffers from imposing stricter standards for relief in the summer of 2019.[20]

An overhaul of higher education financing and even the end of the student loan industry continued to be on the nation's political agenda in 2020, when more than forty-five million owed almost $1.6 trillion. Ideas discussed in the packed Democratic presidential primaries included covering college costs for students from low-income families, tuition-free community colleges, fee-free public universities, interest-rate reductions, stricter standards for for-profits' federal tuition assistance eligibility, prohibiting proprietary outfits from receiving public funds, expanding Pell grants, federal incentives to cajole states into investing in public postsecondary schools, student loan refinancing options, new income-contingent repayment plans, more public service forgiveness opportunities, additional earmarks for HBCUs, and so-called baby bonds—a nest egg that could eventually be tapped to pay for college. Candidates Bernie Sanders and Elizabeth Warren even advocated canceling at least some, if not all, debts.[21]

The COVID-19 outbreak quickly overshadowed the raucous Democratic primaries. The global pandemic laid bare the inadequacies and inequality in what remained of the New Deal's public-private social safety net and the complicated financing needed to afford basic necessities like housing, health care, and education. The virus provided an unintentional lesson in the country's widening class, racial, and gender divides on and off college campuses as Americans strained state unemployment offices, crowded into hospitals, and frantically tried to get tests insurance companies did not necessarily cover. Moving college classes online did not prove a cheap, easy fix to a chronically underfunded academy. Going virtual instead revealed exactly how much American higher education remained as patchwork, piecemeal, and threadbare as the Zook Commission feared federal postsecondary school aid would stay even after the Roosevelt administration's experiments with work-study and the GI Bill. There was a stark digital divide between the wealthy universities with a substantial tech infrastructure and the many small private colleges and large public institutions predominantly serving students of color. Fewer resources left administrators unable to provide wi-fi hot spots and laptops to the estimated 20 percent of students nationwide who did not own computers. Undergraduates able to Zoom into lectures saw the inequality that mass higher education, despite Great Society liberals' hopes, had not ameliorated but actually been complicit in exacerbating. Classmates could be seen sheltering in place from suburban houses, cramped apartments, and dorms for those who had no stable homes or internet options elsewhere.[22]

The fate of those undergraduates, perhaps least likely to return once in-person classes resumed, hung in the balance while Congress debated how much campuses would receive from the stimulus bills meant to keep the economy on life support during the pandemic. Reporters breathlessly noted that total forgiveness of federally held student debt was on the table during tense spring and summer 2020 negotiations over unemployment, direct payment, and small-business provisions. The March CARES Act only gave borrowers paying off some student loans several months of suspended payments and interest charges. That small reprieve actually broke with the tradition of loans accruing interest even if borrowers showed that hardships left them unable to make monthly payments. This temporary help received far more coverage than the limited direct federal support given to colleges and universities, aid that highlighted how lawmakers still shied from decoupling campus financial aid from tuition assistance. The $14 billion allocated for campuses included $6 billion for emergency grants for students. Lawmakers, as they had since the 1972 reauthorization, used Pell grants to calculate how much an individual institution would receive to assist enrollees and to cover costs related to COVID-19. Yet Congress also openly set aside money to aid minority servicing institutions as they had first done during the Great Recession. But higher education lobbyists still worried this relief would not do enough to help campuses reopen in the fall or survive a cataclysmic drop in tuition income. House Education Committee chairman Bobby Scott tried to assure them that CARES had only provided a "down payment" and been "just one step in a long and challenging effort to maintain access to education for students across the country." Yet such promises seemed worthless by August, when infection rates were out of control and key provisions of the CARES Act expired amid continued beltway gridlock. Even though the student loan moratorium had not expired, President Trump still extended it in a flurry of early August executive orders, which many critics considered a desperate, unconstitutional attempt to circumvent Congress and please voters in an election year. [23]

Many Democrats held out hope that newly elected President Joe Biden would use an executive order to wipe out anywhere from $10,000 to $50,000 of an individual's federally held student debt in his first hundred days. On Day One, he prolonged the moratorium. When pressed at a CNN town hall weeks later about debt relief, he quickly replied: "I will not make that happen." He mentioned concerns about "people who have gone to Harvard or Yale," much to the outrage of progressives, like Representative Alexandria Ocasio-Cortez of New York, who tweeted: "Who cares what school someone went to?[24]

Neither a pause nor massive forgiveness would be enough to heal an ailing country or eradicate parasitic student debt. Strike Debt activists recognized that donations, scattershot rallies, and clever campaigns alone could not bring an end to a regressive system that had evolved from efforts to protect states' rights, campus autonomy, and private enterprise, while avoiding meaningful challenges to the systematic inequality the country's public-private social welfare programs, color-blind policies, and government-guaranteed financial products helped sustain. Creatively financing public goods and personal necessities, like higher education, has not been a choice for the majority of Americans for decades. Student lending, in particular, has always relied on questionable consent and the promise of a short, temporary period of indebtedness. Borrowers may have only recently become more outspoken about how their balances have made them feel indentured but there has never been truly equal access to government-guaranteed, campus, and private loans.

Citizens of color, particularly women, have continued to owe disproportionately more for their educations but everyone indebted for degrees or trying to figure out how to eventually pay for college needs to organize in order to elect officials serious about directly funding higher education. Residents must have the kind of genuine public option rightwing CEOs fought in the 1950s. Citizens will also need to hold their elected officials accountable for carrying out, implementing, and enforcing a truly progressive overhaul of the academy. Direct spending always has been and remains a much more cost-effective means of educating the citizenry, providing much-needed research, and ensuring the economic and civic vitality of the many college towns and urban neighborhoods that depend on campuses' survival.

Taking the price tag off a college degree will also recognize that the benefits of higher education are far more than just financial, as Americans both during the Depression and returning from World War II knew. Those tenacious college students proved policymakers and educators wrong about the power, persistence, and potential of ordinary people. Everyday citizens were the ones who forced politicians, bureaucrats, and university administrators to do right by them. Their descendants do not need the ability to borrow for college. They must be able to pursue additional schooling without finding themselves in the paralyzing debt some labeled a new form of unfree labor even before the Great Recession. The American Dream will remain elusive unless education and other basic necessities are finally recognized and treated as rights critical to forming a more perfect union.

APPENDIX 1

Revenue Sources for Higher Education Institutions by Academic Year, 1909–1910 to 1989–1990

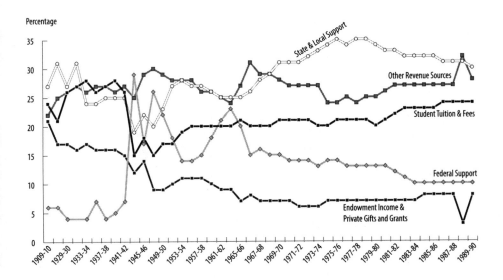

FIG A1 "Other" sources include sales and services, organized activities, hospitals, independent operations, and auxiliary enterprises. Federal officials have sporadically changed how they categorized and counted revenue over the course of the twentieth century, which included, for example, excluding federally funded research and development centers (FFDCs) after 1966–1967, counting federal support under state support in the 1931–1932 school year, and reporting student aid revenue between the 1929–1930 and 1933–1934 academic years as well as between the 1957–1958 and 1973–1974 academic years. Thereafter, that data was cataloged by the source of student aid money. Data source: Thomas Snyder (ed.), *120 Years of American Education: A Statistical Portrait* (National Center for Education Statistics, 1993), 63–94.

APPENDIX 2

Median Household Income by Race and Hispanic Origin, 1967–2018

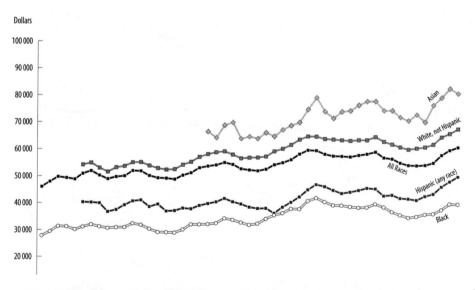

FIG A2 Racial disparities in median household income over time capture how state and federal lawmakers' emphasis on student assistance, particularly lending, has contributed to increasing inequities and widening racial wealth gaps. Families of color have often and continue to borrow more because they lack the inherited wealth to pay for expenses out of pocket. Gender and racial disparities in pay, including for college graduates, have also persisted despite the passage of the 1964 Civil Rights Act. Median household data by race was first available in 1967. Income questions were redesigned in 2013; 2017 data was processed under an updated processing system. Reformatted from Kayla Fontenot, Jessica Semega, and Melissa Kollar, "Current Population Reports. Income and Poverty in the United States: 2017," US Government Printing Office, Washington, DC, 2018, Figure 1.

APPENDIX 3

Consumer Debt since 1945

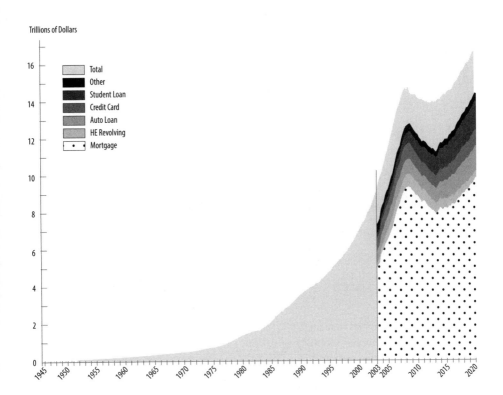

Trillions of Dollars

Total
Other
Student Loan
Credit Card
Auto Loan
HE Revolving
Mortgage

FIG A3 The New York Federal Consumer Credit Panel first gathered data on household borrowing in 1999 but did not begin to separate student loan debt until 2003. For a longer history of household borrowing, New York Federal Reserve economists used data from the Federal Reserve Board's Flow of Funds, now known as the Financial Accounts of the United States, even though it included data on households and nonprofit firms. Although the economists discussed the limitations of combining these two very different data sets, these figures as well as recent efforts to break down the source of household debts underscore how important financial products, including those with a government guarantee (like guaranteed student loans and federal mortgages), were in covering basic expenses before federal officials began to look closer at the sources of household debts, including home, car, and student loans. Data sources: Andrew Haughwout, Donghoon Lee, Joelle Scally, and Wilbert van der Klaauw, "Household Borrowing in Historical Perspective," *Liberty Street Economics Blog*, New York Federal Reserve, https://libertystreeteconomics .newyorkfed.org/2017/05/household-borrowing-in-historical-perspective.html, last accessed July 27, 2020; Households and Nonprofit Organizations; Total Liabilities, Level, Billions of Dollars, Quarterly, Not Seasonally Adjusted. FRED Graph Observations; Federal Reserve Economic Data, Economic Research Division, Federal Reserve Bank of St. Louis, https://fred.stlouisfed.org/series/TLBSHNO; Quarterly Report on Household Debt and Credit, August 2020, Federal Reserve Bank of New York, Research and Statistics, Microeconomic Studies, https://www.newyorkfed.org/microeconomics/hhdc.html.

Notes

Introduction

1. Suren quoted in James B. Steele and Lance Williams, "Who Got Rich Off the Student Debt Crisis?" *Reveal,* June 28, 2016, https://www.revealnews.org/article/who-got-rich-off-the-student -debt-crisis/.
2. Zack Friedman, "Student Loan Debt Statistics for 2020," *Forbes,* February 3, 2020; Finne and Dale quoted in Lance Williams, "In Debt and Out of Hope: Faces of the Student Loan Mess," *Reveal,* June 28, 2016, https://www.revealnews.org/article/in-debt-and-out-of-hope-faces-of-the -student-loan-mess.
3. McClurg quoted in Williams, "In Debt and Out of Hope."
4. Alex and Kate quoted in Amanda Arnold, "4 People on Feeling Crushed by Their Student Debt," *New York,* April 22, 2019; Omar quoted in Gabe Schneider, "Rep. Omar, Alongside Sen. Bernie Sanders, Releases Student-Debt Cancellation Bill," *MinnPost,* June 24, 2019, https://www .minnpost.com/national/2019/06/rep-omar-alongside-sen-bernie-sanders-releases-student -debt-cancellation-bill/.
5. Mahua Sarkar, ed., *Work Out of Place* (Berlin: De Gruyter Oldenbourg, 2018), esp. 1–22, 237– 244; Ellen Brown, "Student Debt Slavery," *Huffington Post,* December 29, 2017; Caroline Rat- cliffe and Signe-Mary McKernan, "Forever in Your Debt: Who Has Student Loan Debt, and Who's Worried?" report, Urban Institute, June 26, 2013, https://www.urban.org/research /publication/forever-your-debt-who-has-student-loan-debt-and-whos-worried; Brandon Jackson and John Reynolds, "The Price of Opportunity: Race, Student Loan Debt, and College Achieve- ment," *Sociological Inquiry* 83, no. 3 (2013): 335–368; John Buell, "Students as Debt Slaves," *Common Dreams,* April 21, 2018, https://www.commondreams.org/views/2018/04/21/students -debt-slaves. For an overview of those arguing against the existence of a student loan crisis, see Elizabeth Tandy Shermer, "The Student Debt Crisis and Its Deniers," *Public Books,* March 15, 2017. See also David Leonhardt, "Eliminating All Student Debt Isn't Progressive," *New York Times,* November 18, 2018.
6. Friedman, "Student Loan Debt Statistics"; Amy Sterling, "Millions of Jobs Have Been Lost to Automation," *Forbes,* June 15, 2019; Stephen Burd, "Undermining Pell: How Colleges Compete

for Wealthy Students and Leave the Low-Income Behind," policy paper, New America Foundation, May 2013, https://www.newamerica.org/education-policy/policy-papers/undermining-pell/; Michael Gaddis, "Discrimination in the Credential Society: An Audit Study of Race and College Selectivity in the Labor Market," *Social Forces* 93, no. 4 (2015): 1451–1479; Raj Chetty, John N. Friedman, Emmanuel Saez, Nicholas Turner, and Danny Yagan, "Mobility Report Cards: The Role of Colleges in Intergenerational Mobility," National Bureau of Economic Research Working Paper 23618, July 2017; Kim Dancy and Ben Barrett, "Is Higher Education the Gateway to the Middle Class?" blog post, New America Foundation, March 6, 2017, https://www.newamerica.org/education-policy/edcentral/higher-education-gateway-middle-class/; Ben Barrett, "College Access Is Still a Problem," blog post, New America Foundation, March 14, 2017, https://www.newamerica.org/education-policy/edcentral/college-access-still-problem; Clare McCann, "Low-Income Students Succeed—When Given the Opportunity," blog post, New America Foundation, April 6, 2017, https://www.newamerica.org/education-policy/edcentral/low-income-students-succeed-when-given-opportunity/.

7. For a comprehensive overview of inequities in campus financial aid, see Chetty et al., "Mobility Report Cards." On propensity for low-income students and women to enroll in less wealthy campuses and financial aid officers expecting families to pay more than their yearly household income see Stephen Burd, "Even at Private Colleges, Low-Income Students Tend to Go to the Poorest Schools," blog post, New America Foundation, May 18, 2017, https://www.newamerica.org/education-policy/edcentral/private-colleges/. On elite schools' competing for wealthy students see Burd, "Undermining Pell." On students' need to work and borrow see Ratcliffe and McKernan, "Forever in Your Debt." On racial and gender disparities on needing to borrow and struggling to repay see Renee Stepler, "Hispanic, Black Parents See College Degree as Key for Children's Success," *Fact Tank,* Pew Research Center, February 24, 2016, https://www.pewresearch.org/fact-tank/2016/02/24/hispanic-black-parents-see-college-degree-as-key-for-childrens-success/; Fenaba R. Addo, Jason N. Houle, Daniel Simon, "Young, Black, and (Still) in the Red: Parental Wealth, Race, and Student Loan Debt," *Race and Social Problems* 8, no. 1 (2016): 64–76; Rachel Fishman, "The Wealth Gap PLUS Debt: How Federal Loans Exacerbate Inequality for Black Families," blog post, New America Foundation, May 15, 2018, https://www.newamerica.org/education-policy/reports/wealth-gap-plus-debt/; Aissa Canchola and Seth Frotman, "The Significant Impact of Student Debt on Communities of Color," blog post, Consumer Financial Protection Bureau, September 15, 2016, https://www.consumerfinance.gov/about-us/blog/significant-impact-student-debt-communities-color/; Michal Grinstein-Weiss, Dana C. Perantie, Samuel H. Taylor, Shenyang Guo, and Ramesh Raghavan, "Racial Disparities in Education Debt Burden among Low- and Moderate-Income Households," *Children and Youth Services Review* 65 (2016): 166–174; Darrick Hamilton, William Darity, Jr., Anne E. Price, Vishnu Sridharan, and Rebecca Tippett, "Umbrellas Don't Make It Rain: Why Studying and Working Hard Isn't Enough for Black Americans," report, New School, Duke University Center for Social Equity and Insight Center for Community Economic Development, April 2015, http://ww1.insightcced.org/uploads/CRWG/Umbrellas-Dont-Make-It-Rain8.pdf; William R. Emmons and Bryan J. Noeth, "Why Didn't Higher Education Protect Hispanic and Black Wealth?" *In the Balance,* Federal Reserve Bank of St. Louis, August 5, 2015, 1–3; Kim Dancy, "Mind the Gap: How Higher Education Contributes to Gender Wage Disparities," blog post, New America Foundation, May 11, 2017, https://www.newamerica.org/education-policy/edcentral/mind-gap-gender

-wage-disparities; Jessica Glazer, "Student Debt Weighs Down Women More," NPR, April 6, 2014, https://www.npr.org/2014/04/03/298800950/student-debt-weighs-down-women -more-blame-the-wage-gap; Kevin Miller, "Deeper in Debt: Women and Student Loans," report, American Association of University Women, May 2017, https://www.aauw.org/aauw _check/pdf_download/show_pdf.php?file=deeper-in-debt.

8. Jennie Woo and Laura Horn, "Reaching the Limit: Undergraduates Who Borrow the Maximum Amount in Federal Direct Loans: 2011–12," Report NCES 2016–408, US Department of Education National Center for Education Statistics, September 2016; Adam Looney and Constantine Yannelis, "How Useful Are Default Rates? Borrowers with Large Balances and Student Loan Repayment," *Economics of Education Review* 71 (2019): 135–145; Maria Danilova, "Full Loan Relief Rare for Students at For-Profit Colleges," *Seattle Times,* September 7, 2018.

9. Woo and Horn, "Reaching the Limit"; Looney and Yannelis, "How Useful Are Default Rates?"; Brown, "Student Debt Slavery"; Government Accountability Office, "Social Security Offsets: Improvements to Program Design Could Better Assist Older Student Loan Borrowers with Obtaining Permitted Relief," Report GAO-17-45, US Government Accountability Office, December 19, 2016.

10. Katie Yu and Lauren Effron, "Tricked-Out College Campuses," ABC News, October 13, 2014, https://abcnews.go.com/Lifestyle/tricked-college-campuses-water-parks-luxury-dorms /story?id=26164491; Sara Goldrick-Rab, Jed Richardson, Joel Schneider, Anthony Hernandez, and Clare Cady, "Still Hungry and Homeless in College," Wisconsin HOPE Lab, September 2018; Sara Goldrick-Rab, *Paying the Price: College Costs, Financial Aid, and the Betrayal of the American Dream* (Chicago: University of Chicago Press, 2016), 83–118; Fishman, "Wealth Gap PLUS Debt"; Judith Scott-Clayton, "The Looming Student Loan Default Crisis Is Worse Than We Thought," Evidence Speaks Reports 2, no. 34, Brookings Institution, January 10, 2018; Barrett, "College Access Is Still a Problem"; Michael Prebil, "Started from the Bottom—and Still Here," blog post, New America Foundation, March 29, 2017, https://www.newamerica.org/education-policy/edcentral/started-bottom-and-still -here; Grinstein-Weiss et al., "Racial Disparities"; Jackson and Reynolds, "The Price of Opportunity."

11. Thomas D. Snyder, "120 Years of American Education: A Statistical Portrait," report, US Department of Education Office of Educational Research and Improvement, January 1993, http://nces.ed.gov/pubs93/93442.pdf; Camille Ryan and Kurt Bauman, "Educational Attainment in the United States: 2015," Report P20-578, US Census Bureau, March 29, 2016, https://www.census.gov/content/dam/Census/library/publications/2016/demo/p20-578 .pdf; Roger Geiger, *History of American Higher Education: Learning and Culture from the Founding to World War II* (Princeton: Princeton University Press, 2015); Roger Geiger, *Research and Relevant Knowledge: American Research Universities since World War II* (New York: Oxford University Press, 1993); Christopher P. Loss, *Between Citizens and the State: The Politics of American Higher Education in the 20th Century* (Princeton: Princeton University Press, 2012); Suzanne Mettler, *Soldiers to Citizens: The G.I. Bill and the Making of the Greatest Generation* (New York: Oxford University Press, 2005); Wayne Urban, *More Than Science and Sputnik: The National Defense Education Act of 1958* (Tuscaloosa: University of Alabama Press, 2010); Hugh Davis Graham, *The Uncertain Triumph: Federal Education Policy in the Kennedy and Johnson Years* (Chapel Hill: University of North Carolina Press, 1984); Shermer, "The Student Debt Crisis and Its Deniers"; Suzanne Mettler, *Degrees of Inequality:*

How the Politics of Higher Education Sabotaged the American Dream (New York: Basic Books, 2014); Goldrick-Rab, *Paying the Price.*

12. "Operations" quote in Lawrence E. Gladieux and Thomas R. Wolanin, *Congress and the Colleges: The National Politics of Higher Education* (Lexington, MA: Lexington Books, 1976), 235; "salamander" quote from John F. Morse, "How We Got Here from There," in Lois D. Rice, *Student Loans: Problems and Policy Alternatives,* ed. Lois D. Rice, 3–15 (New York: College Entrance Examination Board, 1977), 14.

13. Jennifer Klein, *For All These Rights: Business, Labor, and the Shaping of America's Public-Private Welfare State* (Princeton: Princeton University Press, 2003); Sanford Jacoby, *Modern Manors: Welfare Capitalism Since the New Deal* (Princeton: Princeton University Press, 1997); Colin Gordon, *New Deals: Business, Labor, and Politics in America, 1920–1935* (New York: Cambridge University Press, 1994); Lewis Hyman, *Debtor Nation: The History of America in Red Ink* (Princeton: Princeton University Press, 2011); Michael Katz, *The Undeserving Poor: From the War on Poverty to the War on Welfare* (New York: Pantheon, 1989); Ira Katznelson, *When Affirmative Action Was White: An Untold Story of Racial Inequality in Twentieth-Century America* (New York: Norton, 2005); Alice Kessler-Harris, *In Pursuit of Equity: Women, Men, and the Quest for Economic Citizenship in 20th-Century America* (New York: Oxford University Press, 2001); Nelson Lichtenstein, *State of the Union: A Century of American Labor* (Princeton: Princeton University Press, 2002); Judith Stein, *Pivotal Decade: How the United States Traded Factories for Finance in the Seventies* (New Haven: Yale University Press, 2010); Jonathan Levy, *Freaks of Fortune: The Emerging World of Capitalism and Risk in America* (Cambridge, MA: Harvard University Press, 2012); Elizabeth Tandy Shermer, "Financing Security and Opportunity: The New Deal and the Origins of the Millennial Student Debt Crisis," in *Capitalism Contested: The New Deal and Its Legacies,* ed. Romain Huret, Nelson Lichtenstein, and Jean-Christian Vinel, 112–135 (Philadelphia: University of Pennsylvania Press, 2020); Charles Stephens Eaton, "Financialization and the New Organizational Inequality in U.S. Higher Education" (PhD diss., University of California, Berkeley, 2016), 1–8; Sarah Quinn, *American Bonds: How Credit Markets Shaped a Nation* (Princeton: Princeton University Press, 2019); Scott Nelson, *A Nation of Deadbeats: An Uncommon History of America's Financial Disasters* (New York: Knopf, 2012); Richard White, *Railroaded: The Transcontinentals and the Making of Modern America* (New York: Norton, 2012).

14. Robert Hutchins, "The Threat to American Education," *Collier's,* December 1944, 20–21.

15. "Remarks by the President and Dr. Jill Biden at Signing of Health Care and Education Reconciliation Act," White House press release, March 30, 2010, https://obamawhitehouse .archives.gov/the-press-office/remarks-president-and-dr-jill-biden-signing-health-care -and-education-reconciliatio.

1. Honorably Financing College

1. All quotes from Lyndon Baines Johnson from "Remarks at Southwest Texas State College upon Signing the Higher Education Act of 1965," November 8, 1965, in *Lyndon B. Johnson: Containing the Public Messages, Speeches, and Statements of the President: 1965* (Washington, DC: Government Printing Office, 1965–1970), book 2, 1102–1106, quote 1104–1105. For more on LBJ's borrowing and spending in college, see Robert Caro, *The Path to Power: The Years of Lyndon Johnson* (New York: Random House, 1990), 1: 163–165.

2. Morrill quoted in Christopher Loss, "Why the Morrill Land-Grant Colleges Act Still Matters," *Chronicle of Higher Education*, July 16, 2012. On the history of higher education in America, see Roger Geiger, "The Ten Generations of American Higher Education," in *American Higher Education in the Twenty-First Century: Social, Political, and Economic Challenges*, ed. Philip G. Altbach, Robert O. Berdahl, and Patricia J. Gumport, 38–69 (Baltimore: Johns Hopkins University Press, 1999); David Labaree, "A System without a Plan: Emergence of an American System of Higher Education in the Twentieth Century," *Bildungsgeschichte: International Journal for the Historiography of Education* 3, no. 1 (2013): 46–59.

3. Elizabeth Tandy Shermer, "From Educator- to Creditor-in-Chief: The American Presidency, Higher Education, and the Student Loan Industry," in *The President and American Capitalism since 1945*, ed. Mark Rose and Roger Biles, 123–150 (Gainesville: University of Florida Press, 2017); Roger Geiger, *To Advance Knowledge: The Growth of American Research Universities, 1900–1940* (New York: Oxford University Press, 1986), 12–14, 107–110.

4. Virginia Sapiro, "The Life Course of Higher Education Institutions: When the End Comes," unpublished manuscript, 2019, quote on 5, http://blogs.bu.edu/vsapiro/files/2019/02 /SapiroWhentheEndComes2019-1.pdf; Craig Steven Wilder, *Ebony and Ivy: Race, Slavery, and the Troubled History of America's Universities* (New York: Bloomsbury, 2013); Christopher P. Loss, *Between Citizens and the State: The Politics of American Higher Education in the 20th Century* (Princeton: Princeton University Press, 2012), 19–52; John R. Thelin, "Higher Education's Student Financial Aid Enterprise in Historical Perspective," in *Footing the Tuition Bill: The New Student Loan Sector*, ed. Frederick M. Hess, 19–41 (Washington, DC: AEI Press, 2007); Geiger, "Ten Generations," 38–69; Laurence Veysey, *Emergence of the American University* (Chicago: University of Chicago Press, 1970), 1–20; Labaree, "A System without a Plan."

5. Rupert Wilkinson, *Aiding Students, Buying Students: Financial Aid in America* (Nashville: Vanderbilt University Press, 2005), 9–27; Geiger, "Ten Generations," 38–50; Mettler, *Degrees of Inequality*, 111–132; Roger L. Geiger, *The History of American Higher Education: Learning and Culture from the Founding to World War II* (Princeton: Princeton University Press, 2015), 102–122; Veysey, *Emergence of the American University*, 1–20.

6. Paul Dressel, *College to University: The Hannah Years at Michigan State, 1935–1969* (East Lansing: Michigan State University Press, 1987), 17–96; Lyle Blair and Madison Kuhn, *A Short History of Michigan State* (East Lansing: Michigan State College Press, 1955), 5–13; Geiger, "Ten Generations," 38–50.

7. Geiger, *History of American Higher Education*, 287–315; Robert Lee and Tristan Ahtone, "Land-Grab Universities," *High Country News*, March 30, 2020, https://www.hcn.org /issues/52.4/indigenous-affairs-education-land-grab-universities?utm_source=pocket -newtab.

8. Lee and Ahtone, "Land-Grab Universities"; Dressel, *College to University*, 17–96; Blair and Kuhn, *Short History of Michigan State*, 5–13; Verne Stadtman, *The University of California, 1868–1968* (New York: McGraw-Hill, 1970), 45–47.

9. George N. Rainsford, *Congress and Higher Education in the Nineteenth Century* (Knoxville: University of Tennessee Press, 1972), 111–112; Geiger, *History of American Higher Education*, 303–306, 471.

10. Geiger, *To Advance Knowledge*, 58–93.

11. Geiger, "Ten Generations"; Veysey, *Emergence of the American University*, 1–20, 108–110; Merle Curti and Roderick Nash, *Philanthropy in the Shaping of American Higher Education*

(New Brunswick, NJ: Rutgers University Press, 1965), 111–132; Patricia Pelfrey, *A Brief History of the University of California* (Berkeley: University of California Press, 2004), 15–22; Stadtman, *The University of California*, 85–236.

12. Geiger, "Ten Generations"; Veysey, *Emergence of the American University*, 1–20; Curti and Nash, *Philanthropy in the Shaping of American Higher Education*, 111–132.

13. Labaree, "A System without a Plan"; Curti and Nash, *Philanthropy in the Shaping of American Higher Education*, 212–237; David O. Levine, *American College and the Culture of Aspiration, 1915–1940* (Ithaca, NY: Cornell University Press, 1986), 13–22; Ernest Victor Hollis, *Philanthropic Foundations and Higher Education* (New York: Columbia University Press, 1938), 1–6, 268–281; Trevor Arnett, *College and University Finance* (New York: General Education Board, 1922), 1–6.

14. Geiger, "Ten Generations," 38–50; Veysey, *Emergence of the American University*, 1–20, 110–113; Mettler, *Degrees of Inequality*, 111–132, esp. 115–116; Levine, *American College and the Culture of Aspiration*, 13–22.

15. Christina Groeger, *The Education Trap: Schools and the Remaking of Inequality in Boston* (Cambridge, MA: Harvard University Press, 2021), 139–181.

16. Groeger, *Education Trap*, 171, 221–229, 242–248; Eliot quoted in "Our Trade at Stake," *Boston Herald*, October 31, 1899, 12.

17. Geiger, *To Advance Knowledge*, 107–110.

18. Levine, *American College and the Culture of Aspiration*, 113–135; Geiger, *To Advance Knowledge*, 94–139, esp. 128–133; Veysey, *Emergence of the American University*, 263–341.

19. Geiger, "Ten Generations"; Veysey, *Emergence of the American University*, 263–341; Levine, *American College and the Culture of Aspiration*, 39–60, 68–88.

20. Wilkinson, *Aiding Students, Buying Students*, 9–27, esp. 14; Arnett, *College and University Finance*, 1–6, esp. 1n1; Geiger, *To Advance Knowledge*, 12–13, 94–139.

21. Wilkinson, *Aiding Students, Buying Students*, 28–30, 66–70, 107–109; Jackson Toby, "How Scholarships Morphed into Financial Aid," *Academic Questions* 23, no. 3 (September 2010): 298–310; Loss, *Between Citizens and the State*, 19–52; Michael S. McPherson and Morton Owen Schapiro, *The Student Aid Game: Meeting Need and Rewarding Talent in American Higher Education* (Princeton: Princeton University Press, 1998), 105–109; Levine, *American College and the Culture of Aspiration*, 185–189; Thelin, "Higher Education's Student Financial Aid Enterprise."

22. Toby, "How Scholarships Morphed into Financial Aid"; McPherson and Schapiro, *Student Aid Game*, 107–115; Levine, *American College and the Culture of Aspiration*, 185–189; Thelin, "Higher Education's Student Financial Aid Enterprise"; Hollis, *Philanthropic Foundations and Higher Education*, 175–179; Franklin Parker, "George Peabody's Influence on Southern Educational Philanthropy," *Tennessee Historical Quarterly* 20, no. 1 (1961): 65–74.

23. Wilkinson, *Aiding Students, Buying Students*, 22–24; Toby, "How Scholarships Morphed into Financial Aid"; McPherson and Schapiro, *Student Aid Game*, 107–115; Levine, *American College and the Culture of Aspiration*, 188; Thelin, "Higher Education's Student Financial Aid Enterprise."

24. Wilkinson, *Aiding Students, Buying Students*, 14–17, 97–106, quote at 17.

25. D. Bruce Johnstone, *New Patterns for College Lending: Income Contingent Loans* (New York: Columbia University Press, 1972), 1–2; Levine, *American College and the Culture of Aspiration*, 185–189; Dorothy Woolf, "Loans to Students on Business Basis," *New York Times*, November 22, 1931, 77.

26. Wilkinson, *Aiding Students, Buying Students*, 107–109.

27. Wilkinson, *Aiding Students, Buying Students,* 107–109; Woolf, "Loans to Students on Business Basis."

28. Hollis, *Philanthropic Foundations and Higher Education,* 187–189, banker quote 190.

29. Hollis, *Philanthropic Foundations and Higher Education,* 186–190, Harman quote 186; Wilkinson, *Aiding Students, Buying Students,* 107–109, Harman quote 109.

30. Hollis, *Philanthropic Foundations and Higher Education,* 188–190; Woolf, "Loans to Students on Business Basis"; Federal Security Agency, *Final Report of the National Youth Administration: Fiscal Years 1936–1943* (Washington, DC: Government Printing Office, 1944), 46.

31. Levine, *American College and the Culture of Aspiration,* 185–209, Wesleyan President James McConaughy quote 193.

32. Betty Lindley and Ernest K. Lindley, *A New Deal for Youth: The Story of the National Youth Administration* (New York: Viking Press, 1938), 156–160, quote 157; Levine, *American College and the Culture of Aspiration,* 185–209.

33. Lindley and Lindley, *New Deal for Youth,* 185–209; Levine, *American College and the Culture of Aspiration,* 185–209; Geiger, *To Advance Knowledge,* 246–268.

34. Paula Fass, "Without Design: Education Policy in the New Deal," *American Journal of Education* 91, no. 1 (1982): 36–64, quote 39.

35. Fass, "Without Design"; Ronald Story, "New Deal and Higher Education," in *The New Deal and the Triumph of Liberalism,* ed. Sidney M. Milkis and Jerome M. Mileur, 272–296 (Amherst: University of Massachusetts Press, 2002).

36. Fass, "Without Design"; Story, "New Deal and Higher Education."

37. Jerome Karabel, *The Chosen: The Hidden History of Admission and Exclusion at Harvard, Yale, and Princeton* (New York: Houghton Mifflin, 2006), 139–165, quotes 147, 151; James Conant, interview by Isabel Grossner, April 5 and 13, 1967, transcript, quote 6, Carnegie Corporation project, Columbia Center for Oral History, Columbia University, New York.

38. James N. Rule, "Report of the Federal Advisory Committee on Emergency Aid in Education," *NEA Proceedings* 72 (1934), quote 47; Conant speech to Columbia University alumni quoted in "Freedom of Press and Schools Urged," *New York Times,* June 6, 1934, 17; Butler quoted in "'Big Labor' Called Threat by Butler," *New York Times,* March 2, 1935, 4. For discussion, see Fass, "Without Design"; Labaree, "A System without a Plan"; Story, "New Deal and Higher Education."

39. A. Richards to [FDR], May 22, 1933; Grace Sweeny to [FDR], March 19, 1933; Jack Light to The President, July 13 [1933]; John Robinson to [FDR], August 15, 1933; all in box 1, Jan–Sept 1933, Series 107; Thomas Miller to [FDR], December 12, 1933, box 1, Jan–Mar 1934, Series 107; Louis Howe to John Robinson, August 21, 1932, box 1, Jan–Sept 1933, Series 107; all in Papers as President, President's Official File, Franklin Delano Roosevelt Presidential Library and Archive, Hyde Park, NY.

2. Will Work for School

1. Mrs. C. L. Melton to Franklin Delano Roosevelt, July 19, 1933; Louis Howe to George Zook, August 7, 1933; Louis Howe to Mrs. C. Lee Melton, August 12, 1933; all in box 1, folder 1933 Jan–Sept, Series 107, Papers as President, President's Official File, Franklin Delano Roosevelt Presidential Library and Archive, Hyde Park, NY (hereafter FDR-Official).

2. See boxes 1–6, Series 107, FDR-Official; box 12, Series 6, FDR-Official. For specific mentions of funding requests before January 1936, see SEE-44-D Miscel., January 2, 1936, box 12,

Interior Dept., Comm of Ed, 1933–36, Series 6, FDR-Official; Memorandum for Aubrey Williams, August 8, 1936, box 1, Jan–Mar 1934, Series 107, FDR-Official.

3. James MacGregor Burns, *Roosevelt: The Lion and the Fox* (New York: Harcourt, Brace, 1956), 3–22.

4. Burns, *Roosevelt,* Roosevelt quote 19; Franklin Delano Roosevelt, Oglethorpe University address, Atlanta, Georgia, May 22, 1932, Speech File 476, Master Speech File, Franklin Delano Roosevelt Presidential Library and Archive, Hyde Park, NY; Franklin Delano Roosevelt, Milwaukee, Wisconsin Campaign Address, September 30, 1932, Speech File 546, Franklin Delano Roosevelt Presidential Library and Archive, Hyde Park, NY; Harry Zeitlin, "Efforts to Achieve Federal Aid to Education: Developments during the New Deal," *Teachers College Record* 61 (1960): 195–202, "school crowd" quote on 202.

5. Ronald Story, "New Deal and Higher Education," in *The New Deal and the Triumph of Liberalism,* ed. Sidney M. Milkis and Jerome M. Mileur, 272–296 (Amherst: University of Massachusetts Press, 2002).

6. Richard Lowitt and Maurine Beasley, eds., *One Third of a Nation: Lorena Hickok Reports on the Great Depression* (Urbana: University of Illinois Press, 1981), xiii–xvi, 194, 175, quotes on 323, 28, 17.

7. Lowitt and Beasley, *One Third of a Nation,* quotes on 28, 17.

8. Richard Reiman, *The New Deal and American Youth: Ideas and Ideals in a Depression Decade* (Athens: University of Georgia Press, 1992), 56–59; Story, "New Deal and Higher Education," 274–276.

9. Paula Fass, "Without Design: Education Policy in the New Deal," *American Journal of Education* 91, no. 1 (1982): 36–64; Reiman, *The New Deal,* 32–50; Elizabeth Tandy Shermer, "Financing Security and Opportunity: The New Deal and the Origins of the Millennial Student Debt Crisis," in *Capitalism Contested: The New Deal and Its Legacies,* ed. Romain Huret, Nelson Lichtenstein, and Jean-Christian Vinel, 112–135 (Philadelphia: University of Pennsylvania Press, 2020).

10. Fass, "Without Design"; Story, "New Deal and Higher Education"; David Lilienthal, *TVA: Democracy on the March* (New York: Harper, 1944), 34–45, 117–125, 217–227, quote 36; Shermer, "Financing Security and Opportunity."

11. Donald Hamilton, "A History of FERA and WPA Workers' Education: The Indiana Experience, 1933–1943" (PhD diss., Ball State University, 1984), 1–52, Ickes quote 29; Reiman, *The New Deal,* 55–96; Shermer, "Financing Security and Opportunity."

12. Hamilton, "History of FERA and WPA," 1–53, 87–105, Smith quotes 42, 52–53; Shermer, "Financing Security and Opportunity."

13. Hamilton, "History of FERA and WPA," 1–53; Christopher P. Loss, *Between Citizens and the State: The Politics of American Higher Education in the 20th Century* (Princeton: Princeton University Press, 2012), 53–90; Story, "New Deal and Higher Education," 272–273; Richard Novak and David Leslie, "A Not So Distant Mirror: Great Depression Writings on the Governance and Finance of Public Higher Education," in *History of Higher Education Annual 2000,* ed. Roger L. Geiger, 59–78 (New York: Routledge, 2000); Shermer, "Financing Security and Opportunity."

14. Novak and Leslie, "A Not So Distant Mirror"; Jason Scott Smith, *Concise History of the New Deal* (New York: Cambridge University Press, 2014), esp. 1–5, 149–200; Shermer, "Financing Security and Opportunity."

15. Nelson Lichtenstein, *State of the Union: A Century of American Labor* (Princeton: Princeton University Press, 2002), 20–97; Jennifer Klein, *For All These Rights: Business, Labor, and the Shaping of America's Public-Private Welfare State* (Princeton: Princeton University Press, 2003), 78–115; Lewis Hyman, *Debtor Nation: The History of America in Red Ink* (Princeton: Princeton University Press, 2011), 45–97; Shermer, "Financing Security and Opportunity."

16. Hyman, *Debtor Nation*, 45–97; Shermer, "Financing Security and Opportunity"; Jonathan Levy, *Freaks of Fortune: The Emerging World of Capitalism and Risk in America* (Cambridge, MA: Harvard University Press, 2012); John Dean, Saul Moskowitz, and Karen Cipriani, "Implications of the Privatization of Sallie Mae," *Journal of Public Budgeting, Accounting & Financial Management* 11, no. 1 (Spring 1999): 56–80; Dennis Ventry, Jr., "The Accidental Deduction: A History and Critique of the Tax Subsidy for Mortgage Interest," *Law and Contemporary Problems* 73, no. 1 (2009): 233–284.

17. Nelson Lichtenstein, "The United States in Depression and War: Was the Fascist Door Open?" in *Routes into the Abyss: Coping with Crises in the 1930s,* ed. Helmut Konrad and Wolfgang Maderthaner, 115–126 (New York: Berghahn Books, 2013); Alan Brinkley, *Voices of Protest: Huey Long, Father Coughlin, and the Great Depression* (New York: Knopf, 1982); Leo Ribuffo, *Old Christian Right: The Old Christian Right from the Great Depression to the Cold War* (Philadelphia: Temple University Press, 1982); Quote in Lowitt and Beasley, *One Third a Nation,* 364–365; Shermer, "Financing Security and Opportunity."

18. Reiman, *The New Deal,* 31–96, 100–101; Story, "New Deal and Higher Education," 276; Sachi Amatya, "The Role of Student Loan Programs in Higher Education Policy in the United States" (PhD diss., Vanderbilt University, 2008), 46; David O. Levine, *American College and the Culture of Aspiration, 1915–1940* (Ithaca, NY: Cornell University Press, 1986), 194–196.

19. Quoted in George Rawick, "The New Deal and Youth: The Civilian Conservation Corps, the National Administration and the American Youth Congress" (PhD diss., University of Wisconsin, 1957), 175; Reiman, *The New Deal,* 55–73; Levine, *American College and the Culture of Aspiration,* 194–196.

20. Reiman, *The New Deal,* 55–73; John Salmond, *A Southern Rebel: The Life and Times of Aubrey Willis Williams, 1890–1965* (Chapel Hill: University of North Carolina Press, 1983), 64–75; Robert Piercy, "New Deal Administrator: John Lang and the National Youth Administration in North Carolina" (MA thesis, East Carolina University, 1981), 1–23; National Youth Administration, *Report of the National Advisory Committee of the National Youth Administration to the President of the United States* (Washington, DC: Government Printing Office, 1942), 63–67; Palmer Johnson and Oswald Harvey, *National Youth Administration* (New York: Arno Press, 1974), 8–22; Shermer, "Financing Security and Opportunity."

21. Federal Security Agency, *Final Report of the National Youth Administration: Fiscal Years 1936–1943* (Washington, DC: Government Printing Office, 1944), quote 47.

22. Reiman, *The New Deal,* 55–73; Salmond, *Southern Rebel,* 64–75; Piercy, "New Deal Administrator," 1–23; National Youth Administration, *Report of the National Advisory Committee,* 63–67; Johnson and Harvey, *National Youth Administration,* 8–22.

23. Reiman, *The New Deal,* 55–73; Salmond, *Southern Rebel,* 64–75; Piercy, "New Deal Administrator," 1–23; National Youth Administration, *Report of the National Advisory Committee,* 63–67; Johnson and Harvey, *National Youth Administration,* 8–22; Federal Security Agency, *Final Report,* 47–48; Federal Emergency Relief Administration, "Special Bulletin on the Student Aid Program," December 1934, box 22, FERA: Procedural Issuances: Series E (Education),

Papers of Harry L. Hopkins, Franklin Delano Roosevelt Presidential Library and Archive, Hyde Park, NY (hereafter Hopkins papers).

24. "Youth Held Victim of Changed World," *New York Times*, September 17, 1934, Burt quote 19; "Youth Today," *New York Times*, October 31, 1934, quote 18; Benedict S. Alper and George E. Lodgen, "Youth Without Work," *Survey* 70, no. 1 (September 1934), Massachusetts Child Council members quote 285–286; Federal Security Agency, *Final Report*, 10–14; Shermer, "Financing Security and Opportunity."

25. Reiman, *The New Deal*, 74–122; Salmond, *Southern Rebel*, 78–120; Shermer, "Financing Security and Opportunity."

26. Reiman, *The New Deal*, 97–122; Salmond, *Southern Rebel*, 78–120; Loss, *Between Citizens and the State*, 53–90; Webster Peterson, "A National Forum Plan," *New York Times*, September 30, 1934, Studebaker quote XX5.

27. Shermer, "Financing Security and Opportunity"; Salmond, *Southern Rebel*, 78–120; S.T.E., Memorandum for Colonel [Louis] Howe, December 6, 1933, box 1, Jan–Sept 1933, Series 107, FDR-Official; Charles Taussig, "Youth Must Think and Act," transcript, NBC broadcast, June 1, 1934, box 16, Broadcasts; Charles Judd to Charles Taussig, October 22, 1935, box 4, Judd, Dr. Charles 1935; both in Charles W. Taussig Papers, Franklin Delano Roosevelt Presidential Library and Archive, Hyde Park, NY (hereafter Taussig papers).

28. Salmond, *Southern Rebel*, 1–46.

29. Shermer, "Financing Security and Opportunity"; Salmond, *Southern Rebel*, 1–46, Williams quotes 5, 10, 26.

30. Shermer, "Financing Security and Opportunity"; Salmond, *Southern Rebel*, 26–42, Williams quote 32.

31. Shermer, "Financing Security and Opportunity"; Salmond, *Southern Rebel*, 53–120.

32. Shermer, "Financing Security and Opportunity"; Salmond, *Southern Rebel*, 78–120; Reiman, *The New Deal*, 97–122.

33. Shermer, "Financing Security and Opportunity"; Reiman, *The New Deal*, 97–122; Salmond, *Southern Rebel*, 78–120, Studebaker quote 83.

34. Shermer, "Financing Security and Opportunity."

35. Shermer, "Financing Security and Opportunity"; Reiman, *The New Deal*, 120–124; Smith, *A Concise History of the New Deal*, 124–182.

36. Shermer, "Financing Security and Opportunity"; Reiman, *The New Deal*, 120–124; Smith, *A Concise History of the New Deal*, 124–182.

37. Johnson and Harvey, *National Youth Administration*, 8–22; Salmond, *Southern Rebel*, 121–136; National Youth Administration, *Report of the National Advisory Committee*, 38–39; Franklin Delano Roosevelt, Executive Order 7086, June 26, 1935, *American Presidency Project*, University of California, Santa Barbara, https://www.presidency.ucsb.edu/documents/executive-order-7086-establishing-the-national-youth-administration; "Nation's Youth," *Washington Post*, June 30, 1935, B1.

38. Hanna Fried, "America's Jobless Youths Are Tendered a Helping Hand," *Washington Post*, July 7, 1935, B4; George Creel, "Dollars for Youth," *Collier's*, September 28, 1935, 10; Clara Savage Littledale, "Youth Shall Have Its Chance," *Parents' Magazine*, August 1935, 13.

39. American Youth Congress quoted in "Roosevelt Program for Youth Assailed," *New York Times*, September 9, 1935, 14; Student League for Industrial Democracy statement quoted in "U.S. Youth Project Assailed as Peril," *New York Times*, July 1, 1935, 10.

40. Wm. Boutwell to Mr. Strauss, July 1, 1935, p. 1, box 12, Interior Dept., Dept of Ed., 1933–36, Series 6, FDR-Official; "Teachers Warned of Youth Program," *New York Times*, July 25, 1935, 17.

41. Reiman, *The New Deal*, 123–124; Salmond, *Southern Rebel*, 121–136; Rawick, "New Deal and Youth," 199–201.

42. Reiman, *The New Deal*, 123–124; Rawick, "New Deal and Youth," 199–201, Hillman quote 201; Salmond, *Southern Rebel*, 121–136, committee member Selma Borchardt quote 129.

43. Johnson and Harvey, *National Youth Administration*, 8–22; Salmond, *Southern Rebel*, 121–124, Hopkins quote 85; Williams speech to Welfare Council of New York quoted in "What About It?" (editorial), *Boston Evening Globe*, October 18, 1935, 24. For discussion, see Reiman, *The New Deal*, 123–132.

44. Johnson and Harvey, *National Youth Administration*, 8–22; Salmond, *Southern Rebel*, 121–124; Reiman, *The New Deal*, 123–132.

45. Johnson and Harvey, *National Youth Administration*, 8–22; Salmond, *Southern Rebel*, 80–125; Reiman, *The New Deal*, 123–140.

46. Salmond, *Southern Rebel*, 121–136, Williams quote 123; Rawick, "New Deal and Youth," 194–201.

47. Salmond, *Southern Rebel*, 121–124, Weston quote 123, Osborne quote 124; "Williams Accepts Resignation," *New York Times*, November 19, 1935, Williams quote 16.

48. Rawick, "New Deal and Youth," 190–205; Salmond, *Southern Rebel*, 121–127, Williams quote 124; NYA Bulletin #7, September 10, 1936, box 24, WPA National Youth Administration, President's Interdepartmental Committee to Coordinate Health and Welfare Activities, Franklin Delano Roosevelt Presidential Library and Archive, Hyde Park (hereafter FDR-Health-Welfare).

49. "New Opportunities for Negro Youth," October 9, 1936, p. 1, box 24, NYA Memos, Hopkins papers; NYA, "The Tenth Youth," 1938, quoted 1, box 24, WPA National Youth Administration, FDR-Health-Welfare; Rawick, "New Deal and Youth," 190–205; Salmond, *Southern Rebel*, 121–127, Williams quote 126.

50. "New Opportunities for Negro Youth"; Federal Security Agency, *Final Report*, 51–52, quote 51; Rawick, "New Deal and Youth," 190–205; Salmond, *Southern Rebel*, 121–127.

51. Rawick, "New Deal and Youth," 190–205; Arthur Northwood, Jr., president of National Student Federation, quoted in Salmond, *Southern Rebel*, 129, Hopkins quote 131, Williams quote 139; Charles Taussig to [FDR], May 7, 1936, p. 1, box 1643–1661, File 1644, Papers as President, President's Personal File, Franklin Delano Roosevelt Presidential Library and Archive, Hyde Park, NY (hereafter FDR-Personal); Meeting of the National Advisory Committee, quoted 94, box 6, National Advisory Committee, NYA Meetings—Minutes and Correspondence April 28–29, 1936, Taussig papers.

52. Rawick, "New Deal and Youth," 190–205; Salmond, *Southern Rebel*, 121–140; Reiman, *The New Deal*, 123–140.

53. National Youth Administration, *Report of the National Advisory Committee*, 63–68; Betty Lindley and Ernest K. Lindley, *A New Deal for Youth: The Story of the National Youth Administration* (New York: Viking Press, 1938), 158–183; Federal Security Agency, *Final Report*, 49–60; Johnson and Harvey, *National Youth Administration*, 96; "Student Aid Program," NYA Circular No. 10, January 23, 1937, p. 4, box 24, NYA Memos, Hopkins papers.

54. National Youth Administration, *Report of the National Advisory Committee*, 63–68; Lindley and Lindley, *A New Deal for Youth*, 158–183; Federal Security Agency, *Final Report*, 49–60,

quote 59; Johnson and Harvey, *National Youth Administration*, 96; "Student Aid Program," NYA Circular No. 10, January 23, 1937, p. 4, box 24, NYA Memos, Hopkins papers.

55. Levine, *American College and the Culture of Aspiration*, 197–203; Lindley and Lindley, *New Deal for Youth*, 161–162; Johnson and Harvey, *National Youth Administration*, 94–99; National Youth Administration, *Report of the National Advisory Committee*, 61–68.

56. Federal Security Agency, *Final Report*, 67–70.

57. National Youth Administration, *Report of the National Advisory Committee*, 63–68; Lindley and Lindley, *New Deal for Youth*, 158–183.

58. National Youth Administration, *Report of the National Advisory Committee*, 63–68; Lindley and Lindley, *New Deal for Youth*, 158–183, quotes 180, 181, 162.

59. Lindley and Lindley, *A New Deal for Youth*, 167–182, quotes 172, 174, 176.

60. Lindley and Lindley, *A New Deal for Youth*, 158–183, quote 165; Levine, *American College and the Culture of Aspiration*, 197–207; "NYA Students Do Well," *New York Times*, June 20, 1938, 10; National Youth Administration, *Report of the National Advisory Committee*, 63–68.

61. Federal Security Agency, *Final Report*, 61; NYA, "The Tenth Youth," 1938, box 24, WPA National Youth Administration, FDR-Health-Welfare; National Youth Administration, *Report of the National Advisory Committee*, 63–68; Lindley and Lindley, *A New Deal for Youth*, 158–183, quote 166.

62. Federal Security Agency, *Final Report*, Ohio State officials quote 80; [Iowa State official] R. M. Hughes to [George] Zook, May 4, 1937, box 8, Zook, George F., President's Advisory Committee on Education 1936–1939, Franklin Delano Roosevelt Presidential Library and Archive, Hyde Park, NY (hereafter FDR-Advisory); Lindley and Lindley, *A New Deal for Youth*, 158–183; Levine, *American College and the Culture of Aspiration*, 197–207, University of Colorado president quote 204; "NYA Students Do Well," *New York Times*, June 20, 1938, 10; [Temple administrator] John Barr to Aubrey Williams, December 1, 1937, quote 2–3, box 19, Williams, Aubrey 1937–1938, Taussig papers.

63. Lindley and Lindley, *A New Deal for Youth*, 158–183; Levine, *American College and the Culture of Aspiration*, 197–207; Associated Press, "Federal Aid Barred by Hamilton College," *New York Times*, October 11, 1935, Hamilton president quote 23; "Student Aid Grants Made," *Los Angeles Times*, November 11, 1935, Hopkins quote 4; "Yale Agrees to Use Federal Student Aid," *New York Times*, October 26, 1935, Yale officials quote 3.

64. "New Deal Youth Director Flings Mud at Schools," *Chicago Tribune*, October 7, 1936, 11.

65. Floyd Reeves, "Purpose and Functions of the Advisory Committee on Education," typescript, June 28, 1937, chairman quoted 7, box 11, Purpose and Functions, FDR-Advisory; Newton Edwards, Staff Study No. 7, October 1937, college opportunity report quoted 2, box 20 (loose), FDR-Advisory (see boxes 18 and 20 for confidential reports); Palmer Johnson, Staff Study 4b—Preliminary Summary, September 1, 1937, reservoir quote on 3 box 18, Staff Study 4a, b, c, d, e, FDR-Advisory; Johnson and Harvey, *The National Youth Administration*, quote 88; Fass, "Without Design."

66. Shermer, "Financing Security and Opportunity"; Reeves, *Report of the Advisory Committee on Education*.

67. Shermer, "Financing Security and Opportunity"; Salmond, *Southern Rebel*, 99–104, characterization of Williams quote 96; Associated Press, "Racial Problem in Relief Told by WPA Chief," *Washington Post*, November 24, 1935, Williams on African Americans' struggles quote 7; "Youth Director Assails Wealth Centralization," *Washington Post*, November 7, 1937, Williams at United Parents' Association quote R12.

68. Shermer, "Financing Security and Opportunity"; Salmond, *Southern Rebel,* 99–104, quote 103.

69. Shermer, "Financing Security and Opportunity"; Ernest Lindley, "New WPA Head," *Washington Post,* December 23, 1938, 11; Thomas Moodie to Aubrey Williams, December 29, 1938, box 3, 3, Papers of Aubrey Williams, Franklin Delano Roosevelt Presidential Library and Archive, Hyde Park, NY (hereafter Williams papers); "Pinky over Aubrey," *Time,* January 2, 1939, 8; James Shepherd to Aubrey Williams, January 6, 1939, box 3, 3, Williams papers; Edward Day to Aubrey Williams, December 29, 1938, box 3, 3, Williams papers.

70. Shermer, "Financing Security and Opportunity." Aubrey Williams, SEE-444-D, July 23, 1937; Aubrey Williams, SEE-444-D, July 27, 1937; Charles Andrews, SEE-444-D, July 26, 1937; John Sherman, SEE-444-D Mis., July 29, 1937; all in box 2, July–Dec 1937, Series 107, FDR-Official. Rawick, "New Deal and Youth," 215; Lindley and Lindley, *New Deal for Youth,* 161; Salmond, *Southern Rebel,* 133–140; Smith, *Concise History of the New Deal,* 124–148.

71. Shermer, "Financing Security and Opportunity"; Elizabeth Tandy Shermer, *Sunbelt Capitalism: Phoenix and the Transformation of American Politics* (Philadelphia: University of Pennsylvania Press, 2013), 71–92.

72. Johnson quoted in Rawick, "New Deal and Youth," 222–223; Williams quoted in Salmond, *Southern Rebel,* 142. See also Reiman, *The New Deal,* 158–181; National Youth Administration, *Report of the National Advisory Committee,* 28–40.

73. Shermer, "Financing Security and Opportunity"; Rawick, "New Deal and Youth," 222–223; Reiman, *The New Deal,* 158–181; National Youth Administration, *Report of the National Advisory Committee,* 28–40; John Studebaker to William Hassett, July 18, 1941, enclosure, box 2638–2662, File 2652 (in which also see correspondence in box 3, 1940, Series 107, FDR-Official, esp. Edward Hodnett to [FDR], August 16, 1940 and Frank Mossman, telegram, August 24, 1940); Memorandum for Secretary of War and Secretary of the Navy, October 15, 1942, box 4, Jan–April 1943, Series 107, FDR-Official.

74. Shermer, "Financing Security and Opportunity"; Reiman, *The New Deal,* 158–181; Salmond, *Southern Rebel,* 140–143, Johnson quote 143; Rawick, "New Deal and Youth," 225; Charles Taussig, Report of the National Advisory Committee, March 19, 1942, Appendix to Section I, box 6, Advisory Committee, Williams papers.

75. Shermer, "Financing Security and Opportunity"; John Studebaker, memorandum for the president, August 24, 1935, box 12, Interior Dept., Dept of Ed, 1933–36, Series 6, FDR-Official; Aubrey Williams to [Harry] Hopkins, memo, November 19, 1935, box 1712–1734, File 1724, FDR-Personal; Loss, *Between Citizens and the State,* 53–90.

76. Salmon, *Southern Rebel,* 120–146, quote about "school people" and job training on 144, and impressions of educators' trend and Eleanor Roosevelt quotes 145.

77. Shermer, "Financing Security and Opportunity"; Story, "New Deal and Higher Education"; Zeitlin, "Efforts to Achieve Federal Aid to Education"; Reiman, *The New Deal,* 74–96, 126–127; "Colleges Told Their Freedom Is Endangered," *Chicago Tribune,* January 13, 1940, Dickinson College head and Harvard official quotes 2; Fass, "Without Design"; Levine, *American College and the Culture of Aspiration,* Dartmouth professor quote 200–201; Reiman, *The New Deal,* 123–140; Salmond, *Southern Rebel,* 150–160.

78. Presidential Memorandum for Aubrey Williams, April 18, 1942, box 4, Jan–June 1942, Series 107, FDR-Official; Fass, "Without Design"; Levine, *American College and the Culture of Aspiration,* 200–201; Reiman, *The New Deal,* 123–140; Salmond, *Southern Rebel,* 150–160, Williams quote 154–155.

79. Salmond, *Southern Rebel*, 154–157, Benson and Harding students quotes 155, 156; "Aubrey on Economy," *Chicago Tribune*, February 6, 1942, 16. For discussion see Shermer, "Financing Security and Opportunity."

80. Shermer, "Financing Security and Opportunity"; J. H. Reynolds to Aubrey Williams, February 9, 1942; and Guy Masey to Aubrey Williams, February 9, 1942, both in box 25, file 3, Williams papers. Aubrey Williams to R. T. Young, April 27, 1942; John Sands to Aubrey Williams, March 9, 1942; Aubrey Williams to John Sands, February 11, 1942; Aubrey Williams to William LaFollette, February 4, 1942; Aubrey Williams to Harry Berger, January 29, 1942; and Aubrey Williams, January 27, 1942; "'Use Our NYA Checks in War,' Students Ask," January 26, 1942, newspaper clipping; and Statement by Aubrey Williams, January 28, 1942; all in box 10, file 1, Williams papers.

81. Levine, *American College and the Culture of Aspiration*, 200–208; Gene Thomas to Marvin McIntyre, March 12, 1933, file 91, box 88–91, FDR-Personal; Salmond, *Southern Rebel*, 154–157.

82. Salmond, *Southern Rebel*, 144–149; Reiman, *The New Deal*, 158–181; National Youth Administration, *Report of the National Advisory Committee*, 28–32.

83. Kenneth McKellar comments at Hearing before US Senate Labor Committee quoted in "Senator McKellar Demands Abolition of N.Y.A. and C.C.C.," *Los Angeles Times*, March 24, 1942, 11. See also Chesley Manly, "Senators Call for Abolition of CCC and NYA," *Chicago Tribune*, March 24, 1942, 27; David Witwer, *Shadow of the Racketeer: Scandal in Organized Labor* (Urbana: University of Illinois Press, 2009), 147–174; Ernest Lindley, "NYA Record," *Washington Post*, October 6, 1941, 9.

84. "Clinging to the Payroll," March 10, 1942, *Minneapolis Times-Tribune*, clipping, box 13, 7, Williams papers; "Let the N.Y.A. Follow," *Wall Street Journal*, July 2, 1942, 4; "NYA Camouflage," *Chicago Tribune*, June 27, 1942, 12.

85. Paul Garret to [FDR], telegram, May 15, 1942, box 4, Jan–June 1942, Series 107, FDR-Official; Maurice Hartung, "Should the National Youth Administration Be Continued?" *School Review*, May 1943, 264–266; "The Boondoggling Champions," editorial, *Chicago Tribune*, May 27, 1943, 16; Aubrey Williams to Henry Harrison, March 19, 1943, box 25, 2, Williams papers, see entire file for complaints from local business groups.

86. Shermer, "Financing Security and Opportunity"; Rawick, "New Deal and Youth," 267–273; Salmond, *Southern Rebel*, 145–162, Williams quote 157, leading educator's demand 158; Reiman, *The New Deal*, 158–181; "Out with the N.Y.A. and Crop Insurance, Too," *Los Angeles Times*, July 6, 1943, A4.

87. Shermer, *Sunbelt Capitalism*, 71–92.

88. US Congress, House of Representatives, Subcommittee of the Committee on Education and Labor, Scholarship and Loan Program: Hearings before a Subcommittee on Education and Labor, 86th Cong., 1st sess., 1957, 66–67.

89. Federal Security Agency, *Final Report*, 53–56.

90. Federal Security Agency, *Final Report*, 75–78, quotes 75, 76; Hartung, "Should the National Youth Administration Be Saved?" 264–265; Charles Taussig, Report of the National Advisory Committee, March 19, 1942, quotes 81, 84, box 6, Advisory Committee, Williams papers.

91. Federal Security Agency, *Final Report*, 53–56, quote 56; Reiman, *The New Deal*, 158–181; Salmond, *Southern Rebel*, 141–161; National Youth Administration, *Report of the National Advisory Committee*, 8, 40–62; Aubrey Williams to Mary McLeod Bethune, May 20, 1942, quoted 1, box 7, Legislation NYA—1942–43 Program, Williams papers.

92. Associated Press, "N.Y.A. Ends Operations After Eight-Year Trial," *Los Angeles Times*, July 5, 1943, Williams' public remarks quote 2; Federal Security Agency, *Final Report*, Williams quote v; Salmond, *Southern Rebel*, 141–161, Williams to NAC member quote 160.

3. A Bill of Rights for Only Some GIs

1. Thomas Wicks to President Harry Truman, November 23, 1946, folder labeled G.I. Bill of Rights (S. 1767) (1945–July 1947) [2 of 2], box 810; John O. Craig, Jr. and James O. Cochran, Jr. to President Harry S. Truman, December 9, 1946, folder labeled G.I. Bill of Rights (S. 1767) (1945–July 1947) [2 of 2], box 810; Marvin Gerstein to the President, January 13, 1948, folder labeled (1948) [1 of 2], box 811; Untitled Memo about a phone call from Mr. Geo. Antonofsky, January 12, 1948, folder labeled (1948) [1 of 2], box 811; all in Official File, White House Central Files, Harry S Truman Presidential Library, Independence, MO (hereafter Truman-Official). For details on student veterans' financial hardships, see Statement of Chat Paterson, American Veterans Committee, on "Preliminary Report on Cost of Living Surveys Conducted by AVC Chapters on College Campuses," to the US Senate Eightieth Congress, first session, Committee on Labor and Public Welfare, Subcommittee on Veterans' Affairs, Hearings on Education and On-The-Job Training Programs for Veterans, May 7, 1947, 83–144.

2. For discussions of debates surrounding the GI Bill's passage, see Glenn Altschuler and Stuart Blumin, *The GI Bill: A New Deal for Veterans* (New York: Oxford University Press, 2009); Kathleen Frydl, *The GI Bill* (New York: Cambridge University Press, 2009); Keith Olson, "G.I. Bill and Higher Education: Success and Surprise," *American Quarterly* 25, no. 5 (December 1973): 596–610; Ronald Story, "New Deal and Higher Education," in *The New Deal and the Triumph of Liberalism*, ed. Sidney M. Milkis and Jerome M. Mileur, 272–296 (Amherst: University of Massachusetts Press, 2002); Christopher P. Loss, *Between Citizens and the State: The Politics of American Higher Education in the 20th Century* (Princeton: Princeton University Press, 2012), 91–120; Robert Serow, "Policy as Symbol: Title II of the 1944 G.I. Bill," *Review of Higher Education* 27, no. 4 (Summer 2004): 481–499; Suzanne Mettler, *Soldiers to Citizens: The G.I. Bill and the Making of the Greatest Generation* (New York: Oxford University Press, 2005); David Ross, *Preparing for Ulysses: Politics and Veterans during World War II* (New York: Cambridge University Press, 1969).

3. "Fortune Survey," *Fortune*, January 1945, 260; "What Combat Soldiers Think the Biggest Problems Are That Will Be Facing Them after the War," June 20, 1945, 1–3, Attitude Reports of Overseas Personnel, box 1014, entry 94, Records of the Office of the Secretary of Defense, National Archives and Records Administration. For discussion see Christopher Loss, "'The Most Wonderful Thing Has Happened to Me in the Army': Psychology, Citizenship, and American Higher Education in World War II," *Journal of American History* 92, no. 3 (2005): 864–891; James B. Conant, "Wanted: American Radicals," *Atlantic Monthly*, May 1943, 43–44, quote 44; Jerome Karabel, *The Chosen: The Hidden History of Admission and Exclusion at Harvard, Yale, and Princeton* (New York: Houghton Mifflin Harcourt, 2005), 157–161.

4. Altschuler and Blumin, *GI Bill*, 35–41; Elizabeth Tandy Shermer, *Sunbelt Capitalism: Phoenix and the Transformation of American Politics* (Philadelphia: University of Pennsylvania Press, 2013), 71–92; Ross, *Preparing for Ulysses*, 34–66. Walter Cocking, "Assumptions for Planning," undated, box 24, 7; and Walter Cocking to Committee on Program Planning, memo and enclosure, May 15, 1942, box 24, 7; both in Papers of Aubrey Williams,

Franklin Delano Roosevelt Presidential Library and Archive, Hyde Park, NY (hereafter Williams papers). George Zook to Marvin McIntyre, November 16, 1942, box OF5177-OF5223, OF 5182, Papers as President, President's Official File, Franklin Delano Roosevelt Presidential Library and Archive, Hyde Park, NY. Oscar Cox to Harry Hopkins, memo, February 4, 1943, box 210, Post War Employment; and "Jobs after the war," undated enclosure; both in Papers of Harry L. Hopkins, Franklin Delano Roosevelt Presidential Library and Archive, Hyde Park, NY. [Oscar Cox], memorandum to Judge Rosenman, July 28, 1943, p. 2, box 65, Servicemen, Returning—Education and Training, Oscar S. Cox Papers, Franklin Delano Roosevelt Presidential Library and Archive, Hyde Park, NY (hereafter Cox papers).

5. Olson, "G.I. Bill and Higher Education," 600; Altschuler and Blumin, *GI Bill*, 11–34; Frydl, *The GI Bill*, 36–99; Story, "New Deal and Higher Education," 280–283; Ross, *Preparing for Ulysses*, 67–88.

6. Altschuler and Blumin, *GI Bill*, 35–50; Frydl, *The GI Bill*, 36–99; Story, "New Deal and Higher Education," 280–283; Mettler, *Soldiers to Citizens*, 15–23; Franklin D. Roosevelt, Statement on Signing the Bill Reducing the Draft Age, November 13, 1942, *American Presidency Project*, University of California, Santa Barbara, https://www.presidency.ucsb.edu/documents /statement-signing-the-bill-reducing-the-draft-age.

7. Altschuler and Blumin, *GI Bill*, 35–50, primary objective quote 44, exceptionally able quote 47; Mettler, *Soldiers to Citizens*, 15–23; US Congress, Senate, Committee on Education and Labor, *Servicemen's Education and Training Act of 1944*, 78th Cong., 1st sess., 1943, concern states' contributions quote 32.

8. Frydl, *The GI Bill*, 36–99, 122–125; Altschuler and Blumin, *GI Bill*, 35–45; Samuel I. Rosenman, *Working with Roosevelt* (New York: Harper and Brothers, 1952), "entering wedge" quote 395, strategy explained 394–395.

9. Altschuler and Blumin, *GI Bill*, 35–45; Frydl, *The GI Bill*, 36–99.

10. Shermer, *Sunbelt Capitalism*, 71–92; Altschuler and Blumin, *GI Bill*, 41–44.

11. Franklin Roosevelt, Fireside Chat 25, July 28, 1943, https://millercenter.org/the-presidency /presidential-speeches/july-28-1943-fireside-chat-25-fall-mussolini; Altschuler and Blumin, *GI Bill*, 44–51; Olson, "G.I. Bill and Higher Education"; Oscar Cox to Scott Lucas, November 2, 1943, enclosure quoted 5–6, box 65, Servicemen, Returning—Education and Training, Cox papers.

12. Glenn Altschuler and Stuart Blumin, *The GI Bill: The New Deal for Veterans* (Oxford, UK: Oxford University Press, 2009), 44–51, Bridges, Spangler quote 47.

13. *Congressional Record*, 78th Cong., 2d sess., vol. 90, part 3, May 1, 1944, Fish quote 4327; "8-Point Plan Issued to Aid Small Lines," *New York Times*, March 2, 1944, Maverick quoted 23; Olson, "G.I. Bill and Higher Education"; Altschuler and Blumin, *GI Bill*, 51–62; Frydl, *The GI Bill*, 103–105, 121–125.

14. Altschuler and Blumin, *GI Bill*, 1–10, 51–84; Ross, *Preparing for Ulysses*, 275–292; Frydl, *The GI Bill*, 100–145; Christopher Nehls, "The American Legion and Striking Workers during the Interwar Period," in *The Right and Labor in America: Politics, Ideology, and Imagination*, ed. Nelson Lichtenstein and Elizabeth Tandy Shermer, 27–41 (Philadelphia: University of Pennsylvania Press, 2012); Massachusetts Legion quoted in "State Branch, American Legion, Backs Governor," *Boston Globe*, September 14, 1919, 7.

15. Altschuler and Blumin, *GI Bill*, 51–60, Atherton and other Legionnaires quotes 54, 57; Frydl, *The GI Bill*, 104–106; Mettler, *Soldiers to Citizens*, 15–23.

16. Altschuler and Blumin, *GI Bill*, 54–60, Rector quote 58; Frydl, *The GI Bill*, 113–115; Mettler, *Soldiers to Citizens*, 15–23, Stelle quote 21.

17. Altschuler and Blumin, *GI Bill*, 54–57, exceptional ability quote 56; Frydl, *The GI Bill*, 115–122, Colmery quote 120; Louis Keefer, *Scholars in Foxholes: The Story of the Army Specialized Training Program in World War II* (Jefferson, NC: McFarland, 1988), 2–10; Mettler, *Soldiers to Citizens*, 15–23.

18. Altschuler and Blumin, *GI Bill*, 51–54; David Witwer, "Westbrook Pegler and the Anti-Union Movement," *Journal of American History* 92, no. 2 (2005): 527–552; David Nasaw, *The Chief: The Life of William Randolph Hearst* (New York: Houghton Mifflin, 2000), xiii–xv, 564–603, quote xiv; Mettler, *Soldiers to Citizens*, 15–23.

19. *Journal American*, editorial, January 12, 1944, quoted in Altschuler and Blumin, *GI Bill*, 53; Ross, *Preparing for Ulysses*, Hearst newspapers quotes 80 and 81; Frydl, *The GI Bill*, 114–120, Legionnaires quote 115; Mettler, *Soldiers to Citizens*, 15–23.

20. Altschuler and Blumin, *GI Bill*, 54–62, Jack Cejnar of American Legion quote 60; Frydl, *The GI Bill*, 114–120.

21. Altschuler and Blumin, *GI Bill*, 54–62, Atherton quotes 60, 61; Mettler, *Soldiers to Citizens*, 15–23.

22. Altschuler and Blumin, *GI Bill*, 51–62; Frydl, *The GI Bill*, 114–120.

23. Frydl, *The GI Bill*, 103–105; Altschuler and Blumin, *GI Bill*, 51–62, quote 62.

24. US Congress, *Congressional Record: Proceedings and Debates of the 78th Congress, First Session*, vol. 89, part 2 (Washington, DC: U.S. Government Printing Office, 1943), Clark, speaking on March 5, 1943, quote 1606.

25. US Congress, Senate, *Hearings before a Subcommittee of the Committee on Finance, United States Senate, Seventy-eighth Congress, Second Session on S. 1617, a Bill to Provide Federal Government Aid for the Readjustment in Civilian Life of Returning World War II Veterans, January 14, 15, 21, 24; February 11, 14, 23; March 8 and 10, 1944* (Washington, DC: U.S. Government Printing Office, 1944), Wiley quote 172.

26. Altschuler and Blumin, *GI Bill*, 55–65, Barden bill quote 59, Rankin quote 64, 65; James E. McMillan, "Father of the GI Bill: Ernest W. McFarland and Veterans' Legislation," *Journal of Arizona History* 35, no. 4 (1994): 357–376, Taft and Dirksen quote 364; Frydl, *The GI Bill*, 87–130, Wiley quote 127.

27. Altschuler and Blumin, *GI Bill*, 63–66; Frydl, *The GI Bill*, 86–145; Mettler, *Soldiers to Citizens*, 41–58; US Congress, Senate, Committee on Education and Labor, *Servicemen's Education and Training Act of 1944*, 78th Cong., 1st sess., 1943; Shermer, *Sunbelt Capitalism* 50, 87–88; McMillan, "Father of the GI Bill."

28. US Congress, Senate, *Servicemen's Education and Training Act: Hearings Before the Committee on Education and Labor, United States Senate, Seventy-eighth Congress, First Session, on S. 1295, a Bill Providing for Loans to War-service Persons for Educational Purposes and S. 1509, a Bill to Provide for the Education and Training of Members of the Armed Forces and the Merchant Marine after Their Discharge Or Conclusion of Service, and for Other Purposes*, hearings conducted December 13–15, 1943, Pepper quotes 40.

29. US Congress, Senate, *Servicemen's Education and Training Act Hearings*, Pepper quotes 28, 40.

30. Olson, "G.I. Bill and Higher Education," 601; Mettler, *Soldiers to Citizens*, 41–58; Altschuler and Blumin, *GI Bill*, 59–68, Hines's crackpot quote 59, Clark quote 67–68; Frydl, *The GI Bill*, 86–145, Hines's economically quote 141; McMillan, "Father of the GI Bill," Rankin quote 364–365.

31. US Congress, Senate, Committee on Education and Labor, *Servicemen's Education and Training Act of 1944*, 78th Cong., 1st sess., 1943, 87–115, 135–136, quote 114.

32. Loss, "'The Most Wonderful Thing Happened to Me'"; Keefer, *Scholars in Foxholes*, 10–16; Mettler, *Soldiers to Citizens*, 24–40; Loss, *Between Citizens and the State*, 91–120; US Congress, Senate, Committee on Education and Labor, *Servicemen's Education and Training Act of 1944*, 78th Cong., 1st sess., 1943, National Education Association leader quote 83; "College Students Reduce by Third," *New York Times*, December 25, 1944, 22; Charles Hurd, "[Professor Reeves] Says Veterans Aim to Study for Years," *New York Times*, December 11, 1944.

33. Altschuler and Blumin, *GI Bill*, 58–80; Bernard DeVoto, "The Easy Chair," *Harper's Magazine* (May 1943), 645–648, quote 647; Karabel, *Chosen*, Conant's natural aristocracy quote 158; Olson, "G.I. Bill and Higher Education," Conant quote 603–604.

34. "House Is Divided on Veterans' Bill," *New York Times*, May 12, 1944, 10; Dave Camelon, "I Saw the GI Bill Written (conclusion)," *American Legion Magazine*, November 1949, 18–19, 43–48, quote 43–44.

35. "G.I. Enemy No. 1," *The Nation* 58, May 6, 1944, 527–528; Camelon, "I Saw the GI Bill Written (conclusion)," quote 44–45.

36. Camelon, "I Saw the GI Bill Written (conclusion)," 43–48, quotes 47, 48; Altschuler and Blumin, *GI Bill*, 69–72; Mettler, *Soldiers to Citizens*, 15–23; Frydl, *The GI Bill*, 92–95.

37. Altschuler and Blumin, *GI Bill*, 70–72.

38. US Congress, Senate, Committee on Education and Labor, *Servicemen's Education and Training Act of 1944*, 78th Cong., 1st sess., 1943, 19–29, 115–124, quote 118.

39. Associated Press, "Tuition Rates for Veterans Approved," *Washington Post*, September 12, 1944, quote 3; "Floor Is Fixed on Tuition for Returned Vets," *Chicago Tribune*, September 12, 1944, 11; Altschuler and Blumin, *GI Bill*, 85–117.

40. Frydl, *The GI Bill*, 146–185, letter to Rankin quote 146; Altschuler and Blumin, *GI Bill*, 66–67; Olson, "G.I. Bill and Higher Education," veteran quote 602; Victor Colton, "What's Ahead for the Veteran?" *Los Angeles Times*, July 9, 1945, A4.

41. "Big Rush to Colleges Seen after the War," *New York Times*, October 23, 1944, NYU chancellor quote 21; Sarah Riedman, "Expansion of Education Hailed," *New York Times*, November 7, 1944, Riedman quote 26.

42. Harry Ashmore, *Unreasonable Truths: The Life of Robert Maynard Hutchins* (Boston: Little, Brown, 1989), xv–xx, 120–132, 187–209, 233–243, 264–274, impressions of FDR quote 125, predictions government-university relations quote 236, quote about Americans 267.

43. Robert Hutchins, "Threat to American Education," *Collier's*, December 1944, 20–21; Altschuler and Blumin, *GI Bill*, 76–77; Olson, "G.I. Bill and Higher Education," 604–605; Mettler, *Citizens to Soldiers*, 64.

44. Willard Waller, "Which Veterans Should Go to College," *Ladies' Home Journal*, May 1945, quote 142.

45. Edith Efron, "Veterans Storm the Academic Beachhead," *New York Times*, August 12, 1945, quote SM8; Stephen Thompson, "Free Education for Our Veterans," *Science Digest*, February 1945, 35–38.

46. A Soldier, letter to the editor, "Wants Bonus, Not 'Rights,'" *Chicago Tribune*, April 18, 1945, 14; "GI Rights Bill Rated Fraud on Vets, Public," *Chicago Tribune*, May 16, 1945, 27.

47. Frank Gervasi, "No Place to Live," *Collier's*, February 16, 1946, 20–21, 78–83, quote 21; Charles Hurd, "Readjustment," *New York Times*, December 30, 1945, 10; C. S. Forester, "Meet a Student

Veteran," *Ladies' Home Journal*, May 1945, 137–140, 163, quotes 137, 163. For discussion, see Altschuler and Blumin, *GI Bill*, 74–79.

48. Mettler, *Soldiers to Citizens*, 63–64; Ross, *Preparing for Ulysses*, 278–280.

49. Mettler, *Soldiers to Citizens*, 41–86; Altschuler and Blumin, *GI Bill*, 69–84; Olson, "G.I. Bill and Higher Education"; Frydl, *The GI Bill*, 146–185.

50. Mettler, *Soldiers to Citizens*, 41–86; Altschuler and Blumin, *The GI Bill*, 69–84; Olson, "G.I. Bill and Higher Education," 600; Frydl, *The GI Bill*, 146–185; Associated Press, "Broadened GI Bill Is Stripped of Bonus," *New York Times*, July 12, 1945, 12; Associated Press, "House Committee Backs Liberalized G.I. Bill," *Los Angeles Times*, July 12, 1945, 2; "More Liberal Bill Backed for Veterans," *Washington Post*, July 11, 1945, 11; US Congress, Senate, Subcommittee of the Committee on Finance, *Amendments to the Servicemen's Readjustment Act of 1944*, 79th Cong., 1st sess., 1945, 118–131, 288–301, NEA expert quotes 293, 295.

51. Olson, "G.I. Bill and Higher Education," 600–606, Stanford students quote 605; "S.R.O.," *Time*, March 18, 1946, quote 75; Serow, "Policy as Symbol," 482–484.

52. Olson, "G.I. Bill and Higher Education," 605; Story, "New Deal and Higher Education," 280–283; Serow, "Policy as Symbol," 484–486.

53. Thurman Justice, "What Happens to the Veteran in College?" *Journal of Higher Education* 17, no. 4 (April 1946): 185–188, 224–225; Norman Frederiksen and W. B. Schroeder, *Adjustment to College: A Study of 10,000 Veteran and Nonveteran Students in Sixteen American Colleges* (Princeton: Educational Testing Service, 1951), 1–62, quote 21; Mettler, *Soldiers to Citizens*, 59–86.

54. US Congress, House, Subcommittee on Education, Training, and Rehabilitation, *Increasing Subsistence Allowances for Education or Training under the Servicemen's Readjustment Act*, 1947, 100–108, 195–209, veteran quote 199; DDB, summary of December 7, 1946 telegram and actions taken, December 9, 1946, box 810, G.I. Bill of Rights (S.1767) (1945–July 1947) [2 of 2], Truman-Official; DDB, Summary 1/11/1947 letter and actions taken, January 14, 1947, box 810, G.I. Bill of Rights (S.1767) (1945–July 1947) [2 of 2], Truman-Official; Florence Robinson to Harry Truman, August 20, 1947, box 810 G.I. Bill of Rights (S.1767) (August–December 1947) [3 of 3], Truman-Official. For more telegrams and letters, see the cited folders.

55. American Veterans Committee, University of Michigan Chapter, "Cost of Living of Student Veterans at University of Michigan," December 1947, quote 8; Marvin Gerstein to The President, telegram, January 13, 1948; Unauthored, Group of Veterans who had appointment with General Vaught afternoon of 13 January 1948; Unauthored, untitled notes about Operation Subsistence delegation, January 12, 1948; all in box 811, O.F.190-L (1948) [1 of 2], Truman-Official.

56. Justice, "What Happens to the Veteran in College?" 185–188, 224–225; "Housing Shortage Hits College Student Veterans," *Los Angeles Times*, April 21, 1946, A3; John Morris, "Married Veterans Take Over the Campus," *Ladies' Home Journal*, October 1946, 32–39, quote 39; Rosa Lee Jay, "Battle of Subsistence," *Ladies' Home Journal*, November 1947, 252–256, quote 252; Olson, "G.I. Bill and Higher Education," 595–597; Frydl, *The GI Bill*, 311–314; Benjamin Fine, "Education in Review," *New York Times*, February 24, 1946, 75.

57. US Congress, Senate, Subcommittee of the Committee on Education and Labor, *Educational Facilities and Housing for Servicemen*, 79th Cong., 2nd sess., 1946, 3–10, Mead quote 4; Altschuler and Blumin, *GI Bill*, 85–116; Frydl, *The GI Bill*, 301–351; Kiernan, "Federal Aid to Higher Education," 155–157; "2,338,226 Enrolled in Colleges of U.S.," *New York Times*, November 27, 1947; [John Snyder], "The Veteran and Higher Education," quote ii, May 20, 1946,

box 30, Office of War Mobilization & Reconversion [1945–1947], White House Central Files, Confidential File, Harry S Truman Presidential Library, Independence, MO.

58. Altschuler and Blumin, *GI Bill*, 85–116; Frydl, *The GI Bill*, 301–351; Kiernan, "Federal Aid to Higher Education," 155–157.

59. For a contemporaneous discussion of states' initiatives, see [John W. Snyder], "The Veteran and Higher Education: A Report to the President," U.S. Government Printing Office, May 20, 1946, 34–36; "NYU Is to Start Westchester Unit," *New York Times*, May 3, 1946, 38; Altschuler and Blumin, *GI Bill*, 85–116; Frydl, *The GI Bill*, 301–351; Ron Grossman, "University of Illinois at Navy Pier Opened in 1946 to Serve WWII Veterans," *Chicago Tribune*, July 8, 2016; Elizabeth Shermer, "UIC United Faculty on Front Lines of Crisis in Higher Ed," *LaborOnline*, February 5, 2014.

60. "Bias Investigation in Colleges Urged," *New York Times*, July 11, 1946, 25; Mettler, *Soldiers to Citizens*, 72–77; Max Lerner, "Racism at the Grassroots," *PM*, January 24, 1946.

61. James Burwell, "College Priorities," letter to the editor, *Chicago Tribune*, April 19, 1946, 16; Myers quoted in Benjamin Fine, "Educators Fight College Quotas," *New York Times*, February 9, 1945, 32.

62. Mettler, *Soldiers to Citizens*, 65–68.

63. Mettler, *Soldiers to Citizens*, 65–68; Benjamin Fine, "Education in Review," *New York Times*, February 24, 1946, 75; Curtis Avery, "Veterans' Educations in the Universities," *Journal of Higher Education* 17, no. 7 (October 1946): 359–363; Justice, "What Happens to the Veteran in College?" 185–188, 224–225, quote 187–188; Story, "New Deal and Higher Education," 277–280.

64. John Evans, "U. of I. Announces Scholarship Plan for Veterans," *Chicago Defender*, August 20, 1944, E4; Altschuler and Blumin, *GI Bill*, 85–116; Frydl, *The GI Bill*, 310–338; Mettler, *Soldiers to Citizens*, 65–68.

65. Byron H. Atkinson, "The G.I. Bill as a Social Experiment," *School and Society*, July 17, 1948, 43–44, UCLA staff quote 43; Martin Staples Shockley, "The Extra-Curriculum," *Journal of Higher Education* 24, no. 9 (December 1953): 453–459. For discussion see Frydl, *The GI Bill*, 303–351; Olson, "G.I. Bill and Higher Education," 600–606; Serow, "Policy as Symbol," 492–495.

66. Henry Pringle, "Are We Making a Bum Out of G.I. Joe?" *Ladies' Home Journal*, September 1946, 48+; Frydl, *The GI Bill*, 186–221.

67. US Congress, Senate, Subcommittee of the Committee on Finance, *Amendments to the Servicemen's Readjustment Act of 1944*, 79th Cong., 1st sess., 1945, 118–131; "150,000 War Veterans in Business Schools," *New York Times*, November 28, 1947, Executive Secretary quote 38; "North American Newspaper Alliance," *New York Times*, May 18, 1947, quote 52; Frydl, *The GI Bill*, 186–221; Suzanne Mettler, *Degrees of Inequality: How the Politics of Higher Education Sabotaged the American Dream* (New York: Basic Books, 2014), 90–92; Ralph Winkler to Matthew Connely, July 28, 1950, box 95, Educational Appeals Board, Veterans OF 8-G, Truman-Official (for additional appeals see the rest of the folder).

68. Douglas quoted in Hearings before the Special Subcommittee on Veterans' Education and Rehabilitation Benefits for the Committee on Labor and Public Welfare, US Senate, 82nd Cong., 2nd sess., on H.R. 7656, June 10–13 and 17, 1952, 22–23; Rowland Evans, "VA Would Check Some GI Schools," *Washington Post*, August 21, 1949, 15. Alice Keith to Harry Vaughn, February 29, 1949; Alice Keith to M. V. Stirling, March 2, 1949; Stirling quoted in H. V. Stirling to Harry Vaughn, February 10, 1949; Alice Keith to Harry Vaughn, July 16, 1949; and

Alice Vaughn to C. L. Helley, July 15, 1949; all in box 811, O.F.190-L (1949–June 1950) [1 of 2], Truman-Official. Ralph Winkler to Matthew Connely, July 28, 1950, box 95, Educational Appeals Board, Veterans OF 8-G, Truman-Official (for additional appeals see the rest of the folder). For discussion see Frydl, *The GI Bill*, 186–221; Mettler, *Degrees of Inequality*, 90–92.

69. Evans, "VA Would Check Some GI Schools"; "Darden Denies Tuition 'Hike' for Veterans," *Washington Post*, September 14, 1945, 3; Mettler, *Degrees of Inequality*, 90–92; Mettler, *Citizens to Soldiers*, 59–86; Frydl, *The GI Bill*, 186–221.

70. United Press, "Colleges Accused of Treasury Raids," *New York Times*, February 21, 1952, Eckert quote 4; Teague quoted in Hearings before the Special Subcommittee on Veterans' Education and Rehabilitation Benefits for the Committee on Labor and Public Welfare, 22–23; Mettler, *Degrees of Inequality*, 90–92; Mettler, *Citizens to Soldiers*, 59–86; Frydl, *The GI Bill*, 186–221.

71. Forester, "Meet a Student Veteran," quote 163; Harold Anderson to Harry Truman, February 5, 1951, box 811, O.F.190-L (July 1950–Oct. 1951) [1 of 2], Truman-Official; Mettler, *Soldiers to Citizens*, 59–86, other veterans quote 65.

72. John Dee, Jr., to Harry Truman, August 5, 1948, box 811, O.F.190-L (1948) [2 of 2], Truman-Official; Claude and Zella Corbett, May 1, 1949, box 811, O.F.190-L (1949–June 1950) [1 of 2], Truman-Official; William Whittemore to Harry Truman, December 17, 1949, box 811, O.F.190-L (1949–June 1950) [2 of 2], Truman-Official; Mettler, *Soldiers to Citizens*, women veterans quote 151.

73. Avery, "Veterans' Educations in the Universities," 359; Benjamin Fine, "G.I. Called Credit to U.S. Education," *New York Times*, July 23, 1951, Yale officials quote 10; *Report of the President for the Year 1949–1950*, May 1951, Fred quote 8; Charles J. V. Murphy, "G.I.'s at Harvard," *Life*, June 17, 1946, Conant quote 17; Frydl, *The GI Bill*, 303–351; Olson, "G.I. Bill and Higher Education," 600–606.

74. Mettler, *Soldiers to Citizens*, 1–14, 71–73; Ira Katznelson, *When Affirmative Action Was White: An Untold Story of Racial Inequality in Twentieth-Century America* (New York: Norton, 2005); Olson, "G.I. Bill and Higher Education," 602–606; Serow, "Policy as Symbol," 483; Mettler, *Soldiers to Citizens*, 24–40; Frydl, *The GI Bill*, 303–351.

75. Mettler, *Soldiers to Citizens*, 67–69, 136–143; Karabel, *The Chosen*, 183–184, quote 183.

76. Altschuler and Blumin, *GI Bill*, 117–148, quote 128–129; Mettler, *Soldiers to Citizens*, 136–143; Frydl, *The GI Bill*, 188–89, 222–262; Altschuler and Blumin, *GI Bill*, 117–149; R. B. Goldsberry, "Negro Vets Not Wanted in N.U. Dorms," *Chicago Defender*, 3.

77. Mettler, *Soldiers to Citizens*, 65–66, 144–162, 196–197, 208–209; Sarah Rose, "The Right to a College Education? The G.I. Bill, Public Law 16, and Disabled Veterans," *Journal of Policy History* 24, no. 1 (2012): 26–52; Altschuler and Blumin, *GI Bill*, 7–9.

78. Mettler, *Soldiers to Citizens*, 144–162, women veterans quotes 144, 147, 151; Altschuler and Blumin, *GI Bill*, 85–116; Serow, "Policy as Symbol," 482–493; Benjamin Fine, "Education in Review," *New York Times*, October 14, 1945, E9; "College Students Reduce by Third," *New York Times*, December 25, 1944, 22; "2,338,226 Enrolled in Colleges of U.S.," *New York Times*, November 27, 1947, all quotes from 33.

79. Harold W. Stoke, "The Veterans Educate the Nation," *Association of American Colleges Bulletin*, October 1947, quote 4; Mettler, *Soldiers to Citizens*, 41–58; Altschuler and Blumin, *GI Bill*, 85–116; Serow, "Policy as Symbol," 483–494; Frydl, *The GI Bill*, 352–374.

80. Benjamin Fine, "College Fees Up Average of 37%," *New York Times*, September 23, 1947, 27; Arthur Stout, "How Much Does College Really Cost?" *Better Homes and Gardens*, February 1952, 14–17+; United Press, "Colleges Accused of Treasury Raids," *New York Times*,

February 21, 1952, 4; Mettler, *Soldiers to Citizens,* 1–14, 59–86, 163–176; Olson, "G.I. Bill and Higher Education"; Shermer, "From Educator- to Creditor-in-Chief"; Mettler, *Degrees of Inequality,* 90–92, 163–167; Frydl, *The GI Bill,* 215–221.

81. Algo Hendersen, "Plight of the Private Colleges and What to Do about It," Address to 32nd Annual American Council on Education Meeting, May 6–7, 1949, quoted 3, 2, 4, 8, box 48, American Council of Education, James H. Rowe, Jr. Papers, Franklin Delano Roosevelt Presidential Library and Archive, Hyde Park, NY; Benjamin Fine, "Education in Review," *New York Times,* January 15, 1950, E11; Benjamin Fine, "Education in Review," *New York Times,* November 23, 1952, E9.

4. The Fizzled Response to Sputnik

1. Christopher P. Loss, *Between Citizens and the State: The Politics of American Higher Education in the 20th Century* (Princeton: Princeton University Press, 2012), testifying students quotes 159–160. Yale student quote in Eugene Moen to Edith Green, March 27, 1966; and parents quote in Mr. and Mrs. Robert Sleister to Edith Green, March 19, 1966, both in box 137, NDEA-Student Loan Program, Edith Green Papers, Davies Family Research Library, Oregon Historical Society, Portland, OR. Barbara Ransel Gale, "National Defense Student Loan Program: Its History, Significance, and Problems" (PhD diss., George Washington University, 1974), personal interview with official quote 114.

2. For discussion of this misconception, see Barbara Barksdale Clowse, *Brainpower for the Cold War: The Sputnik Crisis and National Defense Act* (Westport, CT: Greenwood Press, 1981), 3–5; Wayne Urban, *More than Science and Sputnik: The National Defense Education Act of 1958* (Tuscaloosa: University of Alabama Press, 2010), 1–9; Loss, *Between Citizens and the State,* 121–164.

3. M. W. Arleigh to Harry Truman, August 18, 1945; Mrs. John S. Mayer to Harry Truman, May 30, 1947, pp. 1–3, self-identified housewife quote 1, 2; Burr Van Hoosean to Harry Truman, September 5, 1945, pages 1–3, quote 1; all in box 608, folder Education, Department of (Proposed), 107a, Official File, White House Central Files, Harry S Truman Presidential Library, Independence, MO.

4. [John Snyder], "The Veteran and Higher Education," quote ii, May 20, 1946, box 30, Office of War Mobilization & Reconversion [1945–1947], White House Central Files, Confidential File, Harry S Truman Presidential Library, Independence, MO.

5. John Salmond, *A Southern Rebel: The Life and Times of Aubrey Willis Williams, 1890–1965* (Chapel Hill: University of North Carolina Press, 1983), 158–160; David Ross, *Preparing for Ulysses: Politics and Veterans during World War II* (New York: Cambridge University Press, 1969), 125–159.

6. George Zook, *Role of the Federal Government in Education* (Cambridge, MA: Harvard University Press, 1945), quote 1–2; Jeffrey Scott Aranguena, "The Zook Commission: Reassessing World War II Veterans' Influence on Higher Education" (MA thesis, California Polytechnic, 2011), 1–8, 54; Philo Hutcheson, "The 1947 President's Commission on Higher Education and the National Rhetoric on Higher Education Policy," *History of Higher Education Annual* 22 (2002): 91–109; Kathleen Frydl, *The GI Bill* (New York: Cambridge University Press, 2009), 338–348; E. C. Wine to Mrs. Kraft, May 3, 1945, Record Group 51, Bureau of the Budget, Records of the Director, National Archives, Box 3.

7. U.S. President's Commission on Higher Education, *Higher Education for Democracy: A Report of the President's Commission on Higher Education* (Washington, DC: U.S. Government Printing Office, 1947), quote 1:36; Hutcheson, "1947 President's Commission"; Frydl, *GI Bill*, 338–348; Loss, *Between Citizens and the State,* 91–120; Michael Fabricant and Stephen Brier, *Austerity Blues: Fighting for the Soul of Public Higher Education* (Baltimore: Johns Hopkins University Press, 2016), 45–50.

8. Hutcheson, "1947 President's Commission," 93–101; James Harlow, "Five Years of Discussion," *Journal of Higher Education* 24, no. 1 (January 1953): 17–24; John Russell, "Higher Education Report Offers Some Challenges," *Washington Evening Star,* clipping, n.p., December 21, 1947, and John Russell, "Report of The President's Commission on Higher Education," January 24, 1948, talk before American Council on Education, both in box 9, John Russell Papers, Harry S Truman Presidential Library, Independence, MO; Edward Elliott, "A Fifty-Year Program?" *Journal of Higher Education* 19, no. 4 (April 1948): 175–180, quote 176; C. G. Woodson, "Review," *Journal of Negro History* 33, no. 2 (April 1948): 234–236, quote 235.

9. Janet Hansen, "Politics of Federal Scholarships: A Case Study of the Development of General Grant Assistance for Undergraduates" (PhD diss., Princeton University, 1977), 1–22.

10. Hansen, "Politics of Federal Scholarships," 1–22; Stephen Brock, "A Comparative Study of Federal Aid to Higher Education: The Higher Education Act of 1965 and Project Upward Bound" (PhD diss., Cornell University, 1968), 9–20; Hutcheson, "1947 President's Commission," 99–101; Frydl, *The GI Bill,* 338–348; Benjamin Fine, "U.S. Student Help Opposed as Peril," *New York Times,* January 11, 1950, Snavely and other educators quote 11.

11. Leonard Buders, "Doubling of Rolls in College Looms," *New York Times,* March 5, 1954, 17; Benjamin Fine, "Education in Review," *New York Times,* October 21, 1956, E9; Thad L. Hungate, *A New Basis of Support for Higher Education: A Study of Current Practices, Issues and Needed Changes* (New York: Bureau of Publications, Teachers College, Columbia University, 1957), 18–29, esp. Figure 1 on 29, quote 4; Roger Geiger, *Research and Relevant Knowledge: American Research Universities Since World War II* (New York: Oxford University Press, 1993), 117–156.

12. Elizabeth Tandy Shermer, *Sunbelt Capitalism: Phoenix and the Transformation of American Politics* (Philadelphia: University of Pennsylvania Press, 2013), 147–224; Elizabeth Tandy Shermer, "Fraught Partnership: Business and the Rise of the American Public University," in *Capital Gains: Business and Politics in Twentieth-Century America,* ed. Kim Phillips-Fein and Richard John, 157–178 (Philadelphia: University of Pennsylvania Press, 2016).

13. John Aubrey Douglass, "Earl Warren's New Deal: Economic Transition, Postwar Planning, and Higher Education in California," *Journal of Policy History* 12, no. 4 (2000): 473–512; Shermer, *Sunbelt Capitalism,* 184–224; Shermer, "Fraught Partnership."

14. Tod Ottman, "Fording SUNY in New York's Political Cauldron," in *SUNY at Sixty: The Promise of the State University of New York,* ed. John Clark, W. Bruce Leslie, and Kenneth O'Brien, 18–28 (Albany: State University of New York Press, 2010); Benjamin Fine, "Education in Review," *New York Times,* February 22, 1948, E9.

15. Ottman, "Fording SUNY in New York's Political Cauldron"; Glenn Altschuler and Stuart Blumin, *The GI Bill: A New Deal for Veterans* (New York: Oxford University Press, 2009), 99–105.

16. Shermer, *Sunbelt Capitalism,* 39–115.

17. Merle Curti and Roderick Nash, *Philanthropy in the Shaping of American Higher Education* (New Brunswick, NJ: Rutgers University Press, 1965), 238–258.

18. Curti and Nash, *Philanthropy*, 226–258; Hutcheson, "1947 President's Commission," 91–93.

19. Quote in *AP Smith Mfg. Co. v. Barlow*, 13 NJ 145 (1953); Curti and Nash, *Philanthropy*, 238–258, examples of corporate efforts divorced from the business right 246–250.

20. Curti and Nash, *Philanthropy*, 238–258; Shermer, *Sunbelt Capitalism*, 225–270.

21. Curti and Nash, *Philanthropy*, 238–258.

22. Curti and Nash, *Philanthropy*, 226–237; Loss, *Between Citizens and the State*, 147–149; Frydl, *GI Bill*, 341–348.

23. Curti and Nash, *Philanthropy*, 245–247.

24. Curti and Nash, *Philanthropy*, 226–249; Elizabeth Tandy Shermer, "Donations for More Than Just Diplomas: Conservative Philanthropy and American Higher Education," blog post, *HistPhil*, April 20, 2018, https://histphil.org/2018/04/20/donations-for-more-than-just -diplomas-conservative-philanthropy-and-american-higher-education/.

25. Shermer, "Donations for More Than Just Diplomas."

26. Frank W. Abrams, "Education Is Everybody's Business," text of speech delivered in New York, ca. 1959, in box 15, Hanover Bank Philanthropy Collection; Council for Financial Aid to Education, *Voluntary Support of Education, 1960* (New York: Council for Financial Aid to Education 1960).]

27. A. H. Raskin, "The Corporations and the Campus," *New York Times*, April 17, 1955, 12, 63–65, Abrams quote 63. Lindsey Kimball to Conference Participants, July 13, 1955, box 354, folder 3661; Wilson Compton to Frank Abrams, February 3, 1956, box 354, folder 3662; Eldredge Hiller to Dr. Kimball, memo, "Advertising in the Interest of Higher Education," September 20, 1956, box 354, folder 3662; Invitation to 1956 Working Conference from Wilson Compton [no addressee], May 1, 1956, box 354, folder 3662; and William Compton to Gentlemen, April 23, 1957, box 354, folder 3663; all in Series 2, General Education Board Archives, Rockefeller Archive Center, Sleepy Hollow, NY (hereafter General Education Board Archives). Anna Clark to Ralph Flynt, November 20, 1953, box 16, Council for Financial Aid to Education, Ralph Flynt Papers, Harry S Truman Presidential Library, Independence, MO (see the rest of this folder for additional CFAE pamphlets). Benjamin Fine, "Education in Review," *New York Times*, January 17, 1954, E9; Benjamin Fine, "Education in Review," *New York Times*, March 13, 1955, E11.

28. "Corporate Support for Higher Education," *Harvard Alumni Bulletin* 57 (1955), quote 621; Curti and Nash, *Philanthropy*, 252–254, University of Vermont staff quote 253.

29. Curti and Nash, *Philanthropy*, 238–258, report quote 255; Benjamin Fine, "Alumni Givers Are Giving Twice," *New York Times*, July 1, 1956, E9.

30. Hungate, *A New Basis of Support for Higher Education*, expert quote 4; John Pollard, *College Scholarships Available—Too Many, Too Few?* (New York: Council for Financial Aid to Education, 1955), CFAE concerns quote 3; Joseph Creech and Jerry Sheehan Davis, "Merit-Based versus Need-Based Aid: The Continual Issues for Policymakers," in *Financing a College Education: How It Works, How It's Changing*, ed. Jacqueline King, 120–136 (Phoenix: American Council on Education Oryx Press, 1999); John Pollard to Lindsley Kimball, June 29, 1955, box 354, folder 3661, General Education Board Archives; Curti and Nash, *Philanthropy*, 252–254; Benjamin Fine, "Education in Review," *New York Times*, October 21, 1956, E9; US Congress, House, Subcommittee of the Committee on Education and Labor, *Scholarship and Loan Program: Hearings before the Subcommittee of the Committee on Education and*

Labor, 58th Cong., 2nd sess., 1958, 1481–1482; "G. M. Doubles Scope of Aid to Education," *New York Times,* May 16, 1956, 20.

31. Hungate, *New Basis of Support for Higher Education,* quote 4; [CFAE] Division of Research, "Staff Memorandum on Student Loan Funds Available, and Their Use," July 23, 1956, box 355, folder 3664, General Education Board Archives; John R. Thelin, "Higher Education's Student Financial Aid Enterprise in Historical Perspective," in *Footing the Tuition Bill: The New Student Loan Sector,* ed. Frederick M. Hess, 19–41 (Washington, DC: AEI Press, 2007), 24–26; John F. Morse, "How We Got Here from There," in *Student Loans: Problems and Policy Alternatives,* ed. Lois Rice, 3–15 (New York: College Entrance Examination Board, 1977), esp. 5–6.

32. "Big Ten Report Criticizes Work-Aid Program as 'Invitation to Hypocrisy,'" *New York Times,* October 16, 1956, 40; Leonard Budard, "'Bidding for Brains' Disturbs Educators," *New York Times,* May 25, 1958, quotes 1, 56.

33. Michael S. McPherson and Morton Owen Schapiro, *The Student Aid Game: Meeting Need and Rewarding Talent in American Higher Education* (Princeton: Princeton University Press, 1998), 5–14; Thelin, "Higher Education's Student Financial Aid," 25–27; Morse, "How We Got Here from There," 6.

34. "Alumni Givers Are Giving Twice," *New York Times,* March 18, 1956, E12; Benjamin Fine, "Education in Review," *New York Times,* July 1, 1956, E9.

35. Milton Friedman, *Capitalism and Freedom* (Chicago: University of Chicago Press, 2002), 99–107; Milton Friedman, "Role of Government in Education," 123–144, in *Economics and the Public Interest,* ed. Robert Solo (New Brunswick, NJ: Rutgers University Press, 1955), quotes 123, 138.

36. John Munro, "Untapped Resource: Loans for Student Aid," *College Board Review,* 1956, 14–18, quotes 14, 17, 18.

37. Benjamin Fine, "Education in Review," *New York Times,* October 21, 1956, E9; Benjamin Fine, "Colleges Urged to Raise Tuition 50% to Ease Financial Plight," *New York Times,* March 6, 1956, 34.

38. Clowse, *Brainpower for the Cold War,* 28–39; Loss, *Between Citizens and the State,* 121–164; George Kizer, "Federal Aid to Education, 1945–1963," *History of Education Society* 10 (1970): 84–102; R. C. Lewontin, "The Cold War Transformation of the Academy," in *The Cold War and the University: Toward an Intellectual History of the Postwar Years,* ed. Noam Chomsky et al., 1–34 (New York: New Press, 1997); Jackson Toby, "How Scholarships Morphed into Financial Aid," *Academic Questions* 23, no. 3 (2010): 298–310, esp. 301; Brock, "Comparative Study of Federal Aid to Higher Education," 9–20; Elizabeth Tandy Shermer, "Financing Security and Opportunity: The New Deal and the Origins of the Millennial Student Debt Crisis," in *Capitalism Contested: The New Deal and Its Legacies,* ed. Romain Huret, Nelson Lichtenstein, and Jean-Christian Vinel, 112–135 (Philadelphia: University of Pennsylvania Press, 2020); Elizabeth Tandy Shermer, "From Educator- to Creditor-in-Chief: The American Presidency, Higher Education, and the Student Loan Industry," in *The President and American Capitalism,* ed. Mark Rose and Roger Biles, 123–150 (Gainesville: University of Florida Press, 2018).

39. Janet Kerr-Tener, "Eisenhower and Federal Aid to Higher Education," *Presidential Studies Quarterly* 17, no. 3 (1987): 473–485; January 17, 1958 Meeting, box 10, Cabinet Series, Dwight Eisenhower Papers as President, Dwight Eisenhower Presidential Library and Archive,

Abilene, KS (hereafter Eisenhower papers); Shermer, "From Educator- to Creditor-in-Chief"; Clowse, *Brainpower for the Cold War,* 28–53.

40. Clowse, *Brainpower for the Cold War,* 28–53, 66–67; Peter Kerr, "Lister Hill, Longtime Senator from Alabama," *New York Times,* December 22, 1984; Urban, *More than Science and Sputnik,* 10–72.

41. Clowse, *Brainpower for the Cold War,* 28–53; Kerr-Tener, "Eisenhower and Federal Aid to Higher Education."

42. Clowse, *Brainpower for the Cold War,* 28–53; Kerr-Tener, "Eisenhower and Federal Aid to Higher Education"; Theodore Thompson, *National Defense Education Act of 1958* (Ithaca, NY: Project One Publication Office, 1964), 3–5; US Congress, House of Representatives, Subcommittee of the Committee on Education and Labor, *Scholarship and Loan Program: Hearings before a Subcommittee on Education and Labor,* 86th Cong., 1st sess., 1957, 45–55, 187–192, 235–245, 257–262, 307–314, 422–425, 620–625, University of Minnesota official quote 244.

43. Shermer, *Sunbelt Capitalism,* 286–292; Clowse, *Brainpower for the Cold War,* 28–53; Robert Griffith, "Dwight D. Eisenhower and the Corporate Commonwealth," *American Historical Review* 87 (1982): 87–122; James Simon, *Eisenhower v. Warren: The Battle for Civil Rights and Liberties* (New York: Liveright, 2018).

44. Hansen, "Politics of Federal Scholarships," Eisenhower's exchange with reporters quote 80; Eisenhower's concerns about federal domination quote from Dwight Eisenhower to Douglas Lawrason, October 30, 1957, DDE Diary Series, box 28, October '57 D.D.E. Dictation, Eisenhower papers; Clowse, *Brainpower for the Cold War,* 28–53, Eisenhower conditions quote 46; Kerr-Tener, "Eisenhower and Federal Aid to Higher Education"; Thompson, *National Defense Education Act of 1958,* 4–7; President's Committee on Education Beyond the High School, *Second Report to the President* (Washington, DC: Government Printing Office, 1957); Urban, *More than Science and Sputnik,* 73–75; Thomas Soapes, "Interview with Dr. Arthur S. Flemming on November 24, 1978 for Dwight D. Eisenhower Library," transcript, Oral History for the Dwight Eisenhower Library, transcript, US National Archives and Records Administration, 6–8, Washington, DC, November 24, 1978, https://www.eisenhowerlibrary.gov/sites/default/files/research/oral-histories/oral-history-transcripts/flemming-arthur-506.pdf.

45. Sanford Jacoby, *Modern Manors: Welfare Capitalism since the New Deal* (Princeton: Princeton University Press, 1997), 57–94.

46. Clowse, *Brain Power for the Cold War,* 28–53, quote 46; M. B. Folsom to the President, January 12, 1956, box 71, folder 2, Series 7, Marion Folsom Papers, Rare Books, Special Collections, and Preservation, River Campus Libraries, University of Rochester, Rochester, NY (hereafter Folsom papers); Urban, *More than Science and Sputnik,* 78–79; Kerr-Tener, "Eisenhower and Federal Aid to Higher Education"; Thompson, *National Defense Education Act,* 4–7; Hansen, "Politics of Federal Scholarships," 80–84. M. B. Folsom to Kenneth Gray, August 31, 1955, box 71, folder 1; M. B. Folsom to John McNulty, January 25, 1955, box 71, folder 2; M. B. Folsom to Paul Jones, January 10, 1956, box 71, folder 2; Marion Folsom to Bracken Lee, January 6, 1956, box 71, folder 2; Harold Hunt to LeRoy Conal, March 14, 1956, box 71, folder 3; and M. B. Folsom to George Montgomery, May 5, 1957, box 72, folder 5; all in Folsom papers.

47. Benjamin Fine, "Satellite Called Spur to Education," *New York Times,* October 12, 1957, 3; Mary Ann Callan, "Crisis Ahead in Education," *Los Angeles Times,* October 22, 1957, A1;

"Sputnik and Survival," *Wall Street Journal*, October 17, 1957, 10; "Sputnik Called a Salutary Jolt," *Washington Post*, November 3, 1957, B2.

48. Minutes of Cabinet Meeting, December 2, 1957, Cabinet series, box 10, Cabinet Meeting of December 2, 1957, Eisenhower papers; Kerr-Tener, "Eisenhower and Federal Aid to Higher Education"; Notes on conversation with Marion Folsom, December 30, 1957, Whitman Diary Series, box 9, A.C.W. Diary Dec 1957, Eisenhower papers; Clowse, *Brainpower for the Cold War*, 53–65, Eisenhower quote 54; Urban, *More than Science and Sputnik*, 80–86; example of Eisenhower being focused more on foreign policy, January 17, 1958 Meeting, box 10, Cabinet Series, Eisenhower papers.

49. Clowse, *Brainpower for the Cold War*, 54–65.

50. Clowse, *Brainpower for the Cold War*, 66–77.

51. Clowse, *Brainpower for the Cold War*, 54–65, Milton Eisenhower quote 61, Conant quote 56, NSF official quote 58.

52. Clowse, *Brainpower for the Cold War*, 5–7, 66–92, Elliott's correspondence quote 90.

53. Clowse, *Brainpower for the Cold War*, 78–104; US Congress, Senate, *National Defense Education Act of 1958*, S. Rept. 2242 to accompany S.4237, 85th Cong., 2d sess., 1958, Senate Miscellaneous Reports on Public Bills, vol. 4, Thurmond quote 51, Goldwater quote 55.

54. Statement of John R. Miles, Chamber of Commerce, to US Congress, *Science and Education for National Defense: Hearings before the Committee on Labor and Public Welfare, United States Senate, Eighty-Fifth Congress, Second Session* (Washington, DC: Government Printing Office, 1958), 1225–1236, quotes 1227, 1235; Statement of Donald J. Hardenbrook, National Association of Manufacturers, to US Congress (March 21, 1958), *Scholarship and Loan Program: Hearings before a Subcommittee of the Committee on Education and Labor, Eighty-Fifth Congress, First Session* (Washington: Government Printing Office, 1958), 1502–1522, quotes 1502, 1520.

55. Congress, Senate, Committee, *Science and Education for National Defense*, student quotes 886–887, Morse quote 1143; Clowse, *Brainpower for the Cold War*, 78–104.

56. Clowse, *Brainpower for the Cold War*, 78–104; David O. Levine, *American College and the Culture of Aspiration, 1915–1940* (Ithaca, NY: Cornell University Press, 1986), 202–204; William Peters, "Battle over Religion in the Schools," *Redbook*, May 1957, 38–39, 105, 108, 110–112; Associated Press, "Jesuits Ask Federal Aid for Schools," *Los Angeles Times*, January 5, 1958, 30; Congress, House, Subcommittee, *Scholarship and Loan Program*, 1623–1630, Catholic academics quote 1626; "Independent Schools," *Washington Post*, January 27, 1958, quote A12.

57. Clowse, *Brainpower for the Cold War*, 78–104; Congress, Senate, Committee, *Science and Education for National Defense*, 871–886; Congress, House, Subcommittee, *Scholarship and Loan Program*, 811–816; Betty Pryor, "House Debates Student Aid Bill," *Washington Post*, August 8, 1958, A12; William Theis, "Skirt Race in School Bill," *Chicago Defender*, August 14, 1958, A4; United Press, "Senate Passes School Aid Bill," *Washington Post*, August 23, 1958, Thurmond quote A2.

58. Clowse, *Brainpower for the Cold War*, 78–104; Thompson, *National Defense Act of 1958*, 28; Hansen, "Politics of Federal Scholarships," Republicans quote 91; Folsom quote in Minutes of Cabinet Meeting, January 17, 1958, Cabinet series, box 10, Cabinet Meeting of January 17, 1958, Eisenhower papers; E. L. Richardson to Clifford Case, April 7, 1959, box 71, folder 8, Folsom papers; Congress, House, Subcommittee, *Scholarship and Loan Program*, 1790–1798, National Student Association quote 1797; Congress, Senate, Committee, *Science and Education for National Defense*, 872–874.

59. Thompson, *National Defense Act of 1958*, 10–11; Congress, House, Subcommittee, *Scholarship and Loan Program*, 1867–1877, 1350–1355; Congress, Senate, Committee, *Science and Education for National Defense*, 15–20, 400–404, 681–712, Kennedy quote 18–19, state university official quote 692; Clowse, *Brainpower for the Cold War*, 78–104.

60. Clowse, *Brainpower for the Cold War*, 78–104; Congress, Senate, Committee, *Science and Education for National Defense*, 389–424, 688–712, 1020–1029, labor leaders quote 1025–1026, state university official quote 693.

61. M. B. Folsom to Leonard Stewart, February 14, 1958, box 71, folder 7, Folsom papers; Thompson, *National Defense Act of 1958*, Coombs quote 10.

62. Congress, House, Subcommittee, *Scholarship and Loan Program*, Pogage quote 1474; Clowse, *Brainpower for the Cold War*, 78–104; Thompson, *National Defense Act of 1958*, research scientists quote 11.

63. Naomi Veronica Ross, "Congresswoman Edith Green on Federal Aid to Schools and Colleges" (PhD diss., Pennsylvania State University, 1980), Green quotes 113, 114. For scholarship on the racism and sexism crafting and dismantling social-welfare programs see, for example, Ira Katznelson, *When Affirmative Action Was White: An Untold Story of Racial Inequality in Twentieth-Century America* (New York: Norton, 2005); Linda Gordon, *Pitied but Not Entitled: Single Mothers and the History of Welfare* (New York: Free Press, 1994); Jill Quadagno, *The Color of Welfare: How Racism Undermined the War on Poverty* (New York: Oxford University Press, 1994).

64. Clowse, *Brainpower for the Cold War*, 78–104; Thompson, *National Defense Act of 1958*, Cooper quote 11–12; Congress, House, Subcommittee, *Scholarship and Loan Program*, 581–583, 1350–1360, National Education Association official quote 1360; Congress, Senate, Committee, *Science and Education for National Defense*, state school official quote 699.

65. M. B. Folsom to Mr. Holtman, February 13, 1958, box 71, folder 7, Folsom papers; E. L. Richardson to Harry Byrd, April 4, 1958, box 71, folder 8, Folsom papers; Urban, *More than Science and Sputnik*, 92–94, 157–159, Folsom quote 92, MIT president quotes 93, 158.

66. Thompson, *National Defense Act of 1958*, 78–92; Azza Salama Layton, "International Pressure and the U.S. Government's Response to Little Rock," *Arkansas Historical Quarterly* 56, no. 3 (1997): 257–272; Clowse, *Brainpower for the Cold War*, 78–104, Hill quote 97.

67. Clowse, *Brainpower for the Cold War*, 78–138, Eisenhower quote 102, Elliott quote 116; Kerr-Tener, "Eisenhower and Federal Aid to Higher Education"; James Leyerzapf, "Interview with Dr. Arthur S. Flemming on June 2 and 3, 1988, for Dwight Eisenhower Library," transcript, National Archives and Records Administration, 44–46, Washington, DC, https://www.eisenhowerlibrary.gov/sites/default/files/research/oral-histories/oral-history-transcripts/flemming-arthur-504.pdf; "Statement by Arthur Flemming," August 8, 1958, box 101, HEW Statements by Secretary Flemming (2), Arthur S. Flemming Papers, Dwight Eisenhower Presidential Library and Archive, Abilene KS.

68. Clowse, *Brainpower for the Cold War*, 115–138, Richardson quote 117.

69. Clowse, *Brainpower for the Cold War*, 115–138, Eisenhower quote 138; Lawrence Gladieux and Thomas Wolanin, *Congress and the Colleges: The National Politics of Higher Education* (Lexington, MA: Lexington Books, 1976), 3–14; Gale, "National Defense Student Loan Program," 49–70.

70. US Congress, House of Representatives, Subcommittee of the Committee on Appropriations, *Review of Activities under National Defense Education Act: Hearings before the Subcommittee of the Committee on Appropriations*, 86th Cong., 2nd sess., 1960, 4–5; J. E. Ryan to Dwight Eisenhower, October 19, 1959, General File, box 994, 127-D Pro R, Eisenhower, Records as President, White House Central Files, Dwight Eisenhower Presidential Library and Archive, Abilene, KS.

71. John Gardner, interview by Isabel S. Grossner, September 28, 29, 1967, and June 24, 25, 1969, 71, Carnegie Corporation Project, Columbia Center for Oral History, Columbia University, New York; Clowse, *Brain Power for the Cold War,* 139–151, Folsom quote 139, Carl Elliott quote 140, Milton Eisenhower quote 144; "Some Aid, Some Trade," *Time,* September 1, 1958, quote 52; "Trojan Horse in the Schools," *Los Angeles Times,* September 7, 1958, B4.

72. Loss, *Between Citizens and the State,* 157–159; Department of Health, Education, and Welfare, *Office of Education Report on the National Defense Education Act: A Summary of Programs Administered by the Office of Education Submitted Under Public Law 85–864* (Washington, DC: Government Printing Office, 1959), 3.

73. Urban, *More than Science and Sputnik,* 2–4; Congress, House, Subcommittee, *Scholarship and Loan Program,* 1604–1608, quote 1607; Gale, "National Defense Student Loan Program," 49–101; Loss, *Between Citizens and the State,* 121–163.

74. Gale, "National Defense Student Loan Program," 49–101; Loss, *Between Citizens and the State,* 121–163.

75. Department of Health, Education, and Welfare, *Report on the National Defense Education Act,* 4–6; Gale, "National Defense Student Loan Program," 49–101; Loss, *Between Citizens and the State,* 121–163.

76. "How the Principal New or Expanded Programs of the Department of Health, Education, and Welfare Will Be Put into Operation," quote 1, released to press, September 10, 1958, box 8, Education (1), Douglas R. Price Papers, Dwight Eisenhower Papers as President, Dwight Eisenhower Presidential Library and Archive, Abilene, KS; Morse, "How We Got Here from There," 3–15, quotes 7–8, 11; US Congress, House of Representatives, Subcommittees of the Committee on Education and Labor, *National Defense Education Act of 1958 (Administration of): Hearings before Subcommittees of the Committee on Education and Labor,* 86th Cong., 1st sess., 1959, 12–29, testifying staff quote 14.

77. R. H. Eckelberry, "National Defense Education Act," *Journal of Higher Education* 30 (January 1959), quote 54; Gale, "National Defense Student Loan Program," staffer interview quote 140–141, staffer signing policy quote 140; Morse, "How We Got Here from There," 3–15, quotes 3, 5; Loss, *Between Citizens and the State,* 121–163.

78. Morse, "How We Got Here from There," quote 4–5; Gale, "National Defense Student Loan Program," 102–168.

79. Congress, Subcommittees, *National Defense Education Act of 1958 (Administration of),* staff testimony to lawmakers quote 7; Gale, "National Defense Student Loan Program," interview with financial aid director quote 105.

80. Morse, "How We Got Here from There," quote 7.

81. McPherson and Schapiro, *Student Aid Game,* 5–14, aid-packaging quote 7, "un-met" need quote 9; Thelin, "Higher Education's Student Financial Aid," 25–27; Morse, "How We Got Here from There," quote 7.

82. Gale, "National Defense Student Loan Program," 102–168, top official quote 120, regional director quote 134.

83. Morse, "How We Got Here from There," 3–15, quote 10–11; Gale, "National Defense Student Loan Program," 130–168.

84. Gale, "National Defense Student Loan Program," 102–168, personal interview quote 111.

85. Morse, "How We Got Here from There," quote 9; US Congress, House of Representatives, Subcommittees of the Committee on Education and Labor, *National Defense Education Act of 1952 (Administration of—Progress Report No. 2): Subcommittees of the Committee on Education and Labor,* 86th Cong., 1st sess., 1959, 27–29. On campus loyalty oath controversies see, for example, Ellen Schrecker, *No Ivory Tower: McCarthyism and the Universities* (New York: Oxford University Press, 1986).

86. Loss, *Between Citizens and the State,* 121–164.

87. Edwin Walker, "A New Plan for Financing a College Education," *School and Society,* January 7, 1956, reprinted *College Review,* 1956, 16; Albert Kraus, "Banks Promote Student Loans," *New York Times,* May 25, 1958, F1, 9; Joe McCormick, "The Direct Loan Demonstration Program: An Analysis of the Legislative Process Involving Federal Student Loan Policy" (PhD diss., University of Texas at Austin, 1994), 85–92; J. D. Boyd, "History of State Involvement in Financial Aid," in *Perspectives on Financial Aid,* 118–128 (New York: College Entrance Examination Board, 1975); Leonard Manning, "Aid to Education—State Style," *Fordham Law Review* 29, no. 3 (1961): 525–552; Richard Norton Smith, *On His Own Terms: A Life of Nelson Rockefeller* (New York: Random House, 2014), 353–354; Ottman, "Fording SUNY in New York's Political Cauldron"; Judith Glazer, *Nelson Rockefeller and the Politics of Higher Education in New York State* (Albany: Nelson Rockefeller Institute of Government, State University of New York, 1989), 1–14.

88. Manning, "Aid to Education—Federal Fashion"; Gladieux and Wolanin, *Congress and the Colleges,* 3–14; US Congress, House, Subcommittees, *National Defense Education Act of 1952,* 24–25; US Congress, House, Subcommittee, *Review of Activities under National Defense Education Act,* 1–2; Gale, "National Defense Student Loan Program," 49–70, 102–129, officials quote 108, red wagon quote 114; Loss, *Between Citizens and the State,* 121–163; Donald Damron, "The Contributions of Carl D. Perkins on Higher Education Legislation, 1948–1984" (PhD diss., Middle Tennessee State University, 1990), 55–102, 105–106.

89. Loss, *Between Citizens and the State,* 121–163; Loren Pope, "Few of Poor Getting Scholarship Funds," *New York Times,* April 5, 1959, 1, quote 84; "Facts about Women in Higher Education," *Women's Studies Newsletter* 6, no. 1 (1978): 26–28.

90. Albert Kraus, "Education Loans Offer Big Market," *New York Times,* October 12, 1958, F1; Erwin Knoll, "Rising Tuitions Raise Fears Only Rich May Go to College," *Washington Post,* June 21, 1959, A14; "More Student Loans Are Urged," *New York Times,* March 22, 1959, Thackrey and National Merit Scholarship head quoted E9.

91. Morse, "How We Got Here from There," 3, 6.

5. Federally Guaranteed Students

1. "Pride of Wahoo," *Newsweek,* August 19, 1968, 76.

2. Paul Boyajian to Editor, *Washington Post, Washington Evening Star, Washington Daily News,* July 22, 1968, folder FA 2 4 / 25 / 68, box 8; Douglass Cater to Jim Jones, July 15, 1968, folder FA 2 4 / 25 / 68, box 8; Paul Boyajian to Jim [Jones], undated, folder FA 2 4 / 25 / 68, box 8; all in White House Central Files, Lyndon Baines Johnson Presidential Library, Austin, TX (hereafter LBJ-WHCF).

3. Julian Zelizer, *Fierce Urgency of Now: Lyndon Johnson, Congress, and the Battle for the Great Society* (New York: Penguin Books, 2015), 303–324; Allen Matusow, *Unraveling of America: A History of Liberalism in the 1960s* (New York: Harper and Row, 1984), 131–274; G. L. Seligman, Jr., "LBJ versus His Interpreters: A Review Essay," 67, no. 3 (1986): 645–652; M. J. Heale, "The Sixties as History: A Review of the Political Historiography," *Reviews in American History* 33, no. 1 (2005): 133–152; Christopher P. Loss, *Between Citizens and the State: The Politics of American Higher Education in the 20th Century* (Princeton: Princeton University Press, 2012), 165–213; Hugh Davis Graham, "The Ambiguous Transformation: Federal Education Policy and the Second Reconstruction," paper presented at the Annual Meeting of the American Educational Research Association, New York, March 19–23, 1982; Hugh Davis Graham, *Uncertain Triumph: Federal Education Policy in the Kennedy and Johnson Years* (Chapel Hill: University of North Carolina Press, 1984), xv.

4. Roger Geiger, *Research and Relevant Knowledge: American Research Universities Since World War II* (New York: Oxford University Press, 1993), 230–269.

5. Geiger, *Research and Relevant Knowledge*, 230–269.

6. Joe McCormick, "The Direct Loan Demonstration Program: An Analysis of the Legislative Process Involving Federal Student Loan Policy" (PhD diss., University of Texas at Austin, 1994), 85–92; J. D. Boyd, "History of State Involvement in Financial Aid," in *Perspectives on Financial Aid*, 118–128 (New York: College Entrance Examination Board, 1975); Leonard Manning, "Aid to Education—State Style," *Fordham Law Review* 29, no. 3 (1961): 525–552; John F. Morse, "How We Got Here from There," in *Student Loans: Problems and Policy Alternatives*, ed. Lois D. Rice, 3–15 (New York: College Entrance Examination Board, 1977); Jose Chavez, "Presidential Influence on the Politics of Higher Education: The Higher Education Act of 1965" (PhD diss., University of Texas at Austin, 1975), 95–96; US Congress, House, Special Subcommittee on Education, *Higher Education Act of 1965: Hearings before the Special Subcommittee on Education*, 89th Cong., 1st session, 1965, 281–283, 482, 497–500, Allen Marshall quote 281.

7. John H. Watson III, *Company Contributions Primer* (New York: National Industrial Conference Board, 1963). Cited by Merle Curti and Roderick Nash, *Philanthropy in the Shaping of American Higher Education* (New Brunswick, NJ: Rutgers University Press, 1965), 256–258.

8. Carnegie Foundation for the Advancement of Teaching, "Twenty-Six Campuses and the Federal Government," *Educational Record* 44, 95–136; Robert Toth, "U.S. Aid to Universities and Colleges Is Called 'Highly Beneficial,'" *New York Times*, July 7, 1963, 28.

9. James Bryant Conant, *Shaping Educational Policy* (New York: McGraw-Hill, 1964), quote 7. For discussion see Wayne Urban, "James Bryant Conant and the Limits of Educational Planning in California and New York," in *SUNY at Sixty: The Promise of the State University of New York*, ed. John B. Clark, W. Bruce Leslie, and Kenneth P. O'Brien, 190–198 (Albany: State University of New York Press, 2010).

10. Elizabeth Tandy Shermer, "A Fraught Partnership: Business and the Rise of the American Public University," in *Capital Gains: Business and Politics in Twentieth-Century America*, ed. Kim Phillips-Fein and Richard John, 157–178 (Philadelphia: University of Pennsylvania Press, 2016); Clark Kerr, interview by Sharon Zane, February 18 and September 14, 1998, transcript, 1–14, 51–74, quote 1–2; Carnegie Corporation Project, Columbia Center for Oral History, Columbia University, New York.

11. Shermer, "Fraught Partnership"; Elizabeth Tandy Shermer, *Sunbelt Capitalism: Phoenix and the Transformation of American Politics* (Philadelphia: University of Pennsylvania Press,

2013), 184–224; Paddy Riley, "Clark Kerr: From the Industrial to the Knowledge Economy," in *American Capitalism: Social Thought and Political Economy in the Twentieth Century*, ed. Nelson Lichtenstein, 71–87 (Philadelphia: University of Pennsylvania Press, 2006).

12. Shermer, "Fraught Partnership"; Shermer, *Sunbelt Capitalism*, 184–224; Paddy Riley, "Clark Kerr"; Clark Kerr, "The Multiversity: Are Its Several Souls Worth Saving?" *Harper's*, November 1963, 37–42, quote 41.

13. Graham, *Uncertain Triumph*, 3–25; George Kizer, "Federal Aid to Education, 1945–1963," *History of Education Society* 10 (1970): 84–102.

14. Francis Keppel, interview by David McComb, April 21, 1969, bank breaking quote 2, Lyndon Baines Johnson Library Oral History Collection, Lyndon Baines Johnson Presidential Library, Austin, TX (hereafter LBJ-OH); Myer Feldman, interview by Charles T. Morrissey, May 29, 1966, annoyed JFK quote 303, John F. Kennedy Library Oral History Program, John F. Kennedy Presidential Library, Boston; Leonard Buder, "School Aid Plan Costing 9 Billion Goes to Kennedy," *New York Times*, January 7, 1961, Kennedy quote 6; "Text of Report on U.S. Aid to Education," *New York Times*, January 7, 1961, 6; Kizer, "Federal Aid to Education." For discussion see Graham, *Uncertain Triumph*, 3–25; Janet Hansen, "Politics of Federal Scholarships: A Case Study of the Development of General Grant Assistance for Undergraduates" (PhD diss., Princeton University, 1977), 28–40.

15. Graham, *Uncertain Triumph*, 3–25.

16. Dennis Hevesi, "Ex-Rep. Edith Green, 77, Is Dead; Early Opponent of Vietnam War," *New York Times*, April 23, 1987; Naomi Veronica Ross, "Congresswoman Edith Green on Federal Aid to Schools and Colleges" (PhD diss., Pennsylvania State University, 1980), 54–107, letter to reporter quote 65; Kizer, "Federal Aid to Education"; Hansen, "Politics of Federal Scholarships," 28–40; Graham, *Uncertain Triumph*, 22–52.

17. John F. Kennedy, "Special Message to the Congress on Education," February 6, 1962, in *Public Papers of the Presidents of the United States: John F. Kennedy, 1962*, 110–117 (Washington, DC: Government Printing Office, 1963), quote 114. For discussion see Kizer, "Federal Aid to Education"; Hansen, "Politics of Federal Scholarships," 28–40; Graham, *Uncertain Triumph*, 22–52.

18. Ashbrook quoted in "College Aid," *Congressional Almanac Quarterly 1962* (Washington, DC: Congressional Quarterly, 1963), http://library.cqpress.com/cqalmanac/cqal62-1326165; Keppel interview by McComb, transcript, 1–5. For discussion see Graham, *Uncertain Triumph*, 22–52.

19. Graham, *Uncertain Triumph*, 22–52; Glenn Fowler, "Francis Keppel Dies at Age of 73; Was Commissioner of Education," *New York Times*, February 21, 1990. James Conant, interview by Isabel Grossner, April 5 and 13, 1967, transcript, 1–30, 56–61, Carnegie Corporation project; Francis Keppel, interviewed by Isabel S. Grossner on June 18, 1982, transcript, Spencer Foundation Project; Francis Keppel, interviewed by Isabel S. Grossner, June 15, 1967, transcript, Carnegie Corporation Project; all in Columbia Center for Oral History, Columbia University, New York.

20. Graham, *Uncertain Triumph*, 22–52, Bureau of Budget staff quote 39; Anthony J. Celebrezze, first of two interviews by William A. Geoghegan, 1965 [NB: the full date not on transcript or finding agreement, gift agreement signed October 1, 1968], transcript, quote 11, John F. Kennedy Library Oral History Program, John F. Kennedy Presidential Library, Boston; Keppel interview by McComb, quote 5.

21. Keppel interview by McComb, quote 5; John F. Kennedy, "Special Message to the Congress on Education," January 29, 1963, *The American Presidency Project*, University of California,

Santa Barbara, https://www.presidency.ucsb.edu/documents/special-message-the-congress
-education; Kizer, "Federal Aid to Education"; Hansen, "Politics of Federal Scholarships,"
28–40; Ross, "Congresswoman Edith Green," 44–46; Graham, *Uncertain Triumph*, 26–52;
Muhammad Attaullah Chaudhry, "Higher Education Act of 1965: An Historical Case
Study" (PhD diss., Oklahoma State University, 1981), 54–57.

22. Lyndon Baines Johnson, "Remarks upon Signing the Higher Education Facilities Act," December 16, 1963, in *Lyndon B. Johnson: Containing the Public Messages, Speeches, and Statements of the President: 1963–64* (Washington, DC: Government Printing Office, 1965–1970), book 1, 57–58, quote 58.

23. Zelizer, *Fierce Urgency of Now*, 303–324; Matusow, *Unraveling of America*, 131–274; Seligman, "LBJ versus His Interpreters"; Heale, "Sixties as History"; Loss, *Between Citizens and the State*, 165–213; Graham, *Uncertain Triumph*, xiii–xxiv; Stephen Brock, "A Comparative Study of Federal Aid to Higher Education: The Higher Education Act of 1965 and Project Upward Bound" (PhD diss., Cornell University, 1968), 9–20; Edward Berkowitz, "Great Society," in *American Congress: The Building of Democracy*, ed. Julian Zelizer, 566–583 (New York: Houghton Mifflin, 2004); Christie Bourgeois, "Stepping over Lines: Lyndon Johnson, Black Texans, and the National Youth Administration, 1935–1937," *Southern Historical Quarterly* 91 (1987): 149–172; Elizabeth Tandy Shermer, "From Educator- to Creditor-in-Chief: The American Presidency, Higher Education, and the Student Loan Industry," in *The President and American Capitalism*, ed. Mark Rose and Roger Biles, 123–150 (Gainesville: University of Florida Press, 2018); Elizabeth Tandy Shermer, "Sunbelt Patriarchs: Lyndon Baines Johnson, Barry Goldwater, and the Unraveling of America," in *The Liberal Consensus Reconsidered: American Politics and Society in the Postwar Era*, ed. Robert Mason and Iwan Morgan (Gainesville: University of Florida Press, 2017).

24. Morse, "How We Got Here from There," quote 12–13; Loss, *Between Citizens and the State*, 165–213; Brock, "Comparative Study of Federal Aid to Higher Education," 9–20; Chavez, "Presidential Influence," 93–94.

25. LBJ quote from Bill Moyers, *Moyers on America: A Journalist and His Times* (New York: New Press, 2004), 167. Also see Shermer, "Sunbelt Patriarchs"; John Tower, interview by Joe Frantz, August 8, 1971, LBJ-OH.

26. Loss, *Between Citizens and the State*, 165–213; Lyndon Johnson, "Commencement Address at the University of Michigan," May 22, 1964, http://lbjmuseum.com/university-of-michigan/; Graham, *Uncertain Triumph*, 53–83.

27. Graham, *Uncertain Triumph*, 53–83; Shermer, "Sunbelt Patriarchs."

28. Shermer, "Sunbelt Patriarchs"; Shermer, *Sunbelt Capitalism*, 270–301.

29. Zelizer, *Fierce Urgency of Now*, 61–84, 163–224; Graham, *Uncertain Triumph*, 53–83, 110–131.

30. Chavez, "Presidential Influence," 50–75, 92–95; Elizabeth Tandy Shermer, "Financing Security and Opportunity: The New Deal and the Origins of the Millennial Student Debt Crisis," in *Capitalism Contested: The New Deal and Its Legacies*, ed. Romain Huret, Nelson Lichtenstein, and Jean-Christian Vinel (Philadelphia: University of Pennsylvania Press, 2020).

31. Graham, *Uncertain Triumph*, 53–83; Chaudhry, "Higher Education Act of 1965," 67–122; Brock, "Comparative Study of Federal Aid to Higher Education," 21–50; Francis Keppel, "The Higher Education Acts Contrasted, 1965–1986: Has Federal Policy Come of Age?" *Harvard Educational Review* 57, no. 1 (1987): 49–67; Chavez, "Presidential Influence," 50–75; Clark Kerr, interview by Janet Kerr-Tener, August 12, 1985, 6–9, LBJ-OH; Keppel interview by McComb, 6–14.

32. Matthew Lassiter, "De Jure / De Facto Segregation: The Long Shadow of a National Myth," in *The Myth of Southern Exceptionalism,* ed. Matthew D. Lassiter and Joseph Crespino, 25–48 (New York: Oxford University Press, 2010); Graham, *Uncertain Triumph,* 53–83; Keppel, "Higher Education Acts Contrasted," 49–67; Marjorie Hunter, "Conferees Clear College Aid Bill," *New York Times,* October 15, 1965, 28; Fred Hechinger, "Education," *New York Times,* June 13, 1965, E8; Kerr interview, August 12, 1985, quote 10–11.

33. Graham, *Uncertain Triumph,* 53–83; Brock, "Comparative Study of Federal Aid to Higher Education," 21–50.

34. Keppel, "Higher Education Acts Contrasted"; Chavez, "Presidential Influence," 50–75, 92–95.

35. Chavez, "Presidential Influence," 50–75, 92–95; Shermer, "Financing Security and Opportunity."

36. Keppel interview by McComb, quote 27; Graham, *Uncertain Triumph,* 53–83; Chaudhry, "Higher Education Act of 1965," 56–58, 67–122.

37. Report on lunch with Green quote from Bill Moyers to Larry O'Brien, memo, January 13, 1965, Box 1, Education [1 of 2], Office Files of Bill Moyers, Papers of Lyndon Baines Johnson President, 1963–1969, Lyndon Baines Johnson Presidential Library, Austin, TX (hereafter LBJ-Papers); Graham, *Uncertain Triumph,* 53–83; Chaudhry, "Higher Education Act of 1965," 67–122; US Congress, House, *Higher Education Act of 1965,* 577–581, 608–640, 651–672, CUNY official quote 578, Lawrence Rogin quote 651; US Congress, Senate, Subcommittee on Education, *Higher Education Act of 1965: Hearings before the Subcommittee on Education,* 89th Congress, 1st sess., 1965, 632–648, 351–356.

38. US Congress, House, *Higher Education Act of 1965,* 28–39, 78–79, 119–120, 201–215, 475–481, 701–712, 753–763, Celebrezze quote 28, Green quote 119, Hill quote 203; Hechinger, "Education"; US Congress, Senate, *Higher Education Act of 1965,* 354–363, 370–371, 385–386, Stahr quote 354.

39. US Congress, House, *Higher Education Act of 1965,* 504–527.

40. US Congress, House, *Higher Education Act of 1965,* 41–42, 58–59.

41. US Congress, House, *Higher Education Act of 1965,* 306–340, 454–465, 482–492, expert quotes 456, 457.

42. US Congress, House, *Higher Education Act of 1965,* 48–53, 621–622, land-grant and state university representative quote 622; Morse, "How We Got Here from There"; Graham, *Uncertain Triumph,* 53–83; Chavez, "Presidential Influence," 89–92; US Congress, Senate, *Higher Education Act of 1965,* 361–362, 374–375, American Council on Education quote 374; Stanley Surrey to Douglass Cater, April 12, 1965, enclosures, box 43, Tax Credit for College Tuition, Office Files of Douglass Cater, LBJ-Papers; William Steif, "College Group Pushing for Tuition Credit Plan," unpaginated clipping, [*Pittsburgh Press,* January 17, 1964].

43. Graham, *Uncertain Triumph,* 53–83; Brock, "Comparative Study of Federal Aid to Higher Education," 21–50.

44. US Congress, House, *Higher Education Act of 1965,* 42–44; Brock, "Comparative Study of Federal Aid to Higher Education," 21–50; US Congress, Senate, *Higher Education Act of 1965,* 129–130, Keppel quote 129.

45. US Congress, Senate, *Higher Education Act of 1965,* 113–116, 181–199, 312–326, 369–370, 647–648, 847–855, Celebrezze quotes 114, 119, Indiana University official quote 369, land-grant administrator quote 648.

46. Barbara Gale, "National Defense Student Loan Program: Its History, Significance, and Problems" (PhD diss., George Washington University, 1974), 102–129, interview with Deakins quotes 116, 118; US Congress, Senate, *Higher Education Act of 1965*, 118–122, Keppel quote 122.

47. US Congress, House, *Higher Education Act of 1965*, 281–294, USAF quote 284; Chaudhry, "Higher Education Act of 1965," 67–122; Brock, "Comparative Study of Federal Aid to Higher Education," 21–50; Morse, "How We Got Here from There," 14–15; Graham, *Uncertain Triumph*, 53–83; Chavez, "Presidential Influence," 95–123.

48. Chaudhry, "Higher Education Act of 1965," 67–122; Brock, "Comparative Study of Federal Aid to Higher Education," 21–50; Morse, "How We Got Here from There," 14–15; Graham, *Uncertain Triumph,* 53–83; Chavez, "Presidential Influence," 95–123; "Banks Urged to Up Loans on Education," *Washington Post,* March 2, 1965, B6; US Congress, Senate, *Higher Education Act of 1965,* 118–122, 1008–1027, 1093–1111, 1028–1057, Javits quote 1021.

49. Chaudhry, "Higher Education Act of 1965," 67–122; Brock, "Comparative Study of Federal Aid to Higher Education," 21–50; Morse, "How We Got Here from There," 14–15; Graham, *Uncertain Triumph,* 53–83; Chavez, "Presidential Influence," 95–123; Elsie Carper, "House Unit Passes School Bill, Changes Key Provisions," *New York Times,* May 19, 1965, C8.

50. Mrs. Jack Fingerhut to Lyndon Johnson, April 21, 1965, and Joe Wood to Lyndon Johnson, April 29, 1965, both in box 45, FI 5-6-1 11/22/63-5/31/65; Marie Newberry to Lyndon Johnson, August 20, 1965; Judy Moore to President Johnson, August 5, 1965, and Karen Slentz to Lyndon Johnson, July 7, 1965, all three in box 45, FI 5-6-1 6/1/65-9/30/65; all in LBJ-WHCF.

51. Graham, *Uncertain Triumph,* 81–83; Shermer, "Financing Security and Opportunity"; Shermer, "From Educator- to Creditor-in-Chief"; Harold Howe II, interview by David G. McComb, October 29, 1968, transcript, 8–9, quote 8, LBJ-OH; Andrew Painter, "Banker Opportunity under the Higher Education and Vocational Acts of 1965," Guaranteed Higher Education Loans forum, Installment Credit Committee of the Connecticut Bankers Association, transcript, quote 6, box 250, "HEA of 1965, Title IV, Part BB-Insured Student Loans," Edith Green Papers, Davies Family Research Library, Oregon Historical Society, Portland, OR (hereafter Green papers).

52. Graham, *Uncertain Triumph,* 81–83; Shermer, "Financing Security and Opportunity"; Shermer, "From Educator- to Creditor-in-Chief"; Chavez, "Presidential Influence," 95–123.

53. Graham, *Uncertain Triumph,* 81–83. See Douglass Cater Papers, boxes 34, 43; James Gaither Papers, boxes 227, 229; White House Central Files, box 37, folders marked LE/FA2; all in LBJ Presidential Library, Austin, TX. See also Suzanne Mettler, *Degrees of Inequality: How the Politics of Higher Education Sabotaged the American Dream* (New York: Basic Books, 2014), 61–63, 219n28.

54. Graham, *Uncertain Triumph,* 53–83; American Bankers Association, press release, September 3, 1965, box 247, "Higher Education General," Green papers.

55. "8.7 Millions Due Colleges in Illinois," *Chicago Tribune,* November 25, 1965, B24; Nathan Spivak, "Higher Education Act of 1965, to Be Signed Today, Extends Aid to New Areas," *Wall Street Journal,* November 8, 1965, 4; William Trombley, "State Education Leaders Puzzled by School Bill," *Los Angeles Times,* November 14, 1965, F1–2; "D.C. to Get $1.3 Million School Aid," *Washington Post,* November 11, 1965, K4.

56. Trombley, "State Education Leaders Puzzled by School Bill"; Spivak, "Higher Education Act of 1965"; Gerald Grant, "College Hopeful?" *Washington Post,* December 9, 1965, H6; "Aid—A New U.S. Concept," *New York Times,* November 14, 1965, E9.

57. Johnson, "Remarks at Southwest State College," 1102–1105. For discussion, see Shermer, "Financing Security and Opportunity"; Shermer, "From Educator- to Creditor-in-Chief."

58. Keppel, "Higher Education Acts Contrasted"; Graham, *Uncertain Triumph,* 53–83; Morse, "How We Got Here from There"; Shermer, "Financing Security and Opportunity"; Shermer, "From Educator- to Creditor-in-Chief."

59. Keppel, "Higher Education Acts Contrasted"; Graham, *Uncertain Triumph,* 53–83; Morse, "How We Got Here from There"; Shermer, "Financing Security and Opportunity"; Shermer, "From Educator- to Creditor-in-Chief."

60. Keppel, "Higher Education Acts Contrasted"; Graham, *Uncertain Triumph,* 53–83; Morse, "How We Got Here from There"; Bruce Johnstone, "Federally Sponsored Student Loans: An Overview of Issues and Policy Alternatives," in *Student Loans: Problems and Policy Alternatives,* ed. Lois D. Rice, 16–41 (New York: College Entrance Examination Board, 1977).

61. Charles Walker to Douglass Cater, November 16, 1966, box 44, FI 5–6 Schools—Institutions of Higher Learning, LBJ-WHCF; Peter Muirhead, Memorandum for Honorable Douglass Cater, October 12, 1965, box 38, LE/FA2 5/20/65-10/16/65, LBJ-WHCF; Office of Education, "The Higher Education Act: A Chance and a Challenge," Opening Address at the Nine Regional Information Briefings, 1965, 3, box 70, HEA of 1965, Department of Health, Education and Welfare, 1963–1969, Lyndon Baines Johnson Presidential Library (hereafter LBJ-HEW); [Office of Education], Invitations to the Higher Education Act Information Sessions, undated, Opening Address at the Nine Regional Information Briefings, box 70, HEA of 1965, LBJ-HEW; Harold Howe, Memorandum for Honorable Douglass Cater, Subject: The Guaranteed Loan Program, April 17, 1966, box 245, FG 165-4 Education, Office of 3/31/66-8/9/66, LBJ-WHCF; Morse, "How We Got Here from There," 14, 15; Howe interview by McComb, 7; Graham, *Uncertain Triumph.* Also see Douglass Cater Papers, boxes 34, 43; James Gaither Papers, boxes 227, 229; and White House Central Files, box 37, folders marked LE/FA2; all in LBJ Presidential Library, Austin, TX. See also C. E. Deakins to Peter Muirhead, memo, "Activity Report for the Insured Loan Branch," March 10, 1966, box 250, "HEA of 1965, Title IV, Part BB-Insured Student Loans," Green papers.

62. Memorandum for the Honorable Douglass Cater, September 12, 1967, box 245, FG 165-4 Education, Office of 4/25/67-10/12/67, LBJ-WHCF; financier quoted in William Reddig, "Tight Money Crisis Engulfs Students Asking College Aid," unpaginated, undated clipping, [August 11, 1966], box 139, "1966: Guaranteed Loan Program," Green papers; Edward Gannon, "A Look at the Student Loan Program," *Banking: Journal of the American Bankers Association,* July 1966, reprint, Box 269, "Guaranteed Loan Programs," Green papers; "3 Banks Stop Lending to Collegians," unpaginated clipping, [*Washington Post,* September 1966], box 351, Higher Education, Office Files of James Gaither, LBJ-Papers; Joseph Barr, Memorandum to the President with enclosures, Guaranteed Student Loan Program, box 43, Guaranteed Loan Program, LBJ-HEW; Division of Student Financial Aid Insured Loan Branch, Student Loan Notes, Number 1, June 8, 1967, box 126, Low Interest Insurance Loans & Interest Benefits–Higher Ed., LBJ-HEW.

63. Barr, Memorandum to the President; James Moore, Memorandum for the Honorable Douglass Cater, September 12, 1967, box 550, Guaranteed Student Loan, Office Files of Frederick Panzer, LBJ-Papers; Graham, *Uncertain Triumph,* 110–180; Graham, "Ambiguous Transformation"; Gale, "National Defense Student Loan Program," 102–129, interview Education Office staff quote 119; Howe interview by McComb, quote on September deadline and program's popularity, 8–9. For Green's mail, see box 137, "1966: Student Loans," Green papers.

64. Telegrams and letters labeled NDEASLP; E. S. Lyons to Edith Green, April 14, 1966; Michael Swozzi to Edith Green, March 27, 1966; Mildred Cummings to Edith Green, March 4, 1966; Eugene Moen to Edith Green, March 27, 1966; Mr. and Mrs. Robert Sleister to Edith Green, March 19, 1966; Joyce Owens to Edith Green, March 11, 1966; all in box 137, "1966: Student Loans," Green papers.

65. Graham, *Uncertain Triumph*, 110–202; Graham, "Ambiguous Transformation"; Gale, "National Defense Student Loan Program," 102–129; Sally Davenport, "Smuggling-In Reform: Equal Opportunity and the Higher Education Act, 1965–1980" (PhD diss., Johns Hopkins University, 1983), 156–166; Lawrence Gladieux and Thomas Wolanin, *Congress and the Colleges: The National Politics of Higher Education* (Lexington, MA: Lexington Books, 1976), 15–32; Sam Halperin, interview by David McComb, February 24, 1969, 17, LBJ-OH. [Office of Education], Comparison of Relative Federal Government Costs for NDEA and Guarantee Student Loan Programs, October 14, 1967, and Office of Education, Comparison of Total Costs to Federal Government NDSL and Guarantee Loan Program, September 19, 1967, both in box 43, Guaranteed Loan Program, LBJ-HEW.

66. Halperin interview by David McComb, 17; Graham, *Uncertain Triumph*, 132–202; Gladieux and Wolanin, *Congress and the Colleges*, 15–32; Davenport, "Smuggling-in Reform," 156–166.

67. Graham, *Uncertain Triumph*, 203–226; Geiger, *Research and Relevant Knowledge*, 198–229; Loss, *Between Citizens and the State*, 165–213, quote 175.

68. Gene Osiri, "Student Loans Go to Affluent," *Baltimore Sun*, unpaginated clipping, August 1, 1968, box 269, "Guaranteed Loan Programs," Green papers; Graham, *Uncertain Triumph*, 203–226; Geiger, *Research and Relevant Knowledge*, 198–229; Loss, *Between Citizens and the State*, 165–213; Adolph Slaughter, "Education: 'The Poor Get Poorer,'" *Chicago Defender*, June 11, 1966, 2; Carolyn Lewis, "New Player in the Cast," *Washington Post*, March 27, 1966, F10; "5 Year Science Project Under Way at Atlanta Universities," *Chicago Defender*, September 24, 1966, 34; "University Exchange Project Gets U.S. $$," *Chicago Defender*, October 23, 1965, 9; Rosemarie Brooks, "Negro College Heads Ungrateful," *Chicago Defender*, November 2, 1965, 2. Edith Green to Harold Pfautz, November 18, 1965, and Harold Pfautz to Edith Green, November 5, 1965; both in box 139, "Higher Education Act of 1965 General" [folder 1 of 2], Green papers.

69. Howe interview by McComb, quote 13; Loss, *Between Citizens and the State*, 165–213; Caroline Ratcliffe and Signe-Mary McKernan, "Forever in Your Debt: Who Has Student Loan Debt, and Who's Worried?" report, *Urban Institute*, June 26, 2013, https://www.urban.org/research/publication/forever-your-debt-who-has-student-loan-debt-and-whos-worried; Brandon Jackson and John Reynolds, "The Price of Opportunity: Race, Student Loan Debt, and College Achievement," *Sociological Inquiry* 83, no. 3 (2013): 335–368; Raj Chetty, John N. Friedman, Emmanuel Saez, Nicholas Turner, and Danny Yagan, "Mobility Report Cards: The Role of Colleges in Intergenerational Mobility," National Bureau of Economic Research Working Paper 23618, July 2017; Fenaba R. Addo, Jason N. Houle, and Daniel Simon, "Young, Black, and (Still) in the Red: Parental Wealth, Race, and Student Loan Debt," *Race and Social Problems* 8, no. 1 (2016): 64–76; Rachel Fishman, "The Wealth Gap PLUS Debt: How Federal Loans Exacerbate Inequality for Black Families," blog post, *New America Foundation*, May 15, 2018, https://www.newamerica.org/education-policy/reports/wealth-gap-plus-debt/; Aissa Canchola and Seth Frotman, "The Significant Impact of Student Debt on Communities of Color," blog post, Consumer Financial Protection Bureau, September 15, 2016,

https://www.consumerfinance.gov/about-us/blog/significant-impact-student-debt
-communities-color/; Michal Grinstein-Weiss, Dana C. Perantie, Samuel H. Taylor, Shenyang
Guo, and Ramesh Raghavan, "Racial Disparities in Education Debt Burden among Low- and
Moderate-Income Households," *Children and Youth Services Review* 65 (2016): 166–174,
Darrick Hamilton, William Darity, Jr., Anne E. Price, Vishnu Sridharan, and Rebecca Tippett, "Umbrellas Don't Make It Rain: Why Studying and Working Hard Isn't Enough for
Black Americans," report, New School, Duke University Center for Social Equity and In-
sight Center for Community Economic Development, April 2015, http://ww1.insightcced
.org/uploads/CRWG/Umbrellas-Dont-Make-It-Rain8.pdf; William R. Emmons and Bryan J.
Noeth, "Why Didn't Higher Education Protect Hispanic and Black Wealth?" *In the Balance, Federal Reserve Bank of St. Louis,* August 5, 2015, 1–3; Kim Dancy, "Mind the Gap: How
Higher Education Contributes to Gender Wage Disparities," blog post, *New America Foundation,* May 11, 2017, https://www.newamerica.org/education-policy/edcentral/mind-gap-gender
-wage-disparities.

70. Thomas D. Snyder, "120 Years of American Education: A Statistical Portrait," report, US Department of Education Office of Educational Research and Improvement, January 1993,
63–94.

71. Morse, "How We Got Here from There," 15; Keppel, "The Higher Education Acts
Contrasted."

72. Cara Pesek, "New Life on a Once-Crumbling Campus," *Lincoln Journal Star,* April 18,
2004, http://journalstar.com/news/local/new-life-on-a-once-crumbling-campus/article
_abf32e6a-e94c-5487-9931-9b4f828cb774.html; Virginia Sapiro, "When the End Comes to
Higher Education Institutions, 1890–2019," blog post, Sapiro website, February 28, 2019, http://
blogs.bu.edu/vsapiro/2019/02/28/when-the-end-comes-to-higher-education-institutions-1890
-2019/; Virginia Sapiro, "The Life Course of Higher Education Institutions: When the End
Comes," unpublished manuscript, 2019, 5–9, http://blogs.bu.edu/vsapiro/files/2019/02
/SapiroWhentheEndComes2019-1.pdf.

6. Reauthorizing the Loan Industry

1. Andrew Pognany to The President [Richard Nixon], July 25, 1972, Alpha Name Files:
Cavanaugh, James, box 15, folder: Education Guaranteed Student Loan Program, White
House Central Files, Richard Nixon Presidential Library, Yorba Linda, CA (hereafter
Nixon-WHCF).

2. [Signature Missing] to Richard Nixon, July 22, 1972; and Fred Jaeger to Richard Nixon,
April 16, 1972, both in Alpha Name Files: Cavanaugh, James, box 15, folder: Education Guaranteed Student Loan Program, Nixon-WHCF.

3. Edward Cannon to Bill Thomas, undated memo, Alpha Name Files: Cavanaugh, James, box
15, folder: Education Guaranteed Student Loan Program, Nixon-WHCF; Bruce Schulman,
The Seventies: The Great Shift in American Culture, Society, and Politics (New York: Da Capo
Press, 2002), 1–52; Nelson Lichtenstein, *State of the Union: A Century of American Labor*
(Princeton: Princeton University Press, 2002), 212–245; Christopher P. Loss, *Between Citi-
zens and the State: The Politics of American Higher Education in the 20th Century* (Princeton:
Princeton University Press, 2012), 165–234.

4. Schulman, *The Seventies;* Lichtenstein, *State of the Union,* 212–245; Bruce J. Schulman and
Julian E. Zelizer, eds., *Rightward Bound: Making America Conservative in the 1970s* (Cam-

bridge, MA: Harvard University Press, 2008); Judith Stein, *Pivotal Decade: How the United States Traded Factories for Finance in the Seventies* (New Haven: Yale University Press, 2010); Beth Bailey and David Farber, eds., *America in the Seventies* (Lawrence: University Press of Kansas, 2004); Jefferson Cowie, "Vigorously Left, Right, and Center: The Crosscurrents of Working-Class America in the 1970s," in *America in the Seventies*, ed. Bailey and Farber, 75–106; Howard Brick, *Transcending Capitalism: Visions of a New Society in Modern American Thought* (Ithaca, NY: Cornell University Press, 2006), 219–274; Jennifer Klein, *For All These Rights: Business, Labor, and the Shaping of America's Public-Private Welfare State* (Princeton: Princeton University Press, 2003), 258–276; Doug Rossinow, *Visions of Progress: The Liberal-Left Tradition in America* (Philadelphia: University of Pennsylvania Press, 2009), 233–260; Michael Kazin, *American Dreamers: How the Left Changes a Nation* (New York: Vintage Books, 2011), 209–251.

5. John Douglass, "Higher Education as a National Resource: A Retrospective on the Influence of the Carnegie Commission and Council on Higher Education," *Change* 37, no. 5 (2005): 30–38; Earl Cheit, *New Depression in Higher Education: A Study of Financial Conditions at 41 Colleges and Universities* (New York: McGraw-Hill, 1971), Table 1 in unpaginated fore-word, quote xviii; Walter Adams, "Financing Public Higher Education," *American Economic Review* 67, no. 1 (1977): 86–89, quote 86; Lawrence E. Gladieux and Thomas R. Wolanin, *Congress and the Colleges: The National Politics of Higher Education* (Lexington, MA: Lexington Books, 1976), 15–32.

6. Patricia Gumport, "Graduate Education and Research: Independence and Strain," in *American Higher Education in the Twenty-First Century: Social, Political, and Economic Challenges*, ed. Philip G. Altbach, Robert O. Berdahl, and Patricia J. Gumport (Baltimore: Johns Hopkins University Press, 1999), 396–426; Joseph Creech and Jerry Sheehan Davis, "Merit-Based versus Need-Based Aid: The Continual Issues for Policymakers," in *Financing a College Education: How It Works, How It's Changing*, ed. Jacqueline King, 120–136 (Phoenix: American Council on Education Oryx Press, 1999); Cheit, *New Depression*, viii–xi; Aims C. McGuinness, "The States and Higher Education," in *American Higher Education*, ed. Altbach, Berdahl, and Gumport, 183–215; Loss, *Between Citizens and the State*, 214–234; Martin Trow, "American Higher Education: Past, Present, and Future," *Educational Researcher* 17, no. 3 (1988): 13–23.

7. William H. Honan, "Claiborne Pell, 90, Patrician Senator behind College Grant Program, Dies," *New York Times*, January 2, 2009, A21; G. Wayne Miller, *Uncommon Man: The Life and Times of Senator Claiborne Pell* (Hanover, NH: University Press of New England, 2011), 10–33, 128–188, biographer quote 188; Gladieux and Wolanin, *Congress and the Colleges*, 83–116, Pell quote 86.

8. Gladieux and Wolanin, *Congress and the Colleges*, 83–116, quote 85; Christopher Michael Kiernan, "Federal Aid to Education: The Pell Grant Program in Historical Perspective" (EdD diss., Boston College, 1992), 191–231.

9. Gladieux and Wolanin, *Congress and the Colleges*, 83–116; Kiernan, "Federal Aid to Education," 191–231; Janet Hansen, "Politics of Federal Scholarships: A Case Study of the Development of General Grant Assistance for Undergraduates" (PhD diss., Princeton University, 1977), 170–221, quote 195–196; Miller, *Uncommon Man*, 101–187.

10. Gladieux and Wolanin, *Congress and the Colleges*, 83–116; Kiernan, "Federal Aid to Education," 191–231; Hansen, "The Politics of Federal Scholarships," 170–221; Miller, *Uncommon Man*, 101–187.

11. Gladieux and Wolanin, *Congress and the Colleges,* 83–116, Pell's sense of himself quote 89; Kiernan, "Federal Aid to Education," 191–231, Pell's placement idea quote 205.

12. Gladieux and Wolanin, *Congress and the Colleges,* 83–116; Kiernan, "Federal Aid to Education," 191–231; Hansen, "Politics of Federal Scholarships," 170–221, aides quote 195–196.

13. Gladieux and Wolanin, *Congress and the Colleges,* 83–116; Kiernan, "Federal Aid to Education," 191–231; Hansen, "Politics of Federal Scholarships," 170–221.

14. Gladieux and Wolanin, *Congress and the Colleges,* 57–82, Nixon aides all quoted 63.

15. Schulman, *The Seventies,* 1–52; Robert Collins, *More: The Politics of Economic Growth* (Oxford: Oxford University Press, 2000), 98–165; Meg Jacobs, "The Politics of Environmental Regulation: Business-Government Relations in the 1970s," in *What's Good for Business: Business and American Politics since World War II,* ed. Julian E. Zelizer and Kim Phillips-Fein, 212–232 (New York: Oxford University Press, 2012); Terry Anderson, *The Pursuit of Fairness: A History of Affirmative Action* (New York: Oxford University Press, 2004), 111–161; Gladieux and Wolanin, *Congress and the Colleges,* 66–83; Robert E. Osborne, "President Nixon and Higher Education Policy Making: Influences and Achievements, 1969–1974" (PhD diss., University of Tulsa, 1990), 83–127.

16. Gladieux and Wolanin, *Congress and the Colleges,* 57–82, Finch quote 60; Associated Press, "Robert H. Finch, 70, Nixon Aide and Former Cabinet Secretary," *New York Times,* October 11, 1995; Osborne, "President Nixon and Higher Education Policy Making," 83–127; "Confidential Report of the Task Force on Education," January 3, 1969, 21, box: Pre-Presidential Task Force Reports, folder: Task Force on Education, Nixon-WHCF.

17. Gladieux and Wolanin, *Congress and the Colleges,* 57–82; McCormick, "Direct Loan Demonstration Program," 20–66, 98–104; Patrick Mungovan, "Role of the U.S. Federal Government in the Student Loan Industry" (MA thesis, MIT Sloan School, 2005), 26–30; Robert W. Hartman, "The National Bank Approach to Solutions," in *Student Loans,* ed. Rice, 74–88; "Confidential Report of the Task Force on Education," quote 17.

18. Erin Dillon, "Leading Lady: Sallie Mae and the Origins of Today's Student Loan Controversy," report, Education Sector, May 2007, 2–3, https://www.immagic.com/eLibrary/ARCHIVES/GENERAL/EDSCTRUS/E070514D.pdf; Gladieux and Wolanin, *Congress and the Colleges,* 57–82; Mungovan, "Role of the U.S. Federal Government," 26–30; John Dean, Saul Moskowitz, and Karen Cipriani, "Implications of the Privatization of Sallie Mae," *Journal of Public Budgeting, Accounting, and Financial Management* 11, no. 1 (1999): 56–80, esp. 56–57; Charles Finn, Memorandum for Ed Morgan, November 24, 1969, FI-5-6-1m box 49, folder: [EX] FI 5-6-1 Credit-Loans / Schools-Institutions of Higher Learning / Student-Teacher [1 of 3], White House Subject Files, Richard Nixon Presidential Library, Yorba Linda, CA (hereafter Nixon-WHSF).

19. Paige Glotzer, *How the Suburbs Were Segregated: Developers and the Business of Exclusionary Housing, 1890–1960* (New York: Columbia University Press, 2020); Richard Rothstein, *The Color of the Law: A Forgotten History of How Our Government Segregated America* (New York: W. W. Norton, 2017); Lewis Hyman, *Debtor Nation: The History of America in Red Ink* (Princeton: Princeton University Press, 2011), 173–219; Gladieux and Wolanin, *Congress and the Colleges,* 57–82; Mungovan, "Role of the U.S. Federal Government," 26–30.

20. Gladieux and Wolanin, *Congress and the Colleges,* 57–82, Nixon aides quote 62–63.

21. Gladieux and Wolanin, *Congress and the Colleges,* 57–82; Frederick Malek, Address to Fifth National College Relations Conference of the National Alliance of Businessmen, March 20, 1970, Alpha Name Files: Malek, Frederic, Series 1, box 7, folder: Speech-Dallas, Nixon-WHCF; Confidential Report of the Task Force on Education, January 3, 1969, quote 17; Ken Cole to

John Ehrlichman, memo with attachment, December 31, 1970, FI5-6, box 48, folder: FI5-6 Credit-Loans/Schools, Institutions of Higher Learning, Nixon-WHSF.

22. Gladieux and Wolanin, *Congress and the Colleges,* 57–82; Confidential Report of the Task Force on Education, January 3, 1969; Ken Cole to John Ehrlichman, memo with attachment, December 31, 1970, FI5-6, box 48, folder: FI5-6 Credit-Loans/Schools, Institutions of Higher Learning, Nixon-WHSF.

23. Richard M. Nixon, "Special Message to the Congress on Higher Education," February 22, 1971, The American Presidency Project, University of California, Santa Barbara, https://www.presidency.ucsb.edu/documents/special-message-the-congress-higher-education.

24. Gladieux and Wolanin, *Congress and the Colleges,* 57–82; Osborne, "President Nixon and Higher Education Policy Making," 83–127.

25. US Congress, House, Subcommittee on Postsecondary Education, *Higher Education Amendments of 1969,* 91st Cong., 1st sess., 1969, Pell quote 1153; Gladieux and Wolanin, *Congress and the Colleges,* 57–82, "mortgage their future" quote 72, White House staff quote 74; Hansen, "The Politics of Federal Scholarships," 170–221; Remarks on Office Log No. 40—Higher Education Legislation, undated, Alpha Name Files: Timmons, William, box 68, folder Higher Education S.3636, H.R. 16621, 18849, Nixon-WHCF.

26. Gladieux and Wolanin, *Congress and the Colleges,* 83–220, Pell quote 94.

27. Gladieux and Wolanin, *Congress and the Colleges,* 57–82; Bart Barnes, "Elliott Richardson Dies at 79," *Washington Post,* January 1, 2000; Elliott Richardson, interview by Frederick Graboske, Washington, DC, May 31, 1988, Nixon Project Oral Histories, Richard Nixon Presidential Library and Museum, Yorba Linda, CA.

28. Gladieux and Wolanin, *Congress and the Colleges,* 57–82; US Congress, House, Special Subcommittee on Education, *Higher Education Amendments of 1971,* 92nd Cong., 1st sess., 1971, Green quote 204.

29. Robert Cohen, "The New Left's Love-Hate Relationship with the University," in *The Port Huron Statement: Sources and Legacies,* ed. Nelson Lichtenstein and Richard Flacks (Philadelphia: University of Pennsylvania Press, 2015), 107–126; Michael Kazin and Maurice Isserman, *America Divided: The Civil War of the 1960s* (New York: Oxford University Press, 2004), 269–300; Michael Kazin, *The Populist Persuasion: An American History* (New York: Basic Books, 1995), 195–220; Ruth Rosen, *The World Split Open: How the Modern Women's Movement Changed America* (New York: Penguin Books, 2000), 63–262; Wesley Hogan, *Many Minds, One Heart: SNCC's Dream for a New America* (Chapel Hill: University of North Carolina Press, 2007); Bethany Moreton, "Make Payroll, Not War: Business Culture as Youth Culture," in Schulman and Zelizer, *Rightward Bound,* 52–70; John A. Andrew III, *The Other Side of the Sixties: Young Americans for Freedom and the Rise of Conservative Politics* (New Brunswick, NJ: Rutgers University Press, 1997), 205–220; US Congress, House, Special Subcommittee, *Higher Education Amendments,* 598–623, 644–677; US Congress, Senate, Subcommittee on Education, *Education Amendments of 1972,* 92nd Cong., 1st sess., 1971, 1392–1393, 1670–75, student quote 1393.

30. US Congress, Senate, Subcommittee, *Education Amendments,* Pell quote 612, Javits quote 760; Gladieux and Wolanin, *Congress and the Colleges,* 35–56; "College-Aid Measure Includes a Set-Up Similar to Fannie Mae," *Wall Street Journal,* August 9, 1971, 4; William Stevens, "Confusion Is Delaying Federal Student Loans," *New York Times,* September 18, 1972, reporter quote 53.

31. Gladieux and Wolanin, *Congress and the Colleges,* 35–56.

32. Gladieux and Wolanin, *Congress and the Colleges,* 83–116, quote 98.

33. Gladieux and Wolanin, *Congress and the Colleges,* 83–116.

34. Gladieux and Wolanin, *Congress and the Colleges,* 83–116, quote 92; Hansen, "Politics of Federal Scholarships," 170–221.

35. US Congress, House, Special Subcommittee, *Higher Education Amendments,* 447–485; US Congress, Senate, Subcommittee, *Education Amendments,* 759–761, 2418–2461, 2526–2534, 1506–1521, 1635–1640, NYU president quote 748, junior college administrator quote 2418, higher education associations representative quote 2460, larger private university president quote 1640.

36. US Congress, Senate, Subcommittee, *Education Amendments,* private college head quote 1508; US Congress, House, Special Subcommittee, *Higher Education Amendments,* 141–208; Gladieux and Wolanin, *Congress and the Colleges,* 83–116; Hansen, "Politics of Federal Scholarships," 170–221; Clark Kerr, interview by Sharon Zane, February 18 and September 14, 1998, transcript, 16–38, 74–88, Carnegie Corporation Project, Columbia Center for Oral History, Columbia University, New York.

37. Philip W. Semas, "Associations Not Helpful, Pell Charges," *Chronicle of Higher Education,* August 2, 1971, Pell quote 3; Eric Wentworth, "Education Aid to Be Reviewed," *Washington Post,* January 12, 1970, A2; Gladieux and Wolanin, *Congress and the Colleges,* 127–134; Naomi Veronica Ross, "Congresswoman Edith Green on Federal Aid to Schools and Colleges" (PhD diss., Pennsylvania State University, 1980), 54–144, Green quote 142; Hansen, "Politics of Federal Scholarships," 170–221; John Skrentny, *Minority Rights Revolution* (Cambridge, MA: Harvard University Press, 2004), 240–243.

38. Gladieux and Wolanin, *Congress and the Colleges,* 127–134; Ross, "Congresswoman Edith Green on Federal Aid," 54–144; Anderson, *Pursuit of Fairness,* 161–216.

39. Ross, "Congresswoman Edith Green on Federal Aid," 54–144.

40. *Congressional Record,* 24 April 1969, Green quote 10230–10231. For discussion see Ross, "Congresswoman Edith Green on Federal Aid," 54–108.

41. *Congressional Record* 118 (1972), Green quote 20283. For discussion see Hansen, "Politics of Federal Scholarships," 170–221; Ross, "Congresswoman Edith Green on Federal Aid," 54–108; Gladieux and Wolanin, *Congress and the Colleges,* 127–134; Schulman, *The Seventies,* 23–52, 102–120.

42. Ira Katznelson, *When Affirmative Action Was White: An Untold Story of Racial Inequality in Twentieth-Century America* (New York: Norton, 2005); Lichtenstein, *State of the Union,* 212–276; Eleanor Krause and Isabel Sawhill, "Seven Reasons to Worry about the American Middle Class," blog post, Brookings Institution, June 5, 2018, https://www.brookings.edu/blog/social-mobility-memos/2018/06/05/seven-reasons-to-worry-about-the-american-middle-class/; Gladieux and Wolanin, *Congress and the Colleges,* 127–134; Ross, "Congresswoman Edith Green on Federal Aid," 54–144, quote 142; Hansen, "The Politics of Federal Scholarships," 170–221. Bernie Granger to Edith Green, March 5, 1971; Gene Lieberman to Edith Green, March 3, 1971; and other letters in box 312, Higher Education Act Letters, Support HR 7248, Series B, Green; and box 198, Student Financial Assistance, Series A, Edith Green Papers, Davies Family Research Library, Oregon Historical Society, Portland, OR (hereafter Green papers).

43. Gladieux and Wolanin, *Congress and the Colleges,* 127–140.

44. Gladieux and Wolanin, *Congress and the Colleges*, 83–144; Robert McFadden, "John Brademas, Indiana Congressman and N.Y.U. President, Dies at 89," *New York Times*, July 11, 2016; Bill Salisbury, "Al Quie: A Life in the Middle," *Pioneer Press*, November 6, 2015, https://www.twincities.com/2013/09/17/al-quie-a-life-in-the-middle/.

45. Skrentny, *Minority Rights Revolution*, 230–248, feminist quote 247; Eric Wentworth, "Women Seek Equality in Universities," *Washington Post*, June 22, 1970, A15; Edwards, "Why Sport? The Development of Sport as a Policy Issue in Title IX of the Education Amendments of 1972," *Journal of Policy History* 22, no. 3 (2010): 300–336; Aaron Zitner, "Rep. Patsy Mink, 74; Legislator from Hawaii," *Los Angeles Times*, September 29, 2002; Elissa Gootman, "Patsy Mink: Veteran Hawaii Congresswoman, Dies at 74," *New York Times*, September 30, 2002.

46. US Congress, Senate, Subcommittee, *Education Amendments*, 2407–2418, American Association of University Women quote 2412; Skrentny, *Minority Rights Revolution*, 230–248, Bayh quote 245; Robert Blaemire, *Birch Bayh: Making a Difference* (Bloomington: University of Indiana Press, 2019), 206–221.

47. *Congressional Record*, August 6, 1971, Dominick quote 30407. For discussion see Skrentny, *Minority Rights Revolution*, 230–248; Gladieux and Wolanin, *Congress and the Colleges*, 83–116, 131–134.

48. Gladieux and Wolanin, *Congress and the Colleges*, 83–121; Don Clausen to the president, July 17, 1969, FHA-mechanism quoted 1, FI5-6, box 48, folder: GEN FI5-6 Credit-Loans/Schools, Institutions of Higher Learning [1 of 2], Nixon-WHSF; Memorandum on Higher Education Bill, April 6, 1970, quote 1, Alpha Name Files: Timmons, William, box 68, folder Higher Education S.3636, H.R. 16621, 18849, Nixon-WHCF (and see the rest of this folder for education experts and college administrators outlining why they could not originate loans).

49. Gladieux and Wolanin, *Congress and the Colleges*, 83–121; "House Approves Plan to Increase Lending to College Students," *Wall Street Journal*, October 29, 1971, 4; "Smith to Propose a New Student Loan Law," *Chicago Tribune*, August 17, 1970, Illinois Republicans quote 20; Wentworth, "Education Aid to Be Reviewed"; "College-Aid Measure Includes a Set-Up Similar to Fannie Mae," *Wall Street Journal*, August 9, 1971, 4; "Plan for Expanded Loans to Students Is Cleared by House Education Panel," *Wall Street Journal*, September 30, 1971, 15; US Congress, Senate, Subcommittee, *Education Amendments*, 2470–2526; US Congress, House, Special Subcommittee, *Higher Education Amendments*, 644–672, banker quote 666. For correspondence examples, see G. C. Stewart to Edith Green, May 8, 1969; Jack Rapp to Edith Green, July 1970; Roma Niel to Edith Green, July 28, 1970; and other letters in box 281, HR 13194 Green and Quie Guaranteed School Loan Program, Series B, Green papers.

50. Edith Green to Charles Walker, July 20, 1970, box 281, HR 13194 Green and Quie Guaranteed School Loan Program, Series B, Green papers; US Congress, Senate, Subcommittee, *Education Amendments*, White House aides quote 438, educators quote 757, Pell quote 756; Gladieux and Wolanin, *Congress and the Colleges*, 83–121; Eric Wentworth, "Hill Fight Looms over Education Aid as Senate Democrats Introduce Bill," *Washington Post*, February 9, 1971, A2.

51. David Trivett, "Proprietary Schools and Postsecondary Education," ERIC Higher Education Research Report No. 2, American Association of Higher Education, 1974; "Profits an Issue in School Ruling," *New York Times*, July 27, 1969, 56; Gene Maeroff, "Regents' Higher-Education Plan Lists Roles for Private Schools," *New York Times*, September 7, 1972, 26.

52. Suzanne Mettler, *Degrees of Inequality: How the Politics of Higher Education Sabotaged the American Dream* (New York: Basic Books, 2014), 33–34, 92–93; US Congress, Senate, Subcommittee, *Education Amendments*, 695–712, 1461–1633, 2383–2385, 2407–2418, HEW official quote 710, American Vocational Association president quote 1582, American Association of University Women representative quote 2411; Trivett, "Proprietary Schools and Postsecondary Education"; "Remarks by Senator Claiborne Pell (D-R.I.) Before the New England Board of Higher Education Conference," December 16, 1971 (typescript), p. 7, box 3, folder 53, Subsection Education: Speeches 1969–1975, Pell; "Remarks of Senator Claiborne Pell to the Rhode Island Business Educators Association—November 15, 1975," 7–8, box 3, folder 54, Subsection Education: Speeches 1969–1975, Senatorial Papers of Claiborne Pell: Congresses 1960–1997, University of Rhode Island Library, Special Collections and University Archives, Kingston, RI (hereafter Pell papers).

53. Brian J. Daugherity and Charles C. Bolton, eds., *With All Deliberate Speed: Implementing Brown v. Board of Education* (Fayetteville: University of Arkansas Press, 2008); Gladieux and Wolanin, *Congress and the Colleges*, 149–160; Skrentny, *Minority Rights Revolution*, 247–248.

54. John N. Erlenborn and anonymous colleague quoted in Marjorie Hunter, "Rep. Carl D. Perkins Dies at 71; Led the Fight for Social Programs," *New York Times*, August 4, 1984; Gladieux and Wolanin, *Congress and the Colleges*, 161–206, Perkins quote 173; Donald Damron, "The Contributions of Carl D. Perkins on Higher Education Legislation, 1948–1984" (PhD diss., Middle Tennessee State University, 1990), 55–102.

55. Gladieux and Wolanin, *Congress and the Colleges*, 161–206, quote 170; Damron, "Contributions of Carl D. Perkins," 55–102.

56. Gladieux and Wolanin, *Congress and the Colleges*, 161–206; Skrentny, *Minority Rights Revolution*, 247–249.

57. Gladieux and Wolanin, *Congress and the Colleges*, 161–206.

58. Gladieux and Wolanin, *Congress and the Colleges*, 161–206.

59. Gladieux and Wolanin, *Congress and the Colleges*, 161–206.

60. Gladieux and Wolanin, *Congress and the Colleges*, 207–220; Claiborne Pell, Conference Report Statement, p. 13, box 1, folder 19, Subsection Education: Speeches 1969–1975, Pell papers.

61. Gladieux and Wolanin, *Congress and the Colleges*, 207–220, lobbyist quote 209, subcommittee member quote 210, staff and congressman quoted 211, assistant quote 217. For concerns and frustrations of college administrators, see contents of box 215, Higher Education Conference Report folders 1–5, Series A, Green papers.

62. Gladieux and Wolanin, *Congress and the Colleges*, senate aide quote 104, aide frustrated about busing quote 217; Osborne, "President Nixon and Higher Education Policy Making," 128–173, aides urging Nixon to fight quote 146, Richardson quote 147.

63. Gladieux and Wolanin, *Congress and the Colleges*, 103–106, 207–220, quote 104, Richardson quote 212, Nixon quote 218–219; Caspar Weinberger, Memorandum for the President, June 19, 1972, Alpha Name Files: Cavanaugh, James, box 15, folder: Education Higher (DGM), Nixon-WHCF; for educators' pleas, see FA3, box 20, folder: GEN FA3 Education 5-1-72-6-30-72, Nixon-WHSF.

64. Richard Nixon, Statement on Signing the Education Amendments of 1972, June 23, 1972, in *Public Papers of the Presidents of the United States: Richard Nixon, Containing the Public Messages, Speeches, and Statements of the President, 1972* (Washington, DC: US Government Printing Office, 1974), 701–703.

65. Miller, *Uncommon Man,* Pell remarks to Senate quote 172; Herbert Stein, "Women's Second Economic Revolution," *Ladies' Home Journal,* October 1972, 28; Gerald Grant, "Universal BA?" *New Republic,* June 24, 1972, 13–16, quote 16.

66. Gladieux and Wolanin, *Congress and the Colleges,* 223–248, Marland quote 232. For contemporaneous news coverage, see Eric Wentworth, "Washington: The Higher Education Act and Beyond," *Change* 4, no. 7 (1972): 10, 63–64; "House Sends Nixon Bill That Would Brake Busing for Integration Pending All Appeals," *Wall Street Journal,* June 9, 1972, 5; Eric Wentworth, "New Programs to Make Mark on Education," *Washington Post,* June 24, 1972, A4; "Breakthrough for Higher Education," *Washington Post,* May 21, 1972, B6; Arthur Siddon, "Amendments Obscure Measure," *Chicago Tribune,* May 30, 1972, A14; Jonathan Spivak, "Money Isn't Everything," *Wall Street Journal,* July 13, 1972, 36.

67. Harold Jenkins, "Legislative-Executive Disagreement: Interpreting the 1972 Amendments to the Guaranteed Student Loan Program," *Harvard Journal on Legislation* 10 (1973): 467–485, National Association of Student Financial Aid Administrators quote 478. See also Gladieux and Wolanin, *Congress and the Colleges,* 223–248; Memorandum to Caspar Weinberger, August 18, 1972, Nixon-WHCF. For evidence of Americans' frustrations with the changes, see box 312, Financials Assistance folders 1–5, Series B, Green papers; Alpha Name Files: Cavanaugh, James, box 15, folder: Education Guaranteed Student Loan Program, Nixon-WHCF; FI-5-6-1, box 49, folder: [GEN] FI 5-6-1 Credit-Loans/Schools-Institutions of Higher Learning/Student-Teacher [4 of 5], Nixon-WHSF.

68. Gladieux and Wolanin, *Congress and the Colleges,* 223–248; Jenkins, "Legislative-Executive Disagreement," 467–485, quote 481; US Congress, House, Special Subcommittee on Education, *Guaranteed Student Loan Program,* 92nd Cong., 2nd sess., 1972.

69. Gladieux and Wolanin, *Congress and the Colleges,* 223–248; Jenkins, "Legislative-Executive Disagreement," 467–485.

70. Gladieux and Wolanin, *Congress and the Colleges,* 223–248, quote 235; Hansen, "Politics of Federal Scholarships," 42–49.

71. Erik Patashnik, "Congress and the Budget since 1974," in *American Congress: The Building of Democracy,* ed. Julian E. Zelizer, 668–686 (New York: Houghton Mifflin, 2004); Osborne, "President Nixon and Higher Education Policy Making," 128–173, quote 163; Gladieux and Wolanin, *Congress and the Colleges,* 223–248; Hansen, "The Politics of Federal Scholarships," 42–49.

72. Gladieux and Wolanin, *Congress and the Colleges,* 223–248, Green on financial aid quote 238; Sally Davenport, "Smuggling-In Reform: Equal Opportunity and the Higher Education Act, 1965–1980" (PhD diss., Johns Hopkins University, 1983), 179–233; Ross, "Congresswoman Edith Green on Federal Aid," 54–107; "Rep. Edith Green Gives Up Post on Education Panel," *Chronicle of Higher Education,* January 22, 1973, Green's resignation quote 3. For protests about the 1973 budget from academics and lawmakers, see FI-5-6-1, box 49, folder: [GEN] FI 5-6-1 Credit-Loans/Schools-Institutions of Higher Learning/Student-Teacher [5 of 5], Nixon-WHSF.

73. Gladieux and Wolanin, *Congress and the Colleges,* 223–248, quote 243; Kiernan, "Federal Aid to Education, 191–231," 259–261.

74. "Sallie Mae's Initial Offer Is Scooped Up by Traders," *Wall Street Journal,* October 3, 1973, skeptical and excited dealers quote 25; "Sallie Mae Reschedules 1st Offering," *Washington Post,* September 27, 1973, D16; "Sallie Mae Will Offer $105 Million of Common," *Wall Street Journal,* July 17, 1973, 35; Edwin Dale, "U.S. Student-Loan Unit Schedules Stock Offering," *New York Times,* July 17, 1973, reporter quote 53; George Gunset, "'Sallie Mae' Chief Here to

Seek Support," *Chicago Tribune,* July 27, 1973, C12; "Student Loan Agency to Offer $100 Million of Notes Next Tuesday," *Wall Street Journal,* September 27, 1973, 31.

75. Thelin, "Higher Education's Student Financial Aid Enterprise in Historical Perspective," in *Footing the Tuition Bill: The New Student Loan Sector,* ed. Frederick M. Hess, 19–41 (Washington, DC: AEI Press, 2007), quote 33; Hartman quote in Hartman, "National Bank Approach to Solutions," 78.

76. "Unrepaid Student Loans," *Chicago Tribune,* January 5, 1972, 16; Robert Cole, "Students' Defaults," *New York Times,* March 30, 1972, 55; Elizabeth Fowler, "Students with Loans for Education in Arrears Facing Action by Lenders," *New York Times,* June 19, 1972, 51; "Defaults Zooming on Student Loans," *US News and World Report,* May 15, 1972, 86.

7. Bankers Lose Their Sweetheart Deal

1. Stanley Ikenberry and Terry Hartle, *Too Little Knowledge Is a Dangerous Thing: What the Public Thinks and Knows about Paying for College* (Washington, DC: American Council on Education, 1998), v, 2.

2. Ikenberry and Hartle, *Too Little Knowledge,* quotes 12, vi, 2, 5.

3. Ikenberry and Hartle, *Too Little Knowledge,* quotes 10, 11, 12.

4. Michael Mumper, "The Student Aid in Industry," in *Financing a College Education: How It Works, How It's Changing,* ed. Jacqueline E. King, 64–77 (Westport, CT: American Council on Education / Oryx Press, 1999).

5. Ruy Teixeira, William H. Frey, and Robert Griffin, "States of Change: The Demographic Evolution of the American Electorate, 1974–2060," report, Center for American Progress and American Enterprise Institute, February 2015, https://cdn.americanprogress.org/wp-content/uploads/2015/02/SOC-report1.pdf; Nikki Graf, Anna Brown, and Eileen Patten, "The Narrowing, but Persistent, Gender Gap in Pay," blog post, Pew Research Center, March 22, 2019, https://www.pewresearch.org/fact-tank/2019/03/22/gender-pay-gap-facts/; Rachel Fishman, "The Wealth Gap PLUS Debt: How Federal Loans Exacerbate Inequality for Black Families," blog post, *New America* Foundation, May 15, 2018; Kevin Miller, "Deeper in Debt: Women and Student Loans," report, American Association of University Women, May 2017.

6. Roger Geiger, *Research and Relevant Knowledge: American Research Universities since World War II* (New York: Oxford University Press, 1993), 230–309; Aims C. McGuinness, Jr., "The States and Higher Education," in *American Higher Education in the Twenty-First Century: Social, Political, and Economic Challenges,* ed. Philip G. Altbach, Robert O. Berdahl, and Patricia J. Gumport, 183–215 (Baltimore: Johns Hopkins University Press, 1999); Elizabeth Tandy Shermer, "*The Great Persuasion: Reinventing Free Markets since the Depression* by Angus Burgin; *Masters of the Universe: Hayek, Friedman, and the Birth of Neoliberal Politics* by Daniel Stedman Jones; *Markets in the Name of Socialism: The Left-Wing Origins of Neoliberalism* by Johanna Bockman," books review, *Journal of Modern History* 86, no. 4 (2014): 884–890; Elizabeth Tandy Shermer, "Books Review: The Ongoing Crisis in American Colleges," *European Journal of American Culture* 37, no. 1 (2018): 90–94.

7. Thomas D. Snyder, "120 Years of American Education: A Statistical Portrait," report, US Department of Education, Office of Educational Research and Improvement, January 1993, fig. 20, p. 71; Geiger, *Research and Relevant Knowledge,* 230–338; McGuinness, "States and Higher Education"; Devin Fergus, *Land of the Fee: Hidden Costs and the Decline of the Amer-*

ican Middle Class (New York: Oxford University Press, 2018), 64–66, 70–75; Sara Goldrick-Rab, *Paying the Price: College Costs, Financial Aid, and the Betrayal of the American Dream* (Chicago: University of Chicago Press, 2016), 1–11, 39–65, 83–118, 139–163; Beth Akers and Matthew Chingos, *Game of Loans: The Rhetoric and Reality of Student Debt* (Princeton: Princeton University Press, 2016), 40–62, esp. 50; Patrick Mungovan, "Role of the U.S. Federal Government in the Student Loan Industry" (MA thesis, MIT Sloan School, 2005), 2–10; Lawrence Gladieux and Jacqueline King, "The Federal Government and Higher Education," in *American Higher Education in the Twenty-First Century: Social, Political, and Economic Challenges,* ed. Philip G. Altbach, Robert O. Berdahl, and Patricia J. Gumport, 151–182 (Baltimore: Johns Hopkins University Press, 1999); Patricia Gumport, "Graduate Education and Research: Independence and Strain," in *American Higher Education,* ed. Altbach, Berdahl, and Gumport, 396–426; Joseph Creech and Jerry Sheehan Davis, "Merit-Based versus Need-Based Aid: The Continual Issues for Policymakers," in *Financing a College Education: How It Works, How It's Changing* ed. Jacqueline King, 120–136 (Phoenix: American Council on Education Oryx Press, 1999); Christopher P. Loss, *Between Citizens and the State: The Politics of American Higher Education in the 20th Century* (Princeton: Princeton University Press, 2012), 214–234; Martin Trow, "American Higher Education: Past, Present, and Future," *Educational Researcher* 17, no. 3 (1988): 13–23.

8. Snyder, "120 Years of American Education," fig. 20, p. 71; John Lee and Sue Cleary, "Key Trends in Higher Education," *American Academic* 1, no. 1 (2004): 21–36, quote 23; Fergus, *Land of the Fee,* 70–75; Goldrick-Rab, *Paying the Price,* 1–11, 39–65, 83–118, 139–163; Akers and Chingos, *Game of Loans,* 40–62; Mungovan, "Role of the U.S. Federal Government," 2–10; Gladieux and King, "Federal Government and Higher Education," 151–182; David Labaree, "A System without a Plan: Emergence of an American System of Higher Education in the Twentieth Century," *Bildungsgeschichte: International Journal for the Historiography of Education* 3, no. 1 (2013): 46–59; Geiger, *Research and Relevant Knowledge,* 230–309; McGuinness, "The States and Higher Education," 183–215.

9. Geiger, *Research and Relevant Knowledge,* 310–338; Creech and Davis, "Merit-Based versus Need-Based Aid," 120–136; Fergus, *Land of the Fee,* 56–59; Loss, *Between Citizens and the State,* 214–238, figures A.2 and A.3; Trow, "American Higher Education"; Nelson Lichtenstein, *State of the Union: A Century of American Labor* (Princeton: Princeton University Press, 2002), 212–245; Suzanne Mettler, *Degrees of Inequality: How the Politics of Higher Education Sabotaged the American Dream* (New York: Basic Books, 2014), 32–34.

10. Snyder, "120 Years of American Education," figs. 4, 8, 10; Geiger, *Research and Relevant Knowledge,* 310–338; Creech and Davis, "Merit-Based versus Need-Based Aid," 120–136; Fergus, *Land of the Fee,* 56–59; Loss, *Between Citizens and the State,* 214–238, figures A.2 and A.3; Trow, "American Higher Education"; Lichtenstein, *State of the Union,* 212–245; Joe Lew McCormick, "Direct Loan Demonstration Program: An Analysis of the Legislative Process Involving Federal Student Loan Policy" (PhD diss., University of Texas at Austin, 1994), 85–98; Susan Hannah, "The Higher Education Act of 1992: Skills, Constraints, and the Politics of Higher Education," *Journal of Higher Education* 67, no. 5 (1996): 498–527; Mettler, *Degrees of Inequality,* 32–34; Kenneth Cooper, "Student Loan Defaults Soaring," *Washington Post,* September 4, 1991, A17.

11. Snyder, "120 Years of American Education," figs. 4, 8, 10; McCormick, "Direct Loan Demonstration Program," 85–98; Hannah, "Higher Education Act of 1992," 508; Mettler, *Degrees of Inequality,* 32–34; Cooper, "Student Loan Defaults Soaring," quote A17.

12. Sally Davenport, "Smuggling-In Reform: Equal Opportunity and the Higher Education Act, 1965–1980" (PhD diss., Johns Hopkins University, 1983), 234–265; Michael Mumper, "The Transformation of Federal Aid to College Students: Dynamics of Growth and Retrenchment," 16, no. 3 (Winter 1991): 315–331; Selma Sa'di Van Eyck, "Political Forces that Shaped the Middle Income Student Assistance Act of 1978" (PhD diss., University of Wisconsin, 1983), 33–142, lawmaker quote 129; Erin Dillon, "Leading Lady: Sallie Mae and the Origins of Today's Student Loan Controversy," report, Education Sector, May 2007, 1–4; Mungovan, "Role of the U.S. Federal Government," 9–10; Hannah, "Higher Education Act of 1992," 507–510.

13. Van Eyck, "Political Forces," 33–142.

14. Dillon, "Leading Lady," 1–4; Davenport, "Smuggling-In Reform," 234–264; Mumper, "Transformation of Federal Aid," 318–326; Van Eyck, "Political Forces," 33–142; Michael Parsons, *Power in Politics: Federal Higher Education Policymaking in the 1990s* (Albany: State University of New York Press, 1997), 57–59.

15. Elizabeth Tandy Shermer, "Collapse or Triumph? A Sixty-Year Assessment of the Modern American Conservative Movement," *American Studies Journal* 65 (2018), http://www .asjournal.org/65-2018/; Elizabeth Tandy Shermer, "Who Is Wagging Whom? Power and the New History of American Populism," *Historical Journal* 57, no. 3 (2014): 1–29; Ellie Shermer, "American Conservatism: A Historiographic Renaissance without Much of a Reconsideration," *Journal of American Studies* 46, no. 2 (2012): 481–488.

16. Mumper, "Transformation of Federal Aid," 321–327; Francis Keppel, "The Higher Education Acts Contrasted, 1965–1986: Has Federal Policy Come of Age?" *Harvard Educational Review* 57, no. 1 (1987): 49–67; Susan Boren et al., *The Higher Education Amendments of 1986: A Summary of Provisions* (Washington, DC: Library of Congress, 1987); Dillon, "Leading Lady," 1–4; Mungovan, "Role of the U.S. Federal Government," 9–10; Hannah, "Higher Education Act of 1992," 507–510; McCormick, "Direct Loan Demonstration Program," 85–90; Fergus, *Land of the Fee,* 6–7, 54–58.

17. Keppel, "The Higher Education Acts Contrasted"; Boren, "Higher Education Amendments of 1986"; Derek Price, *Borrowing Inequality: Race, Class, and Student Loans* (Boulder: L. Rienner, 2004), 33–36.

18. Fergus, *Land of the Fee,* 52–68, Bennett quote 63; David G. Savage, "IRS Confiscates Tax Refunds to Cover Defaulted Loans," *Los Angeles Times,* June 5, 1986, quote 17.

19. Stockman testimony quoted in "A Chat with Dave Stockman," *Columbia Daily Spectator,* October 12, 1981, 1, 3. For discussion see Fergus, *Land of the Fee,* 52–68.

20. Terrel H. Bell, *The Thirteenth Man: A Reagan Cabinet Memoir* (New York: Free Press, 1988), quote 36; T. H. Bell to Ed Meese, January 11, 1982, with unpaginated attachments, "Proposed Changes in Coverage of Title VI, Title IX, and Section 504" and untitled document listing calculations [quoted] as well as other documents in box 56, OA11832, Edwin Meese Collection, Ronald Reagan Presidential Library and Archive, Simi Valley, CA. For discussion see Fergus, *Land of the Fee,* 52–68.

21. Parsons, *Power and Politics,* quote 58; Dillon, "Leading Lady," 1–44; Mungovan, "Role of the U.S. Federal Government," 9–10; Hannah, "Higher Education Act of 1992," 507–510; Price, *Borrowing Inequality,* 27–44; Keppel, "Higher Education Acts Contrasted," 57; Elizabeth Tandy Shermer, "Banking on Government," in *To Promote the General Welfare: The Case for Big Government,* ed. Steven Conn, 65–84 (New York: Oxford University Press, 2012).

22. Joanne Eggert to William Ford, April 19, 1982; Betty Zebecke to William Ford, May 9, 1982; James Lemieux to William Ford, October 8, 1982; Nina Justman to William Ford, May 17, 1982; William Schudlich to William Ford, April 20, 1982; Mike Baldwin to William Ford, April 26, 1982; all in Series 3, Subseries Education & Labor Committee, box 98, folder: Education—Student Aid '82 (f2), William Ford Papers, University of Michigan Archives, Ann Arbor, MI (hereafter Ford papers).

23. Fergus, *Land of the Fee*, 70–75; Goldrick-Rab, *Paying the Price*, 1–11, 39–65, 83–118, 139–163; Akers and Chingos, *Game of Loans*, 40–62; Mungovan, "Role of the U.S. Federal Government," 2–10; Gladieux and King, "Federal Government and Higher Education," 151–182; Hannah, "Higher Education Act of 1992," 508–509; Michael S. McPherson and Morton Owen Schapiro, *The Student Aid Game: Meeting Need and Rewarding Talent in American Higher Education* (Princeton: Princeton University Press, 1998), 108–110.

24. Keppel, "Higher Education Acts Contrasted," quotes 58 and 64; John F. Morse, "How We Got Here from There," in *Student Loans: Problems and Policy Alternatives*, ed. Lois D. Rice, 3–15 (New York: College Entrance Examination Board, 1977), quote 14.

25. Elizabeth Tandy Shermer, *Sunbelt Capitalism: Phoenix and the Transformation of American Politics* (Philadelphia: University of Pennsylvania Press, 2013), 161–176; Kevin Sack, "Nunn, Model Southern Democrat, to Retire from Senate Next Year," *New York Times,* October 10, 1995; Parsons, *Power and Politics,* 107–113.

26. US Congress, Senate, Permanent Subcommittee on Investigations, *Abuses in Federal Student Aid Programs,* 101st Cong., 2nd sess., 1990, 1–3, 81–100, Floridian quote 81.

27. Senate, Permanent Subcommittee on Investigations, *Abuses in Federal Student Aid Programs,* Nunn quote 2; Jill Zuckman, "Education: Nunn Blasts Loan System in Long-Awaited Critique," *CQ Weekly,* May 18, 1991, Ford quote 1288; Kenneth Cooper, "Curbing Student Loan Defaults," *Washington Post,* May 20, 1991, A9; Hilary Stout, "Senate Panel Urges 'Drastic' Reforms for Federal Guaranteed Student Loans," *Wall Street Journal,* May 21, 1991, A24; Parsons, *Power and Politics,* 107–113; Mettler, *Degrees of Inequality,* 96–98; McCormick, "Direct Loan Demonstration Program," 20–66, 96–116; Dillon, "Leading Lady," 3–6.

28. McCormick, "Direct Loan Demonstration Program," 20–66, 96–116; Parsons, *Power and Politics,* 104–107.

29. McCormick, "Direct Loan Demonstration Program," 20–66, 96–116; Dillon, "Leading Lady," 3–6; Parsons, *Power and Politics,* 104–107; Elizabeth Van Nostrand, "U.S. Student Loan Program Buried by Mountain of Debt," *Newsday,* December 31, 1990, 24; "Sallie Mae to Manage 3-Year HEAF Wind Down," *Wall Street Journal,,* November 5, 1990, C15; Kenneth Cooper and Albert Crenshaw, "Student Loan Guarantor Calls for Federal Help," *Washington Post,* July 24, 1990, A5; Anthony Flint, "Cracks in Student-Loan System Kansas-Based Foundation Cause for Concern Along Wall Street," *Boston Globe,* August 3, 1990.

30. Mumper, "Student Aid Industry," Califano quote 68; McCormick, "Direct Loan Demonstration Program," 20–66, 96–116, Education Department official interview quote 111.

31. Dillon, "Leading Lady," lawyer quote 3.

32. McCormick, "Direct Loan Demonstration Program," 20–66, 98–104.

33. Johnson aide quoted in Paul Southwick to Joe Califano, September 7, 1966, memo, box 351, Higher Education, Office Files of James Gaither, Papers of Lyndon Baines Johnson President, 1963–1969, Lyndon Baines Johnson Presidential Library, Austin, TX; Parsons, *Power in Politics,* 135–137; Carnegie Council on Policy Studies in Higher Education, *Next Steps for the 1980s in Student Financial Aid* (San Francisco: Jossey-Bass, 1979), quote 210; McCormick,

"Direct Loan Demonstration Program," 98–128; W. Lee Hansen and Suzanne Feeney, "New Directions in State Loan Programs for Postsecondary Students," in *Student Loans: Problems and Policy Alternatives,* ed. Lois Rice, 48–66 (New York: College Entrance Examination Board, 1977), esp. 55–56.

34. McCormick, "Direct Loan Demonstration Program," 20–66, 96–134, 175–185; Dillon, "Leading Lady," 3–6; Parsons, *Politics and Power,* 137–138.

35. McCormick, "Direct Loan Demonstration Program," 96–134, 175–178, staff's assessment of Darman quotes 116 and 173, aide's impression of Alexander quote 175; Dillon, "Leading Lady," 3–6.

36. McCormick, "Direct Loan Demonstration Program," 96–134; Hannah, "Higher Education Act of 1992," 498–527; US Congress, House, Subcommittee on Postsecondary Education, *Hearing on the Reauthorization of the Higher Education Act of 1965: Sallie Mae—Safety and Soundness,* 102nd Cong., 1st sess., 1991; US Congress, House, Subcommittee on Postsecondary Education, *Hearing on the Reauthorization of the Higher Education Act of 1965: Pell Grants,* 102nd Cong., 1st sess., 1991; US Congress, House, Subcommittee on Postsecondary Education, *Hearing on the Reauthorization of the Higher Education Act of 1965: Title IX, Trip and State Student Incentive Grants, and Campus-Based Programs,* 102nd Cong., 1st sess., 1991; US Congress, House, Subcommittee on Postsecondary Education, *Hearing on the Reauthorization of the Higher Education Act of 1965: Stafford Loans,* 102nd Cong., 1st sess., 1991; US Congress, House, Subcommittee on Postsecondary Education, *Hearing on the Reauthorization of the Higher Education Act of 1965: Program Integrity,* 102nd Cong., 1st sess., 1991; US Congress, House, Subcommittee on Postsecondary Education, *Hearing on the Reauthorization of the Higher Education Act of 1965: Title V,* 102nd Cong., 1st sess., 1991; US Congress, House, Subcommittee on Postsecondary Education, *Hearing on the Reauthorization of the Higher Education Act of 1965: Titles III and VIII,* 102nd Cong., 1st sess., 1991; US Congress, House, Subcommittee on Postsecondary Education, *Hearing on the Reauthorization of the Higher Education Act of 1965: Titles VII and X,* 102nd Cong., 1st sess., 1991; US Congress, House, Subcommittee on Postsecondary Education, *Hearing on the Reauthorization of the Higher Education Act of 1965: Titles I, VI, and XI,* 102nd Cong., 1st sess., 1991; US Congress, House, Subcommittee on Postsecondary Education, *Hearing on the Reauthorization of the Higher Education Act of 1965: Need Analysis,* 102nd Cong., 1st sess., 1991; US Congress, House, Subcommittee on Postsecondary Education, *Hearing on H.R. 2336, the Income-Dependent Assistance Act and H.R. 3050, the Self-Reliance Scholarship Act,* 102nd Cong., 2nd sess., 1992; US Congress, Senate, Committee on Labor and Human Resources, *Access to Higher Education: Increasing Pell Grants and Widening Opportunities,* 102nd Cong., 1st sess., 1991; US Congress, Senate, Committee on Labor and Human Resources, *Reauthorization of the Higher Education Act of 1965,* pts 1–2, 102nd Cong., 1st sess., 1991; US Congress, Senate, Committee on Labor and Human Resources, *Federal Direct Student Loans,* 102nd Cong., 2nd sess., 1992.

37. Thomas DeLoughry, "Preparation Pays Off as Students Address Lawmakers with Testimony on Aid," *Chronicle of Higher Education,* March 27, 1991; Parsons, *Power and Politics,* 124–126; Untitled document, box 103, Testimony Higher Education, Ford papers.

38. McCormick, "Direct Loan Demonstration Program," 96–200, Education Department staffer quote 145, Coleman quote 159, Democratic aide quote 161; Dillon, "Leading Lady," 3–6; Thomas Wolanin, "Reauthorizing the Higher Education Act: Federal Policy Making for Postsecondary Education," 89–105, in *National Issues in Education: The Past Is Prologue,* ed. J. F. Jennings (Bloomington: Phi Delta Kappa, 1993); Pell quote in Thomas J. De-

Loughry, "Introduction of Bill Draws Mixed Reactions," *Chronicle of Higher Education,* March 4, 1992.

39. McCormick, "Direct Loan Demonstration Program," 96–134; Dillon, "Leading Lady," 3–6; Matt Schudel, "Rep. William D. Ford of Michigan Dies at 77," *Washington Post,* August 15, 2004; Mumper, "Transformation of Federal Aid," Ford's concerns quote 329; Hannah, "Higher Education Act of 1992," 498–527, Ford accretion quote 505; Parsons, *Power and Politics,* 130–140, Ford Plastique quote 133, staff convinced colleges quote 136, Nassirian quote 134.

40. Mettler, *Degrees of Inequality,* 87–99, quote 94.

41. Waters quote in Halimah Abdullah, "Are For-Profit Colleges Good for Black Students?" *TheGrio.com,* March 5, 2012; Mettler, *Degrees of Inequality,* 85–90.

42. McCormick, "Direct Loan Demonstration Program," 96–200, Republican conferee quote 162, Democratic staffer quote 132; Parsons, *Power and Politics,* 126–140, impressions of Bush quote 127; Dillon, "Leading Lady," 3–6, 9–11; Wolanin, "Reauthorizing the Higher Education Act," 89–105; Debra Chromy, "FFELP or Direct Lending: A Comparison of the Decision-Making Process at Two Universities" (PhD diss., University of Pennsylvania, 2006), 8–16; Price, *Borrowing Inequality,* 27–44; Hannah, "Higher Education Act of 1992," 508–509; McPherson and Schapiro, *Student Aid Game,* 108–110. Marginalia on February 18, 1992, White House Staff Memorandum, 07786, FOIA2017-1962-F; and Charles Kolb to Clayton Yeutter and Roger Porter, June 19, 1992, 07960, FOIA2017-1962-F, both in George H. W. Bush Presidential Library and Archive, College Station, TX.

43. McCormick, "Direct Loan Demonstration Program," 96–200; Wolanin, "Reauthorizing the Higher Education Act," 89–105; Chromy, "FFELP or Direct Lending," 8–16; Price, *Borrowing Inequality,* 27–44; Hannah, "Higher Education Act of 1992," 508–509; "History of the FAFSA and Needs Analysis," Edvisors, https://www.edvisors.com/fafsa/estimate-aid/history-fafsa-need-analysis/; Parsons, *Power and Politics,* 126–140.

44. McCormick, "Direct Loan Demonstration Program," Republican quote 158; Parsons, *Power and Politics,* 187–210, Carville quote 189; Patrick Maney, *Bill Clinton: New Gilded Age President* (Lawrence: University of Kansas Press, 2016), 9–44; Nigel Hamilton, *Bill Clinton: An American Journey* (East Sussex, UK: Gardners Books, 2004), 20–193, 273–472; Bill Clinton, *My Life* (New York: Knopf, 2004), 69–81; Mumper, "Student Aid Industry"; Susan Fuhrman, "Clinton's Education Policy and Intergovernmental Relations in the 1990s," *Publius* 24, no. 3 (1994): 83–97; Mungovan, "Role of the U.S. Federal Government," 22–44; Fergus, *Land of the Fee,* 77–80.

45. Mumper, "Student Aid Industry"; Fuhrman, "Clinton's Education Policy"; Mungovan, "Role of the U.S. Federal Government," 22–44; Fergus, *Land of the Fee,* 77–80; Parsons, *Power and Politics,* 187–210.

46. Parsons, *Power and Politics,* 187–210, Clinton quote 199; Fergus, *Land of the Fee,* 78–79; Melinsa Amberg-Vajdic, "USA Group Wages Campaign against Clinton's Student Loan Reform Plan," *Indianapolis Business Journal,* May 10, 1993, 9; Roy Nicholson to Members of Congress, with enclosure, July, 26, 1993, General Files, FOIA2017-1069-F, William J. Clinton Presidential Library and Archive, Little Rock, AR (hereafter Clinton Library).

47. McCormick, "Direct Loan Demonstration Program," 96–158, both assessments of Ford quoted 141; Wolanin, "Reauthorizing the Higher Education Act," 89–105; Hannah, "Higher Education Act of 1992"; Price, *Borrowing Inequality,* 27–44; Chromy, "FFELP or Direct Lending," 8–16; Dillon, "Leading Lady," 9–11; Parsons, *Power and Politics,* 188–190.

48. Parsons, *Power and Politics,* 187–210, Kassebaum quote 200.

49. Parsons, *Power and Politics*, 187–210; meeting description quote from Jim Zook, "House Votes to End National-Service Program: Clinton Vows to Veto Bill," *Chronicle of Higher Education*, August 11, 1995, A25; pleas to Pell, see Series VIII-1, Group 71, box 6, folder 40 and box 8, folder 52, Senatorial Papers of Claiborne Pell: Congresses 1960–1997, University of Rhode Island Library, Special Collections and University Archives, Kingston, RI.

50. Parsons, *Power and Politics*, quote 203; Mumper, "Student Aid Industry"; Fuhrman, "Clinton's Education Policy"; Mungovan, "Role of the U.S. Federal Government," 22–44; Fergus, *Land of the Fee*, 77–82; Margot Schenet, *Federal Direct Student Loan Program*, 1995 CRS Report for Congress.

51. Mumper, "Student Aid Industry"; Fuhrman, "Clinton's Education Policy"; Mungovan, "Role of the U.S. Federal Government," 22–44; Elizabeth Shogren, "New Student Loan Plan to Include 6 California Schools," *Los Angeles Times*, November 16, 1993, University of California official quote 3; University of Illinois official quote in Nathaniel Sheppard, Jr., "New Student Loan Program Eases Headaches," *Chicago Tribune*, August 30, 1994, N8; additional students and staff quoted in James Popkin and Viva Hardigg with Susan Headden, "The College Aid Face-Off," *U.S. News & World Report*, March 13, 1995, 64. For discussion see Fergus, *Land of the Fee*, 78–82.

52. Julian Zelizer, *Burning Down the House: Newt Gingrich, the Fall of a Speaker, and the Rise of the New Republican Party* (New York: Penguin, 2020); Mumper, "Student Aid Industry"; Fuhrman, "Clinton's Education Policy"; Mungovan, "Role of the U.S. Federal Government," 22–44; John Dean, Saul Moskowitz, and Karen Cipriani, "Implications of the Privatization of Sallie Mae," *Journal of Public Budgeting, Accounting & Financial Management* 11, no. 1 (Spring 1999): 56–80.

53. Megan Barnett, Julia E. Barnes, and Danielle Knight, "Big Money on Campus: How Taxpayers Are Getting Scammed by Student Loans," *U.S. News & World Report*, October 27, 2003. For discussion see Fergus, *Land of the Fee*, 79–90.

54. Maney, *Bill Clinton*, 1–44, 89–115, 155–181, 167–173, 197–209, 210–236; Nigel Hamilton, *Bill Clinton: Mastering the Presidency* (Philadelphia: Public Affairs, 2007), 302–308, 519–545, 588–595; Timothy Canova, "Legacy of the Clinton Bubble," *Dissent* 55, no. 3 (2008): 41–50; Fergus, *Land of the Fee*, 87–88; Nelson Lichtenstein, "Fabulous Failure: Clinton's 1990s and the Origins of Our Times," *American Prospect*, Winter 2018, https://prospect.org/health/fabulous-failure-clinton-s-1990s-origins-times/; Hamilton, *Bill Clinton: An American Journey*, 20–193, 273–472; Clinton, *My Life*, 69–81.

55. William Clinton, State of the Union Address, January 23, 1996, https://clintonwhitehouse4.archives.gov/WH/New/other/sotu.html; Shermer, "Banking on Government," 65–84.

56. Elizabeth Tandy Shermer, "Financing Security and Opportunity: The New Deal and the Origins of the Millennial Student Debt Crisis," in *Capitalism Contested: The New Deal and Its Legacies*, ed. Romain Huret, Nelson Lichtenstein, and Jean-Christian Vinel, 112–135 (Philadelphia: University of Pennsylvania Press, 2020); Kristin Conklin, *Federal Tuition Tax Credits and State Higher Education Policy: A Guide for State Policy Makers* (San Jose, CA: National Center for Public Policy and Higher Education, 1998), 1–7; Bridget Long, "Impact of Federal Tax Credits for Higher Education Expenses," in *College Choices: The Economics of Where to Go, When to Go, and How to Pay for It*, ed. Caroline Hoxby (Chicago: University of Chicago Press, 2004), 101–168; Patricia Strach, "Making Higher Education Affordable: Policy Design in Postwar America," *Journal of Policy History* 21, no. 1 (2009): 61–88; Creech and David, "Merit-Based versus Need-Based Aid," 120–136; Peter Appelbome,

"Aid Plan That Inspired Clinton Is a Success," *New York Times,* June 6, 1996; Scott Litch to William Galston, April 7, 1993, OA/ID5735, Direct Lending-April 1993, FOIA-2017-1069-F, Clinton; Bobbie Turner to Mr. President, February 28, 1995, OA/ID5735, Direct Loans-I, FOIA-2017-1069-F, Clinton; Bill Clinton to Eric Wiertelak, March 21, 1995, OA/ID5735, Direct Loans-I, FOIA-2017-1069-F (also see this folder for interest-deduction pleas); all in Clinton Library.

57. Clinton quoted in Ronald Brownstein, "Clinton Offers Tax Credit Linked to College Tuition," *Los Angeles Times,* June 5, 1996; Strach, "Making Higher Education Affordable"; Gladieux and King, "Federal Government and Higher Education," 151–182; Clayton Spencer, "New Politics of Higher Education," in *Financing a College Education: How It Works, How It's Changing,* ed. Jacqueline E. King, 101–119 (Westport, CT: American Council on Education/Oryx Press, 1999); Fergus, *Land of the Fee,* 86–88; education policy expert quoted in Applebome, "Aid Plan That Inspired Clinton Is a Success."

58. Strach, "Making Higher Education Affordable"; William Clinton, State of the Union, February 4, 1997, https://clintonwhitehouse2.archives.gov/WH/SOU97/; Conklin, *Federal Tuition Tax Credits*; Long, "Impact of Federal Tax Credits"; Spencer, "New Politics of Higher Education"; Strach, "Making Higher Education Affordable"; "State Colleges and Universities Fees Need a Closer Look," *Atlanta Journal,* January 5, 1998, A6.

59. Conklin, *Federal Tuition Tax Credits*; Long, "Impact of Federal Tax Credits"; William Clinton quote in "Statement on Signing the Taxpayer Relief Act of 1997," August 5, 1997, https://www.govinfo.gov/content/pkg/WCPD-1997-08-11/pdf/WCPD-1997-08-11-Pg1192 .pdf; Strach, "Making Higher Education Affordable."

60. Fergus, *Land of the Fee,* 86–88; Gladieux and King, "Federal Government and Higher Education," 151–182; Conklin, *Federal Tuition Tax Credits*; Long, "Impact of Federal Tax Credits"; Spencer, "New Politics of Higher Education"; Kristin Conklin and Joni Finney, "State Policy Response to the Taxpayer Relief Act of 1997," in *Financing a College Education: How It Works, How It's Changing,* ed. Jacqueline E. King, 151–164 (Westport, CT: American Council on Education/Oryx Press, 1999); Carole Gould, "Education I.R.A.'s Are Already Getting Low Marks," *New York Times,* January 18, 1998, financial planner quote 7; William Clinton quoted in "Radio Address on Higher-Education Opportunities," August 15, 1997, in Lowell Weiss email to Cathy Mays et al., subject: draft of radio address, OA/ID500000, 1997 Taxpayer Relief Act, FOIA-2017-1075-F, Clinton Library; Peter Applebome, "Clinton's College-Aid Plan Faces Doubt from Experts," *New York Times,* March 30, 1997, Dismuke quote 12.

61. Gladieux and King, "Federal Government and Higher Education," 151–182; Conklin, *Federal Tuition Tax Credits,* quote v; Long, "Impact of Federal Tax Credits"; Spencer, "New Politics of Higher Education"; Conklin and Finney, "State Policy Response."

62. Dillon, "Leading Lady"; Dean et al., "Implications of the Privatization of Sallie Mae."

63. Mumper, "Student Aid Industry"; Mungovan, "Role of the U.S. Federal Government," 22–44; Dillon, "Leading Lady"; Dean et al., "Implications of the Privatization of Sallie Mae"; US Congress, House, Subcommittee, *Hearing on the Reauthorization of the Higher Education Act of 1965: Sallie Mae—Safety and Soundness;* Hobart Rowen, "Circling the Wagons around the Treasury," *Washington Post,* July 29, 1990, H1; Maggie Mahar, "How Sallie Will Survive," *Barron's,* June 14, 1990, 10; Stan Hinden, "Singing a Mournful Song for Sallie Mae," *Washington Post,* August 23, 1993, quote 29; James Moore to Bill Clinton, March 1, 1995, ED127563SS, FOIA2017-1074-F, Clinton Library; Gene Sperling and Ellen Seidman, Memorandum for the

President, May 22, 1997, FG255-219440SS, FOIA2017-1074-F, "Issue: Future of Sallie Mae," April 28, 1995, OA/ID5735, Direct Lending April-1993, FOIA2017-1069-F, Clinton Library.

64. William Arceneaux and Lawrence Hough to Bill Clinton, April 13, 1994, FG255-060923; Paul Dimond to Kenneth Apfel, May 30, 1996, 10090; Ellen Seidman to Gene Sperling, April 18, 1996, 10090; Pat Smith and Barry White, April 18, 1996 memo with attachment, 10090; Diane Gilleland to Bill Clinton, September 24, 1996, FG255-188206; Kenneth Apfel email to Ellen Seidman, Subject: Sallie Mae leg meeting with Dem and Rep Senate Staff, November 17, 1995, [5/30/1996–07/24/1997], all in FOIA-2017-1074-F, Clinton Library. Lawrence Hough to William Ford, May 12, 1993, OA/ID57311, Direct Lending April-1993, FOIA-2017-1069-F, Clinton Library.

65. Mumper, "Student Aid Industry"; Mungovan, "Role of the U.S. Federal Government"; Dillon, "Leading Lady"; Dean et al., "Implications of the Privatization of Sallie Mae"; Shermer, "Banking on Government"; "Student Loan Marketing Association," *Washington Post*, April 28, 1997, 48; Kenneth Gilpin, "Struggle over Sallie Mae Sends Message to Boards," *New York Times*, August 10, 1997, 6; Phil Caplan, Memorandum for the President, May 24, 1997, FG001-221069SS, FOIA-2017-1074-F, Clinton Library.

66. John G. Sperling, *Rebel with a Cause: The Entrepreneur Who Created the University of Phoenix and the For-Profit Revolution in Higher Education* (New York: Wiley, 2000), 148, 183. David Longanecker testimony, *Abuses in Federal Student Grant Programs: Hearings before the Permanent Subcommittee on Investigations of the Committee on Governmental Affairs, United States Senate*, 103rd Cong., 1st sess., October 27–28, 1993 (Washington: US Government Printing Office, 1994), 95. For discussion see Mettler, *Degrees of Inequality*, 98–104.

67. For post-1972 efforts see Series III, box 117, Student Aid/GSL/Bankruptcies, Ford papers; Michael Winerip, "Overhauling School Grants," *New York Times*, February 4, 1994, A1; White House, "The Higher Education Amendments of 1998: Five Victories for the Clinton-Gore Administration," press release, October 7, 1998, https://govinfo.library.unt.edu/npr /library/news/100798.html; Mettler, *Degrees of Inequality*, 98–104, Boehner quote 102; Kayla Webley, "Why Can't You Discharge Student Loans in Bankruptcy?" *Time*, February 9, 2012; Jordan Weissmann, "How the Bush Administration Pointlessly Screwed Over Student Borrowers," *Slate*, April 16, 2015, http://www.slate.com/blogs/moneybox/2015/04/16/student_loans _in_bankruptcy_how_the_bush_administration_pointlessly_screwed.html; Stephen P. Strohschein, Jeffrey E. Tate, and Alvin C. Harrell, "2005 Bankruptcy Reform Act," 949–968; Joel Best and Eric Best, *The Student Loan Mess: How Good Intentions Created a Trillion-Dollar Problem* (Berkeley: University of California Press, 2014), 62.

68. Webley, "Why Can't You Discharge Student Loans in Bankruptcy?"; Weissmann, "How the Bush Administration"; Giblin et al., "2005 Bankruptcy Reform Act," 949–968; Elizabeth Tandy Shermer, "Fraught Partnership: Business and the Rise of the American Public University," in *Capital Gains: Business and Politics in Twentieth-Century America*, ed. Kim Phillips-Fein and Richard John, 157–178 (Philadelphia: University of Pennsylvania Press, 2016), esp. 175–178; Mettler, *Degrees of Inequality*, 107–108.

69. Mettler, *Degrees of Inequality*, 101–106, exposé quote 105; Apollo Group goal quote in US Senate, HELP Committee, "Apollo Group, Inc.," 272; Fergus, *Land of the Fee*, 88–91.

70. Price, *Borrowing Inequality*, 27–44; Chromy, "FFELP or Direct Lending," 8–16; Dillon, "Leading Lady," 9–11; Fergus, *Land of the Fee*, 88–91; Nelson Lichtenstein, "Ideology and Interest on the Social Policy Home Front," in *The Presidency of George W. Bush: A First*

Historical Assessment, ed. Julian Zelizer, 169–198 (Princeton: Princeton University Press, 2010).

71. Jonathan Glater, "College Loans by States Face Fresh Scrutiny," *New York Times,* December 9, 2007, findings quote 1; Diana Jean Schemo, "Cuomo Plans to Broaden Student-Lending Inquiry," *New York Times,* June 7, 2007.

72. Schemo, "Cuomo Plans"; college official quoted in Diana Jean Schemo, "Private Loans Deepen a Crisis in Student Debt," *New York Times,* June 10, 2007.

73. Mettler, *Degrees of Inequality,* 139–140; Fergus, *Land of the Fee,* 88–90; Andrew Barr and Sarah E. Turner, "Expanding Enrollments and Contracting State Budgets: The Effect of the Great Recession on Higher Education," *Annals of the American Academy of Political and Social Science* 650, no. 1 (2013): 168–193; American Council on Education, "Summary: The College Cost Reduction and Access Act of 2007," fact sheet, September 7, 2007, http://www.acenet.edu/news-room/Pages/The-College-Cost-Reduction-and-Access-Act-of-2007.aspx.

74. Barr and Turner, "Expanding Enrollments"; Robert Lowry, "Reauthorization of the Federal Higher Education Act and Accountability for Student Learning: The Dog That Didn't Bark," *Publius* 39, no. 3 (2009): 506–526; Brittany McCarthy, "Reauthorizing the Higher Education Act: An Analysis of the Role of the For-Profit Higher Education Sector" (PhD diss., University of Minnesota, 2013); American Council on Education, "ACE Analysis of Higher Education Act Reauthorization," report, August 2008, http://www.acenet.edu/news-room/Pages/Analysis-Higher-Education-Opportunity-Act-of-2008.aspx.

75. American Council on Education, "ACE Analysis"; Barr and Turner, "Expanding Enrollments," Maryland official quote 188; Adam Goldstein and Neil Fligstein, "The Transformation of Mortgage Finance and the Industrial Roots of the Mortgage Meltdown," IRLE Working Paper 133-12, Institution for Research on Labor and Employment, University of California, Berkeley, October 1, 2012, https://irle.berkeley.edu/the-transformation-of-mortgage-finance-and-the-industrial-roots-of-the-mortgage-meltdown/; Shermer, "Banking on Government."

76. Mettler, *Degrees of Inequality,* 138–139; Jonathan Glater, "That Student Loan, So Hard to Shake," *New York Times,* August 24, 2008, Collinge quote BU1; DiPoi quoted in Schemo, "Private Loans Deepen Student-Debt Crisis"; Tara Siegel Bernard, "In Grim Job Market, Student Loans Are a Costly Burden," *New York Times,* April 18, 2009, Kazee and Westby quote B6; Jonathan Glater, "Aspiring Lawyer Finds Debt Is Bigger Hurdle Than Bar Exam," *New York Times,* July 2, 2009, judges quote A1.

77. Barack Obama, *The Audacity of Hope* (New York: Crown, 2006), 159; Obama quoted in David Espo, "Obama Says Clinton, McCain Wrong on Gas Taxes," Associated Press, May 2, 2008; Jill Abramson, "Taking Aim at Elitism," *New York Times,* April 16, 2008, Michelle Obama quote A16; Patrick Healy, "Candidates' Positions on Student Loans Reflect Experience and Market Views," *New York Times,* October 30, 2008, A24.

78. Barr and Turner, "Expanding Enrollments"; Mettler, *Degrees of Inequality,* 147–158.

79. Mettler, *Degrees of Inequality,* 147–158; Jonathan Glater, "Big Changes on the Way in Lending to Students," *New York Times,* February 27, 2009, Duncan and lobbyist quotes A19; Peter Baker, "Obama Calls His Budget Sweeping, Needed Change," *New York Times,* March 1, 2009, Obama quote A17; Phyllis Hooyman to Colleague, September 22, 1997, with enclosures, OA / ID13218, Direct Loan Coalition, FOIA2017-1069-F, Clinton Library.

80. Mettler, *Degrees of Inequality,* 147–158; Obama quoted in David Stout, "Obama Urges Colleges to Curb Rising Tuition," *New York Times,* April 24, 2009.

81. Mettler, *Degrees of Inequality*, 147–158.

82. Mettler, *Degrees of Inequality*, 147–158; Janey Hook, "Overhaul of Student Loans OK'd by House," *Chicago Tribune*, September 18, 2009, Miller quote 19; David Herszenhorn, "Obama Plan to End Role of Banks in Federal Student Loans Wins Support," *New York Times*, July 11, 2009, Bishop quote A9; Alexander and Miller quoted in David Herszenhorn and Tamar Lewin, "Student Loan Overhaul Approved by Congress," *New York Times*, March 25, 2010.

83. Gail Collins, "When Sallie Met Barack," *New York Times*, May 28, 2009, A27; Mettler, *Degrees of Inequality*, 147–159.

84. Shermer, "Financing Security and Opportunity"; Collins, "When Sallie Met Barack"; Peter Baker and David Herszenhorn, "Obama Signs Bill on Student Loans and Health Care," *New York Times*, March 30, 2010; Peter Baker and David Herszenhorn, "Obama Signs Overhaul of Student Loan Program," *New York Times*, March 30, 2010; Obama quote in "Remarks by the President and Dr. Jill Biden at Signing of Health Care and Education Reconciliation Act," March 30, 2010, https://obamawhitehouse.archives.gov/the-press-office /remarks-president-and-dr-jill-biden-signing-health-care-and-education-reconciliation; Mettler, *Degrees of Inequality*, 147–159, confidential source quote 158.

85. "Sallie Mae (SLM) Splits Off Student Loan Segment into Navient (NAVI)," *Equities*, May 1, 2014, https://www.equities.com/news/sallie-mae-slm-splits-off-student-loan-segment-into -navient-navi; Doug Lederman, "USA Funds to End Student Loan Guarantee Business," *Inside Higher Ed*, February 11, 2020; "Everything You Need to Know about Great Lakes Student Loans," *Huffington Post*, July 2, 2016, http://www.huffingtonpost.com/credible/everything-you -need-to-kn_17_b_7718002.html; Fergus, *Land of the Fee*, 94–95.

86. Goldrick-Rab, *Paying the Price*, 1–11.

87. Andrew Fieldhouse, "5 Years after the Great Recession," *Huffington Post*, December 6, 2017, https://www.huffpost.com/entry/five-years-after-the-grea_b_5530597; Michael Grunwald, "Details on the GOP Plot to Obstruct Obama," *Time*, August 23, 2012; Adam Liptak, "Study Calls Snub of Obama's Supreme Court Pick Unprecedented," *New York Times*, June 13, 2016; Peter Schroeder, "Obama's Ultimatum," *The Hill*, October 2, 2015, http://thehill .com/policy/finance/255806-obama-i-will-not-sign-another-short-term-spending-bill.

Epilogue

1. Terrance Ross, "Guardian Angels of Student Debt," *Atlantic*, February 23, 2015; student quoted in Gregory Wallace, "'Corinthian 15' Launch 'Debt Strike' over Student Loans," *CNN*, March 1, 2015; Katie Lobosco, "Corinthian Students Get $480 Million in Debt Relief," *CNN*, February 3, 2015; Jana Kasperkevic, "Occupy Activists Abolish $3.85m in Corinthian Colleges Student Loan Debt," *Guardian*, September, 17, 2014.

2. "Coming out" quote in Andrew Ross and Seth Ackerman, "Strike Debt and Rolling Jubilee: The Debate," *Dissent*, November 13, 2013; Ross, "Guardian Angels of Student Debt"; Lobosco, "Corinthian Students Get $480 Million"; Kasperkevic, "Occupy Activists Abolish $3.85m"; OccupyWallSt, "Debtor assemblies" quote in "Today: Strike Debt Bay Area Presents Oakland's First Debtors' Assembly," blog post, February 2, 2013; "Haunted by Student Debt Past Age 50," *New York Times*, February 13, 2017; Susan Dynarski, "Why Students with the Smallest Debts Have the Larger Problem," *New York Times*, August 31, 2015; Kevin Carey, "Student Debt in America: Lend with a Smile, Collect with a Fist," *New York Times*, November 29, 2015;

Kevin Carey, "Student Debt Is Worse Than You Think," *New York Times,* October 8, 2015; Tara Siegel Bernard, "Many Pitfalls of Private Student Loans," *New York Times,* September 5, 2015; Ron Lieber, "Taking Out Debt, and Refusing to Pay," *New York Times,* June 13, 2015.

3. Charlie Eaton, "Still Public: State Universities and America's New Student-Debt Coalitions," *PS: Political Science and Politics* 50 (2017): 408–413.

4. Philip G. Altbach, "Patterns of Higher Education Development," in *American Higher Education in the Twenty-First Century: Social, Political, and Economic Challenges,* ed. Philip G. Altbach, Robert O. Berdahl, and Patricia J. Gumport, 15–37 (Baltimore: Johns Hopkins University Press, 1998); Sachi Amatya, "The Role of Student Loan Programs in Higher Education Policy in the United States" (PhD diss., Vanderbilt University, 2008), 15–37, 10–16, 27–28; Elizabeth Tandy Shermer, "Fees May Never Fall in the US or South Africa," *South African Labour Bulletin,* September/October 2017, 52–55; Nicholas Hillman, "From Grants for All to Loans for All: Undergraduate Finance from the Implementation of the Anderson Report (1962) to the Implementation of the Browne Report (2012)," *Contemporary British History* 27, no. 3 (2013): 249–270; Philip Oltermann, "Germany Axed Tuition Fees—But Is It Working Out?" *Observer,* June 4, 2016; Ross and Ackerman, "Strike Debt and Rolling Jubilee"; Lobosco, "Corinthian Students Get $480 Million"; Brown quoted in Lydia DePillis, "How One Student Got Burned by a For-Profit College and Bailed Out by Occupy Wall Street," *Washington Post,* September 17, 2014; all other quotes from Kasperkevic, "Occupy Activists Abolish $3.85m."

5. Larson quoted in Ross, "Guardian Angels of Student Debt"; Gokey quoted in DePillis, "How One Student Got Burned."

6. Arianne Hutchins, "What Happened to the Federal Perkins Loan?" *US News & World Report,* July 24, 2019; Suzanne Mettler, *Degrees of Inequality: How the Politics of Higher Education Sabotaged the American Dream* (New York: Basic Books, 2014), 158–160; Binyamin Appelbaum and Michael Shear, "Once Skeptical of Executive Power, Obama Has Come to Embrace It," *New York Times,* August 13, 2016; Kristen Bialik, "Obama Issued Fewer Executive Orders on Average Than Any President since Cleveland," *Fact Tank,* Pew Research Center, January 23, 2017.

7. Andrew Delbanco, "Our Universities: The Outrageous Reality," *New York Review of Books,* July 9, 2015; Kevin Carey, "Programs That Are Predatory: It's Not Just at For-Profit Colleges," *New York Times,* January 13, 2017; US Department of Education, "Departments of Education and Treasury and the Consumer Financial Protection Bureau Announce New Joint Efforts to Protect and Support Student Loan Borrowers," press release, April 28, 2016; US Department of Education, "Education Department Releases Final Debt-to-Earnings Rates for Gainful Employment Programs," press release, January 9, 2017; Fernanda Zamudio-Suaréz, "Here Are the Programs That Failed the Gainful Employment Rules," *Chronicle of Higher Education,* January 9, 2017 (this article contains a link to download the Education Department's spreadsheet).

8. Rachel Fishman, "The Wealth Gap PLUS Debt: How Federal Loans Exacerbate Inequality for Black Families," report, *New America* Foundation, May 15, 2018, 5–6.

9. Fishman, "The Wealth Gap PLUS Debt"; Stephen Burd, "Undermining Pell: How Colleges Compete for Wealthy Students and Leave the Low-Income Behind," policy paper, *New America* Foundation, May 2013; Raj Chetty, John N. Friedman, Emmanuel Saez, Nicholas Turner, and Danny Yagan, "Mobility Report Cards: The Role of Colleges in Intergenerational Mobility," National Bureau of Economic Research Working Paper 23618, July 2017; Kim

Dancy, "Mind the Gap: How Higher Education Contributes to Gender Wage Disparities," blog post, *New America* Foundation, May 11, 2017; Kevin Miller, "Deeper in Debt: Women and Student Loans," report, American Association of University Women, May 2017; Adam Looney and Constantine Yannelis, "How Useful Are Default Rates? Borrowers with Large Balances and Student Loan Repayment," *Economics of Education Review* 71 (2019): 135–145; Judith Scott-Clayton, "The Looming Student Loan Default Crisis Is Worse Than We Thought," *Evidence Speaks Reports* 2, no. 34, Brookings Institution, January 10, 2018; Ben Barrett, "College Access Is Still a Problem," blog post, *New America* Foundation, March 14, 2017; Michael Prebil, "Started from the Bottom—and Still Here," blog post, *New America* Foundation, March 29, 2017; Michal Grinstein-Weiss, Dana C. Perantie, Samuel H. Taylor, Shenyang Guo, and Ramesh Raghavan, "Racial Disparities in Education Debt Burden among Low- and Moderate-Income Households," *Children and Youth Services Review* 65 (2016): 166–174; Brandon Jackson and John Reynolds, "The Price of Opportunity: Race, Student Loan Debt, and College Achievement," *Sociological Inquiry* 83, no. 3 (2013): 335–368; Student Borrower Protection Center, "Educational Redlining," report, February 2020.

10. Sandy Baum, *Student Debt: Rhetoric and Realities of Higher Education Financing* (New York: Palgrave Macmillian, 2016), 83–106; Beth Akers and Matthew Chingos, *Game of Loans: The Rhetoric and Reality of Student Debt* (Princeton: Princeton University Press, 2016), 122–144.

11. Zack Friedman, "25 Colleges with 'No Student Loans,'" *Forbes,* December 19, 2017; Adeel Hassan, "Cornell's Medical School Offers Full Rides in Battle over Student Debt," *New York Times,* September 16, 2019; Tara Siegel Bernard, "Medical, Dental, 401(k)? Now Add School Loan Aid to Job Benefits," *New York Times,* March 25, 2016.

12. Milton Friedman, "The Role of Government in Education," in *Economics and the Public Interest,* ed. Robert A. Solo, 123–144 (New Brunswick, NJ: Rutgers University Press, 1955); D. Bruce Johnstone, *New Patterns for College Lending: Income Contingent Loans* (New York: Columbia University Press, 1972), vii–viii, 51–84; Akers and Chingos, *Game of Loans,* 140–142.

13. Sydney Johnson, "So You Want to Offer an Income Share Arrangement," *EdSurge,* February 15, 2019; Mitchell E. Daniels, Jr., "Could Income-Share Arrangements Help Solve the Student-Debt Crisis?" *Washington Post,* August 20, 2015; "Purdue Research Foundation Raises $10.2 Million for Back a Boiler Income Share Agreement Fund II," press release, Purdue University, December 4, 2018; Stephen Dubner, "The $1.5 Trillion Question: How to Fix Student-Loan Debt?" *Freakonomics Podcast,* Episode 377, May 8, 2019; Andrew Ross Sorkin, "No Tuition, but You Pay a Percentage of Your Income (If You Find a Job)," *New York Times,* January 8, 2019; Matt Reed, "Is Indentured Servitude Really a New Idea," *Inside Higher Ed,* August 30, 2015.

14. Sara Goldrick-Rab, *Paying the Price: College Costs, Financial Aid, and the Betrayal of the American Dream* (Chicago: University of Chicago Press, 2016), 233–260; David Deming, "Tuition-Free College Could Cost Less Than You Think," *New York Times,* July 19, 2019; Caitlin Zaloom, *Indebted: How Families Make College Work at Any Cost* (Princeton: Princeton University Press, 2019), 196.

15. Rick Seltzer, "Tuition Grows in Importance," *Inside Higher Ed,* March 29, 2018; Robert Farrington, "Student Loan Forgiveness Programs by State," *The College Investor,* https://thecollegeinvestor.com/student-loan-forgiveness-programs-by-state/, accessed September 12, 2019; Stacey Cowley and Jessica Silver-Greenberg, "As Paperwork Goes Missing, Private Student Loan Debts May Be Wiped Away," *New York Times,* July 17, 2017; "San Francisco's Kin-

dergarten to College Program Celebrates New Milestone," blog post, *Prosperity Now*, October 19, 2017. For details on San Francisco's publicly funded universal Children's Savings Account program, Kindergarten to College, see its website hosted by the San Francisco Office of the Treasurer and Tax Collector: https://sfgov.org/ofe/k2c; David Chen, "Free Tuition? Tennessee Could Tutor New York," *New York Times*, May 14, 2017; David Chen, "New York's Free-Tuition Program Will Help Traditional, but Not Typical, Students," *New York Times*, April 11, 2017; Jesse McKinley, "Cuomo Proposes Free Tuition at New York State Colleges for Eligible Students," *New York Times*, January 3, 2017; David Chen, "75,000 Apply for State College Scholarships, but Many Won't Qualify," *New York Times*, August 25, 2017; Simon Romero and Dana Goldstein, "New Mexico Announces Plan for Free College for State Residents," *New York Times*, September 18, 2019.

16. Catherine Hill, "Free Tuition Is Not the Answer," *New York Times*, November 30, 2015; Kevin Carey, "Bernie Sanders's Charming, Perfectly Awful Plan to Save Higher Education," *Chronicle of Higher Education*, July 6, 2015; Charles Lane, "College Doesn't Need to Be Free," *Washington Post*, May 21, 2015; Nirvi Shah and Kimberly Hefling, "Hilary's $350 Billion Plan to Kill College Debt," *Politico*, August 10, 2015.

17. Shermer, "Student Debt Crisis and Its Deniers," *Public Books*, March 15, 2017; Jordan Weissmann, "Betsy DeVos Wants to Kill a Major Student Loan Forgiveness Program," *Slate*, May 17, 2017.

18. Danielle Douglas-Gabriel, "Elizabeth Warren Questions the Hiring of For-Profit-College Officials at the Education Department," *New York Times*, March 20, 2017; Susan Dynarski, "The Wrong Way to Fix Student Debt," blog post, *New York Times*, May 6, 2017; Cowley and Silver-Greenberg, "DeVos Halts Obama-Era Plan"; Kevin Carey, "DeVos Is Discarding College Policies That New Evidence Shows Are Effective," *New York Times*, June 30, 2017.

19. Stacey Cowley and Jessica Silver-Greenberg, "Loans 'Designed to Fail': States Say Navient Preyed on Students," *New York Times*, April 9, 2017.

20. Stacy Cowley and Jessica Silver-Greenberg, "Student Loan Collector Cheated Millions, Lawsuits Say," *New York Times*, January 18, 2017; Stacey Cowley, "18 States Sue Betsy DeVos over Student Loan Protections," *New York Times*, July 6, 2017; Danielle Douglas-Gabriel, "Trump Administration Is Sitting on Tens of Thousands of Student Debt Forgiveness Claims," *Washington Post*, July 27, 2017; Stacy Cowley, "Delayed Obama-Era Rule on Student Debt Relief Is to Take Effect," *New York Times*, October 16, 2018; Stacy Cowley, "DeVos Toughens Rules for Student Borrowers Bilked by Colleges," *New York Times*, August 30, 2019.

21. Jillian Berman, "Where the 2020 Candidates Stand on Student Debt and College Affordability," *MarketWatch*, July 30, 2019, https://www.marketwatch.com/story/where-the-2020-candidates-stand-on-student-debt-and-college-affordability-2019-02-20; Friedman, "Student Loan Debt Statistics in 2020."

22. Goldie Blumenstyk, "Partners, 'Vultures,' and Other Dispatches from Higher Ed's Grand Move Online," *Chronicle of Higher Education*, March 25, 2020; Blake Farmer, "Insurers May Only Pay for Coronavirus Tests When They're 'Medically Necessary,'" *NPR*, June 19, 2020, https://www.npr.org/sections/health-shots/2020/06/19/880543755/insurers-may-only-pay-for-coronavirus-tests-when-theyre-medically-necessary; Nicholas Casey, "College Made Them Feel Unequal. The Virus Exposed How Unequal Their Lives Are," *New York Times*, April 4, 2020; Vimal Patel, "Covid-19 Is a Pivotal Moment for Struggling Students. Can Colleges Step Up?" *Chronicle of Higher Education*, April 14, 2020; Tiffany Hsu and Tara Siegel Bernard, "Coronavirus Layoff Surge Overwhelms Unemployment Offices," *New York*

Times, March 19, 2020; "What Is the Cost of COVID-19 Treatment?" *NPR*, March 29, 2020, https://www.npr.org/2020/03/29/823438983/what-is-the-cost-of-covid-19-treatment;   Amy Brittain, Ted Mellnik, Dan Keating, and Joe Fox, "How Surge of Coronavirus Patients Could Stretch Hospital Resources in Your Area," *Washington Post*, April 10, 2020.

23. Kery Murakami, "Emergency Money for Students Arriving Soon," *Inside Higher Ed*, April 10, 2020; Rick Seltzer, "How Much Stimulus Will Your College Receive?" *Inside Higher Ed*, April 10, 2020; Francie Diep and Danielle McLean, "Colleges Are Handing Out Billions in Coronavirus Stimulus Funding to Students. Can They Do It Fairly?" *Chronicle of Higher Education*, April 16, 2020; Anemona Hartocollis, "After Coronavirus, Colleges Worry: Will Students Come Back?" *New York Times*, April 15, 2020; Meghan Lustig, "Coronavirus Stimulus: 5 Things Student Loan Borrowers Should Know," *US News & World Report*, March 31, 2020; Adam S. Minsky, "Second Student Loan Stimulus," *Forbes*, August 5, 2020; Ron Lieber and Stacey Cowley, "Trump's Directives Were Supposed to Offer Relief. Most May Not," *New York Times*, August 10, 2020; Elizabeth Tandy Shermer, "Even Forgiving Student Loans Won't Solve the Higher Education Funding Crisis," *Washington Post*, January 22, 2021.

24. Shermer, "Even Forgiving Student Loans"; Biden and Ocasio-Cortez quoted in Aila Slisco, "'This Is Wrong': Progressives Condemn Joe Biden's Refusal to Cancel $50k in Student Debt," *Newsweek*, February 17, 2021.

Acknowledgments

I am indebted to the many people who made this book possible. The first is Ginny McConnell, who decades ago took an interest in the shy tween living next door. She ended up being more of a parent to me than anyone else. She also gave me a place to stay when I had to return to Northern Virginia in late fall 2015 to move my father into an elder care facility and sell his house. That semester was a blur of wondering how I was going to keep up with both teaching and research while continually going back and forth between the DC area and Chicago. Managing it all seemed hopeless, particularly as I faced the piles of financial and legal documents that my father had been hoarding since the 1960s.

One night, I was standing in Ginny's kitchen shredding tax returns, divorce records, and child custody agreements when I stumbled across the student loan paperwork that I had signed when I was seventeen. I barely recognized the childlike handwriting on forms that I did not remember filling out. I was and still am paying off those debts. Embarrassingly, I knew nothing about that industry or federal tuition assistance, even though I had already published in the fields known as the history of capitalism and policy history. I had also started writing a book on the history of public research universities that I was thinking of titling, "The Business of Education."

My father's needs made finishing in-depth archival research on campuses across the country impossible for the foreseeable future. But, in Ginny's kitchen, I started to imagine how I might be able to delve into the relatively little work on student lending's history and eventually use quick trips to presidential and government repositories to learn more about the tuition assistance that I and so many other Americans had signed up for and have not repaid.

I have spent a lot of time in Ginny's guest room since then, as well as in other friends' spare rooms or on couches when I could squeeze in research. I owe a lot to the patient archivists at the University of Rochester, University of Missouri, University of Illinois Chicago, University of Illinois Urbana-Champaign, Oregon Historical Society, University of Rhode Island, and University of Michigan as well as the staffs at the Franklin Delano Roosevelt, Harry S Truman, Dwight Eisenhower, John F. Kennedy, Lyndon Baines Johnson, Richard Nixon, Ronald Reagan, George H. W. Bush, and William Clinton presidential libraries. Everyone was so patient with me as I asked for materials to be pulled in advance, postponed trips, unexpectedly shortened stays, or requested help finding photographs during the pandemic. A Roosevelt Institute Research Grant, Eisenhower Foundation Abilene Travel Grant, LBJ Foundation Moody Research Grant, Harry S Truman Library Institute Research Grant, and Scowcroft Institute of International Affairs O'Donnell Grant, as well as several Loyola University Chicago summer research stipends, made those research trips possible on a still-indebted assistant professor's salary.

I would never have finished this book without opportunities to get away from campus to write. Wonderful Loyola University Chicago colleagues Bob Bucholz, Kyle Roberts, Tanya Stabler, and Melissa Bradshaw always encouraged me to find the time and space that I needed. My status as a scholar-in-residence gave me the chance to do prodigious amounts of reading for this book at Chicago's Newberry Library, where Brad Hunt, Keelin Burke, Mary Kennedy, Susan Sleeper-Smith, and Kara Johnson let me go on about the intricacies of these complicated financial products. I also relished chances *not* to talk about this project with dear friends in my neighborhood—especially Justine Gianandrea, Carol Semrad, Julia Anderson-Miller, Allison Andrews, Jenn Lyons, Pamela Meyer, Anne Wagner, Tori Simms, Allison Hendron, J'ai Brown, Stella Dimitriou, Odie Schaefer, Joanna Grisinger, and Jessica Katz. I missed them all when I took advantage of short visiting fellowships at the University of California, Santa Barbara's Center for the Study of Work, Labor, and Democracy; University of College London's Institute for the Study of the Americas;

Trinity College Dublin's Trinity Long Room Hub; Rockefeller Foundation's Bellagio Center; Cambridge University's Faculty of History; Wolfson College; and the Obama Institute of the Johannes Gutenberg University in Mainz. I cobbled together a draft from those multiweek stints but needed a full year at Stanford University's Center for Advanced Study in the Behavioral Sciences to edit it. Everything I worked on in and outside Chicago is better because of the questions I got and the painful stories I heard from scholars, journalists, and fellow borrowers.

Most of all, it is friends and loved ones, near and far, who have kept me going as I worked on this book and managed my father's needs. I often came home to Ginny, usually with my cat, Athena, who has sat beside me in my home office as I read various drafts of this book aloud. Research and writing excursions also gave me the chance to reunite with old friends, including Leon Fink, Sue Levine, Betty Wood, John Thompson, Mike Sewell, Andrew Preston, Sarah Pearsall, Gary Gerstle, Jay Kleinberg, Dan Geary, Jennie Sutton, Jonathan Bell, Justin Bengry, Miikka Leskinen, Erika Rappaport, Mary Furner, Leandra Zarnow, Kathleen Belew, and Gerry Cadava. Just as important was the opportunity to meet new comrades, including Ariel Diamond, Linda Haenichen, Patrizia DiLucchio, Eric Arnesen, Katrin Schultheiss, Marshall Steinbaum, Kate Zaloom, Karah Wertz, Kally Forrest, Julia Guarneri, Nick Guyatt, Torsten Kathke, Axel Schäfer, Jane Ohlmeyer, Mitchell Stevens, Nina Bandelj, Mario Biagioli, Christine Ford, Su-Ling Yeh, Cat Ramírez, Paula Moya, Ramón Saldívar, Bruno Perreau, Anita Hardon, Brian Arthur, Mauricio Monico, Gabi Monico, and, of course, Erika Monico. Wherever I went, I knew that I could always text Sarah Watkins and Kate Jewell to vent, cry, or just gab. But I always called Nelson Lichtenstein and Eileen Boris when I needed to discuss ideas, daydream about hiking trips, or admit my doubts that I would ever finish this book.

I never mentioned that doubt to my editor, Kathleen McDermott. She, two generous outside readers, manuscript editor Julia Kirby, graphic designer Isabelle Lewis, and indexer Jim O'Brien helped me make this book much better than it was when I first sent the manuscript in. I also greatly appreciate a book subvention grant from Loyola University Chicago to cover some of the final production costs.

I felt an obligation to make this book as good as I could whenever I stepped into a classroom or held office hours. I wrote it for past, present, and future students who have wondered, and still wonder, how they will pay for college or get out from under all this debt. They include the surgeon, Dr. Chirag Shah, and occupational therapist, Amy Young, who gave me back the full use of my left hand after a bad accident in the midst of writing this book. I am grateful to both of them, and to Dr. Holly García O'Hearn, for helping me recover and get back to this project. Indeed, the first thing I wrote after I could type again was a *Washington Post* op-ed about student loan tax deductions, all the while thinking of Amy telling me how much she pays every month in student loans to *be* an occupational therapist.

Amy should not have to carry such a burden. No one should, for a public good and basic necessity. I continually wonder how much my past and current students have paid and will have to pay for borrowing the same kinds of large amounts while also working the long hours that I did to scrape together the money for fees, books, and living expenses. All students and parents deserve better than just the opportunity to take on debt. I hope this book in some way helps those fighting for a genuine overhaul of the incredibly expensive business of education.

Index

Abrams, Frank, 129–130

AFL-CIO, 146, 151, 181, 284

Ahtone, Tristan, 19

Akers, Beth, 293

Alderman, Lewis, 42, 43

Alexander, Lamar, 259, 284–285

Alfred P. Sloan Foundation, 129

Allen, James, 212, 217

Aluotto, Danielle, 2, 5

American Association of Land Grant Colleges and State Universities, 161

American Association of Teachers Colleges, 90

American Association of University Women (AAUW), 182, 226, 230

American Banker, 159

American Banking Association (ABA), 27, 188, 190, 191, 195, 228, 237

American Conference of Academic Deans, 115

American Council on Education (ACE), 120, 135, 146, 182

American Farm Bureau Federation, 148

American Federation of Teachers, 289

American Jewish Congress, 104

American Legion, 82–83, 148; and GI Bill, 10, 83–87, 92, 93

American Reinvestment and Recovery Act (2009), 283

American Veterans Committee, 94–95, 100

American Vocational Association, 230

Anderson, Harold, 110

Andrew, Rob, 261

Apollo Group, 276, 278. See also University of Phoenix

AP Smith Manufacturing Co. v. Barlow (1953), 127

Arizona State University, 124, 127

Arleigh, M. W., 119

Army Times, 92

Ashbrook, John, 172

Association of American Colleges, 91, 115, 122, 184

Association of American Universities, 26, 115, 129

Atherton, Warren, 83, 86, 92

Avery, Curtis, 110–111

Baby Boomers, 121, 162, 166, 203, 247, 262

bankruptcy, 73; risk of, for some colleges, 9, 16, 28, 96; unavailability of, for student debt, 4, 277, 282

Barden, Graham, 88

Barkley, Alben, 86

Basic Educational Opportunity Grants (BEOGs, basic grants, or Pell grants), 203, 208, 209–211, 215, 229, 244, 248; Claiborne Pell and, 208, 219, 229, 234, 239, 249; differences over, in Congress, 222, 223–224, 231, 232–234, 239; implementation of, 237, 238, 239, 248, 249; increasing inadequacy of, 248, 249

basic grants. *See* Basic Educational Opportunity
  Grants
Baum, Sandy, 293
Bayh, Birch, 226–227, 230–231
Bennett, William, 250
Benson, George, 67–69
Berkeley campus, 20, 24, 169, 206
Berle, Adolf, 45
Bethune, Mary McLeod, 51, 74
Better Homes and Gardens, 115
Biden, Joe, 300
Bishop, Timothy, 285
Boehner, John, 277
Boston American, 85, 86
Bowdoin College, 154
Bowman, Robert, 282
Boyajian, Paul, 163–164
Brademas, John, 225, 233
Bradley, Omar, 98
Bridges, Styles, 81
Brown, Courtney, 290–291
Brown, Jerry, 289
Brown, Richard, 52–53, 54
Brown, Scott, 285
Brown v. Board of Education (1954), 139
Bryn Mawr College, 38, 61
Bundy, McGeorge, 172
Bureau of the Budget, 80, 121, 141, 151, 173. *See also*
  Office of Management and Budget
Burt, Homer, 44
Burwell, James, 105
Bush, George H. W., 263–264, 271, 285–286;
  presidential administration of, 259, 269, 284
Bush, George W., 277; presidential adminis-
  tration of, 278–279
busing, 230–231, 233, 234–235
Butler, Nicholas Murray, 30, 31, 49
Butler University, 58–59
Byrd, Harry, 68, 69, 70

Califano, Joseph, 256
California State University, 289
Cannon, Howard, 227
CARES Act (2020), 299–300
Carleton College, 44
Carnegie, Andrew, 21

Carnegie Commission on Higher Education,
  128, 206, 207, 222, 258
Carnegie Corporation, 131, 172
Carnegie Foundation for the Advancement of
  Teaching, 45, 126, 128–129, 167–168
Carter, Jimmy, 248, 256, 269, 270
Carthage College, 28
Carville, James, 264
Catholic colleges, 103, 120, 137, 144–145, 170,
  182, 198
Celebrezze, Anthony, 172, 173, 181–182
CEOs, 45, 177, 190, 256; conservatism of many,
  125, 130, 146, 177, 190; and support for higher
  education, 123, 124, 126, 128–131, 167, 222
Chalmers, Gordon, 30
Cheit, Earl, 206, 221
Chicago American, 85, 86
Chicago Tribune, 68, 70–71, 96–97, 105, 191
Chingos, Matthew, 293
Chisholm, Shirley, 226
Citizens Committee for Higher Education, 184
City University of New York (CUNY), 107, 181
Civilian Conservation Corps (CCC), 37, 48, 54, 70,
  78, 82; courses offered by, 37; defunding of,
  71, 77, 80, 87
Civil Rights Act of 1964, 5, 165, 178, 183, 188;
  limited impact of, on higher education,
  199, 205–206, 209, 247–248, 273, 304; and
  party politics, 176, 251
Civil War, 17. *See also* Land Grant College Act
Clark, J. Bennett "Champ," 87, 90, 92
Clarkson College, 117
Clinton, Bill, 264–265, 270, 271–272, 273;
  presidential administration of, 268, 269–275,
  277, 283
Clinton, Hillary, 296
Cold War, 116, 125, 126, 161. *See also* Soviet Union
Coleman, Tom, 261
Coles, James, 154
College of the City of New York, 23, 69
College Reform and Access Act (2007), 279–280
College Scholarship Service (CSS), 133, 156–157,
  160–161, 194, 264
Collier's, 50, 97
Collinge, Alan, 281
Colmery, Harry, 83–85, 93

Colorado State University, 268

Columbia University, 24, 34, 51, 96, 134, 137, 139, 149, 208. *See also* Butler, Nicholas Murray

Commons, John R., 47

Compton, Wilson, 129

Conant, James, 30–31, 136, 142, 172, 190, 280; as critic of New Deal, 30, 31, 40, 49; and GI Bill, 91, 111, 112; as Harvard president, 30–31, 43, 111, 112, 172, 223; views of, on mass higher education, 9, 31, 91, 168, 190

Congressional Black Caucus, 263, 277, 292

Conrad, Kent, 285

Contract with America, 268

Coombs, Philip, 147

Cooper, John, 149

Corinthian Colleges, 288–289, 290, 292, 297

Cornell University, 19, 25, 64, 106, 110

corporate elite, 126. *See also* CEOs

Coughlin, Father Charles, 41

Council on Financial Aid to Education (CFAE), 129–132, 134, 136, 146; conservative views of, 129, 130, 138, 148, 161

COVID-19 pandemic, 298–299

Creel, George, 50

Cunningham, Glenn, 51

Cuomo, Andrew, 279, 296

Curtice, Harlow, 131–132

Dale, Ashley, 1–2

Daniels, Mitch, 294

Darman, Richard, 259

Dartmouth College, 18, 25–26, 67

Deakins, Clarence, 186–187

debt forgiveness. *See* debt relief

debt relief, 14, 155–156, 267, 296, 298; proposals for, 170, 264, 288–291, 293, 296, 299, 300

Dee, John, 110

default rates, 5, 186, 219, 240, 255

defense loan program. *See* National Defense Student Loan Program

Deming, David, 295

Des Moines Forum, 45, 66

de Sola Pool, David, 51

"developing institutions" (term), 181–182, 198–199, 203, 280; use of, for HBCUs, 178–179, 191, 193, 198–199, 214, 280

DeVos, Betsy, 297, 298

DeVoto, Bernard, 91

Dewey, Thomas E., 124, 125, 159, 161

Dillow, Theodore, 163–164

"diploma mills," 6, 182, 262, 280

DiPoi, Lucia, 282

direct funding (of colleges and universities), 16–17, 167–168, 199, 210, 221–222, 232, 245; opposition to, 219–220, 222, 245; some, in original Higher Education Act, 179, 181, 191, 193, 198–199, 212

direct lending, 13, 257–258; debate over, and partial victory for, in 1990s, 258–269, 270, 275; and defense loans, 257–258; distinction between, and grants, 261; money saved by, 257, 258–259, 261, 267, 283–284; pilot program for, 13, 263–264, 267, 285–286; student loan industry's efforts to block, 13, 268, 271. *See also* William D. Ford Direct Lending Program

Dirksen, Everett, 88

Disabled American Veterans, 82, 97

Dismuke, Audrey, 273

Dodd, Chris, 260

Dominick, Peter, 225, 227, 229

Douglas, Paul, 109

Duke, James B., 21

Duke University, 21, 294

Duncan, Arne, 283

du Pont Fund, 27

Durr, Clifford, 47–48

Durr, Virginia, 47–48

Earhart, Amelia, 51

East Central Junior College, 58

Eckert, Charles, 109

Educational Development Bank, proposal, 228–229

Education Amendments of 1972 (1972 reauthorization of the Higher Education Act), 12–13, 202–208, 234–241, 243; congressional negotiations over, 208–211, 216–234; and end of direct funding, 245; Richard Nixon and, 202–203, 211, 212–218, 234–235, 238, 239. *See also* Pell grants; Student Loan Marketing Association; Title IX

Education Finance Institute, 294
Education Office. *See* Office of Education
Efron, Edith, 96
Eisenhower, Dwight D., 137, 138–139, 177, 211, 270; and federal aid to education, 139, 140, 141–142, 146, 149, 150–151, 160, 177, 217
Eisenhower, Milton, 142, 152
Elementary and Secondary Education Act of 1965, 180–181
Eliot, Charles, 22
Elliott, Carl, 137–138, 142–143, 144, 151, 152, 171
Elliott, Edward, 121
Emergency Education Program, 36, 42
Emergency Relief Appropriation Act (1935), 50
Equal Opportunity Grants, 195, 209–210
Equal Rights Amendment, 203, 227
extension services, 36, 37, 39, 45

Fannie Mae. *See* Federal National Mortgage Association
Federal Credit Reform Act (1990), 258
Federal Emergency Relief Association (FERA), 42, 43, 44, 48, 52
Federal Family Education Loan Program, 12, 264. *See also* Guaranteed Student Loan Program
Federal National Mortgage Association (FNMA, Fannie Mae), 40–41, 162, 228; exacerbation of inequality by, 162, 213; as model for student loan program, 12, 205, 213
Federal Security Administration (FSA), 65, 78, 80, 88, 90
Feild Cooperative Loan Fund, 27
Field, Marshall, 21
Filene, Edward, 41
"financial aid" (term), 16–17
Finch, Robert, 212, 217
Finne, Hilary, 1, 2
Fish, Hamilton, 82
Flint, Ross, 110
Folsom, Marion, 140, 141, 146, 147, 150, 152, 188
Ford, Edsel, 128
Ford, Henry, 128
Ford, William D., 255–256, 260, 261–262, 266–268, 281. *See also* William D. Ford Direct Lending Program

Ford Foundation, 128–129, 131, 147, 157, 206
Ford loans. *See* William D. Ford Direct Lending Program
Forester, C. S., 97
for-profit schools, 21–22, 247, 288–289; aggressive tactics of some, 255, 278; and defaults, 5, 251, 255; elite schools' war against, 32, 43, 97, 108, 122; exclusion of, from work-study programs, 108, 205; kinds of students drawn to, 3, 4, 14, 22, 25, 32, 43, 60, 108, 114, 122, 205, 286
for-profit schools, and tuition assistance programs, 7, 8, 13, 14, 256, 262, 291–292; and GI Bill, 94, 97, 108–109, 205, 229, 276; and Higher Education Act, 183, 204, 211, 229–230, 236, 247; and NDEA, 153, 160; political influence used in, 276–278, 297
Fortune, 77
foundations, 21, 25, 26–27, 126, 129–130. *See also individual foundations*
Fred, E. B., 111
Free Application for Federal Student Aid (FAFSA), 156, 264
Fresno Junior College, 107
Fried, Hannah, 50
Friedman, Milton, 134, 215, 258, 294, 295
Fund for Adult Education, 128
Fund for the Advancement of Education, 128

Gardner, John, 178
gay and lesbian students, 113
Gearhart, Bertrand, 88
General Accounting Office, 109, 250, 277
General Electric (GE), 45, 130. *See also* Young, Owen
General Motors (GM), 129, 131–132
GI Bill. *See* Servicemen's Readjustment Act
Gibson, John, 92–93
Gingrich, Newt, 268
Gokey, Thomas, 291
Goldrick-Rab, Sara, 295
Goldwater, Barry, 137, 139, 143–144, 146, 184, 220; 1964 campaign of, 177, 184, 190, 220, 249
Goodling, Bill, 265
graduate students, 54, 106, 143, 151, 207
Graham, Hugh Davis, 164

Gray, Philip, 97

Great Depression, 9–10, 28–29, 41, 47, 128, 169, 206, 281. *See also* New Deal

Great Lakes Higher Education Corporation, 286

Great Recession, 270, 281; highlighting of student debt problems by, 4–5, 14, 281–283, 286, 289–291, 300

Great Society, 12, 164, 190, 191, 197, 239; and higher education, 5, 164, 176, 190, 197, 253, 257, 299; turn away from, 212, 214, 215–216, 239

Green, William, 51

Green Edith Starrett, 148, 171, 222–224, 228, 237–238, 281; background of, 148, 171, 226; as champion of loans as opposed to grants, 148, 171, 222, 239; concern of, for middle-income families, 181, 183, 218, 224; and Higher Education Act deliberations, 181, 182, 183, 188, 199; and NDEA, 148, 166, 171, 172, 196; and 1972 HEA reauthorization, 217, 218, 222–225, 226, 228, 232–234; and women's equality, 226

GSEs (government-sponsored enterprises), 213–214, 228, 274–275, 276. *See also* Federal National Mortgage Association; Student Loan Marketing Association

Guaranteed Student Loan Program (GSLP), 12–14, 180; creation of, 164–165, 177–191; end of, 14, 286. *See also* Student Loan Marketing Association

guaranteed student loans, 6–7, 12–13; ending of, 14, 291; greater cost of, than of direct lending, 257, 258–259, 261, 267, 283–284. *See also* Guaranteed Student Loan Program; National Defense Student Loan Program; student loan industry; Student Loan Marketing Association

Hamilton College, 61

Harding College, 67–68, 69

Harmon, William, 27

Harmon Foundation, 27, 135

Harper's Magazine, 91

Harrington, Francis, 63

Harrington, Michael, 204

Harris, Seymour, 161

Hartle, Terry, 242, 243, 274, 286

Hartung, Maurice, 70

Harvard University, 30–31, 34, 168, 172–173; admissions policies of, 106; cost of attending, 10, 94, 109, 282, 292; donations to, 24, 26–27; and GI Bill, 111, 112; student body composition of, 22, 30, 43, 69, 112; student loans at, 132, 134–135, 153, 158

Hatch Act (1887), 20

HCBUs (historically Black colleges and universities), 51, 179, 214, 279, 280, 292, 293; and Higher Education Act, 178–179, 182, 183, 1912, 193, 194–195, 198–199, 222–223, 269; and National Youth Administration, 51, 55, 280; and term "developing institutions," 178–179, 191, 193, 198–199, 214, 280

Health Care and Educational Reform Reconciliation Act (2010), 286, 287

Hearst, William Randolph, 85–86, 97

Henderson, Algo, 115

Henry, David, 161

Hickok, Lorena, 35–36, 39, 41, 50

Higher Ed, Not Debt coalition, 289

Higher Education Act (HEA, 1965), 5, 12, 160, 295; congressional negotiations over, Francis Keppel and, 173, 174, 179, 180, 186, 187, 254; initial implementation of, 191–201; limited direct funding in, 179, 181, 191, 193, 198–199, 212; loans as central aspect of, 165–166, 178–180, 183–191; Lyndon Johnson and, 12, 65, 164, 186, 189–190, 192–193, 197–198, 203, 245

Higher Education Act (HEA, 1965), reauthorizations of, with changes, 193, 200, 249, 258, 277, 295; in 1968, 200–201, 203, 206, 254; in 1986, 250, 271; in 1992, 258–265, 285–286; in 2008, 279–280, 281, 292. *See also* Education Amendments of 1972

Higher Education Assistance Foundation (HEAF), 256, 258; collapse of, 256–257, 258, 274

Higher Education Facilities Act (HEFA, 1963), 174, 175–176, 177–178, 181

Hill, Alfred, 182

Hill, Lister, 137, 138, 142–143, 144, 145, 150, 171

Hillman, Sidney, 51, 52
Hines, Frank, 90
Hoffman, Paul, 128
Hogan, Cicero, 97
Hoover, Herbert, 26, 29, 31, 69
Hope Scholarship Program (Georgia), 271
Hopkins, Harry, 35, 37–38, 41, 43, 44, 52; and
 Aubrey Williams, 46, 47, 48, 50, 51, 52, 63;
 and Franklin Roosevelt, 35, 42, 45, 63, 64–65;
 and National Youth Administration, 42,
 43, 46–48, 49, 51, 53, 55, 61, 64–65; reports
 to, by Lorena Hickok, 35–36, 41; and Works
 Progress Administration, 39, 48, 50, 52
Hopkins, Johns, 21, 142
Housing Act of 1934, 40, 189, 205. *See also*
 Federal National Mortgage Association
Howard University, 59
Howe, Harold, 189
Howe, Louis, 45
Hull, J. W., 53
Humphrey, Hubert, 163, 184
Hungate, Thad, 123, 132
Hunter, John, 100
Hutchins, Robert, 42, 95–96, 128; and GI Bill,
 10, 96, 99, 107, 109

Ickes, Harold, 37–38, 48–49
Ikenberry, Stanley, 242, 243, 274, 286
impoundment, 238
Indiana State Teachers College, 60
Internal Revenue Service (IRS), proposed use
 of, for debt collection, 213, 258, 261, 265, 266,
 286, 292
Iowa State University, 60–61, 268
Iowa Student Loan Liquidity Corporation, 279
Ivy League universities, 17, 20–21, 22, 38, 99,
 221, 226; cost of attending, 133, 136, 246–247;
 donations to, 20–21, 126; in 1930s, 61, 67,
 94. *See also individual schools*

Javits, Jacob, 188, 219
Jay, Rose Lee, 101
Jefferson, Thomas, 24, 31, 161, 238
Jeffords, Jim, 266
Jesuits, 145
John F. Kennedy College, 163, 200, 206

Johns Hopkins University, 21, 142
Johnson, Campbell, 112
Johnson, Louis, 64
Johnson, Lyndon Baines ("LBJ"), 12, 53, 164,
 174–178; college experience of, 15, 16, 22–23,
 192, 195; in Congress, 65, 71, 141, 162, 175; and
 Higher Education Act, 12, 65, 164, 186, 189–190,
 192–193, 197–198, 203, 245; and National
 Defense Education Act, 196–197, 257
Johnson, Mordecai, 51
Jotsen, George, 110
Journal of Higher Education, The, 107
Judd, Charles, 46

Kasich, John, 268–269
Kassebaum, Nancy, 266
Kazee, Ezra, 282
Kearney, Pat, 92
Kennedy, John F. ("JFK"), 146–147, 169–172, 238;
 presidential administration of, 170–174,
 176, 178, 180–181, 190, 250
Keppel, Francis, 172–173; and Higher Educa-
 tion Act, 173, 174, 179, 180, 186, 187, 254
Kerr, Clark, 168–169, 178; on aid policies, 179,
 194, 207, 222; background of, 168–169;
 vision of, for mass higher education, 169,
 172, 173, 183, 193, 204
Killian, James, 149
Kleberg, Richard, 53
Klinefelter, Cyril, 42, 43
Korean War, 115, 263
Krowen, Jackie, 2, 4
Kutcher, Ashton, 294

Ladies Home Journal, 97, 101, 107, 235–236
LaFollette, Robert M., Jr., 68, 88
Lambda School, 294
Land Grant College Act (Morrill Act, 1862),
 16, 18–20, 29, 124, 179
Lang, John, 44
La Raza, 284
Larson, Ann, 291
Lasser, David, 63
Laughlin, Anne, 53
Lee, Robert, 19
Lerner, Max, 105

Lilienthal, David, 37
Lily Endowment, 242
Lindley, Ernest H., 51, 63
Long, Huey, 41
Los Angeles Times, 71, 95, 140, 152, 191
Loyola University Chicago, 1
Lucy, Autherine, 150

Marland, Sidney, 236
Maryville College, 46
Massachusetts Higher Education Assistance Corporation, 159, 166, 167
Massachusetts Institute of Technology (MIT), 19, 24, 57, 129, 132, 135, 149
mass higher education, 62, 116; Clark Kerr's vision for, 169, 172, 173, 183, 193, 204; GI Bill and, 115; growing acceptance of, 121, 168–169, 172, 182–183, 194; inequality within, 299; James Conant on, 9, 31, 91, 168, 190
Maverick, Maury, 82
McCain, John, 283
McClurg, Vanessa, 2, 5
McCormack, John, 86
McCurdy, R. W., 83
McFadden, Bernarr, 51
McFarland, Ernest, 89
McGrath, Earl, 135
McKellar, Kenneth, 70
McMurrin, Sterling, 172
McWilliams, Carey, 169
Mead, James, 101–102
Melton, Mrs. C. L., 33–34, 57
Miami University, 60
Michigan State University, 18
Middle Income Student Assistance Act (MISAA, 1978), 248–249
Miller, George, 284–285
Miller, Zell, 271
Mink, Patsy, 226
Mockler, Garrett, 282
Mondale, Walter, 220–221
Montana School of Mines, 57
Montana State University, 103, 253
Moon, Rexford, Jr., 160–161
Morrill, Justin, 16, 19, 21. *See also* Land Grant College Act

Morse, John, 162
Morse, Wayne, 144, 181, 208
mortgage program. *See* Federal National Mortgage Association
"multiversities," 169–170
Munro, John, 134–135
Myers, Alfonso, 105

NAACP, 145, 284
Nasaw, David, 85
Nation, the, 92
National Advisory Committee on Education, 29–30
National Association of Manufacturers, 144, 148
National Association of Student Financial Aid Administrators, 236–237
National Council of Business Schools, 108
National Defense Education Act (NDEA, 1958), 11, 117, 171; congressional negotiations over, 11, 142–151, 166, 170, 177, 217; Eisenhower Administration and, 141–142, 147, 149, 150–151, 177, 217; implementation of, 152–162, 166, 186; later efforts to change, 172, 181, 186, 196; limited scope of, 118–119, 154–155; loans as central feature of, 11–12, 117, 118–119, 158–162, 166. *See also* National Defense Student Loan Program
National Defense Student Loan Program (NDSLP, defense loan program), 117, 118–119, 152–158, 183–184, 257–258, 267; defaults under, 186, 244; differences between, and guaranteed loans, 180, 257, 269; funding for, 195, 196, 238; help rendered by, 183–184; later folding of, into Higher Education Act; opponents of, 187, 196–197, 257
National Education Association (NEA), 123, 139, 152; and GI Bill, 91, 98–99; and NDEA, 146, 149, 151; and New Deal, 30, 31, 44, 51
National Education Improvement Act, proposed, 173–174
National Housing Agency, 102–103
National Industrial Conference Board, 167
National Institutes of Health (NIH), 136
National Merit Scholarship Corporation, 131, 148, 161

National Resources Planning Board (NRPB), 73, 78

National Science Foundation (NSF), 136

National Student Association, 145, 146

National Student Federation of America, 44, 50, 55

National Student League, 50

National War Labor Board, 169

National Youth Administration (NYA), 9–10; Aubrey Williams as director of (*see under* Williams, Aubrey); background of, in Great Depression, 33–48; creation of, 48–50; Franklin Roosevelt and, 50, 51, 52, 53, 55, 64–65; Harry Hopkins and, 42, 43, 46–48, 49, 51, 53, 55, 61, 64–65; Lyndon Johnson as a state director in, 141, 162, 175; National Advisory Council (NAC) of, 50, 51–52, 53, 55, 57, 59, 67, 73, 74, 124; after start of World War II, 64–75, 80, 90; termination of, by Congress (1943), 10, 77, 80, 81, 291

National Youth Administration (NYA), work-study program of, 9–10, 48, 55–62, 64, 65, 72–74, 194; extent of, 55, 56–57, 73; opposition to, 66–71; and students of color, 10, 54–55, 62, 63–64, 74, 112, 119, 175, 280; women in, 54, 73–74

Nelson, Ben, 285

neoliberalism, 245–246

New Deal, 7, 32, 34, 40–41, 49–50; public-private character of, 8, 40, 41, 45, 56. *See also* Civilian Conservation Corps; Federal National Mortgage Association; National Youth Administration

New Depression in Higher Education, The (Cheit), 206

"New Federalism," 212

New Republic, 236

Newsweek, 81, 163

New York Journal American, 85

New York Post, 105

New York State Teachers Guild, 104

New York Times, 27, 44, 96, 97, 104, 140, 191, 207, 292

New York University (NYU), 28, 44, 95, 96

Nixon, Richard, 211, 212, 223, 238; as candidate, 170, 211; "grief mail" to, from

students and parents, 202–203, 224, 245, 253, 281; and HEA reauthorization, 202–203, 211, 212–218, 234–235, 238, 239

North Carolina State University, 1–2

Northwestern University, 103, 113

Notre Dame University, 106, 227

Nunn, Sam, 254–255, 256, 258, 262

Obama, Barack, 14, 282–283, 284, 286–287, 291; presidential administration of, 14, 283–292, 298

Obama, Michelle, 282

Ocasio-Cortez, Alexandria, 300

Occupy Student Debt Campaign, 289. *See also* Strike Debt

O'Dwyer, William, 103–104

Office of Education: in 1930s, 29–30, 38, 44, 45, 48–49, 66, 67; in 1940s, 72, 82, 90, 114, 119, 121, 122; in 1950s, 138, 142, 153, 154–160; in 1960s, 182, 191, 195, 198, 236, 237, 240, 257; in 1970s, 236, 237, 239, 240. *See also* US Department of Education

Office of Management and Budget, 212, 238, 251, 259. *See also* Bureau of the Budget

Office of War Mobilization and Reconversion, 102, 119

Oglethorpe University, 34–35

Ohio State University, 59–60, 110

Oklahoma Agricultural and Mechanical College, 58

Olds, Irving, 130

Olson, Keith, 78

Omar, Ilhan, 2

Operation Subsistence, 100

Osborn, Frederick, 89

Osborne, Fairfield, Jr., 53

Peabody Education Fund, 25

Pell, Claiborne, 207–211, 266, 275, 286; background of, 207–208, 230; belief of, in right to an education, 216, 218, 232, 261, 285; as champion of basic grants, 203–204, 208–211, 219, 229, 239, 261; grants named for (*see* Pell grants); and 1972 Higher Education Act reauthorization, 208–211, 215, 217, 218, 220, 221, 222, 228–229, 230, 233, 235

Pell grants, 12–13, 203–204, 261, 299–300; as basic grants, 223, 229; Claiborne Pell's campaign for, 204, 207–211, 215, 218, 219, 220–221, 222, 229, 232, 233, 239; efforts to turn into an entitlement, 261, 263, 284–285; and for-profit schools, 262; funding of, 250, 264, 279–280; renaming of, in Pell's honor, 249; and students of color, 13, 203

Pennsylvania State University (Penn State), 106, 142

Pepper, Claude, 89

Perkins, Carl, 160, 231–232, 233–234; loan program named for, 291

Perkins, Frances, 44–45

Perkins loan program, 291

philanthropies, 9, 20–21, 24–25, 26–27, 126–132, 147

Player, Willa, 198

Poage, W. R., 148

Pognany, Andrew, 202, 205, 236

Powell, Adam Clayton, Jr., 145

Princeton University, 57, 58, 61, 67, 127, 175, 207

privatization, 268, 270, 274–275, 276

proprietary schools. *See* for-profit schools

Protestants United for the Separation of Church and State, 145

Prouty, Winston, 220

Public Sector Loan Forgiveness Program, 296, 297

Purdue University, 227, 294

Quie, Albert, 225

quota system, 23, 103, 112, 114, 118, 160; protests against, 95, 105, 112, 118, 122, 124–125, 132

racial segregation, 118, 121–122, 160, 235; challenges to, 105, 137, 139, 145, 165, 166, 178; as issue in formulating student assistance policies, 9, 137, 145, 150, 230; 1964 Civil Rights Act and, 165, 178; and origins of HBCUs, 20, 55

racial wealth gap, 3–4, 11, 14, 271, 293, 304

racism, 48, 92. *See also* racial segregation; racial wealth gap

Rankin, John, 86–87, 88, 90, 91–92, 94, 233

Rayburn, Sam, 86

Reagan, Ronald, 168, 177, 249–250; presidential administration of, 250–252, 269

Rector, Stanley, 84

Rensselaer Polytechnic Institute, 132

Ribicoff, Abraham, 172, 176, 184

Richardson, Elliott, 140; in Eisenhower Administration, 140, 141, 146, 149, 151; in Nixon Administration, 140, 217–218, 229, 234, 238

Riedman, Sarah, 95

Riley, Frank, 86

Roberts, John, 252

Rockefeller, John D., 21

Rockefeller Foundation, 126, 128–129

Rogers, Edith Nourse, 87, 89–90

Rogers, John, 87

Rogin, Lawrence, 181

Rolling Jubilee, 289–291

Roosevelt, Eleanor, 45, 48, 53, 54, 66

Roosevelt, Franklin Delano ("FDR"), 31–33, 238; and academic leaders, 31–35, 67–68, 96, 105, 120; background of, 34–35; and creation of National Youth Administration, 42–49, 50, 51, 52, 53, 55, 64–65; critics of, 31–32, 64, 81, 85–87, 95; and GI Bill, 78, 79, 80, 81, 85–87, 114, 205

Rorex, Sam, 83

Rule, James, 31

Ruml, Beardsley, 47–48

Rural Rehabilitation Administration, 250

Russell, John, 121

Rutgers University, 58, 107

Sallie Mae. *See* Student Loan Marketing Association

Sanders, Bernie, 296, 298

Saturday Evening Post, 97

School Review, 70

Scott, Bobby, 300

secondary market, 13, 213–214, 228–229, 252, 274, 276. *See also* Student Loan Marketing Association

Second Morrill Act (1890), 20

Selective Service Act (1940), 79

"self-help" (term), 25

Service Employees International Union (SEIU), 284

Servicemen's Readjustment Act (GI Bill, 1944), 93–97; American Legion and, 10, 83–87, 92, 93; congressional negotiations over, 77, 80, 86–90, 91–92; Franklin Roosevelt and, 79, 81, 85–87, 114, 205; Harry Truman and, 76, 98, 100, 101, 102, 110, 122; job placement services in, 88, 93, 97, 107–108; Veterans Administration of, 93–94, 97–102, 106–109, 112–113, 133, 205, 220

Servicemen's Readjustment Act (GI Bill, 1944), 93–97, Title II of (student assistance), 91, 96, 97–116, 153, 158; congressional maneuvering over, 77, 80, 81–93; criticism of, 91, 94–95, 96, 97, 98; effects of, on higher education, 106–107, 114–115; enthusiasm for, 110–111; expansion of, in 1945 revisions, 97–98; and for-profit schools, 94, 97, 108–109, 115, 205, 229, 276; racial and gender disparity in, 112–114; small stipends under, 98–103

Sharp, Ann, 110

Sinclair, Upton, 83

Slaughter, Adolph, 198

Sloan, Alfred P., 129, 132

Smith, Hilda, 38, 39, 41, 106, 128, 172–173

Snavely, Guy, 122

Social Security Act (1935), 40, 140

Soviet Union, 141; education in, 136, 161. *See also* Cold War; Sputnik launch

Spangler, Harrison, 81

Sperling, John, 276, 278

Sproul, Robert, 169

Sputnik launch (1957), 118; and US higher education programs, 11, 118, 140–142, 150, 151, 206, 220, 252

Stahr, Elvis, 182

Stanford, Leland, 21

Stanford University, 21, 24, 26, 99, 191

state universities, 20, 99, 133, 166, 246. *See also* *individual institutions*

Stein, Herbert, 235–236

Stelle, John, 83–84

Stirling, H. V., 109

Stockman, David, 251

Stoke, Harold, 114

St. Olaf College, 225

Strike Debt, 289–291, 300

Stroup, Sally, 278

Studebaker, John, 45, 48–49, 51, 66, 67

student assistance. *See* student loans; work-study

student loan industry, 6–7, 245, 268–269, 279; attempts to rein in, 7, 256–257, 264–267, 279–280, 291–292, 296, 298, 300–301; encouragement of, by federal policies, 6–7, 13, 116, 165, 180, 194, 200–201, 205, 245, 249–254; huge debt collectively owed to, 1, 240, 250; lives ruined by, 1–3, 241, 279; opposition of, to direct lending programs, 13, 268, 271; political power of, 13, 265, 268, 275, 297; slack regulation of, 13, 250–251, 256–257, 297

StudentLoanJustice.org, 281

Student Loan Marketing Association (SLMA, Sallie Mae), 13, 239–241, 249–250, 281, 286, 298; as boost to student loan industry, 13, 240, 243, 252–253, 274, 297; creation of, 13, 204, 205, 213–214, 227–232; early implementation of, 236–237, 239–240; fight of, against direct lending, 265, 268, 270, 284; and growth of student debt, 240–241, 282; and privatization, 268, 270, 274–276; as secondary market, 13, 213–214, 228–229, 252, 274, 276

Student Loan Marketing Association Reorganization Act (1996), 275–276

Student Loan Reform Act (1993), 265, 266, 267, 268

student loans. *See* direct lending; guaranteed student loans

Students for Democratic Action, 144

Supplemental Educational Opportunity Grants (SEOG), 209

Suren, Jessie, 1, 4, 5

Swing, Raymond Gram, 81

Syracuse University, 106, 111–112, 129

Taft, Robert A., 88

Taussig, Charles, 41, 45–46; and National Youth Administration, 48, 49, 51–52, 53, 55, 66, 67, 73 tax credits and deductions, 126–128; failed proposals for, 146, 177, 178, 181, 212; for tuition, 8, 41, 184–185, 248, 271–273, 283

Taylor, Paul, 169

Teachers Union, 95

Teague, Olin, 109

Temple University, 61, 152

Tennessee Valley Authority (TVA), 37, 70

Thackrey, Russell, 161

Thomas, Clarence, 252

Thomas, Elbert, 82, 83, 84, 86

Thomas, Norman, 46

Thompson, Stephen, 96

Thurmond, Strom, 143, 145, 177, 227

Tillman, Ben, 20

Title IX (of Higher Education Act), 12, 203, 235–236; congressional passage of, 204, 226–227, 232; efforts to undermine, 251, 252; limited impact of, on underlying inequality, 244, 247, 248

Topper, Roy, 86

Tower, John, 176, 184

Truman, Harry S., 87, 119–120, 217, 238; and GI Bill, 76, 98, 100, 101, 102, 110, 122

Trump, Donald, 296–297, 298, 300

tuition rates, 28, 73, 131, 166, 200, 203, 246; and the G.I. Bill, 94, 98, 114–115; in the Great Recession, 281

Tuskegee University, 269

United States Aid Funds (USAF), 167, 183–184, 187–188, 191, 195, 252

United States Student Association, 284, 289

University of Alabama, 137, 150

University of California (UC), 19, 24, 101, 191, 267–268, 289; Berkeley campus of, 20, 169; Clark Kerr and, 168, 169

University of Chicago, 21, 25, 27, 95, 97, 106, 109

University of Cincinnati, 47, 91, 265

University of Colorado, 61

University of Florida, 268, 269

University of Idaho, 57

University of Illinois, 57–58, 60, 103, 106, 161, 242, 267; Chicago campus of, 103, 104

University of Indiana, 186, 227

University of Iowa, 57, 101

University of Michigan, 18, 24, 100

University of Minnesota, 19, 43, 58, 59, 111, 138, 156

University of Missouri, 76, 101, 102

University of Nebraska, 110

University of Nevada, 36

University of North Carolina, 44, 124

University of North Dakota, 28, 58

University of Pennsylvania, 24, 107

University of Phoenix, 276, 278, 292

University of Rochester, 140

University of South Carolina, 18, 20, 36

University of Vermont, 130

University of Virginia, 24, 27, 31, 227

University of West Virginia, 36

University of Wisconsin, 20, 24, 35, 37, 47, 100, 111, 265

upward mobility, 5–6, 183

USA Group Foundation, 242, 267, 274, 275

US Chamber of Commerce, 144, 148

US Children's Bureau, 44–45

US Consumer Financial Protection Bureau, 288, 297, 298

US Department of Education, 250–251, 261, 279–280, 297–298; creation of, 249; earlier proposals for, 29–30, 37, 119, 217; and for-profit schools, 276, 278, 291–292; and student loan industry, 250–251, 256–257, 267, 275, 278–279, 291–293

US Employment Service, 88, 93, 97, 98

US Public Interest Research Group, 284

US Supreme Court, 18, 29, 50, 95, 105, 252, 287; and the New Deal, 50, 64

Vanderbilt University, 58

Van Hoosean, Burr, 119

Vassar College, 61

veterans, 78–79, 81, 82–83, 98; African American, 112–113; female, 113–115. *See also* Servicemen's Readjustment Act

Veterans Administration (VA), 77, 80, 84–85, 88, 90, 92; administration of GI Bill by, 93–94, 97–102, 106–109, 112–113, 133, 205, 220

Veterans of Foreign Wars, 82

Vietnam War, 12, 165, 175, 191, 197, 202, 218; protests against, 202, 218, 260

Wagner, Robert F., 88

Waldrip, W. B., 83

Waller, Willard, 96

Wall Street Journal, 70, 191, 228

War Manpower Commission, 70

War on Poverty, 5, 12, 176, 185, 190

Warren, Earl, 123, 139, 169

Warren, Elizabeth, 297, 298

Washington, George, 18

Washington Post, 50, 63, 140, 145, 226, 290–291

Waters, Maxine, 262–263

Wayne State University, 100, 269

wealth gap. *See* racial wealth gap

Weber College, 107

Weinberger, Caspar, 238

Wesleyan University, 28

Westby, Gregory, 282

Weston, Burns, 53

Whitney Benefits, 27

Whittemore, William, 110

Wickenden, Elizabeth, 47–48

Wicks, Thomas, 76, 101

Wiley, Alexander, 88

William D. Ford Direct Lending Program, 266–268, 270, 278–279

Williams, Aubrey, 46–50, 61, 137; anti-racism of, 46, 47, 48, 54, 62, 63–64, 74, 112, 175, 280; background of, 46–49; and creation of National Youth Administration, 48–49, 50; and Franklin Roosevelt, 48, 53, 63, 67

Williams, Aubrey, as NYA director, 50–55, 62–74; achievements of, 52, 55, 64, 72–73; criticisms of, 51, 63, 67–71; and National Advisory Committee, 51–52, 54–55; and state directors, 53, 54, 55, 65; and students of color, 54–55, 62, 63–64, 74, 175, 280

Williams, Harrison, 225

Williams College, 24

Wine, E.C., 121

women, 3–4, 26, 38, 135, 182, 247–248; of color, 3, 5, 6; and for-profit schools, 22, 230; and GI Bill, 11, 104, 113–114; greater debt burden for, 3–4, 5, 14, 244–245, 253; and National Defense Education Act, 119, 149, 160; and National Youth Administration work-study program, 54, 73–74; as proportion of all students, 4, 247; and wealth gap, 14, 293. *See also* Title IX

Women's Equity League, 226

Woodson, Carter, 121–122

Woolf, Dorothy, 27

Workers Alliance for America, 63

Workers Education Project, 38, 106

Workers Service Program. *See* Workers Education Project

work-study, 121, 169, 225; for-profit schools ineligible for, 108, 205; Higher Education Act and, 195, 248, 250, 254, 295; National Youth Administration and, 9–10, 34, 48, 55–62, 64, 65, 67–70, 72–74, 79, 194; opponents of, 34, 48–49, 61, 67–69, 70, 168; War on Poverty and, 176

World War I, 30, 46–47, 82

World War II: colleges and universities during, 70, 93, 111, 120, 199; education offered to troops during, 111, 120, 139. *See also* Servicemen's Readjustment Act

Wright, Houston, 53

Yale University, 19, 61, 111, 112, 117, 135, 158, 294

Young, Owen, 51, 124

Zaloom, Caitlin, 295

Zook, George, 38, 90, 120–121, 152, 262. *See also* Zook Commission

Zook Commission, 120–121, 123, 139; conclusions drawn by, 121–122, 125, 126, 173, 208, 296, 299; limited response to, 123, 128–129, 136, 152, 208–209, 271, 284–285